VMware Performance and Capacity Management

Second Edition

Master SDDC operations with proven best practices

Iwan 'e1' Rahabok

PUBLISHING

BIRMINGHAM - MUMBAI

VMware Performance and Capacity Management
Second Edition

First published: March 2016

Production reference: 1230316

Published by Packt Publishing Ltd.
Livery Place
35 Livery Street
Birmingham B3 2PB, UK.

ISBN 978-1-78588-031-5

www.packtpub.com

Credits

Author

Iwan 'e1' Rahabok

Reviewers

Mark Achtemichuk

Sunny Dua

Commissioning Editor

Karthikey Pandey

Acquisition Editor

Vinay Argekar

Content Development Editor

Viranchi Shetty

Technical Editor

Vishal Mewada

Copy Editor

Madhusudan Uchil

Project Coordinator

Izzat Contractor

Proofreader

Safis Editing

Indexer

Hemangini Bari

Graphics

Kirk D'Penha

Production Coordinator

Shantanu N. Zagade

Cover Work

Shantanu N. Zagade

Foreword

I first ran across Iwan Rahabok, the author of this book, in late 2013 when my company, Blue Medora, began shipping our first software solutions that were built on top of vRealize Operations. By that point, Iwan had established himself as one of the top 2–3 authorities on the planet on vRealize Operations; its capabilities were that it was strong, but still immature, and the key role the product had been playing in the Cloud Systems Management journey early adopters of the product were embarking on. Blue Medora's first encounter with Iwan was via a series on VMware internal training classes that Iwan had developed based on his early experiences with the product, with an emphasis on how it optimizes its configuration to solve real-world customer challenges. In short, in those early days of vRealize Operations, Iwan was playing an integral role in educating others in VMware on the product, its capabilities, and how to relate that to real-world customer environments.

vRealize Operations has become the foundational component of, according to IDC, the #1 Cloud Systems Management platform, considering market share available today. Over the past 2 years, VMware has continued to invest heavily in expanding vRealize Operations, both in terms of scalability, usability, and consumability as well as adding or deeply enhancing core features, including anomaly detection, predictive analytics, capacity planning, right-sizing, and workload placement. These new capabilities have been rolled out of a short 15-month time period via 3 significant updates: version 6.0 in December 2014, version 6.1 in August 2015, and version 6.2 in January 2016. VMware has successfully evolved vRealize Operations from a vSphere-centric tool to a broad-based SDDC management tool perfectly suited to monitoring and managing mixed-hypervisor environments, compute, storage, network, converged, infrastructure, as well as Tier-1 business critical applications.

Given those changes, Iwan rightly decided that in order to keep this book relevant and up to date with the incredible pace of change within the vRealize Operations platform since this book's first publication, which he needed to go back and rewrite it from the ground up. This edition is the labor of those efforts.

This book is required by all vRealize Operations admins and users—whether you are a first-time user of vRealize Operations or a seasoned professional, managing large-scale hybrid enterprise environments. Iwan is one of the most recognized vRealize Operations experts in the world, and the content of this book belies his deep personal experience with the product as well as Iwan's ongoing interactions with VMware staff, partners, and customers who are architecting configuring, installing, and using the product.

Nathan Owen
CEO, Blue Medora

Foreword

Bridging the gap between R&D, the people who build products, the field, the people who sell solutions that include those products, and customers who consume those solutions, is critical to VMware's success. They are connected so that each can be effective. Customer intimacy and feedback into R&D drives more relevant innovation and compelling products. A clear channel from R&D and the CTO office to our customers ensures that our customers understand the broad context for VMware's solutions and are equipped to take the maximum advantage of them. In between is the field, and in the field are the CTO Ambassadors, whose specific mission is to provide that bridge.

Iwan is a great example of a CTO Ambassador—passionate and knowledgeable about technology, committed to our customers' success, and always going above and beyond. He was elected the CTO Ambassador program in 2014 among 100 ambassadors. The program is run by the VMware Office of the CTO, and the individual CTO Ambassadors are members of a small group of our most experienced and talented customer facing, individual contributor technologists. They are presales Systems Engineers (SEs), Technical Account Managers (TAMs), professional services consultants, architects, and global support services engineers.

The ambassadors are able to articulate VMware strategy and have a keen understanding of the big picture. They typically specialize in certain technology or business areas and are subject matter experts in their chosen fields. These ambassadors help to facilitate an effective collaboration between R&D and our customers so that we can address current customer issues and future needs as effectively as possible.

There are many tangible results of the program, and this book is a good example. Iwan took advantage of the bridge made possible through the program, collaborating with R&D and his peers. I supported his first edition, and it's my pleasure to write a foreword for this second edition also. This book demonstrates that breadth and depth of knowledge. It covers the overall Software-Defined Data Center (SDDC) architecture, which is relevant for everyone interested in virtualization and cloud computing, before diving into a number of performance and capacity management topics, providing the depth and detail needed by engineers and architects.

A non-negotiable requirement to be accepted into the CTO Ambassador program is direct customer relationships. A deep understanding of customers' requirements and how they expect VMware to be their partner are expected of our Ambassadors. As you read this book, it will be clear to you that it is written from the customers' viewpoint, and not from the product's perspective. It looks at what it takes to operationalize performance and capacity management of your SDDC.

I hope that you found the book immensely valuable in your IT transformation.

Paul Strong
CTO, Global Field, VMware

About the Author

Iwan 'e1' Rahabok was the first VMware SE for strategic accounts in ASEAN. Joining VMware in 2008 from Sun Microsystems, he has seen how enterprises adopt virtualization and cloud computing and reap the benefits while overcoming the challenges. It is a journey that is very much ongoing and the book reflects a subset of that undertaking. Iwan was one of the first to achieve the VCAP-DCD certification globally and has since helped others to achieve the same, via his participation in the community. He started the user community in ASEAN, and today, the group is one of the largest VMware communities on Facebook. Iwan is a member of VMware CTO Ambassadors program since 2014, representing the Asia Pacific region at the global level and representing the product team and CTO office to the Asia Pacific customers. He is a vExpert since 2013, and has been helping others to achieve this global recognition for their contribution to the VMware community. After graduating from Bond University, Australia, Iwan moved to Singapore in 1994, where he has lived ever since.

Acknowledgments

Behind an author, there are always many people involved to make a book possible. I am grateful for the feedback, help and encouragement provided by the following individuals.

VMware vRealize Operations & Log Insight product team:

- Anil Gupta, Senior Director
- Bill Erdman, Product Manager
- Dave Overbeek, Director, Technical Marketing & Enablement
- Hicham Mourad, Staff Technical Marketing Manager
- James Ang, Staff Engineer
- Michael Beckmann, Senior Director
- Monica Sharma, Group Product Manager
- Steven Flanders, Consulting Architect
- Tom Findling, Staff Engineer

VMware Education team:

- Linus Bourque, Principal Instructor

VMware Asia Pacific team:

- Mike Sumner, Senior Director, Systems Engineering

VMware ASEAN team:

- Ron Goh, VP and GM
- Santoso Suwignyo, Senior Director, Systems Engineering
- Eng Soo Jing, Senior Manager, Systems Engineering

VMware Office of the CTO:

- Paul Strong, CTO, Global Field
- Shannon Schofield, Program Manager, CTO Ambassador program

Members of CTO Ambassador program and vRealize Operations Curators:

- Scott Carpenter
- Kim Jahnz
- Cheryl Eagan
- Martin Banda
- Jodi Shely
- Paul James
- Jim Medeiros
- Bill Hunter
- Jim Silvera

About the Reviewers

Mark Achtemichuk currently works as a staff engineer within VMware's Central Engineering Performance team, focusing on education, benchmarking, collaterals, and performance architectures. He has also held various performance-focused field, specialist and technical marketing positions within VMware over the last 6 years. Mark is recognized as an industry expert and holds a VMware Certified Design Expert (VCDX#50) certification, one of less than 250 worldwide. He has worked on engagements with Fortune 50 companies, served as a technical editor for many books and publications, and is a sought-after speaker at numerous industry events.

Mark is a blogger and has been recognized as a VMware vExpert from 2013 to 2016. He is active on Twitter at @vmMarkA where he shares his knowledge of performance with the virtualization community. His experience and expertise from infrastructure to application helps customers ensure that performance is no longer a barrier, perceived or real, to virtualizing and operating an organization's software-defined assets.

Sunny Dua works as a senior consultant for VMware's professional services organization, which is focused on ASEAN countries. In addition to his PSO role in VMware, he is also an ambassador of the VMware CTO Office. He is a four-time vExpert (2013, 2014, 2015, and 2016) and an active member of the VMware community.

With his industry experience of more than 12 years, he has worked on large-scale virtualization and cloud deployments in various roles at VMware, Hewlett Packard, and Capgemini. In his current role, he is focusing on providing IT transformation roadmaps to large-enterprise customers on their journey toward the adoption of cloud computing. He also helps enterprise shops by providing them with directions on virtualizing business-critical applications on the VMware virtualization platform.

Operations management in the virtual infrastructure is one of his core competencies, and he has been sharing his experience on the transformation of IT operations through his personal blog, `http://www.vxpresss.blogspot.com/`. He is a guest blogger on VMware management and consulting blogs as well. The industry and vCommunity have recognized his work as his blog ranks in the top 50 in the virtualization and cloud industry. He is also a coauthor for vSphere Design Pocketbook, published by Create Space Independent Publishing Platform, written by highly respected members of the VMware virtualization community.

I would like to thank Iwan who gave me the opportunity to review his work. I would also like to thank my parents, my wonderful wife Roomi, and my son Samar to support and allow me to spend my personal time on projects like this.

www.PacktPub.com

eBooks, discount offers, and more

Did you know that Packt offers eBook versions of every book published, with PDF and ePub files available? You can upgrade to the eBook version at www.PacktPub.com and as a print book customer, you are entitled to a discount on the eBook copy. Get in touch with us at customercare@packtpub.com for more details.

At www.PacktPub.com, you can also read a collection of free technical articles, sign up for a range of free newsletters and receive exclusive discounts and offers on Packt books and eBooks.

https://www2.packtpub.com/books/subscription/packtlib

Do you need instant solutions to your IT questions? PacktLib is Packt's online digital book library. Here, you can search, access, and read Packt's entire library of books.

Why subscribe?

- Fully searchable across every book published by Packt
- Copy and paste, print, and bookmark content
- On demand and accessible via a web browser

Instant updates on new Packt books

Get notified! Find out when new books are published by following @PacktEnterprise on Twitter or the *Packt Enterprise* Facebook page.

Table of Contents

Preface

First of all, thank you for the feedback on the first edition. You will see that this second edition goes above and beyond the feedback. It actually has more new content than the existing content, enabling us to cover the topic deeper and wider.

The strongest feedback Packt Publishing and I got was to make it more pleasant to read as infrastructure is a dry topic. The topics we cover in the book are complex in nature, and the book goes deep into operationalizing performance and capacity management.

Another common feedback was to give more examples on the dashboards. You want more practical solution that you can implement. You want the book to guide you in your journey to operationalize your IaaS platform.

These two feedback plus other feedback and goals made the publisher and me took a fresh look on the topic. You will find the 2nd edition more complete, yet easier to read.

- In terms of ease of read, we have made the writing style more conversational. It should read less like a formal technical whitepaper and more like a spoken conversation among colleagues. We've also made the pictures clearer and added more diagrams to explain the topics better. We use more bullets and tables to improve the layout. We use shorter sentence, hence, we only use she instead of she/he in the book. It applies to both genders.

- In terms of completeness, you will find that the topics are expanded significantly. For example, the 2nd edition has five chapters on dashboards, compared with just one chapter on the 1st edition. Chapter wise, the book now has 15 chapters instead of 8 in the 1st edition.

What this book covers

Content wise, the book is now distinctly split into three main parts. Each part happens to have five chapters each:

- Part 1 provides the technical foundation of SDDC management. It aims to correct deep-rooted misunderstanding of knowledge that is considered basic. Terms such as VM and SDDC will be redefined, and we hope that you will gain new perspective. Part 1 is also written for VMware specialists who need to explain these topics to their peers, customers, or management.

- Part 2 provides the actual solution that you can implement in your environment. We provide the reasons behind each dashboard, so you get the understanding on why it is required and what problem it solves.

- Part 3 acts as a reference section. If you need to know the meaning behind a specific counter and how it relates to other counters, Part 3 has over 100 pages on this topic.

Chapter 1, VM – It Is Not What You Think!, aims to clear up the misunderstandings that customers have about virtualization. It explains why a VM is radically different from a physical server.

Chapter 2, Software-Defined Data Centers, takes the concept further and explains why a virtual data center is fundamentally different from a physical data center. You will see how it differs architecturally in almost all aspects.

Chapter 3, SDDC Management, covers the aspects of management that are affected with the new architecture.

Chapter 4, Performance Monitoring, takes the topic of the previous chapter deeper by discussing how performance management should be done in a virtual data center. It introduces a new paradigm that redefines the word Performance.

Chapter 5, Capacity Monitoring, complements Chapter 4 by explaining why capacity management needs to take into account performance before utilization. This chapter wraps up Part 1 of the book.

Chapter 6, Performance-Monitoring Dashboards, kicks off Part 2, where we cover the practical aspects of this book, as they show how sample solutions are implemented. We start by showing the steps to implement dashboards to monitor performance.

Chapter 7, Capacity-Monitoring Dashboards, takes the dashboards in *Chapter 6* further by adding capacity monitoring requirement. You will see how they are closely related.

Chapter 8, Specific-Purpose Dashboards, complements those dashboards by covering specific use cases. They are often used by specific roles, such as network team, storage team, and senior management.

Chapter 9, Infrastructure Monitoring Using Blue Medora, takes the dashboards beyond VMware. It covers non-VMware components of your IaaS. Blue Medora is contributing their expertise here.

Chapter 10, Application Monitoring Using Blue Medora, completes our scope by going above the infrastructure layer. It covers commonly used applications in your VMware-based SDDC. This chapter also wraps up Part 2 of the book.

Chapter 11, SDDC Key Counters, sets the technical foundations of performance and capacity management by giving you a tour of the four infrastructure elements (CPU, RAM, network, and storage). It also maps these four elements into all the vSphere objects, so you know what is available at each level.

Chapter 12, CPU Counters, covers CPU counters in detail. It is the first of four chapters that cover the core infrastructure element (CPU, RAM, network, and storage). If you do not fully understand the various counters in vSphere and vRealize Operations, how they impact one another, and what values you consider healthy, then these four chapters are good for you. They dive deep into the counters, comparing the counters in vCenter and vRealize Operations. Knowing the counters is critical, as choosing the wrong counters or interpreting the values wrongly will lead to a wrong conclusion.

Chapter 13, Memory Counters, continues the deep dive by covering memory counters. It explains why memory is one of the most complex area to monitor and troubleshoot in SDDC.

Chapter 14, Storage Counters, continues the deep dive by covering storage counters. It explains the multiple layers of storage that occur as a result of virtualization. It also explains that distributed storage requires different monitoring approach.

Chapter 15, Network Counters, completes the deep dive by covering network counters and wraps up the book.

What you need for this book

We assume that you have the products installed and configured. VMware vSphere, vRealize Operations, and Log Insight are the products used in this book. There are many blog articles and YouTube videos on design, installation, configuration, and product overview. Some of the bloggers, such as Sunny Dua, have many other materials, which will complete your learning. At a personal level and as a father of two young kids, I'm not keen on killing trees unless it's really necessary.

The book takes advantage of all relevant new features in the latest release. That means vSphere 6.0 Update 2, vRealize Operations 6.2, and Log Insight 3.3. As this is not a product book, almost all the content of the book can be implemented using earlier release. To assure you that you can do that, we've kept screenshots from older versions whenever possible.

The detailed steps of implementation will certainly vary if you are using the older release. For example, instead of using the View widget in vRealize Operations 6, you will have to use the Metric Graph and XML in vRealize Operations 5.8.

If the solution cannot be implemented with the previous release, we'd highlight it. For example, the data transformation feature in the View widget is hard to replicate in vRealize Operations 5.8.

Who this book is for

This book is for VMware professionals. This can be a VMware administrator, architect, consultant, engineer, or technical support. You may be working for VMware customers, partners, or VMware itself. You may be an individual contributor or a technical leader.

This book is an intermediate-level book. It assumes that you have hands-on experience of vSphere, vRealize Operations, and Log Insight, and you are capable of performing some level of performance troubleshooting. You also have good overall knowledge of vCloud Suite, Virtual SAN, Horizon View, and NSX. Beyond VMware, you should also have intermediate knowledge of operating systems, storage, network, disaster recovery, and data center.

This book is also for IT professionals who deal with VMware professionals. As such, there is a wide range of roles, as virtualization and VMware cover many aspects of IT. Depending on your role, certain chapters will be more useful to you.

What this book is not

This book is a solution book, not a product book. It uses vRealize Operations and Log Insight to apply the solution. You can probably use other products to implement the dashboards.

Because it is not a product book, it does not cover all modules of vRealize Operations Suite. vCenter Infrastructure Navigator and VMware Configuration Manager are not covered. If you need a product book, Scott Norris and Christopher Slater have published one. There are also many blogs that cover installation and configuration.

The book focuses on the management of the SDDC. It does not cover the architecture. So no vCloud Suite design best practices are present in this book. It also does not cover all aspects of operation. For example, it does not cover process innovation, organizational structure, financial management, and audit. Specific to management, the book only focuses on the following most fundamental areas:

- Performance
- Capacity

This book does not cover other areas of management, such as configuration, compliance, and availability management.

Conventions

In this book, you will find a number of text styles that distinguish between different kinds of information. Here are some examples of these styles and an explanation of their meaning.

Code words in text, database table names, folder names, filenames, file extensions, pathnames, dummy URLs, user input, and Twitter handles are shown as follows: This includes the drive where the OS resides (the `c:\` drive in Windows systems).

A block of code is set as follows:

```
max(${adaptertype=VMWARE, objecttype=VirtualMachine,
attribute=cpu|capacity_contentionPct, depth=2})
max(${adaptertype=VMWARE, objecttype=VirtualMachine,
attribute=mem|host_contentionPct, depth=2})
Max(${adaptertype=VMWARE, objecttype=VirtualMachine, attribute=virtual
Disk|totalLatency, depth=2})
Max(${adaptertype=VMWARE, objecttype=VirtualMachine,
attribute=net|droppedPct, depth=3})
```

New terms and **important words** are shown in bold. Words that you see on the screen, for example, in menus or dialog boxes, appear in the text like this: A popular technology often branded under virtualization is **hardware partitioning**.

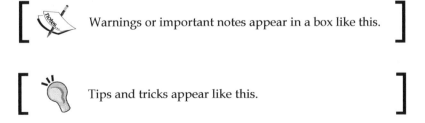

Warnings or important notes appear in a box like this.

Tips and tricks appear like this.

Reader feedback

Feedback from our readers is always welcome. Let us know what you think about this book—what you liked or disliked. Reader feedback is important for us as it helps us develop titles that you will really get the most out of.

To send us general feedback, simply e-mail feedback@packtpub.com, and mention the book's title in the subject of your message.

If there is a topic that you have expertise in and you are interested in either writing or contributing to a book, see our author guide at www.packtpub.com/authors.

Customer support

Now that you are the proud owner of a Packt book, we have a number of things to help you to get the most from your purchase.

Downloading the color images of this book

We also provide you with a PDF file that has color images of the screenshots/diagrams used in this book. The color images will help you better understand the changes in the output. You can download this file from http://www.packtpub.com/sites/default/files/downloads/VMwarePerformanceAndCapacityManagementSecondEdition_ColorImages.pdf.

Errata

Although we have taken every care to ensure the accuracy of our content, mistakes do happen. If you find a mistake in one of our books—maybe a mistake in the text or the code—we would be grateful if you could report this to us. By doing so, you can save other readers from frustration and help us improve subsequent versions of this book. If you find any errata, please report them by visiting http://www.packtpub.com/submit-errata, selecting your book, clicking on the **Errata Submission Form** link, and entering the details of your errata. Once your errata are verified, your submission will be accepted and the errata will be uploaded to our website or added to any list of existing errata under the Errata section of that title.

To view the previously submitted errata, go to https://www.packtpub.com/books/content/support and enter the name of the book in the search field. The required information will appear under the **Errata** section.

Piracy

Piracy of copyrighted material on the Internet is an ongoing problem across all media. At Packt, we take the protection of our copyright and licenses very seriously. If you come across any illegal copies of our works in any form on the Internet, please provide us with the location address or website name immediately so that we can pursue a remedy.

Please contact us at copyright@packtpub.com with a link to the suspected pirated material.

We appreciate your help in protecting our authors and our ability to bring you valuable content.

Questions

If you have a problem with any aspect of this book, you can contact us at questions@packtpub.com, and we will do our best to address the problem.

Part 1
Technical Introduction

Part 1 provides the technical foundation of SDDC Performance and Capacity Management. It aims to correct deep-rooted misunderstanding of many terms that are considered basic. Terms such as VM and SDDC will be redefined, and I hope you will gain new perspective.

It consists of 5 chapters

- Chapter 1 covers VM
- Chapter 2 covers SDDC
- Chapter 3 covers SDDC management
- Chapter 4 covers performance monitoring
- Chapter 5 covers capacity monitoring

Chapter 1 and 2 redefine what we know as VM and SDDC. Once these core entites (VM and SDDC) are redefined, how we manage them changes drastically. Chapter 3 explains what exactly needs to be changed. Chapter 4 and 5 dive deeper into the two most fundamental of SDDC management, which are performance and capacity.

1

VM – It Is Not
What You Think!

In this chapter, we will dive into why a seemingly simple technology, a virtualized x86 machine, has huge ramifications for the IT industry. In fact, it is turning a lot of things upside down and breaking down silos that have existed for decades in large IT organizations. We will cover the following topics:

- Why virtualization is not what we think it is
- Virtualization versus partitioning
- A comparison between a physical server and Virtual Machine

Our journey into the virtual world

Virtual Machines, or simply, VMs—who doesn't know what they are? Even a business user who has never seen one knows what it is. It is just a physical server, virtualized—nothing more.

Wise men say that small leaks sink the ship. I think that's a good way to explain why IT departments that manage physical servers well struggle when the same servers are virtualized.

We can also use the Pareto principle (80/20 rule): 80 percent of a VM is identical to a physical server. But it's the 20 percent of differences that hits you. We will highlight some of this 20 percent portion, focusing on areas that impact data center management.

The change caused by virtualization is much larger than the changes brought about by previous technologies. In the past two or more decades, we transitioned from mainframes to the client/server-based model and then to the web-based model. These are commonly agreed upon as the main evolutions in IT architecture. However, all of these are just technological changes. They changed the architecture, yes, but they did not change the operation in a fundamental way. Both the client-server and web shifts did not talk about the "journey". There was no journey to the client-server based model. However, with virtualization, we talk about the virtualization journey. It is a journey because the changes are massive and involve a lot of people.

Gartner correctly predicted the impact of virtualization in 2007 (`http://www.gartner.com/newsroom/id/505040`). More than 8 years later, we are still in the midst of the journey. Proving how pervasive the change is, here is the summary of the article from Gartner:

> Virtualization will be the most impactful trend in infrastructure and operations through 2010, changing:
> * How you plan
> * How, what and when you buy
> * How and how quickly you deploy
> * How you manage
> * How you charge
> * Technology, process, culture
>
> **— Gartner**

Notice how Gartner talks about a change in culture. So, virtualization has a cultural impact too. In fact, if your virtualization journey is not fast enough, look at your organization's structure and culture. Have you broken the silos? Do you empower your people to take risks and do things that have never been done before? Are you willing to flatten the organizational chart?

 The silos that have served you well are likely your number one barrier to a hybrid cloud.

So why exactly is virtualization causing such a fundamental shift? To understand this, we need to go back to the basics, which is exactly what virtualization is. It's pretty common that **chief information officers (CIOs)** have a misconception about what it is.

Take a look at the following comments. Have you seen them in your organization?

- VM is just a physical machine that has been virtualized. Even VMware says the Guest OS is not aware it's virtualized and it does not run differently.

- It is still about monitoring CPU, RAM, disk, network, and other resources—no difference.

- It is a technological change. Our management process does not have to change.

- All of these VMs must still feed into our main enterprise IT management system. This is how we have run our business for decades, and it works.

If only life were that simple; we would all be 100-percent virtualized and have no headaches! Virtualization has been around for years, and yet, most organizations have not mastered it. The proof of mastering it is if you complete the journey and reach the highest level of the virtualization maturity model.

Not all virtualizations are equal

There are plenty of misconceptions about the topic of virtualization, especially among IT folks who are not familiar with virtualization. CIOs who have not felt the strategic impact of virtualization (be it a good or bad experience) tend to carry these misconceptions. Although virtualization looks similar to a physical system from the outside, it is completely re-architected under the hood.

So let's take a look at the first misconception: what exactly is virtualization?

Because it is an industry trend, virtualization is often generalized to include other technologies that are not virtualized. This is a typical strategy of IT vendors that have similar technology. A popular technology often branded under virtualization is **hardware partitioning**; once it is parked under the umbrella of virtualization, both are expected be managed in the same way. Since both are actually different, customers who try to manage both with a single piece of management software struggle to do well.

Partitioning and virtualization are two different architectures in computer engineering, resulting in major differences between their functionalities. They are shown in the following screenshot:

Virtualization versus partitioning

With partitioning, there is no hypervisor that virtualizes the underlying hardware. There is no software layer separating the VM and the physical motherboard. There is, in fact, no VM. This is why some technical manuals about partitioning technology do not even use the term "VM". They use the terms "domain", "partition", or "container" instead.

There are two variants of partitioning technology, hardware-level and OS-level partitioning, which are covered in the following bullet points:

- In hardware-level partitioning, each partition runs directly on the hardware. It is not virtualized. This is why it is more scalable and has less of a performance hit. Because it is not virtualized, it has to have an awareness of the underlying hardware. As a result, it is not fully portable. You cannot move the partition from one hardware model to another. The hardware has to be built for the purpose of supporting that specific version of the partition. The partitioned OS still needs all the hardware drivers and will not work on other hardware if the compatibility matrix does not match. As a result, even the version of the OS matters, as it is just like the physical server.

- In OS-level partitioning, there is a parent OS that runs directly on the server motherboard. This OS then creates an OS partition, where another "OS" can run. I use double quotes as it is not exactly the full OS that runs inside that partition. The OS has to be modified and qualified to be able to run as a Zone or Container. Because of this, application compatibility is affected. This is different in a VM, where there is no application compatibility issue because the hypervisor is transparent to the Guest OS.

Hardware partitioning

We covered the difference from an engineering point of view. However, does it translate into different data center architectures and operations? We will focus on hardware partitioning as there are fundamental differences between hardware partitioning and software partitioning. The use cases for both are also different. Software partitioning is typically used in native cloud applications.

With that, let's do a comparison between hardware partitioning and virtualization. Let's take availability as a start.

With virtualization, all VMs become protected by **vSphere High Availability (vSphere HA)** — 100 percent protection and that too done without VM awareness. Nothing needs to be done at the VM layer. No shared or quorum disk and no heartbeat-network VM is required to protect a VM with basic HA.

With hardware partitioning, protection has to be configured manually, one by one for each **Logical Partition (LPAR)** or **Logical Domain (LDOM)**. The underlying platform does not provide it.

With virtualization, you can even go beyond five nines, that is, 99.999 percent, and move to 100 percent with **vSphere Fault Tolerance**. This is not possible in the partitioning approach as there is no hypervisor that replays CPU instructions. Also, because it is virtualized and transparent to the VM, you can turn on and off the Fault Tolerance capability on demand. Fault Tolerance is fully defined in the software.

Another area of difference between partitioning and virtualization is **Disaster Recovery (DR)**. With partitioning technology, the DR site requires another instance to protect the production instance. It is a different instance, with its own OS image, hostname, and IP address. Yes, we can perform a **Storage Area Network (SAN)** boot, but that means another **Logical Unit Number (LUN)** is required to manage, zone, replicate, and so on. DR is not scalable to thousands of servers. To make it scalable, it has to be simpler.

Compared to partitioning, virtualization takes a different approach. The entire VM fits inside a folder; it becomes like a document and we migrate the entire folder as if it were one object. This is what **vSphere Replication** in vSphere or **Site Recovery Manager** does. It performs a replication per VM; there is no need to configure SAN boot. The entire DR exercise, which can cover thousands of virtual servers, is completely automated and has audit logs automatically generated. Many large enterprises have automated their DR with virtualization. There is probably no company that has automated DR for their entire LPAR, LDOM, or container.

In the previous paragraph, we're not implying LUN-based or hardware-based replication to be inferior solutions. We're merely driving the point that virtualization enables you to do things differently.

We're also not saying that hardware partitioning is an inferior technology. Every technology has its advantages and disadvantages and addresses different use cases. Before I joined VMware, I was a Sun Microsystems sales engineer for 5 years, so I'm aware of the benefit of UNIX partitioning. This book is merely trying to dispel the misunderstanding that hardware partitioning equals virtualization.

OS partitioning

We've covered the differences between hardware partitioning and virtualization.

Let's switch gears to software partitioning. In 2016, the adoption of Linux containers will continue its rapid rise. You can actually use both containers and virtualization, and they complement each other in some use cases. There are two main approaches to deploying containers:

- Running them directly on bare metal
- Running them inside a Virtual Machine

As both technologies evolve, the gap gets wider. As a result, managing a software partition is different from managing a VM. Securing a container is different to securing a VM. Be careful when opting for a management solution that claims to manage both. You will probably end up with the most common denominator. This is one reason why VMware is working on vSphere Integrated Containers and the Photon platform. Now that's a separate topic by itself!

Virtual Machine – it is not what you think!

A VM is not just a physical server that has been virtualized. Yes, there is a **Physical-to-Virtual (P2V)** process; however, once it is virtualized, it takes on a new shape. This shape has many new and changed properties, and some old properties are no longer applicable or available. My apologies if the following is not the best analogy:

We P2V the soul, not the body.

On the surface, a VM looks like a physical server. So, let's actually look at VM properties. The following screenshot shows a VM's settings in vSphere 5.5. It looks familiar as it has a CPU, memory, hard disk, network adapter, and so on. However, look at it closely. Do you see any properties that you don't see in a physical server?

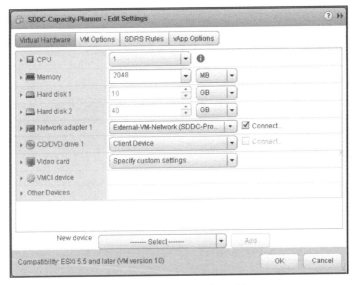

VM properties in vSphere 5.5

Let's highlight some of the virtual server properties that do not exist in a physical server. I'll focus on the properties that have an impact on management, as management is the topic of this book.

At the top of the dialog box, there are four tabs:

- **Virtual Hardware**
- **VM Options**
- **SDRS Rules**
- **vApp Options**

The **Virtual Hardware** tab is the only tab that has similar properties to a physical server. The other three tabs do not have their equivalent physical server counterparts. For example, **SDRS Rules** pertains to **Storage DRS**. It means that the VM storage can be automatically moved by vCenter. Its location in the data center is not static. This includes the drive where the OS resides (the c:\ drive in Windows systems). This directly impacts your server management tool. It has to have awareness of **Storage DRS** and can no longer assume that a VM is always located in the same datastore or **Logical Unit Number** (**LUN**). Compare this with a physical server. Its OS typically resides on a local disk, which is part of the physical server. You don't want your physical server's OS drive being moved around in a data center, do you?

In the **Virtual Hardware** tab, notice the **New device** option at the bottom of the screen. Yes, you can add devices, some of them on the fly, while an OS such as Windows or Linux is running. All the VM's devices are defined in the software. This is a major difference compared to a physical server, where the physical hardware defines it and you cannot change it. With virtualization, you can have a VM with five sockets on an ESXi host with two sockets. Windows or Linux can run on five physical CPUs even though the underlying ESXi actually only runs on two physical CPUs.

Your server management tool needs to be aware of this and recognize that the new **Configuration Management Database** (**CMDB**) is vCenter. vCenter is certainly not a CMDB product. We're only saying that in a situation when there is a conflict between vCenter and a CMDB product, the one you trust is vCenter. In a **Software-Defined Data Center** (**SDDC**), the need for a CMDB is further reduced.

The following screenshot shows a bit more detail. Look at the CPU device. Again, what do you see that does not exist in a physical server?

VM CPU and network properties in vSphere 5.5

Let's highlight some of the options.

Look at the **Reservation**, **Limit**, and **Shares** options under **CPU**. None of them exist in a physical server, as a physical server is standalone by default. It does not share any resource on the motherboard (such as CPU or RAM) with another server. With these three levers, you can perform **Quality of Service (QoS)** on a virtual data center. So, QoS is actually built into the platform. This has an impact on management, as the platform is able to do some of the management by itself. There is no need to get another console to do what the platform provides you out of the box.

Other properties in the previous screenshot, such as **Hardware virtualization**, **Performance counters**, **HT Sharing**, and **CPU/MMU Virtualization**, also do not exist in a physical server. It is beyond the scope of this book to explain every feature, and there are many blogs and technical papers freely available on the Internet that explain them. Two of my favorites are http://blogs.vmware.com/performance/ and http://www.vmware.com/vmtn/resources/.

The next screenshot shows the **VM Options** tab. Again, which properties do you see that do not exist in a physical server?

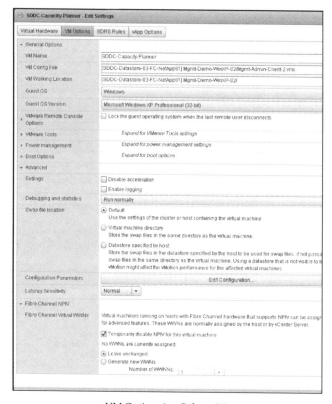

VM Options in vSphere 5.5

I'd like to highlight a few of the properties present in the **VM Options** tab. The **VMware Tools** property is a key component. It provides you with drivers and improves manageability. The **VMware Tools** property is not present in a physical server. A physical server has drivers, but none of them are from VMware. A VM, however, is different. Its motherboard (virtual motherboard, naturally) is defined and supplied by VMware. Hence, the drivers are supplied by VMware. The **VMware Tools** property is the mechanism of supplying those drivers. The **VMware Tools** property comes in different versions. So, now you need to be aware of **VMware Tools** and it is something you need to manage.

We've just covered a few VM properties from the VM settings dialog box. There are literally hundreds of properties in VMs that do not exist in physical systems. Even the same properties are implemented differently. For example, although vSphere supports **N_Port ID Virtualization (NPIV)**, the Guest OS does not see the **World Wide Name (WWN)**. This means that data center management tools have to be aware of the specific implementation of vSphere. And these properties change with every vSphere release. Notice the line right at the bottom of the screenshot. It says **Compatibility: ESXi 5.5 and later (VM version 10)**. This is your VM motherboard. It has a dependency on the ESXi version and yes, this becomes another new thing to manage too.

Every vSphere release typically adds new properties too, making a VM more manageable than a physical machine and differentiating a VM further from a physical server.

Physical server versus Virtual Machine

Hopefully, I've driven home the point that a VM is different from a physical server. I'll now list the differences from a management point of view. The following table shows the differences that impact how you manage your infrastructure. Let's begin with the core properties:

Properties	Physical server	Virtual Machine
BIOS	Every brand and model has a unique BIOS. Even the same model (for example, HP DL 380 Generation 9) can have multiple BIOS versions. The BIOS needs updates and management, often with physical access to a data center. This requires downtime.	This is standardized in a VM. There is only one type, which is the VMware motherboard. This is independent from the ESXi motherboard. The VM BIOS needs far fewer updates and management. The inventory management system no longer needs the BIOS management module.

Properties	Physical server	Virtual Machine
Virtual HW	Not applicable.	This is a new layer below the BIOS. It needs an update after every vSphere release. A data center management system needs to be aware of this as it requires a deep knowledge of vSphere. For example, to upgrade the virtual hardware, the VM has to be in the powered-off state.
Drivers	Many drivers are loaded and bundled with the OS. Often, you need to get the latest drivers from their respective hardware vendors. All these drivers need to be managed. This can be a complex operation, as they vary from model to model and brand to brand. The management tool has rich functionalities, such as being able to check compatibility, roll out drivers, roll them back if there is an issue, and so on.	Relatively fewer drivers are loaded with the Guest OS; some drivers are replaced by the ones provided by VMware Tools. Even with NPIV, the VM does not need the FC HBA driver. VMware Tools needs to be managed, with vCenter being the most common management tool.

How do all these differences impact the hardware upgrade process? Let's take a look:

Physical server	Virtual Machine
Downtime is required. It is done offline and is complex. OS reinstallation and updates are required, hence it is a complex project in physical systems. Sometimes, a hardware upgrade is not even possible without upgrading the application.	It is done online and is simple. Virtualization decouples the application from hardware dependencies. A VM can be upgraded from 5-year-old hardware to a new one, moving from the local SCSI disk to 10 Gigabit **Fiber Channel over Ethernet (FCoE)**, from a dual-core to an 18-core CPU. So yes, MS-DOS can run on 10 Gigabit Ethernet, accessing SSD storage via the PCIe lane. You just need to migrate to the new hardware with vMotion. As a result, the operation is drastically simplified.

In the preceding table, we compared the core properties of a physical server with a VM. Every server needs storage, so let's compare their storage properties:

Physical server	Virtual Machine
Servers connected to a SAN can see the SAN and FC fabric. They need HBA drivers and have FC PCI cards, and they have **multipathing** software installed. They normally need an advanced file system or volume manager to **Redundant Array of Inexpensive Disks (RAID)** local disk.	No VM is connected to the FC fabric or SAN. The VM only sees the local disk. Even with **N_Port ID Virtualization (NPIV)** and physical **Raw Device Mapping (RDM)**, the VM does not send FC frames. Multipathing is provided by vSphere, transparent to the VM. There is no need for a RAID local disk. It is one virtual disk, not two. Availability is provided at the hardware layer.
A backup agent and backup LAN are required in a majority of cases.	These are not needed in a majority of cases, as backup is done via the vSphere VADP API, which is a VMware vStorage API that backs up and restores vSphere VMs. An agent is only required for application-level backup.

There's a big difference in storage. How about network and security? Let's see:

Physical server	Virtual Machine
NIC teaming is common. This typically requires two cables per server.	NIC teaming is provided by ESXi. The VM is not aware and only sees one vNIC.
The Guest OS is VLAN-aware. It is configured inside the OS. Moving the VLAN requires reconfiguration.	The VLAN is generally provided by vSphere and not done inside the Guest OS. This means the VM can be moved from one VLAN to another with no downtime. With network virtualization, the VM moves from a VLAN to VXLAN.
The AV agent is installed on the Guest and can be seen by an attacker.	An AV agent runs on the ESXi host as a VM (one per ESXi). It cannot be seen by the attacker from inside the Guest OS.
The AV consumes OS resources. AV signature updates cause high storage usage.	The AV consumes minimal Guest OS resources as it is offloaded to the ESXi Agent VM. AV signature updates do not require high **Input/Output Operations Per Second (IOPS)** inside the Guest OS. The total IOPS is also lower at the ESXi host level as it is not done per VM.

Finally, let's take a look at the impact on management. As can be seen here, even the way we manage a server changes once it is converted into a VM:

Property	Physical server	Virtual Machine
Monitoring approach	An agent is commonly deployed. It is typical for a server to have multiple agents. In-Guest counters are accurate as the OS can see the physical hardware. A physical server has an average of 5 percent CPU utilization due to a multicore chip. As a result, there is no need to monitor it closely.	An agent is typically not deployed. Certain areas, such as application and Guest OS monitoring, are still best served by an agent. The key in-Guest counters are not accurate as the Guest OS does not see the physical hardware. A VM has an average of 50 percent CPU utilization as it is rightsized. This is 10 times higher compared to a physical server. As a result, there is a need to monitor it closely, especially when physical resources are oversubscribed. Capacity management becomes a discipline in itself.
Availability approach	HA is provided by clusterware, such as Microsoft **Windows Server Failover Clusters (WSFC)** and **Veritas Cluster Server (VCS)**. Clusterware tends to be complex and expensive. Cloning a physical server is a complex task and requires the boot drive to be on the SAN or LAN, which is not typical. A snapshot is rarely made, due to cost and complexity. Only very large IT departments are found to perform physical server snapshots.	HA is a built-in core component of vSphere. From what I see, most clustered physical servers end up as just a single VM since vSphere HA is good enough. Cloning can be done easily. It can even be done live. The drawback is that the clone becomes a new area of management. Snapshots can be made easily. In fact, this is done every time as part of the backup process. Snapshots also become a new area of management.

Property	Physical server	Virtual Machine
Company asset	The physical server is a company asset and it has book value in the accounting system. It needs proper asset management as components vary among servers. Here, an annual stock-take process is required.	A VM is not an asset as it has no accounting value. It is like a document. It is technically a folder with files in it. A stock-take process is no longer required as the VM cannot exist outside vSphere.

Summary

I hope you enjoyed the comparison and found it useful. We covered, to a great extent, the impact caused by virtualization and the changes it introduces. We started by clarifying that virtualization is a different technology compared to partitioning. We then explained that once a physical server is converted into a Virtual Machine, it takes on a different form and has radically different properties. The changes range from the core property of the server itself to how we manage it.

The changes create a ripple effect in the bigger picture. The entire data center changes once we virtualize it, and this the topic of our next chapter.

2
Software-Defined Data Centers

In this chapter, we will take the point introduced in *Chapter 1, VM – It Is Not What You Think!*, further. We will explain why the **software-defined data center** (**SDDC**) is much more than a virtualized data center.

We will cover the following topics:

- What exactly is a software-defined data center?
- SDDCs and the cloud.
- A comparison between a physical and a virtual data center.

The software-defined data center

In *Chapter 1, VM – It Is Not What You Think!*, we covered how a VM differs drastically from a physical server. Now, let's take a look at the big picture, which is at the data-center level. A data center consists of three major functions—**compute**, **network**, and **storage**. Security is not a function on its own, but a key property that each function has to deliver. We use the term "compute" to represent processing power, namely, CPU and memory. In today's data centers, compute is also used when referencing converged infrastructure, where the server and storage have physically converged into one box. The industry term for this is **Hyper-Converged Infrastructure** (**HCI**). You will see later in the book that this convergence impacts how you architect and operate an SDDC.

VMware has moved to virtualizing the network and storage functions as well, resulting in a data center that is fully virtualized and thus defined in the software. The software is the data center. This has resulted in the term "SDDC". This book will make extensive comparisons with the physical data center. For ease of reference, let's call the physical data center the **hardware-defined data center** (**HDDC**).

In SDDC, we no longer define the architecture in the physical layer. The physical layer is just there to provide resources. These resources are not aware of one another. The stickiness is reduced and they become a commodity. In many cases, the hardware can even be replaced without incurring downtime on the VMs running on top.

The next diagram shows one possibility of a data center defined in software. I have drawn the diagram to state a point, so don't take this as the best practice for SDDC architecture. In the diagram, there are many virtual data centers (I have drawn three due to space constraints). Each virtual data center has its own set of virtual infrastructure (server, storage, network, and security). They are independent of one another.

A virtual data center is no longer contained in a single building bound by a physical boundary. Although bandwidth and latency are still limiting factors in 2016, the main thing here is that you can architect your physical data centers as one or more logical data centers. You should be able to, with just a few clicks in VMware **Site Recovery Manager (SRM)**, automatically move thousands of servers from data center 1 to data center 2; alternatively, you can perform **Disaster Recovery (DR)** from four branch sites to a common HQ data center.

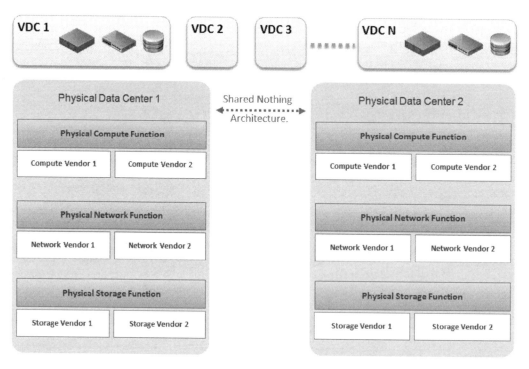

An example SDDC

In our example, the virtual data centers run on top of two physical data centers. Large enterprises will probably have more than this (whether it is outsourced or not is a different matter). The two physical data centers are completely independent. Their hardware is not dependent on each other:

- The **compute** function: There is no stretched cluster between two physical sites. Each site has its own vCenter. There is no need to protect vCenter with DR.

- The **network** function: There is no stretched VLAN between two physical sites. You do not have to worry about a spanning tree or broadcast storm hitting multiple data centers. The physical sites can even be on different networks. Site 1 might be on the `10.10.x.x` network, while site 2 might be on `20.20.x.x`.

- The **storage** function: There is no array-based replication. Replication can be done independently using a storage protocol (FC, iSCSI, or NFS) and **Virtual Machine Disk (VMDK)** type (thick or thin). vSphere has built-in host-based replication via TCP/IP, simply named **vSphere Replication**. It can replicate individual VMs, and it provides finer granularity than replication based on a **Logical Unit Number (LUN)** . You might decide to keep the same storage vendor and protocol, but that's your choice, not something forced upon you.

I have drawn two vendors for each layer to show you that the hardware does not define the architecture. It is there to support the function of that layer (for example, compute). So, you can have 10 vSphere clusters, of which three could be using Vendor 1 and seven could be using Vendor 2.

We are taking the shared-nothing architecture approach. This is a good thing, because you can contain the failure domain. Ivan Pepelnjak, an authority on data center networking architecture, stated the following:

> *"Interconnected things tend to fail at the same time."*

You can find more details at `http://blog.ipspace.net/2012/10/if-something-can-fail-it-will.html`. While you are on the site, check out `http://blog.ipspace.net/2013/02/hot-and-cold-vm-mobility.html`.

In 2016, cloud computing is set to rise even further, with adoption accelerating. The SDDC fits better in the cloud strategy than HDDC, as it's not bound by the rigidity of physical hardware. You can certainly incorporate a public cloud in your SDDC architecture. Your cloud extends from private to public, hence creating a hybrid cloud.

You have three options when it comes to the deployment of your hybrid cloud.

The first choice is that all data centers are on-premises. They can be on your premises or on the managed hosting company's.

The second choice is a hybrid of on-premises and off-premises data centers. The off-premises data centers do not have to be pure cloud ones. They can be managed vSphere environments, where you are not paying for VMware licenses. There are at least three sub-models for off-premises VMware, as follows:

- **Pure cloud**: This is a multi-tenant, shared environment. You pay per VM per month. You own neither VMware licenses nor any hardware.
- **Managed VMware (shared)**: You have a dedicated vSphere cluster, but you don't manage vSphere. You do not dictate the version of vCenter. You may or may not have your own LUN. You pay per cluster per month, and it gives you unlimited VMs. You own no VMware licenses nor any hardware.
- **Managed VMware (dedicated)**: You have a dedicated vCenter. You may or may not manage it. You can dictate your vCenter version, which can be useful since, as you know, some features need the latest version of vCenter. You may own VMware licenses and some hardware.

The third choice is to have both off-premises:

- Just like the second option, you have sub-choices here. You do not have to choose from the same provider. You can have two VMware cloud partners since both use the same architecture, providing you with compatibility.
- You may choose the same VMware cloud partner if you want to leverage their global presence and private network. There are customers who do not want their data going over a public network, even though it may be encrypted.

We've covered SDDCs a fair bit. What do they look like? For those who are not familiar with VMware products, let's take a quick tour.

The next screenshot shows what vCenter looks like in vSphere, the foundation of vCloud Suite:

The vCenter 5.5 overall UI with the Summary tab

I will zoom in to a part of the screenshot as it's rather small. The left-hand part of the screenshot, shown next, shows that there are three vCenter servers, and I've expanded each of them to show their data centers, clusters, hosts, and VMs:

Let's take a closer look at the following screenshot to better understand what is displayed.

The left part of the screenshot, shows that there are three vCenter servers, with their Data Centers, Clusters, Hosts, and VMs.

From here, we can tell that we no longer need another inventory management software, as we can see all objects, their configurations, and how they relate to one another. It is clear from here how many data centers, clusters, ESXi hosts, and VMs we have.

We also get more than static configuration information. Can you see the live or dynamic information is that presented here?

We are able to see the current state of each component, such as the powered state (on/off) or object status (in error, warning, or clear). This is not the type of information you get from CMDBs or inventory management systems.

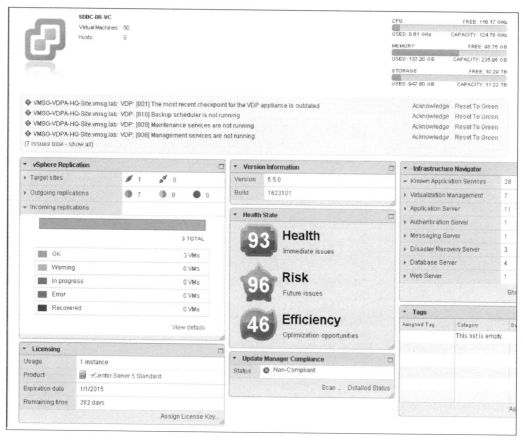

vCenter 5.5 – the Summary tab

You will notice from the preceding screenshot that we get warnings and alerts, so this is a live environment. We also get information on the capacity and health. In the upper-right corner of the screen, you can see the data center's **CPU**, **MEMORY**, **STORAGE** capacity, and their usage. In the **vSphere Replication** box, you can see the VM's replication status. For example, you can see that it has **7** outgoing replications and **3** incoming replications. In the middle of the screen, you can see **Health State**, which, by the way, comes from vRealize Operations. In the **Infrastructure Navigator** box, you get to see which applications are running, such as the **Application Server** and **Database Server**. This information also comes from vRealize Operations. So, many management functions are provided out of the box. These functions are an integral part of vCloud Suite.

The compute function

Many of us virtualization engineers see a cluster as the smallest logical building block in vSphere. We treat it as one physical computer. We perform capacity management at the cluster level and not at the host level. This is because a VM moves around within a cluster with DRS and storage DRS. In a virtual data center, we think in terms of a cluster and not a server.

Let's take a look at the cluster called **SDDC-DR-Workload-Cluster**, shown in the next screenshot. We can tell that it has **3 Hosts, 24** processors (that's cores, not sockets or threads), and almost 140 GB of RAM (about 4 GB is used by the three instances of vmkernel). We can also tell that it has **Enhanced vMotion Compatibility (EVC)** mode enabled, and it is based on the **Intel® "Nehalem" Generation**. This means we can add an ESXi host running a newer Intel processor (for example, Skylake) live inside the cluster and perform vMotion across the CPU generations.

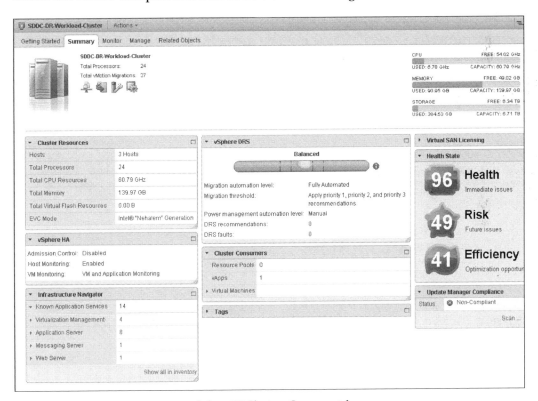

vSphere 5.5 Cluster – Summary tab

In the top-right corner, we can see the capacity used, just like we can see it at the vCenter level. In a sense, we can drill down from the vCenter level to the cluster level.

We can also see that vSphere **High Availability (HA)** and **Distributed Resource Scheduler (DRS)** are turned on. DRS is set to fully automated, which is recommended as you do not want to manually manage the ESXi hosts one by one. There are whole books on vSphere Cluster, as there are many settings for this feature. My favorite is by Duncan Epping and Frank Denneman, which is available at http://www.yellow-bricks.com/my-bookstore/.

The ramification of this is that the data center management software needs to understand vSphere well. It has to keep up with the enhancements in vSphere and vCloud Suite. A case in point: vSphere 5.5, in the update 1 release, added Virtual SAN, a software-defined storage integrated into vSphere. Virtual SAN has been updated several times, demonstrating the rapid changes in SDDC.

Notice **Health State**. Again, this information comes from vRealize Operations. If you click on it, it will take you to a more detailed page, showing charts. If you drill down further, it will take you to vRealize Operations.

Now look at the the **Infrastructure Navigator** area. It is useful to know which applications are running on your cluster. For example, if you have a dedicated cluster for Microsoft SQL Server (as you want to optimize the license) and you see SQL in another cluster (which is not supposed to run the database), you know you need to move the VM. This visibility is important because as an infrastructure team, you typically do not have access to go inside the VM. You do not know what's running on top of Windows or Linux.

The network function

We covered compute. Let's move on to network. The next screenshot shows a distributed virtual switch. As you can see, the distributed switch is an object at the data-center level. Therefore, it extends across clusters. In some environments, this can result in a very large virtual switch with more than 1,000 ports. In the physical world, this would be a huge switch indeed!

A VM is connected to either a standard switch or a distributed switch. It is not directly connected to the physical **network interface card (NIC)** in your ESXi host. The ESXi host's physical NICs become the virtual switch's uplinks instead, and I recommend you have at least two 10 Gigabit Ethernet ports. This means that the traditional **Top-Of-Rack (TOR)** switch has been entirely virtualized. It runs completely as software, and the following screenshot is where you create, define, and manage it. This means that the management software needs to understand the distributed vSwitch and its features. As you will see later, vRealize Operations understands virtual switches and treats networking as a first-class object.

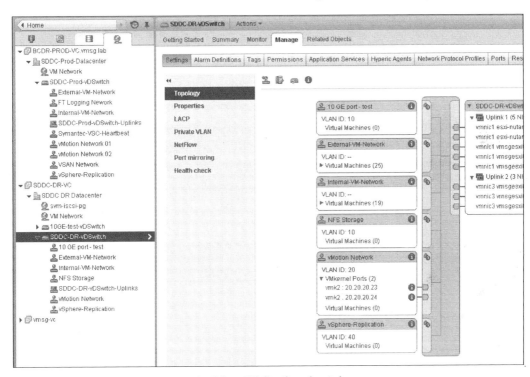

A vSphere 5.5 distributed switch

The previous screenshot also shows that the virtual switch has six port groups and two uplinks. Let's drill down to one of the port groups, as shown in the next screenshot. A port group is a feature that is optional in physical switches, but mandatory in virtual ones. It lets you group a number of switch ports and give them a common property. You can also set policies. As shown in the **Policies** box, there are many properties that you can set. A port group is essential to managing all the ports connected to a switch.

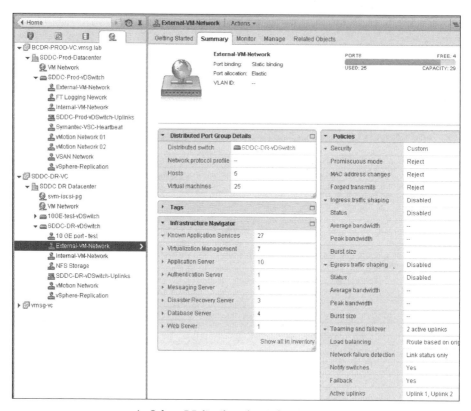

A vSphere 5.5 distributed-switch port group

In the top-right corner, you see the capacity information, so you know how many ports you configured and how many ports are being used. This is where virtual networking is different from virtual compute and virtual storage. For compute and storage, you need to have the underlying physical resources to back them up. You cannot have a VM with a 32-core vCPU if the underlying ESXi has less than 32 physical threads. vSphere will let you create it but not power it on. Virtual networks are different. A network is an interconnection; it is not a "node" like compute and storage. It is not backed by physical ports. You can increase the number of ports to basically any number you want. The entire switch lives in memory! You power off the ESXi and the switch is no more.

In the **Infrastructure Navigator** widget, you will again see the list of applications. **Infrastructure Navigator** is embedded into the vSphere Web UI, making you feel as if it's a single application, like a single pane of glass. Over the past several releases of VMware products, they have been becoming one integrated suite, and this trend is set to continue.

The storage function

Let's now move to storage. The next screenshot shows a vSphere 5.5 datastore cluster. The idea behind a datastore cluster is similar to that of a compute cluster.

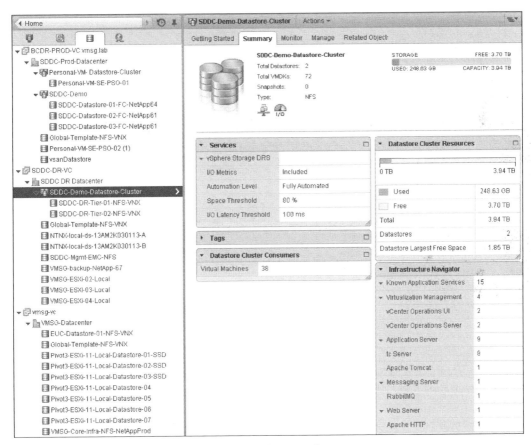

A vSphere 5.5 datastore cluster

Let's use an example since it's easier to understand. Say you have a cluster of eight ESXi hosts, with each host sporting two sockets, 36 cores, and 72 threads. The entire cluster has 288 physical cores and 576 physical threads. In this cluster, you run 200 VMs, giving you a 25:1 consolidation ratio. Based on the guideline that Intel Hyper-Threading gives around a 25-percent performance boost, you can use 360 cores as the max thread count. This gives you around 1.8 cores per VM, which is possible assuming your VMs have two to four vCPUs and around 50-percent utilization. These 200 VMs are stored in four datastores, that is, around 50 VMs per datastore.

With the compute node, you need not worry about where a VM is running in that cluster. When you provision a new VM, you do not necessarily need to specify which host will run it. You let DRS decide. As the workload goes up and down, you do not want to manage the placement on an individual ESXi host for 200 VMs. You let DRS do the load balancing, and it will use vMotion automatically. You treat the entire cluster as if it were a single giant box.

With the storage node, you can do the same thing. When you provision a new VM, you do not specify a datastore for it. If you want to specify it manually, you need to check which datastore has the most amount of space and the least amount of IOPS. The first piece of information is quite easy to check, but the second one is not!

[Balancing VM performance across datastores is hard]

This is the first benefit of a datastore cluster. It picks a datastore based on both capacity and performance. The second benefit is based on the ongoing operation. As time passes, the VM grows at different rates in terms of both capacity and IOPS. Just like the well-known DRS, storage DRS monitors this and makes recommendations for you. The major difference here is the amount of data to be migrated:

- In vMotion, we normally migrate somewhere between 1 GB to 10 GB of RAM, as the kernel only copies the used RAM (and not the configured RAM).
- In storage vMotion, we potentially copy 100 GB of data. This takes a lot longer and hence has a greater performance impact. As such, storage DRS should be performed a lot less frequently, perhaps once a month.

A datastore cluster helps in capacity management, as you basically treat all the datastores as one. You can easily check key information about the datastore cluster, such as the number of VMs, total storage, capacity used, and largest amount of free space you have.

As usual, vRealize Operations, via its Infrastructure Navigator component, provides information about which applications are running in a datastore cluster. This is handy information in a large environment, where you have specific datastores for specific applications.

All together now

We covered all the three elements—compute, storage, and network. How are they related? The next screenshot shows the relationship between the key objects managed by vCenter.

It's handy information in a small environment. If you have a large environment, maps such as the one shown in the next screenshot really become much more complex! In this map, we only have three ESXi hosts and seven datastores, and we already have to hide some relationships. Notice that I did not select the **Host to VM** and **VM to Datastore** relationship options, because the diagram got complicated when I did. These can be added to the maps easily to give an even more detailed view of the datacenter.

The point of sharing the screenshot is to tell you that you really have your data center in software with the following characteristics:

- You have your VM as the consumer. You can show both powered-on and powered-off VMs.
- You have your compute (ESXi), network (port group), and storage (datastore) as the provider. You can show the relationships between your compute, network, and storage.
- You have the information about the network, storage, and compute your VM is connected to.

Think about it: how difficult would it be to have this type of relationship mapped in a large physical data center? We have all heard comments from customers that they do not know exactly how many servers they have, which network they are connected to, and which applications run on a box. A powered-off server is even harder to find! Even if you can implement a datacenter management system, which can give you the map, one or two years later, you cannot be sure that the map is up to date. The management system has to be embedded into the platform. In fact, it's the only point of entry to the virtual platform. It cannot be a separate, detached system.

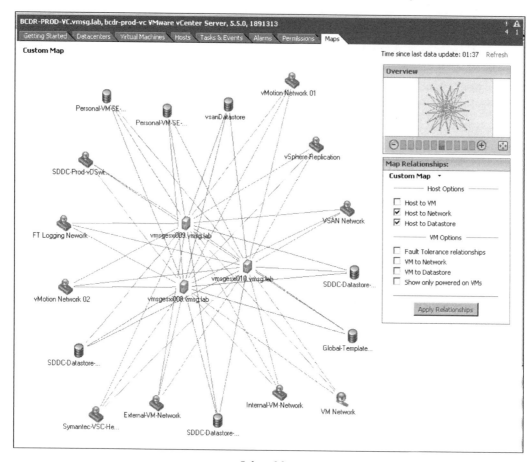

vSphere Maps

The last point I'd like to bring up is that an SDDC is a world in itself. It's not simply your data center that has been virtualized. Look at the following table. It lists some of the objects in vSphere. We have not included NSX, Virtual SAN, or vRealize Suite objects here. These objects do not have their physical equivalents. If they do, they have different properties, generate different events, and are measured by different counters. Plus, all these objects have some relationship with one another. You need to look at vCloud Suite in its entirety to understand it well.

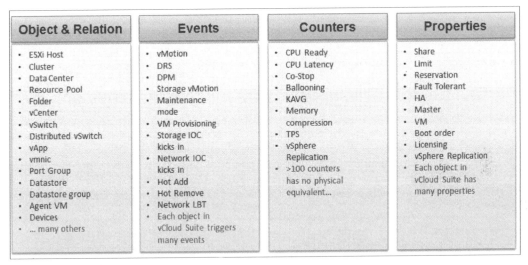

Object & Relation	Events	Counters	Properties
• ESXi Host • Cluster • Data Center • Resource Pool • Folder • vCenter • vSwitch • Distributed vSwitch • vApp • vmnic • Port Group • Datastore • Datastore group • Agent VM • Devices • ... many others	• vMotion • DRS • DPM • Storage vMotion • Maintenance mode • VM Provisioning • Storage IOC kicks in • Network IOC kicks in • Hot Add • Hot Remove • Network LBT • Each object in vCloud Suite triggers many events	• CPU Ready • CPU Latency • Co-Stop • Ballooning • KAVG • Memory compression • TPS • vSphere Replication • >100 counters has no physical equivalent...	• Share • Limit • Reservation • Fault Tolerant • HA • Master • VM • Boot order • Licensing • vSphere Replication • Each object in vCloud Suite has many properties

vSphere objects and their relationships

The downside of an SDDC is that the upgrade of such a "giant machine" is a new project for IT. It has to be planned and implemented carefully because it is as good as upgrading the data center while the servers, storage, and network are all still running. Using a physical-world analogy, it's like renovating your home while living in it.

SDDC versus HDDC

We have covered SDDCs to a certain depth. We can now summarize the key differences between a physical data center and a virtual one. To highlight the differences, we're assuming in this comparison that the physical data center is zero-percent virtualized and the virtual data center is 100-percent virtualized. For the virtual data center, we're assuming you have also adjusted your operation method, because operating a virtual data center with a physical operation mindset results in a lot of frustration and suboptimal virtualization. This means that your processes and organizational chart have been adapted to a virtual data center.

Data Center

The following table compares the key properties of HDDCs and SDDCs. As Disaster Recovery across the data center is the litmus test that defines whether your data center is an HDDC or SDDC, we have included the DR properties as well.

HDDC	SDDC
Data-center migration is a major and expensive project.	The entire virtual DC can be replicated and migrated. I have a customer who performed long-distance vMotion over eight weekends, hence achieving data-center migration with zero downtime.
Architecturally, DR is done on a per-application basis. Every application has its bespoke solution.	DR is provided as a service by the platform. It provides one solution for all applications. This enables DC-wide DR.
A standby server is required on the DR site. This increases the cost. Because the server has to be compatible with the associated production server, this increases complexity in a large environment.	There is no need for a standby server. The vSphere cluster on the DR site typically runs the non-production workload, which can be suspended (hibernate mode) during DR. The DR site can be of a different server brand and CPU.
DR is a manual process, relying on a run book written manually. It also requires all hands on deck. An unavailability of key IT resources when disaster strikes can impact the organization's ability to recover.	All the DR steps can be automated. Once management decides to trigger DR, all that needs to be done is to execute the right recovery process in VMware SRM. No manual intervention is required.
A complete DR dry run is rarely done, as it is time consuming and requires production to be down.	A DR dry run can be done frequently, as it does not impact the production system. This is made possible by having a virtual network that isolates the VMs participating in a DR dry run. As a result, the dry run can even be done the day before the actual planned DR.
The report produced after a DR exercise is manually typed. It is not possible to prove that what is documented in the Microsoft Word or Excel document is what actually happened in the data center.	The report is automatically generated, with no human intervention. It timestamps every step and provides a status whether it was successful or not. The report can be used as audit proof.

Compute

The following table compares the compute element of HDDCs versus SDDCs:

HDDC	SDDC
It has 1,000 physical servers (just an example, so we can provide a comparison).	The number of VMs will be more than 1,000. It may even reach 2,000. The number of VMs is higher for multiple reasons: VM sprawl; the physical server tends to run multiple applications or instances whereas a VM runs only one; DR is much easier and hence, more VMs are protected.
Growth is relatively static and predictable, and it is normally just one-way (adding more servers).	The number of VMs can go up and down due to dynamic provisioning.
Downtime for hardware maintenance or a technology refresh is a common job in a large environment due to component failure.	Planned downtime is eliminated with vMotion and storage vMotion.
5-10 percent average CPU utilization is present, especially in a CPU with a high core count.	There is 50-80 percent utilization of both VM and ESXi.
There are racks of physical boxes, often with a top-of-rack access switch and UPS. The data center consumes a lot of power.	Rack space requirements shrink drastically as servers are consolidated and the infrastructure is converged. There is a drastic reduction in overall space and power, although power consumption per rack is higher.
It has low complexity. There is a lot of repetitive and coordination work, but not a lot of expertise is required.	It has high complexity. Less quantity but deep expertise is required. There are far fewer people, but each one is an expert.
Availability and performance is monitored by management tools, which normally use an agent. It is typical for a server to have many agents.	Availability and performance monitoring happens via vCenter Server, and it's agentless for the infrastructure. All other management tools get their data from vCenter Server, not an individual ESXi or VM. Application-level monitoring is typically done using agents within the Guest OS.

HDDC	SDDC
The word "cluster" generally means two or more servers joined with a heartbeat and shared storage, which is typically a SAN. In another context, a cluster means a single application using shared-nothing hardware. A typical example here is a Hadoop cluster.	The word has a different meaning here. It's a group of ESXi hosts sharing the workload, normally, 8-16 hosts, not 2-4.
High Availability is provided by clusterware, such as Microsoft MSCS and Veritas. Every cluster pair needs shared storage, which is typically a SAN. Typically, one service needs two physical servers with a physical network heartbeat; hence, most servers are not clustered, as the cost and complexity are high.	HA is provided by vSphere HA. All VMs are protected, and not just by a small percentage. The need for traditional clustering software has reduced, and a new kind of clustering software has emerged. It has full awareness of virtualization and integrates with vSphere using vSphere API.
Fault tolerance is rarely used due to cost and complexity. You need specialized hardware, such as Stratus ftServer.	Fault tolerance is an on-demand feature as it is software based. For example, you can temporarily turn it on during batch job runs.
Antivirus software is installed on every server. Management is harder in a large environment.	The antivirus runs as an Agent VM on each ESXi host. It is agentless to the Guest OS and hence, it is no longer visible by malware. A popular solution is Trend Micro Deep Security.

Storage

The following table compares storage in HDDCs and SDDCs:

HDDC	SDDC
It has 1,000 physical servers (just an example so that we can provide a comparison), where IOPS and capacity do not impact each other. It is a relatively static environment from a storage point of view because normally, only 10 percent of these machines are on a SAN/NAS due to cost.	It has a maximum of 2,000 interdependent VMs, which impact one another. It is a very dynamic environment where management becomes critical because almost all VMs are on shared storage, including distributed storage.
Every server on a SAN has its own dedicated LUN. Some data centers, such as databases, may have multiple LUNs.	Most VMs do not use RDM. They use VMDKs and share the VMFS or NFS datastore. The VMDK files may reside in different datastores.
Storage migration causes major downtime, even within the same array. A lot of manual work is required.	Storage migration is live with storage vMotion. Intra-array migration is faster due to the VAAI API.

HDDC	SDDC
Backup, especially in the x64 architecture, is done with backup agents. As a SAN is relatively more expensive and SAN boot is complex at scale, backup is done via the backup LAN and with the agent installed. This creates its own problem, because the backup agents have to be deployed, patched, upgraded, and managed.	The backup service is provided by the hypervisor. It is agentless as far as the VM is concerned. Most backup applications use the VMware VADP API to back up by taking snapshots. Windows **Volume Shadow Services** (**VSS**) provides application-consistent backups by quiescing an application during backup. Non-VSS environments can use pre-post thaw scripts to stop necessary services prior to taking a VM snapshot in order to provide crash-consistent backups of applications and the underlying OS.
The backup process creates high disk I/O, impacting application performance. Because the backup traffic is network intensive and carries sensitive data, an entire network is born for backup purposes.	Because backup is performed outside the VM, there is no performance impact on the application or Guest OS. There is also no security risk, as the Guest OS admin cannot see the backup network.
The storage's QoS is taken care of by an array, although the array has no control over the demand of IOPS coming from servers.	The storage's QoS is taken care of by **vSphere Storage I/O Control**, which has full control over every VM.

Network

The following table compares networks in HDDCs and SDDCs:

HDDC	SDDC
The access network is typically 1 GE, as it is sufficient for most servers. Typically, it is a top-of-rack entry-level switch.	The top-of-rack switch is generally replaced with an end-of-row distribution switch, as the access switch is completely virtualized. ESXi hosts typically use 10 GE connections, with some having four 10-GE connections.
A VLAN is normally used for segregation. This results in VLAN complexity.	A VLAN is not required (traffic within the same VLAN can be controlled) for segregation by NSX.
It is impacted by the spanning tree.	There is no spanning tree.
A switch must learn the MAC address as it comes with the server.	There is no need to learn the MAC address as it's given by vSphere.
Network QoS is provided by core switches.	Network QoS is provided by vSphere and NSX.

HDDC	SDDC
The DMZ is physically separate. Separation is done at the IP layer. IDS/IPS deployment is normally limited in the DMZ due to cost and complexity.	The DMZ is logically separate. Separation is not limited to IP addresses and is done at the hypervisor layer. IDS/IPS is deployed in all zones as it is also hypervisor-based.
No DR test network is required. As a result, the same hostname cannot exist on a DR site, making a true DR test impossible without shutting down production servers.	A DR test network is required. The same hostname can exist on any site as a result. This means that a DR test can be done anytime as it does not impact production.
The firewall is not part of the server. It is typically centrally located. It is not aware of the servers as it's completely independent from them.	The firewall becomes a built-in property of the VM. The firewall policy follows the VM. When a VM undergoes a vMotion to another host, the policy follows it and is enforced by the hypervisor.
The firewall scales vertically and independently from the workload (demand from servers). This makes sizing difficult. IT ends up buying the biggest firewall they can afford, hence increasing the cost.	The firewall scales horizontally. It grows with demand, since it is deployed as part of the hypervisor (using NSX). Upfront cost is lower as there is no need to buy a pair of high-end firewalls upfront.
Traffic has to be deliberately directed to the firewall. Without it, the traffic "escapes" the firewall.	All traffic passes the firewall as it's embedded into the VM and hypervisor. It cannot escape the firewall.
Firewall rules are typically based on the IP address. Changing the IP address equals changing the rules. This results in a database of long and complicated rules. After a while, the firewall admin dare not delete any rules as the database becomes huge and unmanageable.	Rules are not tied to the IP address or hostname. This makes rules much easier. For example, we can say that all VMs in the **Contractor Desktop** pool cannot talk to each other. This is just one rule. When a VM gets added to this pool, the rule is applied to it.
The load balancer is typically centrally located. Just like the firewall, sizing becomes difficult and the cost goes up.	The load balancer is distributed. It scales with the demand. Adding a hypervisor means adding load-balancing capability.

Application

The application is at the heart of an SDDC. It is a common mistake to think of an SDDC as a platform. Since an SDDC lends itself to IaaS, there is often the tendency to build it without considering the applications. Different groups of applications can benefit from a different SDDC architecture. Examples are:

- End-user computing
- Mission-critical applications
- Cloud-native applications
- General-purpose, platform 2 applications

Each of these applications has different infrastructure requirements. You could certainly build the same SDDC for all of them, but you will not optimize your cost. For each of the applications, think of the areas shown by the following diagram:

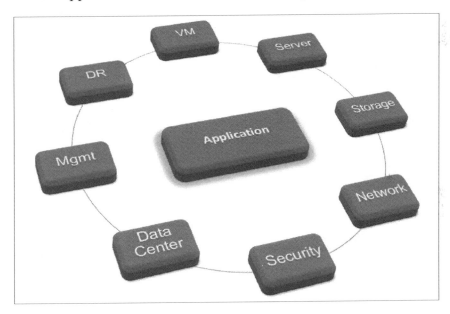

Besides these considerations, there are the following differences between HDDCs and SDDCs:

HDDC	SDDC
Licensing is bound by the physical server. It is a relatively simple thing to manage.	Licensing is bound by an entire cluster or per VM. It can be more expensive or cheaper; hence, it is complex from a management point of view.
All applications are supported.	Most applications are supported. The ones that are not supported are primarily due to the perception of being outdated by **Independent Software Vendors** (**ISVs**). When more apps are developed in the virtual environment, this perception will go away.

Summary

I hope you enjoyed the comparison and found it useful. We covered, to a great extent, the impact caused by virtualization and the changes it introduces. We started by clarifying that virtualization is a different technology compared to partitioning. We then explained that once a physical server is converted into a virtual machine, it takes on a very different form and has radically different properties. The changes range from the core property of the server itself to how we manage it. This, in turn, creates a ripple effect in the bigger picture. The entire data center changes once we virtualize it.

In the next chapter, we will cover SDDC management in greater depth, as it is an area that is made more complex once you virtualize your data center.

3
SDDC Management

SDDC management changes drastically with virtualization. In this chapter, we will learn why it is one of the areas that are greatly impacted by virtualization. We will cover the following topics:

- Why the very thing you manage has changed and how it directly impacts management
- The restaurant analogy
- Contention versus utilization
- Monitoring versus troubleshooting
- The primary counters for monitoring
- Planning for the dashboards

What you manage has changed

Before we cover management, it is important to understand what it is exactly that needs to be managed. This is because it changes drastically. We will use the physical aspect of SDDCs to drive the point. It is easy to use the physical element as that's where our experience comes from, and it's also easy to mentally picture it.

Ponder the following question: how many people does it take to manage one rack's worth of hardware?

Your answer is likely "Not many." After all, it is just one standard rack. The entire thing barely occupies a small server room.

If your entire data center can fit inside one standard rack of equipment, that makes it a small operation. It is indeed a small operation for physical systems. However, in SDDC, you can achieve 1000-2000 VM per rack from a performance point of view. We're using a standard 30:1 consolidation ratio, which is possible with Intel Xeon E5-2699 v3. With 18 cores per socket, you have 36 physical cores in a dual-socket ESXi host. Add 50 percent of Intel Hyper-Threading benefit, and you can easily support 25 VMs with two to four vCPUs each, as there are enough physical cores to schedule the VMs.

I published a calculation in this blog post, which has resonated well with readers: `http://virtual-red-dot.info/1000-vm-per-rack-is-the-new-minimum/`.

The calculation takes into account your Infrastructure VM. Infrastructure functions that used to be provided by hardware (for example, storage replication, firewall, load balancer) are now delivered as VMs. You may run a hundred such VMs, depending on the type of services that your SDDC needs to provide.

This is not just my opinion. Ivan Pepelnjak, a networking authority, in fact shared back in October 2014 that *2000 VMs can easily fit onto 40 servers*. He elaborates the calculation in this blog article: `http://blog.ipspace.net/2014/10/all-you-need-are-two-top-of-rack.html`. He further updates it in his November 2015 blog post at `http://blog.ipspace.net/2015/11/1000-vm-per-rack-is-perfectly-realistic.html`.

Greg Ferro, cofounder at Packet Pushers Interactive, also wrote a good article on why it is possible to have high VM density. He shared an example where you exceed 1000 at `http://etherealmind.com/response-number-of-vms-per-rack-its-more-than-1000-dell-ms-for-example/`. It all depends on the applications.

The key to having this kind of density is a converged infrastructure. In the Example Lab, we have chosen a 2RU 4-node form factor. You can find many models from Super Micro and Dell that use this form factor. From their websites, you can tell that they have a lot of other form factors to choose from.

I hope that you are convinced that 1000 VMs per rack, complete with storage, network, and security, is achievable. Assuming enough power supply per rack, you will practically shrink your data center.

How does that impact your **Infrastructure as a Service (IaaS)** operation? Here's how:

- You will no longer need many teams (Architect, Implement, Operate)
- You will no longer need silos (Network, Server, Storage, Security)
- You will no longer need layers (Admin, Manager, Director, Head)

It's an important question, so it's worth pondering: How should the IT department be structured if it only has 25 percent of the team left?

By team, I mean all types of members, be it your own permanent staff, monthly contractors, or per-project outsourced vendors.

You still need the doers and the experts. The layer you can cut is the middle management.

Indeed, we are entering a period of tectonic shift in Data Center Management.

The changes to SDDC management can be largely grouped into two areas:

- **Architecturally**: The infrastructure moves from a bespoke system to standardized hardware. The application team no longer needs to dictate the specifications of the hardware. For example, they do not need to specify a server brand, model, and CPU frequency. They need only specify how many virtual CPUs they need. Sometimes, especially in a large environment, they need only choose small, medium, or large vCPUs, and all of these will have been preconfigured.

- **Operationally**: Virtualization changes the IT infrastructure team from system builders to service providers. The application team no longer owns the physical infrastructure, and it is now a shared infrastructure.

Let's summarize the points. The following table compares the operations of HDDCs and SDDCs:

HDDC	SDDC
There's a clear silo between the compute, storage, and network teams. In organizations where the IT team is big, the DR, Windows, and Linux teams could also be separate teams. There is also a separation between the engineering, integration (projects), and operations (business as usual) teams. The team, in turn, needs layers of management. This results in rigidity in IT.	With virtualization, IT is taking the game to the next level. It's a lot more powerful than the previous architecture. When you take the game to the next level, the enemy is also stronger. In this case, the expertise required is deeper and the experience requirement is more extensive.
A relatively higher headcount is required in IT, with lower skill sets.	Earlier, you may have needed 10 people to manage 1,000 physical servers. With virtualization, you might only need three people to manage 2,000 VMs on 80 ESXi hosts. However, these three people have deeper expertise and longer experience than the 10 people combined.

HDDC	SDDC
DevOps is a concept that applies to the developer or application team. It does not apply to the Infrastructure team.	The IaaS team needs to have its own DevOps too. As the infrastructure becomes software, there is a need for a continuous flow of Architect | Engineer | Implement | Operate | Upgrade.

Management changes in SDDC

I stated earlier that the very thing you manage has changed. SDDC changes the architecture of data centers, turning operation as usual from best practice to dated practice. The following table explains the operations in more detail so that we can see the impact on a specific discipline:

Area	Reason
Performance management	This is actually a brand new discipline in itself. As you will see in *Chapter 4, Performance Monitoring*, it is not what you think it is.
	This gets harder as the performance of ESXi, VM, and datastores can impact one another. The entire environment is no longer static. VM activities such as vMotion, Storage vMotion, provisioning, and power on also add to the workload. So, there is VM workload and infrastructure workload. Performance issues can originate from any component.
	Troubleshooting something that is dynamic is difficult. Unlike a physical data center, the first thing we need to check is the overall health, because of the interdependency. Only when we are satisfied that the problem is not widespread do we zoom in to a specific object (for example, VM, ESXi, or datastore).
	Performance degradations can also be caused by configuration changes. These configuration changes occur more frequently than in a physical data center as many of them can be done live.
	QoS becomes mandatory due to shared resources.
	A new requirement is application visibility. We can no longer troubleshoot in isolation without knowing which applications run inside that VM. If you do not know which applications are running inside all those VMs, you're flying blind.

Area	Reason
Availability management	vCloud Suite relies heavily on shared storage. The availability of this storage becomes critical. Enterprise should consider storage as an integral part of the platform and not a subsystem managed by a different team.
	Clustering software is mostly replaced by vSphere.
	Backup is mostly agentless and LAN-free.
	DR becomes a service provided by the platform.
Capacity management	Capacity management now needs to take into account performance (read: VM contention) and not just utilization. We will cover this in more detail in *Chapter 5, Capacity Monitoring*.
	It also becomes a complex process. You need a tool that understands the dynamic nature of SDDC.
Compliance management	Compliance becomes more complex due to the lack of physical segregation and ease of changes.
	vCloud Suite itself is a big area that needs to be in compliance.
Security management	Access to vCloud Suite needs to be properly controlled. The security team needs to be more involved with architecture discussion as security becomes integral.
Configuration management (related to change management and patch management)	vCloud Suite became the new source of truth, displacing the **Configuration Management Database (CMDB)**, as it is detached from the environment it manages. The need for another database to manage the virtual environment has to be considered in as there is already a *de facto* database, which is vCenter. For example, if vCenter shows that a VM is running but there is no record in the CMDB, do you power off and delete the VM? Certainly not. As a result, CMDB becomes less important as vCloud Suite itself provides the data.
	The SDDC itself becomes another area where configuration management needs to be applied. The data center is a collection of software, which needs to be patched and upgraded. This can be automated to a large extent.
	Because the SDDC itself is software, it needs to have a non-production copy.
	VM configuration changes need to be tracked. Changes happen more often and faster.
	Although **Information Technology Infrastructure Library (ITIL)** principles do not change, the details of a lot of processes change drastically. We covered some of them previously.

Area	Reason
Financial management	Chargeback (or showback at the minimum) becomes mandatory as the infrastructure is no longer owned by the application team. Shared resources means your customers do not expect to pay the full price of dedicated hardware.
Asset management	This is drastically simplified as the VM is not an asset. Most network and storage appliances become software.
	ESXi is the new asset, but it can't be changed without central management (vCenter) being alerted. The configuration is also standardized.
	Stock-take is no longer applicable for the VM and top-of-rack access switch. Inventory is built-in in vSphere and NSX.

The restaurant analogy

We've covered how all aspects of data center management have changed. These fundamental changes also change your IT business.

You are now a service provider. While your engineering or technical knowledge is still important, your customer measures you on your business service level. There is a subtle difference between what they care about and what they measure you on.

Sunny Dua and I use the restaurant analogy when explaining the need for a formal **Service Level Agreement (SLA)**. The analogy has resonated well with many customers. Humans can always relate to food!

Essentially, a restaurant has two areas, often with a clear demarcation:

- The dining area
- The kitchen

Think of your IaaS business like a restaurant business. It has a dining area, where your customers live, and a kitchen, where you prepare the food. Guess which one is more important?

You're right. The dining area.

If everything runs smoothly in the dining area, customers are being served on time and with quality food, and they are paying you well, it is a good day for the business. Whether you're running around in the hot kitchen is a separate, internal matter. The customers need not know about it.

We use the analogy to drive the message that you need to focus on the customers first and your IaaS second. While this sounds obvious, we rarely see customers implement it. The vRealize Operations dashboards you will see in *Chapter 5*, *Capacity Monitoring*, and *Chapter 6*, *Performance-Monitoring Dashboards*, will surprise you, as they are nothing like what you have in your Network Operating Center.

If you take care of your customers well, and they are happy with your service, the problem you have in your IaaS is a secondary and internal matter. Consider this:

- The dining area is the **Consumer Layer**. Look at the next diagram. It is where your customers' VMs live.

- The kitchen is the **Provider Layer**. This is your infrastructure layer, where VMware and the hardware reside.

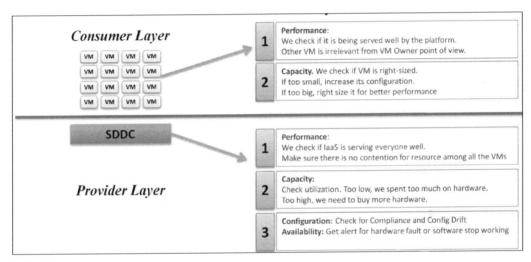

The two layers of IaaS business

There is clearly a line of demarcation between the two layers. Your customers should not care about the details of your SDDC. The VM owner does not care if you are firefighting in the data center. Because they do not care, whether you are using vSphere 5.1 Update 3 or vSphere 6 Update 1 is not something you want them to dictate upon you. The same goes with your choice of hardware brand and specification.

The application team becomes a consumer of a shared service — the virtual platform. Depending on the **Service Level Agreement (SLA)**, the application team can be served as if they have dedicated access to the infrastructure, or they can take a performance hit in exchange for a lower price. For SLAs where performance is guaranteed, the VM running in the cluster should not be impacted by any other VMs. The performance must be as good as if it is the only VM running in the ESXi.

Ponder the previous paragraph and diagram for a moment.

Think of the implication. This is because they do not exist in HDDC. Can you see the impact if you are not 100-percent virtualized?

If you are not 100-percent virtualized yet, you need to have two modes of operation. Yes, it is that big a change.

The consumer layer

The following are the properties of the consumer layer:

- vSphere is well known for its stability. As a result, availability is not something you need to deal with daily. In the event of failure, vSphere HA will bring up the affected VMs within a few minutes, probably before the VM owner notices, if it happens during non-peak hours.

- Performance, on the other hand, is something that needs to be managed daily and monitored in minutes. In fact, this is generally the number one source of disagreement between the application team and Infrastructure team. That's why we put a large "number one" next to performance. As you know well, a VM owner only cares about their VM. Other VMs in the ESXi host or vSphere cluster are irrelevant. When a VM owner complains that her VM performance is slow, can you prove within one minute that your IaaS is serving that VM well? If you cannot, that is a sign you do not have performance SLA.

- When performance is taken care of, you can look at capacity. There is no point in discussing capacity when there is a performance issue. This is why it is given the number-two spot.

- Capacity for a VM is a matter of rightsizing. In general, it's the responsibility of the application team. As an IaaS provider, you can add value by recommending the right size.

The provider layer

The following are the properties of the provider layer:

- The IaaS layer is where you have, or should have, complete control and visibility. If you do not have it, you need to fix it, as your customers assume and expect you to.

- At this layer, you care about everyone, not just a specific VM. You have to care about both the VM and infrastructure, because you want to be assured that the shared infrastructure is not a bottleneck. The big picture is the key here. This is the layer where you answer questions such as "How healthy is my VMware environment?"

- Good performance means everyone is served well. The definition of "well" here is that the level of contention for any given VM is below what you officially promise.

- Good capacity means you are balancing your hardware procurement. Neither high utilization nor low utilization is good for your IaaS business.

- Configuration management becomes critical in your SDDC as it is easy to make changes. However, it is below performance and capacity in terms of business priority as it impacts your customers less directly.

- Availability management is important due to overcommitment. It is less critical relative to performance and capacity because generally, you have redundancy and are protected by vSphere HA. In SDDC, availability management has to cover Infrastructure VM. For example, you need to ensure the uptime of all your NSX Edge VMs and TrendMicro VMs, because they are in the data path.

Contention versus utilization

Because each layer has its own set of requirements, this translates into two sets of counters or metrics. Each group has its own metrics.

At the VM layer, we care whether a particular VM is being served well by the platform. Other VMs are irrelevant from the VM owner's point of view. So the key counter here is VM contention. Infrastructure metrics are irrelevant here. Only when we are satisfied that there is no contention can we proceed to check whether the VM is sized correctly or not. Most people check for utilization first because that is what they are used to monitoring in the physical infrastructure. In a virtual environment, we should check for contention first.

At the Infrastructure layer, we care whether it serves everyone well. Make sure that there is no contention for resources among all the VMs in the platform. Only when the infrastructure is clear from contention can we troubleshoot a particular VM. If the infrastructure is having a hard time serving a majority of the VMs, there is no point troubleshooting a particular VM. Notice all the previous sentences are about the VM. Yes, the Infrastructure counters are not that relevant.

Showing every single VM in a single screen is certainly impossible; hence, we need to have a metric that can track across all VMs. As you can guess, this metric does not exist in vSphere. vRealize Operations complements vSphere by allowing you to create super metrics. As you will see in the next four chapters, we use super metrics extensively.

 Super metrics allow you to get the big picture without losing the details.

This two-layer concept is also implemented by vSphere in compute and storage architectures. For example, there are two distinct layers of memory in vSphere. There is the individual VM memory provided by the hypervisor, and there is the physical memory at the host level. For an individual VM, we care whether the VM is getting enough memory. At the host level, we care whether the host has enough memory for everyone. Because of the difference in goals and because existing metrics in vSphere cannot provide the insight, we need to rely on vRealize Operations super metrics.

Performance and capacity management

We have seen that there are two sets of metrics. Before we go into the metrics, we need to cover one more thing so that we are clear about the scope of our discussion.

The word "management" in SDDC covers the entire spectrum of activity required to keep the SDDC running well. In some situations, we need to use a narrower word, such as monitoring, planning, or troubleshooting.

Since the book focuses on performance and capacity, let's distinguish the areas within them:

- Performance management has two sub-activities:
    - Monitoring
    - Troubleshooting

- Capacity management has two sub-activities:
    - Planning
    - Monitoring

Performance

In a virtual environment, performance monitoring and performance troubleshooting are relatively more distinct from each other than they are in a traditional physical environment. As resources are shared, performance management becomes more important in order to reduce the need to troubleshoot often. Here is a breakdown of the differences between performance monitoring and performance troubleshooting.

Performance monitoring	Performance troubleshooting
Monitoring is about preventing the problem in the first place.	Troubleshooting means you currently have or you had a problem. Even if the problem is no longer active, you normally need to know what caused it.
Monitoring is about optimizing and planning.	Troubleshooting is about correcting the problem.
Monitoring tends to start from the big picture. You need to ensure the overall situation is good before diving into a particular trouble spot.	Troubleshooting tends to start from a specific problem (for example, a VM running slow, the network dropping packets, or the storage array having high latency).
When you are monitoring, you are focused on the future, anticipating problems, and taking action before they occur. In some sense, performance monitoring is related to capacity management. This relationship is reflected in the vRealize Operations dashboard, where the major capacity management badge is risk — indicating the risk of future health and performance problems.	When you are troubleshooting, you are focused on the present, as you have a live fire to put out. You do not care about capacity unless it's impacting performance.
In monitoring, you care about utilization and track it so that it does not grow beyond your physical resources and become a problem in the future.	In troubleshooting, the utilization of the resource is secondary. A VM can generate 10,000 IOPS, it might be using 128 GB vRAM, and so on. So long as its high demands are being met, there is no performance problem. In troubleshooting, we are concerned with demands not being met. The utilization of the VM and the infrastructure are technically irrelevant.
Monitoring consists of repeatable steps that you perform regularly, preferably daily. You can create a **Standard Operating Procedure** (**SOP**) out of it.	Troubleshooting is a realm by itself, and the steps vary depending on what you're trying to troubleshoot. You may write a guideline, but not an SOP.

The preceding differences directly impact how we use the vRealize Operations dashboards. From experience, performance troubleshooting requires on-demand dashboards in addition to the dashboards used for performance monitoring. Depending on the symptoms, we would either clone existing dashboards or create a brand new one. The dashboard may require new super metrics, groups, views, or tags. Depending on the complexity of the problem, we may need to create multiple widgets or dashboards. This is why this book devotes almost 100 pages to covering all the counters, as you need to know exactly what they mean. Even if you choose the right counters, the wrong interpretation will still lead to the wrong conclusion.

Because of this wide variation, this chapter only focuses on monitoring. Creating troubleshooting dashboards on the fly is a skill best picked up with experience.

Capacity

We saw that there are two aspects of capacity: planning and monitoring. Let's compare them in more detail now:

Capacity planning	Capacity monitoring
You look at future demand and future supply. You typically do a what-if analysis.	You look at the present situation and compare with the threshold.
You are required to know the hardware delivery lead time and your procurement process. In large organizations, there can be a separate team that determines the brand, model, and specifications of what you can buy. You may plan to buy a particular model as per what you always do, but the engineering team may advise to wait one more month because they are certifying a new model.	You do not have to know about hardware supply. You work with Operations instead of Engineering.
Capacity planning is not something you do daily. Perhaps you do it every month. Some customers do it every quarter to align with their fiscal quarter and minimize procurement work.	Capacity monitoring is something you do daily, or at the most, weekly. You are tracking, ensuring what you planned earlier is still valid.
You do not set alerts for capacity planning. OK, perhaps you set a calendar entry to remind you not to postpone it yet again.	You can, and should, set alerts for capacity monitoring.

This book will focus on capacity monitoring; it will touch on capacity planning only briefly.

As a summary, the book will cover performance monitoring and capacity monitoring. Performance troubleshooting and capacity planning will not be covered.

With the preceding concept in mind, we are ready to choose the correct counters for monitoring.

Primary counters for monitoring

vSphere 6 comes with many counters, many more than what a physical server provides. There are new counters that do not have a physical equivalent, such as memory ballooning, CPU latency, and vSphere replication. In addition, some counters have the same name as their physical-world counterparts but behave differently in vSphere. Memory usage is a common one, resulting in confusion among VMware system administrators. For those counters that are similar to their physical-world counterparts, vSphere may use different units, such as milliseconds instead of percentage.

vSphere has many objects. It is important that you pick the right counters for each object. In *Chapter 10, Application Monitoring Using Blue Medora*, to *Chapter 13, Memory Counters*, we're dedicating over 100 pages to covering all the counters.

As a result, experienced IT administrators find it hard to master vSphere counters by building on their existing knowledge. Instead of trying to relate each counter to its physical equivalent, it is useful to group them according to their purpose. There are two main purposes:

- Performance
- Capacity

For performance, the key counter is VM contention. A VM will experience suboptimal performance when it is experiencing contention.

For capacity, the key counter is workload. Workload is more than just utilization. The main limitation of utilization is it does not reflect the true demand. If a VM wants to use 80 percent of its CPU but ESXi can only deliver 50 percent, the utilization counter will show 50 percent. The workload counter takes into account the unmet demand and will show 80 percent.

I've listed all the vSphere objects in the following table. For each object, a **No** under the **Contention counter** column means you will not find a counter named **Contention** for that object. The same goes for the **Workload counter** column. This is because the Contention counter and Workload counter do not exist for all objects. For example, a distributed switch does not have a Contention counter, but it does have a Workload counter.

When there is no actual counter called Contention or Workload, you can use other counters as a workaround. For example, you can use Latency (millisecond) as a replacement for Contention (%).

Object	Contention counter	Workload counter	Remarks
VM	Overall: No. CPU: Yes. RAM: Yes. Storage: No. Network: No.	Overall: Yes. CPU: Yes. RAM: Yes. Storage: Yes. Network: Yes.	For storage, use the Latency counter. It is available for datastores only and not for RDM.
ESXi	Overall: No. CPU: Yes. RAM: Yes. Storage: No. Network: No.	Overall: Yes. CPU: Yes. RAM: Yes. Storage: Yes. Network: Yes.	Same as **VM**.
Cluster	Overall: No. CPU: Yes. RAM: Yes. Storage: No. Network: No.	Overall: Yes. CPU: Yes. RAM: Yes. Storage: Yes. Network: Yes.	Same as **VM**.
Data center	Overall: No. CPU: Yes. RAM: Yes. Storage: No. Network: No.	Overall: Yes. CPU: Yes. RAM: Yes. Storage: Yes. Network: Yes.	Same as **VM**.

Object	Contention counter	Workload counter	Remarks
vCenter	Overall: No. CPU: Yes. RAM: Yes. Storage: No. Network: No.	Overall: Yes. CPU: Yes. RAM: Yes. Storage: Yes. Network: Yes.	Same as **VM**.
World	Overall: No. CPU: No. RAM: Yes. Storage: No. Network: No.	Overall: Yes. CPU: Yes. RAM: Yes. Storage: Yes. Network: Yes.	Same as **VM**.
Distributed switch	Network: No.	Network: Yes.	CPU, RAM, and Storage are not relevant for this object, hence they are not shown. Use the Dropped Packet counter to measure contention.
Distributed port group	Network: No.	Network: Yes.	Same as **Distributed Switch**.
Datastore	Storage: No.	Storage: Yes.	CPU, RAM, and Network are not relevant for this object. Use the Latency counter to measure contention.
Datastore Cluster	Storage: No.	Storage: No.	Same as **Datastore**.

Who uses which dashboards

As you create many dashboards for different roles in your organization, you will find that some of the information or widgets apply to more than one user or role. For example, the VMware administrator may need a dashboard that shows information about VMs, ESXi, network, and storage on a single screen. The network widget in that dashboard is also useful for the network administrator. So don't worry if you find yourself duplicating information as you build your dashboards. This is why we prefer to use the **View** widget in vRealize Operations, as it can be shared across dashboards. What start as very similar dashboards may evolve over time as user requirements change.

In general, there are some differences between dashboards for senior management (for example, the CIO) and dashboards for the ground-level technical team (for example, a VMware administrator). This table lists the main differences:

Senior management	Ground-level team
A simple dashboard with minimal interaction and widgets. The dashboard fits into a notebook's display.	A rich dashboard, which may have complex interaction and many widgets. Ideally, the dashboard occupies a full HD screen.
It shows the big picture. It also tends to be application focused.	It shows the big picture but it is complemented with detailed information. It focuses on the infrastructure or application, depending on the role.
The number presented is relative, normalized to 0 to 100 for ease of comparison and understanding.	The data presented shows both the absolute data (raw figure) and the normalized data. It requires technical knowledge on counters.
It focuses on the long-term timeline (normally 1-3 months). The data is averaged out. A 30-minute spike will not show up.	Some dashboards will focus on the long-term timeline, whereas others will focus on the short term. For the short-term timeline, it tends to show both peak and average values. A five-minute spike will be visible in the chart.
Normally, it is updated daily. Users are not expected to log in multiple times a day.	The short-term dashboard will be updated every five minutes. Users may have the dashboard open all the time.

You will also tailor the built-in dashboards to fit your needs. Do not be afraid to change them in any way, as they do not impact the way vRealize Operations works. The dashboards that you create should complement the built-in dashboards, as there is no point in duplicating them.

Duplicate the built-in dashboards instead of modifying them. The built-in dashboards may get updated in a vRealize Operations upgrade.

How many dashboards do I need?

The number of dashboards you will have depends on the size of the environment and the number of people managing it. An environment with 100 VMs in just five hosts and one cluster will need far fewer dashboards than an environment with 100,000 VMs spread over 5,000 ESXi, 500 clusters, 20 data centers, and 15 vCenter servers.

In a large environment, where you have many physical data centers and even more vSphere clusters, you will likely need to display the information per physical data center. There are several reasons for this:

- Aggregating data at a global level, which spans many physical data centers, will hide too much information. Presenting data at such a level means you are getting an average of thousands of objects. If your environment is generally healthy (and it should be), the average will logically fall within a healthy range.

- In most cases, the performance in a given physical data center is independent from that of other data centers. For example, your Singapore data center typically does not impact the performance of your London data center. An exception to this case is when you link your data center at the network (stretched L2) and storage layers (synchronous replication). From experience in troubleshooting such a scenario, I recommend you keep the physical layers independent from one another. Assuming your data centers are independent, it makes more sense to display the chart on a per data center basis.

- VMs typically do not move from one physical data center to another (unless they are paired with storage replication and your network is stretched), so an imbalance among multiple data centers does not translate into a realistic rebalancing action.

The following figure should help you visualize the situation. Imagine you have two vCenter servers. They manage five large data centers, located in different cities or countries. Each data center has multiple clusters. From here, you can plan what data you want to see at which level. Think of both techniques of rolling up (across time and across member), which we covered earlier.

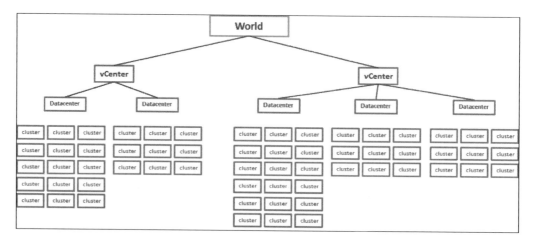

Summary

We have covered why SDDC management differs drastically from HDDC management, so much that you have to have two different modes of separation if you are not 100-percent virtualized.

We used the restaurant analogy to see that you need to shift your focus from your infrastructure to your customer. A lot of IT departments struggle because they did not shift their management focus to the consumer layer. The shift also requires the use of new counters, and we introduced the Contention counter. We also saw that you need super metrics in this new management.

We closed the chapter by providing guidance on the vRealize Operations dashboard. The next four chapters will share some dashboards that demonstrate how vRealize Operations helps in performance and capacity management. There are many possibilities for these dashboards. For example, you can enhance them to include availability-related information, since a fault can certainly impact performance. You may also decide to combine performance, capacity, and configuration into a series of dashboards that you check as one set.

4
Performance Monitoring

In this chapter, we will dive into performance, a well-known term that has taken a completely new meaning in SDDC. In fact, if you use the definition from HDDC, you will have difficulty reaching an agreement with the application team (your customers) on where the performance issue lies.

After setting the scene with a familiar story, we will cover the following topics:

- What exactly is performance?
- How performance, capacity, and availability are related.
- Performance SLA, with actual sample values you can use as a guide.

A day in the life of a VMware Admin

To understand what performance actually is, it is always good to begin with the customer. As shared in the previous chapter, the SDDC is providing a service, not a system. We have seen this in almost all customers. Whether the application team or VM owner pays for the service or not, it is a service. The existence of a chargeback model is practically optional. VM owners no longer own, hence care, about the underlying infrastructure.

Here is a common story often told in the virtualization community, which will resonate with you as an IaaS provider:

A VM owner complains to you that her VM is slow. It was not slow yesterday. Her application architect and lead developer have verified that:

- The VM CPU and RAM utilization did not increase. They are also within a healthy range. The application team has verified that the **CPU run queue** is also in the healthy range.

- The disk latency is good. It is below 10 milliseconds.

- The network isn't dropping any packets.

- There is no change in the application settings. In fact, the application has not had any changes made in the past month.

- There hasn't been any recent patch to Windows.

- There was no reboot.

She says that your VMware environment is a shared environment, and perhaps an increase in the number of Virtual Machines and in the workload of other Virtual Machines is straining your IaaS.

She also says that her other VM, which was P2V recently, was performing much faster in physical mode.

You are right – she is saying it's your fault.

What do you do?

It is certainly a difficult situation to be in. You are in charge of more than 1,000 Virtual Machines. You have successfully consolidated them into 50 ESXi 6.0 hosts, saving the company 950 servers, not to mention a lot of money. You built your reputation in the process, so this matter is not just that her VM is not performing.

You also recall that your team has been adding new VM regularly in the past several months, so she could be right. But why did it happen today, and not, say, 3 days ago?

What exactly is performance?

To answer her question, we need to define performance. It's a software-defined era, so performance needs to be redefined as the architecture has changed.

In *Chapter 3, SDDC Management*, we leaned that there are two layers:

- **The VM layer**: This is where her complaint lies
- **The Infrastructure layer**: This is where you are looking for the solution, as you are not familiar with her application and do not have access to the VM

You see the problem?

Yup, there is a major disconnect. You are trying to help in an area that you neither have access to nor knowledge of. You have no expertise in the application, and you don't have full admin rights on the Guest OS.

Is there hope?

There is, if you are willing to let go your status of a superhero. Ponder the new nature of your business. In SDDC, you are an IaaS service provider. In HDDC, you are a system builder.

At the core, an IaaS provides these four basic resources to a VM:

- CPU
- RAM
- Network
- Storage

You need to ensure that you deliver the amount of resources that the VM asks whenever it needs them.

Your IaaS is performing fast if it delivers the amount that the VM asks for within your performance SLA. If you promise a 20-millisecond disk latency, your IaaS is doing well if you return all the I/O issued by the VM within 20 milliseconds. Whether 20 milliseconds is good enough for the custom application is not within your scope. If you promise a maximum of one dropped packet in any given 5-minute interval because you are catering for vMotion, then your IaaS is performing if it is only dropping one packet during the period where the VM was not performing. If your IaaS dropped two packets in any given 5-minute period, you have failed your performance SLA.

You are in charge of your IaaS performance, not her VM performance. Your IaaS can perform fast, even exceeding the SLA you promise, but that does not guarantee that her VM meets her performance criteria. Generally speaking, application-level performance SLA is business centric (for example, 8 seconds per financial transaction), so it is beyond the control of your IaaS.

Let's use a table to summarize what exactly IaaS performance is:

IaaS performance is	IaaS performance is not
The boundary of your IaaS and VM: The line in between the two layers.	The VM layer: The OS and applications are not something you own or control. The Infrastructure layer: This layer is irrelevant to the VM owner, and hence, the metrics are not something she is interested in.
VM contention.	VM utilization: From your viewpoint as an IaaS provider, this is a capacity matter, not a performance matter. ESXi or Infrastructure utilization: She is not interested anyway.
SLA-driven: Formally agreed and stated in your service catalog. If you fail, you can proactively improve without having to wait for complaints.	Case-by-case: Another phrase is complaint-by-complaint.
Varies by service tier: You promise higher performance (read: less contention experienced by the VM) on higher tiers.	Same for everyone: If you only have one tier, that tier will be benchmarked by physical-world standards by default. While you can certainly match physical systems, the cost will not be low. Do not let your performance SLA be defined and driven by those who do not architect your IaaS.

Once you determine that your IaaS is serving her VM well, you are done with your scope. You may decide to come back to your hero status and help her troubleshoot that in-house custom application that you're not familiar with. That's a value-added service from you. Your IaaS stops at Infrastructure.

Performance versus capacity

Now that we know what IaaS performance is, what metric should we use to measure it?

A lot of customers mistake capacity with performance. They associate low utilization with high performance, for example:

- Low ESXi CPU utilization means its performance is good (it is fast)
- Low VM CPU utilization means its performance is good (it is fast)

If you ponder these points, you will see the failure in the logic. There are several reasons why your ESXi utilization is irrelevant:

- Whether the ESXi has high or low utilization has nothing to do with its performance. An ESXi does not become slower as its utilization goes from 5 percent to 50 percent. It's still running at the same speed!

- An ESXi with low utilization has a better chance of serving all its VM better than an ESXi with high utilization. There is certainly a correlation. The question is, how do you quantify that correlation? You cannot say that 25 percent ESXi CPU utilization means none of its VMs has CPU contention. Defending your IaaS by citing your ESXi utilization is not a good idea.

- VM utilization can certainly impact its own performance. While that specific issue is about performance, it is not about your IaaS performance. If a VM has four vCPUs, and it's using all four at 100 percent, your IaaS role is to provide the resources as per your SLA. Whether that's enough to meet the VM's business requirement is between the VM owner and the business owner. A VM can certainly have performance issues while your IaaS has excellent performance.

Let's use a table to compare performance and capacity. It helps to disassociate VM performance from IaaS performance:

IaaS performance	IaaS capacity
The focus is on the VM. It does not apply to IaaS. From the VM owner's viewpoint, the performance experienced by other VMs is irrelevant.	The focus is on the IaaS. For compute, this typically means a vSphere cluster, not ESXi host, due to HA and DRS.
The primary counter is VM contention or VM latency. IaaS utilization is irrelevant.	The primary counter is contention or latency. The secondary counter is utilization.
It does not take into account availability SLA.	It takes into account availability SLA. Tier 1 is in fact availability-driven. It is not performance-driven, as performance is essentially guaranteed.
You measure on a short-term basis. A good practice is to measure every 5 minutes.	You measure on a long-term basis. The time period is typically 1-3 months, as you are checking for overall trends and not a one-off spike.

Now that we know their differences, we can expect that they use *different* counters:

IaaS area	IaaS performance	IaaS capacity
CPU	VM CPU contention.	VM CPU contention (not Cluster CPU contention).
		vSphere Cluster CPU utilization.
RAM	VM RAM contention.	As above, but for RAM.
Network	VM network latency.	ESXi vmnic network utilization.
	VM network dropped packets.	Physical switch utilization.
	VM packet retransmits.	
Storage	VM disk latency.	VM disk latency (not datastore disk latency).
		Datastore disk space utilization.

Can you notice which counters are not included in the preceding table?

Commonly used counters such as VM CPU utilization and VM RAM utilization have been excluded. As discussed, these counters are not counters you can use to quantify your IaaS performance or IaaS capacity. They are counters for individual VMs.

Bonus question! Can you notice what else is missing?

There are counters that are specific to SDDC that give you a clue on the performance of your IaaS. A poor value on these counters will hit performance. Examples include:

- VM kernel network latency, network dropped packets, and packet retransmits
- vMotion stunned time and vMotion downtime
- VSAN SSD cache hit rate
- NSX Edge VM performance (as it is is in the datapath)
- F5 load balancer (as it in the datapath)
- Horizon View Security Server performance (as it is is in the datapath)
- Trend Micro Deep Security virtual appliance (as it is in the datapath)

Do you then monitor them all?

No. They are secondary counters. All these counters are required for performance troubleshooting. They are not required for performance monitoring. If you need more details, review *Chapter 3, SDDC Management*, where we covered the difference between monitoring and troubleshooting.

I think by now it should be clear to you. To help you explain it to your management and customers, I've created the following diagram:

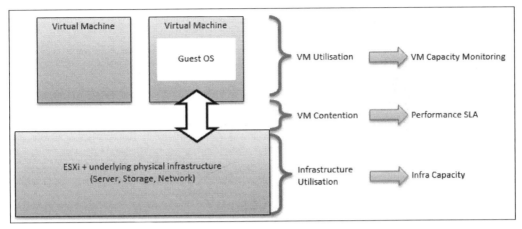

Performance and Capacity

Performance SLA

We have covered the metrics; how do we put them to use?

As usual, let's begin with the customer. In this case, it is your CIO or head of Infrastructure, as the scope now is all VMs, and not just one VM.

For performance, the main requirement from your CIO or management is typically around your IaaS system's ability to deliver. They want your IaaS to perform, as their business runs on it. The question is this:

How do you prove that… not a single VM… in the past 1 month… suffers unacceptable performance hit because of non-performing IaaS?

That's an innocent, but loaded, question. You need to consider the impact carefully before answering, "That's easy!"

If you have 1000 VMs, you need to answer for 1000 VMs. For each VM, you need to answer for CPU, RAM, disk and network. That's 4000 metrics. If your management or customer agrees on a 5-minute sampling period, you have 12 samples in 1 hour. In 1 day, you have 288 samples. In 1 month, you have nearly 8750 samples (30.4 days on average). For 1000 VMs, this means 4000 x 8750 = 35,000,000 chances where your IaaS can fail in serving the customers! 35 million chances in a month, and you need to repeat this performance every month.

You are right! As an IaaS architect, you are actually a magician. The way you achieve that feat is via service tiering. You should always have at least two tiers. The VM owner is used to the physical environment. She will compare you with the physical world as that represents the ideal. So if you only have one tier, you will have no choice but to deliver a tier that can match a physical server. As a physical server is dedicated, it means you will not be able to overcommit. If you overcommit, you run the risk of contention, and hence, failure to meet performance SLA.

Having just a single tier means any mission-critical VM is getting the same class of service as a development VM—sacrificing either the performance of mission critical VMs or the cost of the overall solution. On the other hand, having too many tiers adds operational complexity and hence increases cost.

We use three service tiers as that provides a good balance. The table in the following figure provides an example that is suitable for a large environment:

Service Tier	Purpose	Compute	Storage
1 (highest)	Production	No oversubscription. As a result, there is no need for reservation. All hosts are identical in specification.	All Flash
2	Production Non Production	~2 times oversubscription for CPU and ~1.5 times for RAM. An ESXi host with 36 cores, 72 threads and 256 GB RAM may run 72 vCPUs and 384 GB vRAM.	Hybrid, but with Class E SSD.
3 (lowest)	Non Production	~3 times oversubscription for CPU and ~2 times for RAM.	Hybrid, with Class C SSD

This table should look logical to you. One thing that you need to pay attention to is the oversubscription ratio. You should emphasize to your customers that they are nothing but rough guidelines. You may go above them if the performance is still acceptable.

In a small environment, you should have just two tiers. Performance and capacity are much more easily done on a per-cluster basis. Having just two tiers means you can go as low as two clusters.

In a very large environment, with more than 100,000 VMs, you should also have just three tiers. Avoid having four or five tiers as that complicates operation. Providing too many choices can result in more confusion and frustration. Remember, each tier carries a different pricing. I'd make the gap large enough so it's easy to choose.

Do not confuse the SLA you promise with the design you implement to achieve it. Your customers only care, and should only care, about the SLA. The design is your internal matter.

As the performance SLA is driven by the quality of the design, you need to be clear on the key design differentiators. In the preceding table, I've provided my key design differentiators. Your design may differ. That is perfectly fine. The key thing is your customers, not just you, must be able to see the difference. If they cannot, that means your tiers are too close to each other.

Here are a few highlights of my design:

- Tier 1 is your "physical tier". It matches the performance of a physical server. This is possible as it does not have CPU or RAM over commitment. No VM needs to wait or contend for resources. As a result, reservation is not even applicable. We can guarantee that the value of the CPU contention metric will be near zero, and the value of RAM contention will be zero.

- All hosts in the Tier 1 cluster are also identical. This means the specifications of all the hosts are identical. This makes performance predictable. We cannot make such a guarantee in Tier 2 and Tier 3. The cluster may start with four identical nodes, but over time may grow into 16 nodes. The 16-node cluster is certainly not identical in terms of performance as the new nodes will sport faster technology.

- Tier 2 is where the majority of production VMs live. If the majority of your production VMs are in Tier 1, there is something wrong with your definition of critical. It is not granular enough. Yes, all VMs in production are important. However, some are more important than others.

- In Tier 1, the virtual disk (VMDK) is thick provisioned, so there is no performance penalty in the first write. We do not provide the same service quality in lower tiers.

With these guidelines, you have a clear 3-tier IaaS based on performance. Let's now cover the actual performance SLA that you put in the contract with your customers. You need to define the service for each of the four infrastructure components (CPU, RAM, disk, and network). For each one, specify the actual value and metric to track.

The table in the following figure provides an example of server VMs. For VDI VMs, we need to have a different definition. It is also a sample recommendation. This is not an official guideline from VMware but is just my experience. The actual numbers you set may not be the same as mine. You should choose numbers that you are comfortable with and have been agreed upon by your customers (the application team or business units).

If you have no idea what numbers you should set, use vRealize Operations to look at your actual data in the past so that your number is backed by fact. It is sufficient to go back a few months. The larger your sample, the shorter you can look back. For example, if you have, say, 100 clusters, you can in fact just take a few clusters and go back 1 month on each:

Service Tier	CPU	RAM	Network	Storage
1 (highest)	<1% CPU Contention	0% RAM Contention	0 drop packet	10 ms latency
2	<3% CPU Contention	5% RAM Contention	0 drop packet	20 ms latency
3 (lowest)	<13% CPU Contention	10% RAM Contention	0 drop packet	30 ms latency

Notice what's missing? It's something that you normally have if you are doing capacity management using a spreadsheet.

Yup, it's the famous **consolidation ratio**. In fact, your entire infrastructure is no longer there. It is all about the VM. The values apply to VMs, not to your infrastructure.

It's not there because it's not relevant. Mark Achtemichuk, an expert on VMware performance, explains it in his article at `https://blogs.vmware.com/vsphere/2015/11/vcpu-to-pcpu-ratios-are-they-still-relevant.html`. As explained in the blog, oversubscription is an incomplete policy. It fails to take into account contention. I've seen this in a global bank, where the higher tier performed worse than the lower tier. Once you oversubscribe, you are no longer able to guarantee consistent performance. Contention can happen, even if your ESXi utilization is not high.

You should have two numbers:

- One is the SLA your customers agree on
- The other is an internal number for your own proactive monitoring

The second number is naturally lower. For example, you may set 10 percent as the official SLA and 8 percent as the internal threshold for you to start proactive adjustment. The delta is a buffer you have for proactive troubleshooting.

With that, let's look at each component.

CPU SLA

Tier 1 is not 0 percent as the CPU ready counter in vCenter does not hit zero even if there is no contention. From my experience, a 5 minute average of 0.5 percent is a perfectly achievable SLA when a VM experiences no contention.

Tier 2 is set at 3 percent, as that's a reasonable drop from 1 percent. You can set yours to 5 percent if you want a wider gap or if your customer can tolerate slower performance.

Tier 3 is set at 13 percent as it is no longer using the maximum CPU power management setting. It is left at the default setting, which is **Balanced**. This impacts the latency counter; hence, we have to set a lower SLA. If you set CPU power management to maximum, then you should lower the number to 5-6 percent.

Memory SLA

For CPU and RAM, you can notice that their numbers are not consistent. This is because their nature is different. RAM is not affected by power management, so consistent scaling can be used.

Tier 1 is 0 percent because every single VM has its memory backed by the hypervisor. There will be no ballooning, swap, or compression. As a result, the value for contention in Tier 1 will be 0 percent.

Network SLA

Ideally, you use network latency as the metric. Latency, by definition, is the time taken between a source and destination pair. Different pairs can, and generally will, certainly have different latencies.

Network has a fundamentally different nature to compute and storage. Network is an interconnect, not a node. A VM does not "deal with" the network. It communicates with other VMs or physical machines, using the network as the medium. So, the destination is not constant. A VM may have network latency at 9 in the morning. Say it is a server that serves a thousand users in the same office building. By the time you get the information, that VM may have stopped communicating with the same users and is now serving other users. It is hard to troubleshoot the network latency as the pair has changed.

This unique nature of network is elaborated in *Chapter 9, Infrastructure Monitoring Using Blue Medora*. For the purpose of SLA, we need to pick a counter that your customers can accept. We pick the drop packet counter as it's the best we can do without injecting a lot of extra packets and doing a lot of measurement. Performance monitoring needs to be light, else the monitoring itself will degrade the performance. I'm sure you have experienced issues where the performance monitoring agent is the one causing the performance issue. Yup, it's typically the collector agent.

VM dropped packets is actually not a good proxy for all cases. A VM may drop packets if its CPU is saturated. It may also drop packets if its network is wrongly configured. As a result, you should complement it with drop packet monitoring at the ESXi vmnic level.

You may notice that I used the same performance SLA as for service tiers. This is because your network should not be dropping packets.

Storage SLA

The performance SLA is set at 10, 20, and 30 milliseconds for each tier, respectively. This is reasonable given that it is a 5-minute average. A VM that generates 500 IOPS for 5 minutes is performing 500 x 60 x 5 = 150,000 SCSI commands. It is possible that one of the commands does not return within the stipulated SLA.

Just a recap: do you know why we do not track the latency at the datastore level?

You are right. It is irrelevant.

VDI SLA

The previous SLAs are for server workload. What about for VDI? To me, VDI needs to be high-performance:

- From an employee's viewpoint, if a $500 PC can give me good performance, I certainly expect the same performance on a VDI.

- From a business viewpoint, let's consider a staff salary of $50,000 per year. The total loaded cost for that person will be around $100,000. We calculate VDI TCO every 3 years. For someone who is costing the business $300,000 in 3 years, a 5-percent drop in productivity because the employee is frustrated with the VDI costs the business $15,000. Here is another way of looking at it: if you are an employee, and you feel frustrated with your slow desktop/ laptop, does it make business sense to get you a better one?

Based on this, we'd set the VDI performance SLA as shown here:

Component	SLA
CPU	<2% CPU Contention
RAM	<1% RAM Contention
Disk	<15 ms disk latency
PCoIP	<1% packet loss

As you can see, there are other counters that define a high-performance VDI. They are not in the SLA. They belong to capacity, not performance.

You should only include metrics that you can control. Be careful of including PCoIP packet loss in the SLA, because the **Wide Area Network (WAN)** is not within your control. The network may not drop the packet, but PCoIP counts it as packet loss if it cannot use it. If a user accesses the VDI from a mobile network (4G), latency can be erratic and high. When this happens, PCoIP will experience dropped packets as it's constantly adjusting its bandwidth even though there is no dropped packet at the TCP/IP layer.

Summary

If you are like my typical customers, you would have found the concepts in this chapter a breath of fresh air. They were the missing pieces in your performance management.

We saw what exactly performance is, as a lot of VMware architects, engineers, and administrators are mistaken about it. Once defined, we looked at a sample set of guidelines on the value you can use for your operation.

In the next chapter, we will cover capacity management in greater depth, as it is an area that is made more complex once you virtualize your data center.

Capacity Monitoring

5

Capacity management changes drastically with virtualization. In this chapter, we will learn why it is one of the areas that are greatly impacted by virtualization. We will cover the following topics:

- The changes in capacity management
- How you should perform capacity management
- How many resources are consumed by the SDDC itself
- When peak utilization is not what it actually is
- How you should perform capacity management
- VM rightsizing

Some well-meaning but harmful advice

Can you figure out why the following statements are wrong? They are all well-meaning pieces of advice on the topic of capacity management. I'm sure you have heard them, or even given them.

Regarding cluster RAM:

- We recommend a 1:2 overcommit ratio between physical RAM and virtual RAM. Going above this is risky.
- Memory usage on most of your clusters is high, around 90 percent. You should aim for 60 percent as you need to consider HA.
- Active memory should not exceed 50-60 percent. You need a buffer between **active memory** and **consumed memory**.
- Memory should be running at a high state on each host.

Regarding cluster CPU:

- The CPU ratio in cluster X is high at 1:5, because it is an important cluster.

- The rest of your clusters' overcommit ratios look good as they are around 1:3. This gives your some buffer for spike and HA.

- Keep the overcommitment ratio at 1:4 for tier 3 workload.

- CPU usage is around 70 percent on cluster Y. Since they are **User Acceptance Testing (UAT)** servers, don't worry. You should be worried only when they reach 85 percent.

- The rest of your clusters' CPU utilization is around 25 percent. This is good! You have plenty of capacity left.

The scope of these statements is obviously a VMware vSphere Cluster. From a capacity-monitoring point of view, a cluster is the smallest logical building block, due to HA and DRS. So, it is correct that we perform capacity planning at the cluster level and not at the host or data center level.

Can you figure out where the mistakes are?

You should notice a trend by now. The statements have something in common. Here is another hint—review this great blog by Mark Achtemichuk, a performance expert on VMware: `https://blogs.vmware.com/vsphere/2015/11/vcpu-to-pcpu-ratios-are-they-still-relevant.html`. In the blog, he explains why static counters such as vCPU:pCPU are no longer sufficient. You need something that reflects the actual live situation in the data center.

The earlier statements are wrong as they focus on the wrong item. They are looking at the cluster, when they should be looking at the VM.

Remember the restaurant analogy we covered in *Chapter 3, SDDC Management*? Those well-meant pieces of advice were looking at the supplier (provider), when they should have been focusing on the consumer (customer). What's important is your VM.

 The way you perform capacity monitoring changes drastically once you take into account performance and availability.

A shift in capacity management

Before we discuss how to perform capacity management in SDDC, let's discuss what changes drastically.

Let's take our restaurant analogy further:

Do you know how much food your diners should consume? You probably do. You've seen a lot of people dining in your restaurant, and you know roughly how much food a person, given his size and age, can consume.

Now, do you have authority on how much food they can order? No, you do not. If a diner wants to order three servings of fried rice for himself, it is his right. You can advise him, but you know you are not the one eating.

Let's take this to our IaaS now. It is up to the VM owner how big a VM he wants to order. In other words, capacity management no longer covers the VM. This is a big shift in capacity management. There is no capacity management for VMs. It has been replaced by VM rightsizing, which is handled by the application team.

Your scope has been reduced to the SDDC layer. Does it become simpler?

Not at all.

The SDDC layer needs to be planned as one integrated block. Remember, the SDDC transforms the infrastructure team into the service provider model. You need to see the application team as a customer who does not need to know about the detailed specification of your infrastructure. You provide them a service. To achieve this, you need to unify the three components (compute, network, and storage) as one integrated capacity planning model. It is no longer sufficient to look at them as three separate components managed by three different teams.

There is another reason why it is harder. SDDC means what used to be storage, network, and security are now taking the form of software. So there is no longer a physical boundary that says, "This is where server ends and storage starts."

With that, let's look at the three resources.

SDDC capacity planning

As the SDDC architect, you look at the big picture. Hence, it is important that you know your architecture well. One way to easily remember what you have is to keep it simple. Yes, you can have different host specifications—CPU speed, amount of RAM, and so on—in a cluster. But that would be hard to remember if you have a large farm with many clusters.

You also need to know what you actually have at the physical layer. If you don't know how many CPUs or how much RAM the ESXi host has, then it's impossible to figure out how much capacity is left. Sounds obvious, right? Who does not know how much physical resource he has!

Well, it's not so easy, actually.

We will use storage as an example to illustrate why it is hard to know what you actually have. Do you know how many IOPS your storage actually has?

Indeed. You only know roughly. There are too many "it depends" factors in the answer.

Once you know the actual raw capacity, you are in a position to figure out the usable portion. The next figure shows the relationship. The raw capacity is what you physically have. The Infrastructure as a Service (IaaS) workload is all the workload that is not caused by a VM. For example, the hypervisor itself consumes CPU and RAM. When you put an ESXi host into maintenance mode, it will trigger a mass vMotion for all the VMs running on it. That vMotion will take up the CPU and RAM of both ESXi hosts and the network between them. So, the capacity left for VM, the usable capacity, is **Raw Capacity (IaaS workload + Non vSphere workload)**.

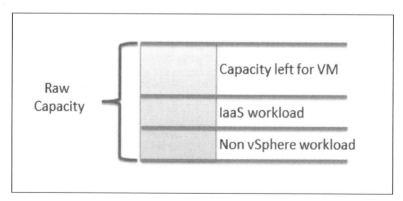

The main consumers of the IaaS capacity

So what are these IaaS workloads?

Think of the S in SDDC.

All the services or functionalities your SDDC provides to the consumer (the VM) run as software. Storage services (for example, Virtual SAN and vSphere Replication), network services (for example, an L3 switch in NSX and a firewall), security services (for example, Trend Micro antivirus), and availability services (for example, Storage vMotion) the list goes on. It is software, and software consumes physical resources. The next table lists all the IaaS workloads. It is possible that the list will get outdated as more and more capabilities are moved into software. For each of the workloads, I have not put an estimate on the impact, as it varies widely. Let's consider two examples:

- Performing vMotion on a small and idle VM will have minimal impact. Putting a host into maintenance mode, and hence triggering mass vMotion on ten large memory-intensive VMs, will have high impact.

- Replicating an idle VM with a **Recovery Point Objective (RPO)** of 24 hours will generate minimal traffic. Replicating many write-intensive VMs with an RPO of 15 minutes will generate high network traffic.

The blank spaces are for you to fill. Going through the exercise will make you think and understand your environment better.

IaaS workload	Compute impact	Network impact	Storage impact
vMotion and DRS.			
Storage vMotion and storage DRS.			
VM operation—snapshot, cloning, hibernate, shutdown, bootup.			
Fault-tolerant VM.			
HA and cluster maintenance (can result in all VMs being evacuated from an affected host).			
Hypervisor-based storage services: vSphere Replication.			
Virtual storage (for example, VSAN, SimpliVity, and so on).			

IaaS workload	Compute impact	Network impact	Storage impact
Backup (for example, VDP, VADP API) with de-dupe. Backup vendor can provide the info here. For VDP, you can see the actual data in vSphere.			
Hypervisor-based network services: AV, IDS, IPS, FW, and L3 switch (NSX).			
Edge-of-network services (for example, NSX Edge, and F5).			
DR test or actual (with SRM).			

Can you notice a popular workload that has not been included in the table? It's something that you probably already have.

You are right—**Virtual Desktop Infrastructure (VDI)**.

VMware Horizon workloads behave differently than server workloads, so they need their own separate breakdowns of workload, which have not been included in the table. A VDI (desktop) and VSI (server) farm should be separated physically for performance reasons and so that you may upgrade your vCenter servers independently. If that is not possible in your environment, then you need to include IaaS workloads specific to VMware Horizon (recompose, refresh, rebalance, and so on) in your calculations. If you ignore these and only include desktop workloads, you may not be able to perform desktop recomposition during office hours.

 Good capacity management begins with a good design.

A good design creates standards that simplify capacity management. If the design is flawed and complex, capacity management may become impossible.

Capacity planning at the compute level

In a large environment, having dedicated clusters for each service tier makes capacity management easier. We can compare the task of managing the needs of virtual machines to how an airline business manages the needs of passengers on a plane: the plane has dedicated areas for first class, business class, and economy class. It makes management easier as each class has a dedicated amount of space to be divided among the passengers, and the passengers are grouped by service level, so it is easier to tell whether the service levels for each class are being met overall. You also avoid a situation where a first-class passenger complains of slow service because your resources are busy serving the economy class passengers.

With this operations consideration in mind, we can see that three smaller clusters will be easier to manage than one large, mixed cluster serving all three tiers. Of course, there are situations where it is not possible to have small clusters; it all depends on the requirements and budget. Additionally, there are benefits of having one large cluster, such as lower cost and more resources to handle peak periods. In situations where you choose to mix VMs of different tiers, you should consider using shares instead of reservations.

You should use reservation sparingly as it impacts vSphere HA slot size, increases management complexity, and prevents you from oversubscribing. In tier 1, where there is no oversubscription because you are guaranteeing resources to every VM, reservation becomes unnecessary from a capacity-management point of view. You may still use it if you want a faster boot, but that's not concerned with the capacity point of view. In tier 3, where cost is the number-one factor, using reservation will prevent you from oversubscribing. This negates the purpose of tier 3 in the first place.

You should avoid using limits as they lead to unpredictable performance. The Guest OS does not know that it is artificially limited.

Capacity planning at the storage layer

For the storage node, capacity management depends on the chosen architecture. Storage is undergoing an evolution with the arrival of converged storage, which introduces an alternative to the traditional, external array.

In the traditional, external storage model, there is a physical array (for example, EMC VNX, HDS, HUS, and NetApp). As most environments are not yet 100-percent virtualized, the physical array is shared by non-ESXi servers (for example, Unix). There is often a physical backup server (for example, Symantec NetBackup) that utilizes the VMware VADP API.

The array might have LUNs replicated to a DR site. This replication certainly takes up bandwidth, FC ports, the array CPU, and bandwidth on the lines between your data centers.

If the array does not support VAAI (or this feature has not yet been implemented at the VM kernel level), then the traffic will traverse the path up and down. This can mean a lot of traffic going from the spindle to ESXi and back.

Some storage models support dynamic tiering (high IOPS, low latency storage fronting the low IOPS, and high latency spindles). In this configuration, the underlying physical IOPS varies from minute to minute. This creates a challenge for ESXi and vRealize Operations to determine the actual physical limit of the array, so you need to take extra care to ensure you accurately account for the resources available. A change in the array configuration can impact your capacity planning. Changing the tier preference of a given LUN can probably be done live, so it can be done without you being informed.

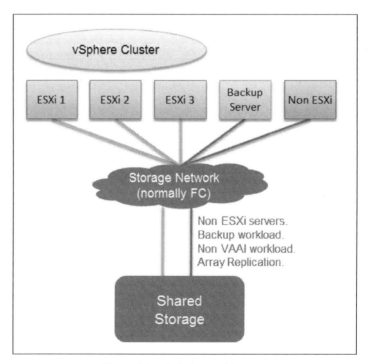

The traditional vSphere architecture

In the latter example, there is no longer a separate physical array. It has been virtualized and absorbed into the server. It has truly become a subsystem. Some example products in this category are SimpliVity and Virtual SAN. So, the object labeled **Storage 1** in the next diagram is just a bunch of local disks (magnetic or solid-state) in the physical server. Each ESXi host runs a similar group of local drives, typically with flash, SSD, and SATA. The local drives are virtualized. There is no FC protocol; it's all IP-based storage.

To avoid a single point of failure, the virtual storage appliance is able to mirror or copy in real time and there is a need to provide a bandwidth of 1 Gbps or higher for this. Use 10 GB infrastructure for your ESXi if you are adopting this distributed storage architecture, especially in environments with five or more hosts in a cluster. The physical switches connecting your ESXi servers should be seen as an integral part of the solution, not a "service" provided by the network team. Architectural choices such as ensuring redundancy for **network interface cards** (**NICs**) and switches are important.

The following diagram also uses vSphere Replication. Unlike array replication, this consumes the resource of ESXi and the network.

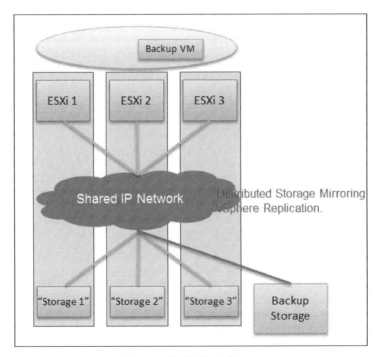

vSphere with distributed storage

Once you have confirmed your storage architecture, you will be in a position to calculate your usable capacity and IOPS. Let's now dive deeper into the first architecture, as this is still the most common architecture.

The next diagram shows a typical mid-range array. We're only showing **Controller 1** since our focus here is capacity, not availability. The topmost box shows the controller. It has CPU, RAM, and cache. In a tiered storage systems, there will be multiple tiers and the datastore can write into any of the tiers seamlessly and transparently. You do not need to have per-VM control over it. The control is likely at the LUN level. We've covered what this means in terms of performance (IOPS and latency).

What I'd like to show you in this diagram is the tradeoff in design between the ability to share resources and the ability to guarantee performance. In this diagram, the array has three volumes:

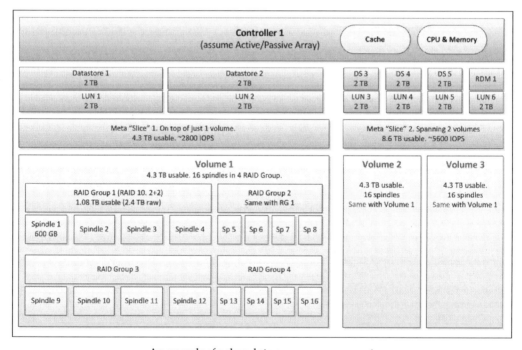

An example of a shared storage array component

Each volume consists of 16 spindles. In this specific example, each volume is independent of every other. If **Volume 1** is overloaded with IOPS but **Volume 2** is idle, it cannot offload the IOPS to **Volume 2**. Hence, the storage array is not exactly one array. From a capacity and performance point of view, it has hard partitions that cannot be crossed.

Does this then mean that you create one giant volume so that you can share everything?

Probably not; the reason is that there is no concept of shares or priority within a single volume. From the diagram, **Datastore 1** and **Datastore 2** live in **Volume 1**. If a non-production VM in **Datastore 1** is performing a high-IO task (say someone runs IOmeter), it can impact a production VM in **Datastore 2**.

Storage I/O control (SIOC) will not help you in this case. The scope of SIOC is within a datastore. It does not ensure fairness across datastores. Review Cormac Hogan's blog at `http://cormachogan.com/2013/07/11/sioc-and-datastores-spread-across-all-spindles-in-the-array`. Duncan Epping has also written articles on the topic, and a good starting point is this one: `http://www.yellow-bricks.com/2010/10/19/storage-io-control-best-practices`. If you have many datastores, SIOC has the highest chance of hitting fairness across datastores when the number of VMs per datastore is consistent.

As a VMware admin performing capacity management, you need to know the physical hardware your VMware environment is running on at all layers. As VMware professionals, we often stop at the compute layer and treat storage as just a LUN provider. There is a whole world underneath the LUNs presented to you.

Now that you know your physical capacity, the next thing to do is estimate your IaaS workload. If you buy an array with 100,000 IOPS, it does not mean you have 100,000 IOPS for your VM. In the next example, you have a much smaller number of usable IOPS. The most important factors you need to be aware of are:

- Frontend IOPS
- Backend IOPS

There are many calculations on IOPS as there are many variables impacting it. The numbers in this table are merely examples. The point I hope to get across is that it is important to sit down with the storage architect and estimate the number for your specific environment.

Components	IOPS	Remarks
Raw capacity	100,000	Backend IOPS.
Front-end IOPS	50,000	Use RAID 10. RAID 5 or RAID 6 will be slower.
Non ESXi workload	5,000	Not recommended to mix this as we cannot perform QoS or storage IO control.

Components	IOPS	Remarks
Back up workload	5,000	You can get the data from the physical array since the backup server is typically a physical server connected to the array. Included in vSphere if VDP is used.
Array replication	5,000.	If used.
vSphere replication	5,000.	If used.
Distributed storage mirroring	0.	Not applicable in this example as it uses a shared array.
Net available	30,000.	Only 30 percent left for the VM workload!

Capacity planning at the network layer

Similar to calculating capacity for storage, understanding capacity requirements for your network requires knowledge of the IaaS workloads that will compete with your VM workload. The following table provides an example using IP storage. Your actual design may differ compared to it. If you are using **fiber channel** storage, then you can use the available bandwidth for other purposes.

Purpose	Bandwidth	Remarks
VM	4 Gb	For around 20 VMs. An NSX Edge VM needs a lot of bandwidth as all the traffic passes through it. Ideally, you dedicate a separate cluster for network edge functions.
ESXi Agent		An appliance VM that exists per ESXi. For example, a Trend Micro Deep Security appliance.
Heartbeat	1 Mb	Minimal as it's purely for the heartbeat. Used by Symantec Veritas clusters.
FT network	2 Gb	Four vCPU FTs can easily hit more than 1 Gb, especially if you are planning to have more than one FT VM.

Purpose	Bandwidth	Remarks
IP Storage (serving VM)	6 Gb	NFS, iSCSI, or distributed storage. Doesn't need 10 Gb as the storage array is likely shared by 10-50 hosts. The array may only have 40 Gb in total for all these hosts (assuming it uses four 10 GE cables). In this example, seven hosts are enough to saturate it already if each host has 6 Gb.
vMotion & Storage vMotion	6 Gb	vSphere is capable of shared-nothing live migration. This increases the demand as the VMDK is much larger than the vRAM. Include multi-NIC vMotion for faster vMotion when there are multiple VMs to be migrated.
Management	1 Gb	Copying a powered-off VM to another host without a shared datastore takes this much bandwidth.
vSphere Replication	1 Gb	Should be sufficient as the WAN link is likely the bottleneck.
Total	Around 20 Gb	

When is a peak not a true peak?

One common requirement I get from customers is the need to size for peaks. I've seen many mistakes in defining what a peak actually is.

So, let's elaborate on peaks.

How do you define peak utilization or contention without being overly conservative or aggressive?

There are two dimensions of peaks: you can measure them across time or across members of the group.

Let's take a cluster with eight ESXi hosts as an example. The following chart shows the **ESXi Hosts Utilization** for the eight hosts.

What's the cluster peak utilization on that day?

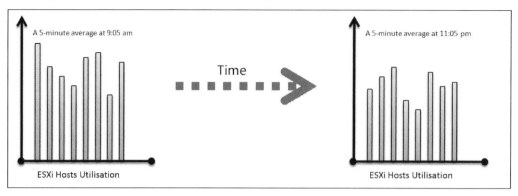

The two dimensions of peaks

As you can see from the graphs, it is not so simple. Let's elaborate:

- **Approach 1**: You measure across time. You take the average utilization of the cluster, roll up the time period to a longer time period, and calculate the peak of that longer time period. For example, the average cluster utilization peaks at 65 percent at 9:05 am. You roll up the data for one day. This means the peak utilization for that day is 65 percent. This is the most common approach. The problem of this approach is that it is actually an average. For the cluster to hit 80 percent average utilization, some hosts have to hit over 80 percent. This means you can't rule out the possibility that one host might hit near 100 percent. The same logic applies to a VM. If a VM with 16 vCPUs hits 80 percent utilization, some cores probably hit 100 percent. This method results in under-reporting since it is an average.

- **Approach 2**: You measure across members of the group. For each data sample, calculate the utilization from the host with the highest utilization. In our cluster example, at 9:05 am, host number 1 has the highest utilization among all hosts. It hits 80 percent. We then infer that the peak cluster utilization at 9:05 am is also 80 percent. You repeat this process for each sample period. You may get different hosts at different times. You will not know which host provides the peak value as it varies from time to time. This method results in over-reporting, as it is the peak of a member. You can technically argue that this is the true peak.

The second approach is useful if you want to know detailed information. You retain the 5-minute granularity. With the first approach, you lose the granularity and each sample becomes 1 day (or 1 month, depending on your timeline). You do not know what time of the day it hits the peak. The first approach will result in a higher average than the second one, because in most cases, your cluster is not perfectly balanced (identical utilization).

In a tier 1 cluster, where you do not oversubscribe, the second approach is better as it will capture the host with the highest peak. The second approach can be achieved using super metrics in vRealize Operations. The first approach requires the **View** widget with data transformation. As shown in the following screenshot, choose **Maximum** from the **Transformation** drop-down field:

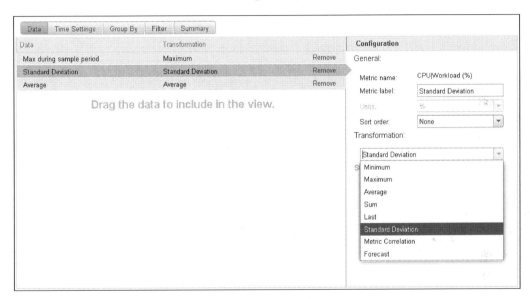

The data transformation feature of vRealize Operations

Does this mean you always use the second approach? The answer is no. This approach can be too conservative when the number of members is high. If your data center has 500 hosts and you use the second approach, then your overall data center peak utilization will always be high. All it takes is one host to hit a peak at any given time.

The second approach fits a use case where automatic load balancing should happen. So you expect an overall balanced distribution. A DRS cluster is a good example.

Putting it all together

We've covered a lot of foundation. This is important as we need to get the theory right so we know that we understand reality correctly, because it will match the theory. You should have the expected result or baseline.

The way you perform capacity management changes drastically once you take into account performance and availability. Let's consider an example to drive the point. We'll take storage, as it's the easiest example:

- Say your physical SAN array has 200 TB usable capacity.
- It supports 1000 VMs, which take up 100 TB.
- It has 100 TB usable capacity left. That's plenty of space.
- Assuming an average VM occupies 100 GB of space, you can fit almost 1000 VMs!

My question is this: how many additional running VMs can that array support?

1000? 500? 1?

You are right—it depends on the VM IOPS. Just because there is space does not mean the array can handle the workload.

Now, what if the existing 1000 VMs are already experiencing high latency? Users are complaining as latency is hitting 100 milliseconds, impacting many VMs randomly.

Should you add more VMs? The answer is clearly no. Adding VMs will make performance worse. For all practical purposes, the array capacity is full.

It is common practice to perform capacity management by looking at the utilization of the infrastructure (**IaaS Utilization**). That's a costly mistake. You should stop looking at it as the primary indicator.

The following diagram shows that **Performance** and **Availability** are driving your **Capacity**. **IaaS Utilization** and **IaaS Workload** are in fact the last things you consider.

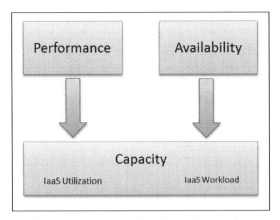

Capacity management based on business policy

You only look at the utilization of your infrastructure when you pass your performance and availability SLAs. If all the VMs are performing fast, then you check your ESXi utilization to see whether you can add more VMs. If the VMs are not performing fast, the utilization of your ESXi is irrelevant.

You may recall from *Chapter 4, Performance Monitoring*, that the primary counter for capacity is workload (or utilization). You will see later on that we do not in fact use them as part of capacity monitoring. We only use performance and availability metrics.

Availability – service definition

We covered performance in great depth in *Chapter 4, Performance Monitoring*. Assuming you read that, let's proceed to covering availability.

For the compute node, the table in the following diagram provides an example cluster design for virtual machine tiers. Your design will likely differ from the following table, as your requirements may differ. The main thing is that you need to have a design that clearly defines your service. I've used properties such as maximum cluster size and maximum number of VMs as part of my availability policy. I'm using the cluster size to define my failure domain. The maximum number of VMs helps you assure your customers on the extent of the "damage" when a host or cluster goes down.

You may, and probably do, use other properties in your environment.

Service Tier	vSphere HA	Max Cluster Size	Max No of VM
1 (highest)	2 HA Host (N+2)	8 nodes	15 VM per host 100 VM per cluster
2	1 HA Host (N+1)	12 nodes	30 VM per host 250 VM per cluster
3 (lowest)	1 HA Host (N+1)	16 nodes	60 VM per host 750 VM per cluster

This is for the compute portion. It is not applicable to the network portion as it is an interconnect, as described in *Chapter 11, SDDC Key Counters*.

Let's now look at the storage portion. It depends on the architecture. The principle of availability remains the same, though. As you know well, mission-critical VMs have to be better protected than development VMs. You would go the extra mile to ensure redundancy. In the event of failure, you also want to cap the degree of the damage. You want to minimize the chance of human error too.

I've provided an example in the following diagram. Just like the compute portion, you need to come up with your own policy. For example, if you are using VMFS, you may have a policy that says no more than 50 mission-critical VMs are allowed in a single VMFS datastore:

Service Tier	No of copies	Disk Failure Tolerance	Snapshot
1 (highest)	2 copies	2 disk failure	Every 2 hours
2	1 copy	1 disk failure	Every 12 hours
3 (lowest)	1 copy	1 disk failure	Upon request

Let's now see how we can translate this policy into a solution.

We are using line charts so that we can see the trend across time. All the timelines should be about 1 month, with a maximum of 3 months. This allows you to spot trends early, as it takes weeks to buy hardware. A timeline longer than 3 months will result in you buying hardware too early.

Let's begin with tier 1 as it's the easiest. We'll cover tier 2 and tier 3 together, as they have the same nature. They both have overcommitment.

Network will be covered separately as it has the same solution for all tiers.

Tier 1 compute monitoring

For the compute portion of capacity management, monitoring becomes much simpler, as there is no overcommitment. Your ESXi will have low utilization almost all of the time. Even if all VMs are running at 100 percent, the ESXi will not hit contention as there are enough physical resources for everyone. As a result, there is no need to track contention as there won't be any. This means you do not need to check capacity against your performance SLA. You just need to check against your availability SLA.

To help you monitor, you can create five line charts, three for compute and two for storage. Here are the line charts for compute:

- A line chart showing the total number of vCPUs left in the cluster
- A line chart showing the total number of vRAM left in the cluster
- A line chart showing the total number of VMs left in the cluster

Look at the previous three charts as one group. Take the one with the lowest number.

If the lowest number is approaching a low number, it's time to add capacity. How low that number should be depends on how fast you can procure hardware. I will explain this in detail in *Chapter 7, Capacity-Monitoring Dashboards*.

Yup, that's all you need for compute. There's nothing about ESXi or vSphere Cluster utilization as they are irrelevant. In tier 1, you are driven by availability, not performance.

Tier 2 and 3 compute monitoring

For the compute portion, tier 2 and 3 are more complex than tier 1, as there is now the possibility of contention. You need to check against both the performance and availability SLAs.

Here are the line charts for compute:

- A line chart showing the maximum and average CPU contention experienced by any VM in the cluster

- A line chart showing the maximum and average RAM contention experienced by any VM in the cluster

- A line chart showing the total number of VMs left in the cluster

How do you use the maximum and average lines to track capacity? Here's how:

- The maximum number has to be lower than the SLA you promise at all times. If the maximum latency number hits your threshold, it's time to add capacity. Adding a VM will breach your performance SLA.

- If the maximum is below your SLA but your minimum number is approaching your threshold, the capacity is near full. Adding VMs may breach your performance SLA as the maximum number may exceed it.

- If the maximum is well below your SLA, it means that you overprovisioned the hardware.

Look at these three charts as one group. Take the one with the value closest to your SLA. The first two lines are from your performance SLA and the third line is from your availability SLA.

Storage monitoring

I've separated storage as you can use the same solution for all tiers. You will use the same line charts. The only difference is your threshold. Keeping a consistent solution makes operations simpler.

Unlike compute, storage is driven by performance and utilization for all service tiers. Here are the line charts for storage:

- A line chart showing the maximum and average storage latency experienced by any VM in the datastore cluster

- A line chart showing the disk capacity left in the datastore cluster

You should group your datastores into a datastore cluster. Other than the primary benefits, it also makes capacity management easier. If you use it, you need not manually exclude local datastores. You also need not manually group shared datastores, which can be complex if you have multiple clusters.

Can you guess why the first line chart is based on the datastore cluster, since it was based on the compute cluster when we discussed it in *Chapter 4, Performance Monitoring*?

The reason is that we use the compute cluster when we track performance based on ease of operation. In addition, performance is about the VM, not your IaaS. It does not matter where the VM disk resides; slow means slow.

Capacity is different. It is about your IaaS, not the VM. There are two reasons why storage capacity monitoring cannot be based on the compute cluster:

- **Local datastores**: They complicate capacity monitoring because they are included by default in the compute cluster storage capacity. You do not include local datastores in capacity management.

- **A datastore spanning multiple compute clusters**: You will get partial data if you perform calculations based on the compute cluster. This is another reason why your design should have a 1:1 mapping between the datastore cluster and compute cluster.

With these line charts, we are tracking both performance and utilization. Take the *lower* of these two dimensions, because adding one capacity dimension gives you the other. This also keeps your storage in a simple building block.

What if you are using all-flash storage?

All-flash storage is becoming a common option in 2016. With SSDs, even with large capacity ones, there is a chance of you being bound by disk space and not performance. The second line chart helps you track the space left (in GB).

What if you are using distributed storage, such as VSAN?

This changes capacity management as you cannot perform compute and storage differently.

Since your storage is part of your compute, you need to look at them as one unit. So, look at the five line charts together.

Adding compute means adding storage. It is true that adding storage does not mean adding compute if you have spare physical slots. However, that requires advance planning and intentionally choosing a server model with enough disk slots.

For VSAN, there is only one datastore, so there is no need for a datastore cluster.

Network monitoring

For network, you should use the same standard regardless of the tier. You should not expect dropped packets in your data center.

The ideal counter to measure is network latency. However, this is costly to measure at the VM level. It is also costly to measure for all packets. You could certainly generate a sample packet that measures the point-to-point latency at a given interval. However, that is not the actual latency experienced by the business. As a result, we have to use dropped packets as a proxy.

It's 2016. Your SDDC should be on 10 GE, as the chance of ESXi saturating one GE is not something you can ignore. The chance of ESXi saturating two 10 GE links is relatively lower, unless you run vSphere FT and VSAN (or another form of distributed storage).

To help you monitor, you can create the following:

- A line chart showing the maximum network dropped packets at the physical data center level. It is applied at the physical data center and not the vSphere cluster, as they eventually share the same core switches.
- A line chart showing the maximum and average ESXi vmnic at the same level as in the previous point. This will tell you whether any of your vmnics are saturated.

Here's a quiz to help you figure out the logic:

- In the first line chart, notice it only has the maximum line. We're not tracking the average dropped packets. Why is that so?
- In the second line chart, we're tracking at the vmnic level, not any other level (for example, distributed port group, distributed switch, or ESXi). Why is that so?

Conclusion

I hope the discussion in this section has given you a fresh perspective on how you should do capacity management in SDDC. Indeed, a few line charts are all you need for managing capacity. Yes, it is not a fully automated solution. However, our customers will find it logical and easy to understand. It follows the 80/20 principle, where you are given 20 percent room to make a judgement call as the expert.

Ronald Buder and Sunny Dua, in their review of this book, shared that there are situations where you need to use the 95th percentile. This lets you have greater confidence in your monitoring, as you can see whether the 5 percent is an exception. We will include this when we implement the dashboards in *Part 2* of the book.

VDI capacity planning

We've covered a lot about SDDC. Let's include VDI, as it shows how capacity management changes when you include higher-level services (above your IaaS).

VDI differs from SDDC at the business level. It is much more than server workload versus desktop workload. With VDI, it is DaaS, which runs on top of the IaaS. So, the scope goes beyond IaaS. It includes the VDI VM (for example, Windows 7 and Windows 2008) and the Horizon infrastructure VM.

As a result, there are three areas where you need to monitor for capacity:

- **The user's VDI VM**: This is typically Windows 7 or Windows 10 64-bit. Different users have different workload profiles, even though they may use the same set of applications. I've seen users who use Microsoft Excel with large files and it needs six vCPUs!
- **The Horizon server VM**: This includes non-VMware products that complete your DaaS offering. Some products, such as F5 and Trend Micro, are in the data path, so you need to monitor them as their performance can impact the users' experience.
- **The IaaS layer**: This includes vSphere and the layer below it.

Other than the scope of the business, the workload itself differs. The table in the following figure summarizes the key differences:

Server Workload	VDI Workload
1 apps	Many apps
Long live apps	Many apps launched and closed.
Varies	Many files opened and closed
No Internet browsing	Internet browsing (movie!)
Workload predictable	Workload spiky and unpredictable
Varies (UI-less)	Flash, Java, JavaScript (UI heavy)

VM rightsizing

Remember the story in *Chapter 4, Performance Monitoring*, where you got blamed for a non-performing VM?

Well, part of it was your fault. You meddled with someone else's business.

Many IaaS teams are eager to help application teams downsize the VM. The number one reason is to save the company money. However, this approach is wrong. You need to approach it with respect to benefit, not cost.

There are some tips you can give your customers and policies you can set to encourage VM rightsizing from the beginning.

For a start, keep the building blocks simple—one VM, one OS, one application, and one instance. So, avoid doing things such as having one OS running the web, app, and DB server or one Microsoft SQL server running five instances of databases. The workload can become harder to predict as you cannot isolate them.

Implement a chargeback model that encourages the right behavior (for example, non-linear costing, where an eight-vCPU VM is charged more than eight times the cost of a one-vCPU VM).

Adjust the size based on the peak workload for a production environment. A month-end VM needs to be sized based on the month-end workload. For a non-production environment, you may want to tell the application team to opt for a smaller VM, because the vSphere cluster where the VM is running is oversubscribed. The large VM may not get the CPUs it asks for if it asks for too many.

Be careful with VMs that have two distinct peaks, one for CPU resources and another for memory resources. I have seen this with a telecommunications client running Oracle Hyperion. For example, the first peak needs eight vCPUs and 12 GB vRAM, and the second peak needs two vCPUs and 48 GB vRAM. In this case, the application team tendency is to size for 8 vCPUs and 48 GB vRAM. This results in an unnecessarily large VM, which can result in poor performance for both peaks. It is likely that there are two different workloads running in the VM, which should be split into two VMs.

Size correctly. Educate the application team that oversizing results in slower performance in the virtual world. Besides wasting company resources, there are several disadvantages of oversized VMs:

- It takes longer to boot. If a VM does not have a reservation, vSphere will create a swap file the size of the configured RAM.

- It takes longer to vMotion.

- The RAM or CPU may be spread over a single socket. Due to the NUMA architecture, the performance will be inferior.

- It will experience higher CPU co-stop and CPU ready time. Even if not all vCPUs are used by the application, the Guest OS will still demand all the vCPUs be provided by the hypervisor.

- It takes longer to snapshot, especially if a memory snapshot is included. With newer technology such as Virtual SAN, snapshots are faster and more scalable. Regardless, you should still aim for the right size.

- The processes inside the Guest OS may experience ping-pong. Depending on your configuration, the Guest OS may not be aware of the NUMA nature of the physical motherboard and may think it has a uniform structure. It may move processes within its own CPUs, as it assumes it has no performance impact. If the vCPUs are spread into different NUMA nodes, for example, a 20-vCPU VM on an ESXi host with two sockets and 20 cores, it can experience a ping-pong effect. For more details, read `http://blogs.vmware.com/vsphere/2013/10/does-corespersocket-affect-performance.html` by Mark Achtemichuk.

- There is a lack of performance visibility at the individual vCPU or virtual core level. As covered earlier in this book, a majority of the counters are at the VM level, which is an aggregate of all of its vCPUs. It does not matter whether you use virtual sockets or virtual cores.

Although standardization of VM size helps in making operations simpler, you should be flexible for large cases. For example, once you pass six vCPUs, you need to consider every additional CPU carefully and ensure that the application can indeed take advantage of the extra threads.

You also need to verify that the underlying ESXi has sufficient physical cores, as it will affect your consolidation ratio and, hence, your capacity management. You may see an ESXi that is largely idle yet the VMs on it are not performing, therefore impacting your confidence about adding VMs.

At the VM level, you need to monitor the following five components:

- Virtual CPU
- Virtual RAM
- Virtual network
- Virtual disk IOPS
- Usable disk capacity left in the Guest OS

Getting vCPUs and vRAM into a healthy range requires finding a balance. Undersizing leads to poor performance and oversizing leads to monetary waste as well as poor performance. The actual healthy range depends upon your expected utilization, and it normally varies from tier to tier. It also depends on the nature of the workload (online versus batch). For example, in tier 1 (the highest tier), you will have a lower range for the OLTP type of workload as you do not want to hit 100 percent at peak. The overall utilization will be low as you are catering for a spike. For batch workloads, you normally tolerate a higher range for long-running batch jobs, as they tend to consume all the resources given to them.

In a non-production environment, you normally tolerate a higher range, as the business expectation is lower (because they are paying a lower price).

Between CPU and RAM, you focus on CPU first. Here are the reasons why reducing RAM should come secondary:

- If the VM has no RAM shortage, reducing RAM will not speed up the VM. With CPU, the VM will perform faster as it will have lower CPU contention.
- RAM monitoring is best done with counters inside the Guest OS. If you do not have this visibility, your recommendation can be wrong.

- Reducing RAM requires manual reduction for apps that manage their own RAM (such as Java, SQL, and Oracle). VMware vCenter, for example, has three JVM instances and each has its RAM recommendation documented in vSphere.

- Reducing RAM can trigger more internal swapping in the Guest. This in turn generates I/O, making the storage situation worse.

- It's hard enough to ask the application team to reduce CPU, so asking them to reduce both CPU and RAM will be even harder. It's better that you ask for one thing and emphasize it well. In addition, if there is any issue after you reduce both CPU and RAM, you have to bring both back up, even though it was caused by just one of them.

Generally speaking, a virtual network is not something that you need to worry about from a capacity point of view. You can create a super metric in vRealize Operations that tracks the maximum of your entire vNIC utilization from all VMs. If the maximum is, say, 80 percent, then you know that the rest of the VMs are lower than that. You can then plot a chart that shows this peak utilization in the last three months. We will cover this in more detail in one of the use cases discussed in the final chapter.

You should monitor the usable disk capacity left inside the Guest OS. Although vCenter does not provide this information, vRealize Operations does—provided your VM has VMware Tools installed (which it should have, as part of best practice).

Chapter 7, Capacity-Monitoring Dashboards, will include a dashboard that helps you rightsize VMs.

Summary

In this chapter, we discussed how you should approach capacity management in a virtual data center. We saw that there is a fundamental shift, resulting in a two-tier model. The application team performs capacity management at the VM layer, and the infrastructure team performs it at the infrastructure layer.

In the infrastructure layer, we covered the three service tiers and how they differ in terms of capacity management. We covered the actual line charts you need for each service tier.

In *Chapter 4, Performance Monitoring*, we learned in depth how you should monitor things. We are now ready to dive deeper into the actual dashboards. *Chapter 6, Performance-Monitoring Dashboards*, will kick off the dashboard series. I'll start by showing you the performance dashboards.

Part 2
Dashboards

Part 2 provides the actual dashboards to implement the concept we introduce in Part 1. It consists of 5 chapters

- Chapter 6 covers performance monitoring
- Chapter 7 covers capacity monitoring
- Chapter 8 covers complementary dashboards to use cases covered in previous 2 chapters. They are typically used by specific roles.
- Chapter 9 covers non VMware components of your IaaS. It leverages management packs from Blue Medora.
- Chapter 10 covers application level monitoring.

Most of these dashboards are real-life examples of dashboards that customers have used.

For each use case, we will provide the rationale behind it. This will enable you to review the context and requirements behind the dashboard, so you can then tailor the dashboard to your own needs. Each use case may need more than one dashboard, as a big dashboard takes longer to load and increases complexity. Having said that, use full HD resolution whenever possible.

The use cases given in this chapter are only a subset of the possible use cases for vRealize Operations dashboards. Sunny Dua shares more examples at http://vxpresss.blogspot.com/. We have minimized duplication with what he has covered in his blog.

In general, if we find a dashboard available freely on the Internet, we would provide the link to the dashboard instead of duplicating the information here.

Providing a step-by-step guide on how to build the vRealize Operations dashboards in the use cases is out of the scope of this book. There are 2 reasons for this:

- Materials on how to build vRealize Operations dashboards is freely available online. There are many bloggers who provide the info. The purpose of this book is to help you work out what to build.

- It keeps this book version independent. We use virtual-red-dot.info site to provide information that is version dependent, as it can be updated anytime.

6
Performance-Monitoring Dashboards

This chapter demonstrates how you can use vRealize Operations and vRealize Log Insight to monitor performance. To some extent, it will help in performance troubleshooting too. This chapter deliberately separates capacity from performance in order to further drive the point that they are different.

We group the dashboards into use cases and will cover the following use cases:

- How is the overall IaaS performance? Is any VM not getting the resources promised as per the performance SLA?
- Is virtualization causing the problem? This dashboard lets the help desk team quickly determine where a performance problem lies when a VM owner complains.
- Is vMotion impacting VM performance?
- Is any VM abusing the shared IaaS?

What is the overall IaaS performance?

Let's recap from *Chapter 4, Performance Monitoring*, the main question asked by the CIO about your IaaS platform:

"How do you prove that not a single VM in the past month has suffered an unacceptable performance hit because of non-performing IaaS?"

Chapter 4, Performance Monitoring, then went on to explain that you implement service tiering to help you defend your IaaS. *Chapter 5, Capacity Monitoring*, supported the idea by incorporating performance into capacity management.

For each service tier, we need to cover the four components of infrastructure, which are:

- CPU
- RAM
- Disk
- Network

You need to ensure that not a single VM experiences a contention that exceeds the agreed-upon SLA on that service tier. Naturally, there is different SLA for each tier. This means you need to plot one chart for each service tier.

Based on the performance SLA defined in *Chapter 4, Performance Monitoring*, these are the required line charts:

- A line chart showing the maximum CPU contention experienced by any VM in the cluster
- A line chart showing the maximum RAM contention experienced by any VM in the cluster
- A line chart showing the maximum storage latency experienced by any VM in the cluster

Can you guess why we use clusters and not ESXi hosts?

You are right: due to HA and DRS, a vSphere cluster is the smallest logical building block. With technology like VSAN, it further emphasizes that a cluster should be seen as one unit.

You will need a minimum of four super metrics, which are:

- Maximum VM CPU contention in the cluster
- Maximum VM RAM contention in the cluster
- Maximum VM disk latency in the cluster
- Maximum VM dropped packets in the data center

We're not tracking the network at the cluster level as it's something you can do at higher levels. You should not expect any dropped packets within your data center.

Can you guess why we only display the maximum value and not the average?

There is no need to display the average value. Our focus here is performance, not capacity. Remember, performance is something you check daily, while capacity is something you check quarterly.

While this dashboard is for day-to-day monitoring, it is a good starting point for any performance troubleshooting. You need to know the overall situation before diving into a particular problem. There is no point troubleshooting a particular VM's performance if the whole cluster has a performance issue.

This dashboard is not for the overall health. Health is more than performance. It takes into account anomalies and availability. Health is also affected when the capacity is near full as it takes into account the vSphere HA setting.

With that, let's proceed.

Creating the super metrics

The following screenshot shows the super metric formula to get the maximum CPU contention experienced among all VMs in the cluster. I have enlarged the original dialog box so that the text is large enough to read on a tablet and printed copy.

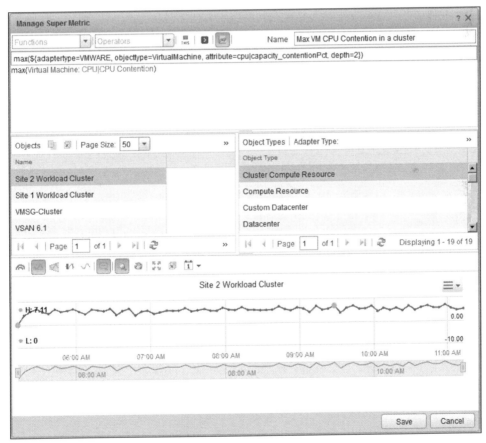

Maximum VM CPU contention in a cluster

If you are not sure how to create a super metric, follow the instructions at `http://virtual-red-dot.info/how-to-create-a-super-metric-in-vrealize-operations-6/`.

The following screenshot shows the **Super Metric** formula to get the maximum memory contention of all the VMs in the cluster. It's similar to CPU contention, but just using a different metric.

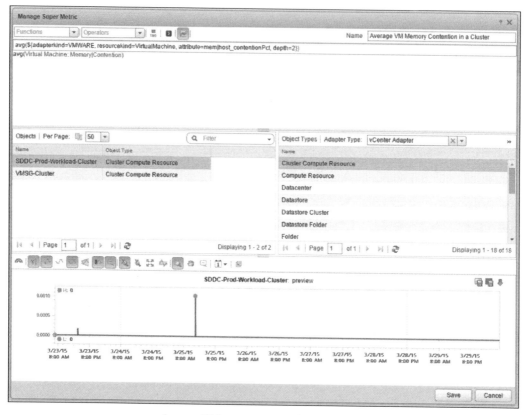

Average VM memory contention in a cluster

For storage, we have a few counters to choose from as VMs have multiple storage counters. We've chosen a counter at the **Virtual Disk** level, so it does not matter whether it is VMFS, NFS, or VSAN. It also works on RDM, although you should avoid using RDM in the first place.

The following screenshot shows the **Super Metric** formula to get the maximum disk latency of all the VMs in the cluster:

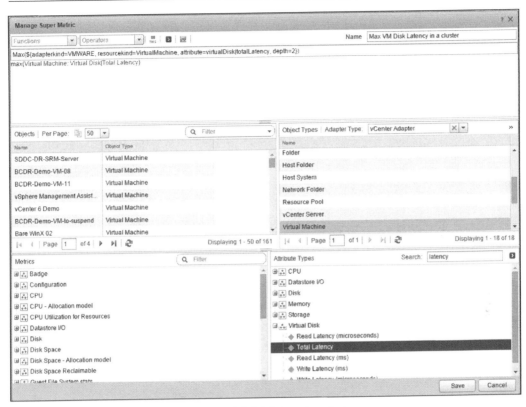

Maximum VM disk latency in a cluster

For network, we need a line chart showing the maximum network dropped packets at the physical data center level. We use a physical data center and not a vSphere cluster, as both share the same core switches.

It's also easier to manage the network per physical data center. Unless your network is stretched, problems do not span across. If you are planning to span your network across multiple sites, review the article by Ivan Pepelnjak at `http://blog.ipspace.net/2012/10/if-something-can-fail-it-will.html`.

The problem is how to choose ESXi from the same physical data center. It is possible for a physical data center to have multiple vCenter servers. On the other hand, it is also possible for a vRealize Operations world object, or even a single vCenter, to span multiple physical data centers.

Based on your environment, determine the right vRealize Operations object so that you get all the ESXi hosts in that physical data center. For example, if you have one vRealize Operations instance managing two physical data centers, you definitely cannot use the World object. It will span across both data centers.

In this example, the environment has one virtual data center mapped to one physical data center. None of the clusters span across physical data centers. In this case, we can choose a vCenter virtual data center.

The following screenshot shows the super metric formula to get the maximum network dropped packets in a vCenter data center object. Notice the formula has **depth=3**, as the data center object is three levels above the VM object:

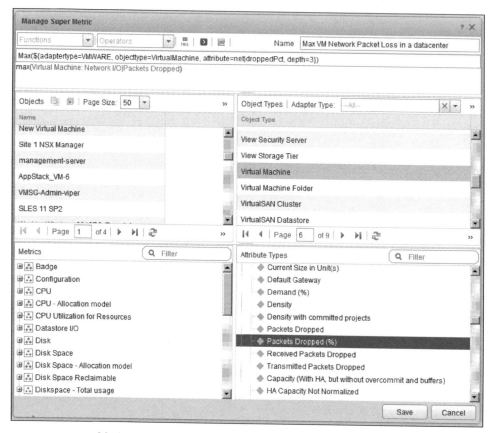

Maximum VM network dropped packets in a vCenter data center

Applying the super metrics

Once you create the super metrics, you need to apply them to the objects. If you are not sure how to apply super metrics to objects, follow the instructions at http://virtual-red-dot.info/vrealize-operations-how-to-add-supermetric/.

By the way, if you prefer to copy and paste the **Super Metrics**, here are the actual formulas:

```
max(${adaptertype=VMWARE, objecttype=VirtualMachine,
attribute=cpu|capacity_contentionPct, depth=2})
max(${adaptertype=VMWARE, objecttype=VirtualMachine,
attribute=mem|host_contentionPct, depth=2})
Max(${adaptertype=VMWARE, objecttype=VirtualMachine, attribute=virtual
Disk|totalLatency, depth=2})
Max(${adaptertype=VMWARE, objecttype=VirtualMachine,
attribute=net|droppedPct, depth=3})
```

Creating the dashboard

There are many resources on the Internet showing you how to create dashboards, so I hope you agree that there is no need to kill trees when the information is readily available using Google. The actual steps also differ slightly for each vRealize Operations edition.

The dashboard we use here leverages the **View** widget.

View is a new feature in version 6.0. In version 5.x, you needed to create a custom XML file to display specific metrics in a widget. In version 6, you just need to create a view for a specific metric. There is no need to manually edit and upload an XML file. The catch is that you get one chart per view, which cannot be split. If you want multiple charts, you need to have multiple views, and hence, multiple widgets.

Always prefix the View objects that you create. vRealize Operations has over 200 out-of-the-box views, so it can be difficult to find yours if you do not tag them somehow. In the following example, we have prefixed our view with **E1**. A good prefix for you will be the short name of your company (for example, MSFT or AWS).

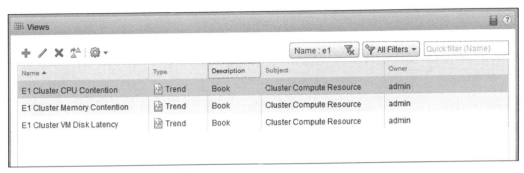

vRealize Operations — Views list with filters

You need to create three **View** objects. Each of them is a line chart. As part of the creation, you need to do the following:

1. Click on the **Presentation** tab in the wizard's dialog box and choose **Trend**. This stands for line chart.

2. In the **Subjects** dialog box, choose **Cluster**. You want to get the **Super Metric** you created earlier.

3. In the **Data** tab, choose the relevant **Super Metric**. For CPU, choose **CPU contention**.

4. In the **Configuration** area, deselect **Trend** under historical data and forecast data. You only need the actual historical data. A trend line will complicate the chart.

5. Now, in the **Time Settings** tab, choose the time duration that suits your need. I recommend **12 hours** as the default. This means you should check the environment twice a day, which is a good practice.

When you are done, it will look like the following screenshot. This example is for CPU:

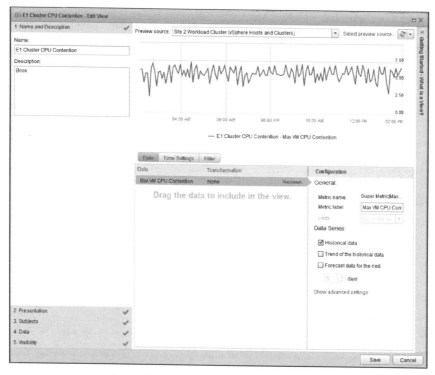

vRealize Operations—the View wizard dialog box

Once all the View widgets are created, it is a matter of adding them to a dashboard. Here are the steps you need to carry out:

1. Create a new dashboard. Name it **IaaS Overall Performance**, or something that makes sense to you.

2. From the **Widget List** submenu, choose an **Object List**. Customize it to show the cluster objects.

3. Add three **View** widgets. Associate each with the views you created earlier (CPU, RAM, storage, and so on).

4. Make your dashboard a two-column dashboard.

5. Define an interaction between the widgets, as shown in the following screenshot:

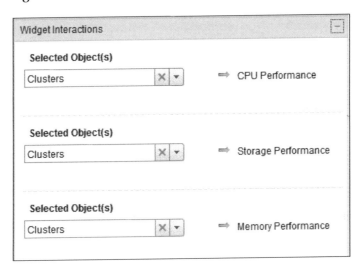

6. Save the dashboard.

That's it!

Here is what it should look like. The screenshot shows we have created a two-column dashboard. It has a list of clusters. Choosing a cluster from the list will automatically show the relevant performance line charts in the three **View** widgets:

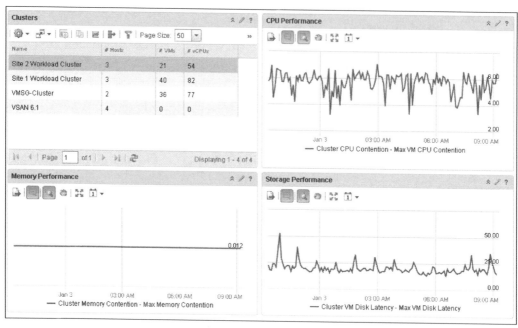

The performance monitoring dashboard

The performance SLA line

The preceding dashboard is good and simple. In a very large environment, where there are many people using the dashboard, it will be useful to add the SLA threshold. This helps everyone visually tell whether the threshold is breached or not.

This means we enhance the dashboard by adding:

- VM CPU performance SLA for that tier
- VM RAM performance SLA for that tier
- VM Disk performance SLA for that tier

We also can add an alert. The alert should tell us the VM name and which SLA was hit (CPU, disk, RAM, network, and so on).

Can you think of the complexity required to realize this? The following questions come to mind:

- How does vRealize Operations know which cluster is on which tier, since even vSphere does not know?
- How do we associate the SLA with each object?
- How do we associate the SLA with a new VM? It has to inherit from the cluster it belongs to.

There are a few ways to implement this, as we have two tools (vSphere and vRealize). In this example, we will not touch vCenter and do all the implementation in vRealize Operations. This is simpler as organizations typically have multiple vCenter servers but one vRealize Operations server.

vRealize Operations does not allow you to apply a Super Metric to a group, so there is some workaround required. You might feel that we are performing a lot of steps, so a diagram will help. The numbers in the following diagram correspond to the steps we will perform:

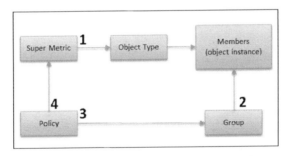

Step 1 – create a super metric to define the SLA

We cannot create a property in vRealize Operations and attach a value to it. What we can do is create a metric and attach a constant value. Brandon Gordon shared this idea when we met during VMworld.

The following example shows how to set the VM CPU SLA to 5 percent. There is no need to specify percentage or other units.

vRealize Operations | Super Metric | edit dialog box

You may be surprised that all you need to do is specify the value. Here is what it looks like after it's created:

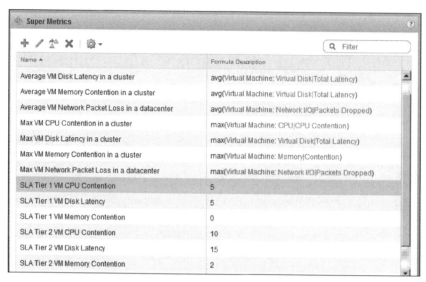

vRealize Operations | Super Metric | main screen

Now, we need to attach the right SLA to the right cluster. This means we need to map each cluster to the right tier. One way to do this is to create a group for each tier and add all the associated clusters as members.

Step 2 – create a group for each tier

In the following example, we have created three groups, one for each tier:

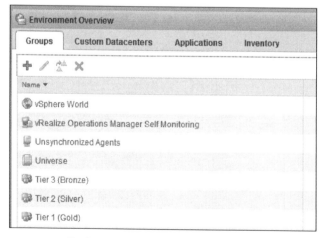

vRealize Operations | Group | main screen

The group members are the associated clusters. There are two ways you can do this, as shown in the following diagram. You can use either a dynamic (**1**) or static membership (**2**):

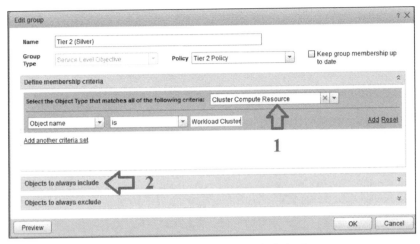

vRealize Operations | Group | edit dialog box

The first option works when you have a clear naming convention for each tier. You can include all clusters whose names or properties match a pattern.

The second option works if you do not have a clear naming convention. In this situation, you simply include the object manually, as shown in the following screenshot:

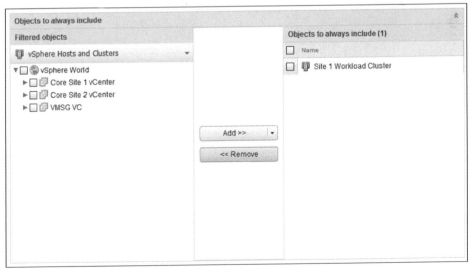

vRealize Operations | Group | edit dialog box | static membership

Step 3 – create policies for each group

The group we created only has members. It does not have its own SLA yet. In other words, it does not have a policy, since an SLA is a form of policy. By default, vRealize Operations only has one active policy. So, we need to create three more policies. We have created two in the following example, as the environment does not need more than that:

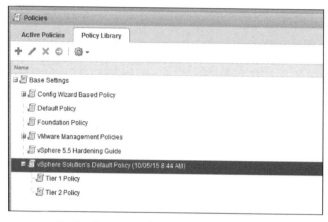

vRealize Operations | Policy | Policy Library tab

Now that we have multiple policies, we need to associate each one to the group we created earlier. Here is how you do it:

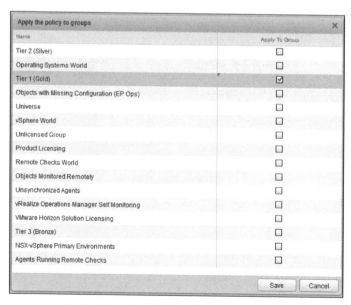

vRealize Operations | Policy | Applying to groups

When you are done, the result will look like the following. Notice it shows the number of objects for each group.

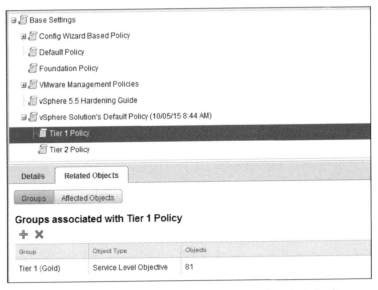

vRealize Operations | Policy | Groups mapped to the selected policy

Step 4 – map super metrics to policy

We have the group and we have the Super Metric. The next step is to associate them. Association between metrics and objects is done using policies, which is why we created the policies in the previous step. This screenshot shows you how to map them:

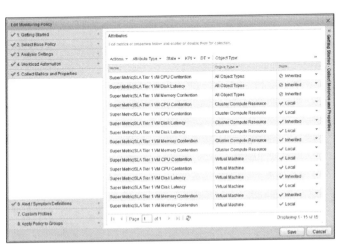

vRealize Operations | Policy | mapping super metrics

Once you do the mapping, you will see the effect on the **Super Metrics** screen. Click on the **Policies** tab, and you will see the policy tied to the super metric. This means that this Super Metric will not be tied to objects that do not belong to this policy.

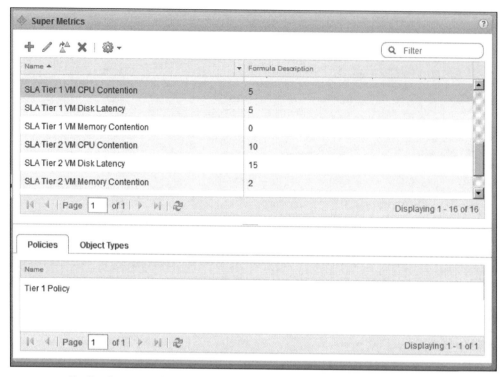

vRealize Operations | Super Metric | Policies mapped to the selected super metric

Step 5 – add the SLA to each line chart

Finally, we are ready to add the SLA line to each of the **View** widgets. To do this, you need to copy each widget for each tier because they have different SLAs.

For each tier, add the Super Metric. We have added the tier one CPU SLA Super Metric to the tier one **CPU** widget, as shown in the following screenshot:

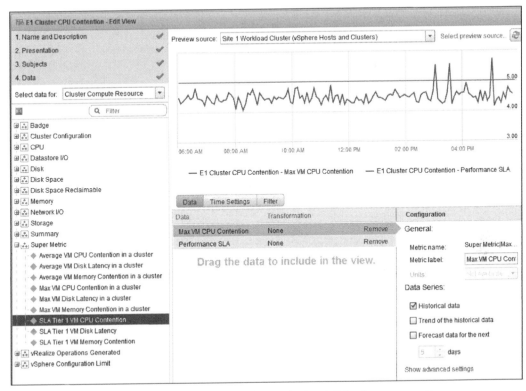

vRealize Operations | View | wizard dialog box

The resultant dashboard

This is what the dashboard looks like for the tier 1 cluster. You will need to have a separate dashboard for tier 2 and tier 3.

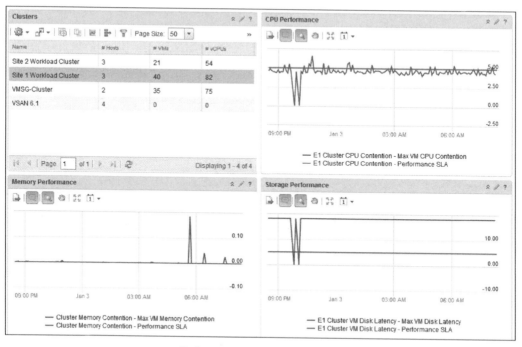

Performance monitoring with SLA

Alerts

The next possible enhancement is to have an alert. An alert is triggered when a symptom occurs, so let's define the symptom. An example symptom is VM CPU contention exceeding the tier 1 CPU SLA. Another example is VM disk latency exceeding the tier 3 disk SLA.

To create a symptom, go the **Symptom Definitions** UI and create a new one based on metrics. It will show you the following window:

vRealize Operations | Create a new symptom definition

In the previous screenshot, choose **Virtual Machine** as the object.

Next, find **CPU Contention** and drag it to the right. We did this in the previous example.

Change **Static Threshold** to **Compare**. You will get the following screen, which enables you to compare values instead of hardcoding a static threshold:

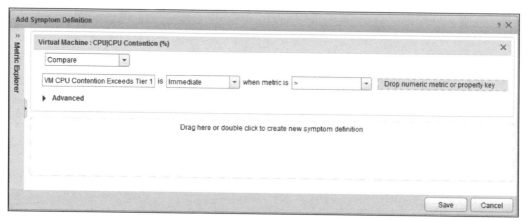

vRealize Operations | Create a new symptom definition

Once you have that, simply drag the Super Metric counter.

At the end, you will have a symptom for each tier and SLA.

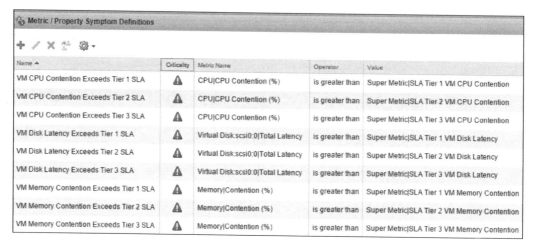

vRealize Operations | the symptom definition main screen

Once you have the symptom, you can create an alert. An alert can be triggered by a complex set of logic involving many symptoms. In our case, we will keep things simple and have just one symptom, as shown in the following screenshot:

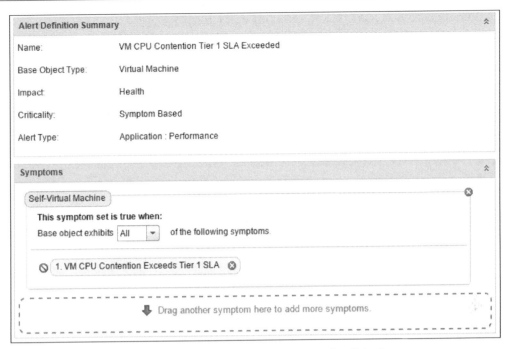

vRealize Operations | Alert | the Create new alert dialog box

Repeat the steps for each alert, mapping it to each symptom. At the end, you will get a list of alerts, as shown in the following screenshot:

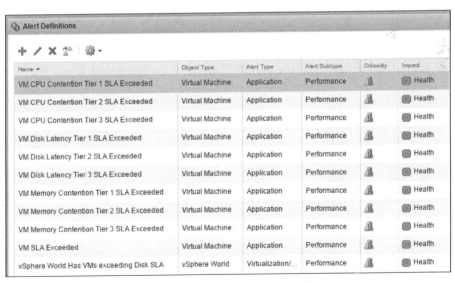

vRealize Operations | Alert Definitions | Main screen

You do not need to activate the alerts. They are active by default.

If indeed your environment is unable to meet the SLA, you will start getting alerts.

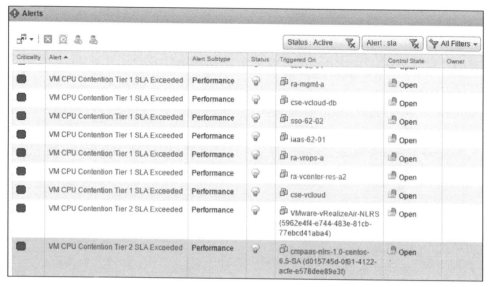

vRealize Operations | Alerts | list of active alerts

You can click on each of them to assign them to a different person. The **Owner** column is blank by default. The date it was triggered was cropped from the previous screenshot to fit the book.

When you click on an alert, you get more details, including the actual chart for when it was breached.

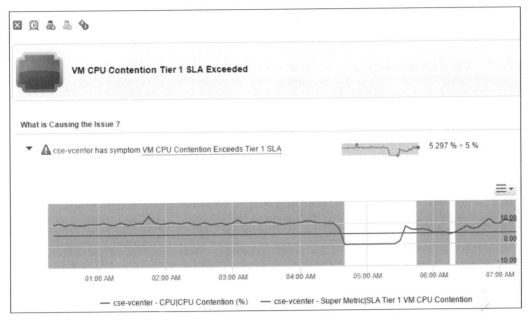

vRealize Operations | Example of an alert being triggered

Which VMs are affected?

Alerts are good when they are triggered. It is a form of reactive management. Sometimes, you want to see the overall picture and see how many VMs are near the alerts, not just the ones that hit the alert.

This is where the **Top-N** widget comes in. It is a simple widget that lists objects based on your chosen time and metric value.

Let's create a simple dashboard with four independent **Top-N** widgets. It will look like this:

List of affected VMs

These four widgets are driven from the cluster that we created in the first dashboard. To enable that interaction, perform these steps:

1. Edit the first dashboard.

2. Click on **Dashboard Navigation**, as shown in the next screenshot.

3. From the dropdown, choose the **Top-N** dashboard you created earlier.

4. Click on all its **Top-N** widgets. You want to drive all the widgets.

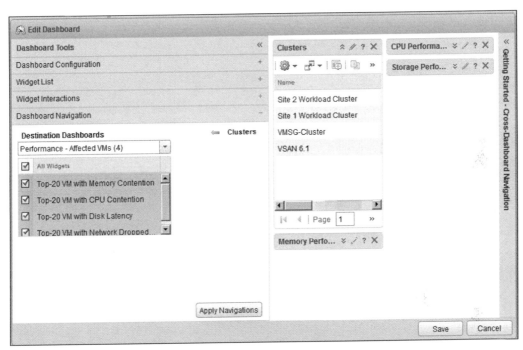

vRealize Operations | Dashboard | edit dialog box

5. Click on **Save**, and you are done. This dashboard will now drive the other dashboard.

How do you actually use it, as in navigate from one dashboard to another? The following screenshot shows this. From the **Clusters** list, click on **Navigate**, and then choose the dashboard you want to go to. You can link more than one dashboard. We have linked three dashboards to be driven from this dashboard.

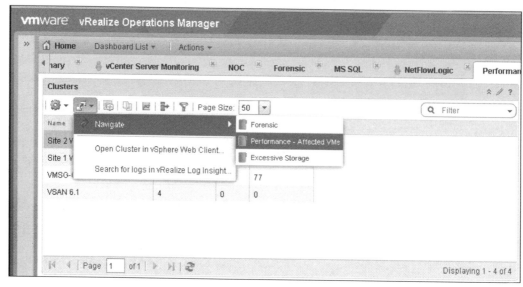

vRealize Operations | transitioning from one dashboard to another

Adapting the dashboards to different environments

We've covered an environment where a vSphere cluster is dedicated to a service tier. What if your environment is much smaller? Due to cost reasons, you have to mix multiple service tiers in a cluster. As a result, you need to manually create groups. Create one group for each tier, and place the VMs in their respective tiers.

What about the other extreme? You have way too many clusters, and it's hard to monitor them one by one. You want to monitor at the Tier level first before drilling into a specific cluster.

You need to create a group for each tier. Add the clusters to their groups. This is a one-time setup that you need to do for each cluster. In an environment where you have many physical data centers, these groups can contain clusters from different vCenter Servers and physical data centers. A tier 1 VM is a tier 1 VM, regardless of where it physically resides. You should have consistent SLAs throughout your organization.

When you create the group, the group will naturally be an object that is one level higher, as it has to encompass all the members of the group. Remember to increase your **super metric depth value** by **1**.

Are you serving my VM well?

It is common for the application team (or the VM owner) to suspect that virtualization is behind any performance degradation. After all, resources are shared and there are many IaaS workloads.

We start with a single VM, as we need to ensure we can handle one VM before we consider handling all VMs. A common use case here is that a VM owner (your customer) complains that his VM is slow. You need to come up with a dashboard that enables the help desk to quickly and easily identify where the problem is. Is it with Infrastructure or with the VM? Is it related to CPU, RAM, disk, or network? How severe is the problem?

To prove that the IaaS is meeting its performance SLA, we need to show the following information about the VM:

- CPU contention
- Memory contention
- Disk latency
- Network dropped packets (as covered in *Chapter 15, Network Counters,* vCenter does not provide network latency information)

All the preceding information has to be provided in a line-chart format so that any peak in the past can be shown. The line chart will also enable the operations team to look back to see whether the problem has occurred previously or not.

If all the four counters are below the performance SLA that you have agreed to with your customer, your IaaS is delivering its obligation. In other words, it performs well. All other counters are irrelevant.

If any of the four counters is above the official threshold you promised, you've failed to deliver and need to take action so that the affected VM is given the promised SLA. You may need to do performance troubleshooting or move some VMs out.

With that, let's go build the dashboard.

The dashboard contains several widgets with interactions among them. The first widget is **Object List**, which lists all the VMs in the environment. This is ideally a **World** level object, so you get all the VMs from all vCenter servers. Perform the following configuration on the widget:

1. Choose **Virtual Machine** as the object type. This will filter all other objects.

2. Choose **Collecting** as the **Collection States** option. This will filter out VMs that are not in the collection state.

3. Choose **Powered On** from **VM Entity Status**. This will filter out powered-off VMs as they do not cause performance problems.

4. Display additional columns. I have provided a few examples in the following screenshot:

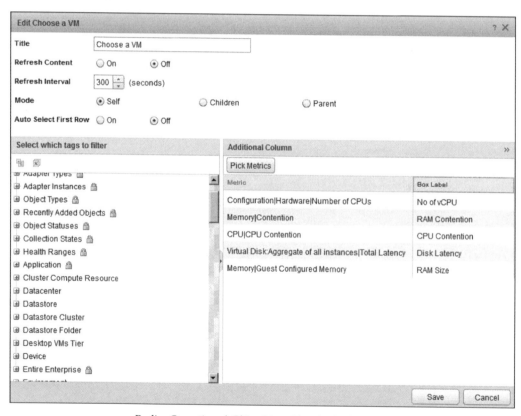

vRealize Operations | Object List widget | edit dialog box

5. Click on **Save** to close the dialog box.

The resultant widget looks like this:

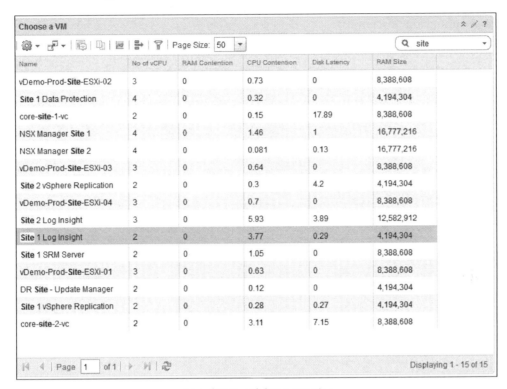

List of VMs with key properties

From here, you can also search for a VM. In the preceding example, we searched for VMs whose names contain the word **site**.

This list of VM widgets drives four other widgets. We choose a **View** widget instead of a **Metric Chart** widget as it is more flexible. The four **View** widgets are:

- CPU contention
- Memory contention
- Disk latency
- Network dropped packets

You can set the default information to display data at any length of time. We choose 1 day as it is a good balance between the details and the big picture. Ideally, your screen resolution is full HD, so the line charts can display sufficient information.

You can display the performance SLA if you create one dashboard for each tier. This is because you need to choose the metric, as each tier has its own metric (which defines the threshold).

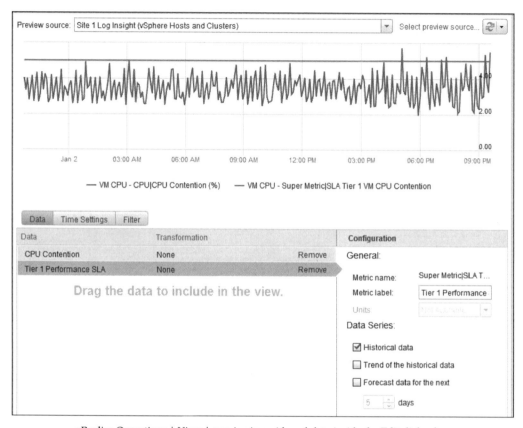

vRealize Operations | View | previewing with real data inside the Edit dialog box

Once you have created the four **View** widgets, do not forget to apply the interaction.

The resultant dashboard looks like the following:

The "Are you serving my VM well?" dashboard

In the preceding example, notice that we have included the performance SLA line. To achieve that, you need to create one dashboard for each service tier.

This dashboard is meant to be simple and quick for level 1 or level 2 support in a large organization with thousands of VMs. If you want to enhance it, here are some ideas you can use:

- VM CPU demand and memory usage can be included to verify whether the slowness is because of high utilization. Please note that memory usage is best taken from inside the Guest OS using the vRealize Operations End Point agent.

- Provide individual vCPU utilization. This provides visibility into whether any cores are saturated. This covers the situation of a large VM with multiple vCPUs, where the VM does not use all its given cores.

- Provide individual VMDK latency. The information at the VM level is an average of all its VMDK files.

- If your environment has a standard where the Guest OS page file is always on a separate VMDK (for example, `scsi1:0`), you can use vRealize Operations to display its read/write information without the need for an agent.

Is vMotion causing performance hit?

When a vMotion is done, a VM is stunned by the kernel. While this should not impact VM performance in most cases, there can be situations where it takes longer.

There are two values in the ESXi log files that capture the actual time taken to flip the VM:

- Pre-copy stunned time
- vMotion downtime

Both values are in microseconds. The time should be kept minimal. In general, less than 0.5 seconds (500,000 microseconds in the log) is a good threshold for either number.

In a VDI use case, if the end user happens to be using the computer (for example, watching a video), she may see the impact if the vMotion takes longer than 0.5 seconds. If she is watching a 30-frame/second video, she will miss around half the frames.

Log Insight provides a built-in variable for the pre-copy stunned time. You just need to select it from the dropdown and specify that the value exists. The following screenshot shows how we perform the query. We simply add a filter and select the field from the drop-down menu. We then specify the condition that it exists.

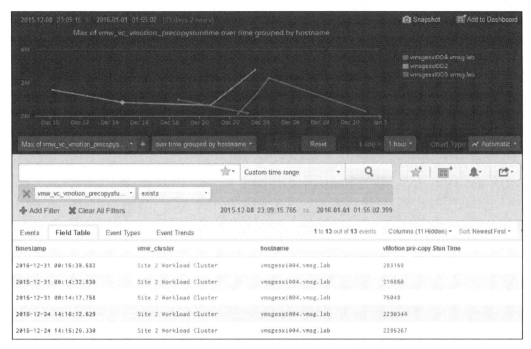

Log Insight | vMotion pre-copy stunned time line chart

The second value is not provided out of the box. You need to create a field. To do this, you can search for the string `vmotion result has downtime value`. From the returned results, select one and choose **Extract** field from the context-sensitive menu. Once you do this, follow the example shown in the following screenshot:

Log Insight | Creating a few field

In the previous example, we called the field `vMotion_Downtime`. It is identified by the string `vmotion result has downtime value`. Once the field is created, we can use it just like other fields. The following screenshot shows the result when you check for the time taken for the downtime value. The numbers are certainly too high; they should be below 500,000 microseconds:

Log Insight – using custom field in chart

Is any VM abusing the shared IaaS?

One characteristic of virtual environments is sharing. The VMs share the physical resources. Excessive usage by just one or two VMs can impact the overall IaaS performance. I have published a technical guide on how you can track excessive usage at `http://virtual-red-dot.info/any-vm-abusing-your-iaas-by-doing-excessive-workload/`. It has resonated well with the audience and I have updated it while writing this book.

Summary

We covered four of the use cases you need. The first one is what you need as your daily check. Make it part of your **standard operating procedure** (SOP) so that the admin team gains insight into what's normal in your environment.

Make it clear if you think you need additional dashboards as part of your daily checks. Keep it simple so that you are not lost in a forest of screens and reports. From experience, customers who want more dashboards mistake monitoring with troubleshooting.

In the next chapter, we will cover capacity management in greater depth, as it is an area that is made more complex once you virtualize your data center.

7
Capacity-Monitoring Dashboards

In this chapter, we will implement the capacity-monitoring solution we discussed in *Chapter 5, Capacity Monitoring*. We will cover each service tier from compute, storage, and network components. Due to the similarity in the approach, we can cover them in the following sequence:

- Tier 1 compute
- Tier 2 and 3 compute
- Storage (common for all service tiers)
- Network (common for all service tiers)

This will cover IaaS capacity monitoring. As overprovisioned VMs are a common problem, we will also cover VM rightsizing. We will cover both downsizing and upsizing scenarios.

Tier 1 compute

Let's recap from *Chapter 5, Capacity Monitoring*, what we need to produce to monitor capacity in tier 1 compute:

- A line chart showing the total number of vCPUs left in the cluster
- A line chart showing the total number of vRAM left in the cluster
- A line chart showing the total number of VMs left in the cluster

Tier 1 compute – CPU

Let's look at the first line chart. The number of vCPUs left is essentially supply and demand. The supply and demand can be defined as the following:

- Supply = (The total physical cores of all ESXi hosts) - (HA buffer)
- Demand = The total vCPUs for all the VMs

On the supply side, we can choose physical cores or physical threads. One will be conservative while the other will be aggressive. The ideal number is 1.5 times the physical core, as that's the estimated performance improvement from Hyper-Threading.

My recommendation is to count the cores, not the threads. There are two reasons for this:

- This is tier 1, your highest and best tier. If you are counting the threads, or using a 1.5x multiplier, you can no longer promise it is as good as physical. Contractually, you should also adjust your SLA accordingly from 1 percent CPU contention to perhaps 2-3 percent.
- The vmkernel itself takes up CPU, albeit minimal. It will take up more if you are running kernel modules such as VMware VSAN and VMware NSX. If you are counting the cores, you have more than enough buffer.

That's it for the supply side.

The demand side is simpler. It is simply the sum of all the vCPUs in all the VMs in the cluster.

Count the ESXi agent VMs too. This includes basic VMs such as a Nutanix **Controller Virtual Machine** (**CVM**) or Trend Micro Deep Security VM. Regardless of their functionality, they are consuming CPU resources.

If you are using virtual threads in your VM, then count them as if they are full vCPUs. For example, a VM with two vCPUs and two threads per core should be counted as four vCPUs.

In logic, the super metric formula is:

- Supply = (Number of Physical Cores in the cluster) - (HA buffer)
- Demand = Number of running vCPUs in the cluster

vRealize Operations has a metric that takes HA into account. You do not need to manually build the formula any more.

The following screenshot shows the actual super metric formula:

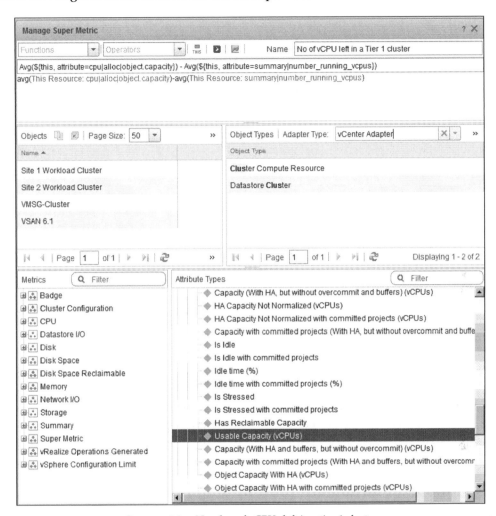

Super metric – Number of vCPUs left in a tier-1 cluster

Since we need to apply the formula to the vSphere cluster in question, we need to use the **THIS** option. Click on the little blue icon above the formula bar, as shown in the following diagram, then double-click on the formula you want to use:

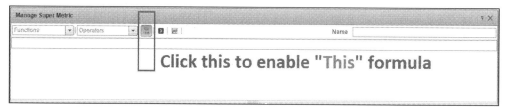

Super metric – enabling the THIS formula

The actual formula is as follows:

```
Avg(${this, attribute=cpu|alloc|object.capacity}) -
Avg(${this, attribute=summary|number_running_vcpus})
```

Tier 1 compute – RAM

We've covered CPU. RAM follows a similar logic. The amount of vRAM left is also based on supply and demand, where:

- Supply = (The total physical RAM of all ESXi hosts) - (HA buffer)
- Demand = The total vRAM for all the VMs

There is no need to include ESXi vmkernel RAM as it is small enough to ignore. In addition, almost no VM uses its configured RAM, and you have **Transparent Page Sharing**. These two reasons are also why we do not see the need to add a threshold.

If you need to include one, review *Chapter 13, Memory Counters*.

If you are using VSAN and NSX, you can add some buffer if you think that's necessary. For VSAN 6.1, Cormac Hogan explains this at `http://cormachogan.com/2015/11/10/vsan-design-sizing-memory-overhead-considerations/`. In most cases, we can ignore both NSX and VSAN overhead.

You do not need to include virtual appliances as they take the form of a VM; hence, they will be included in the demand.

If you find the formula complex, you can actually split them into two super metrics first. Work out supply, then work out demand.

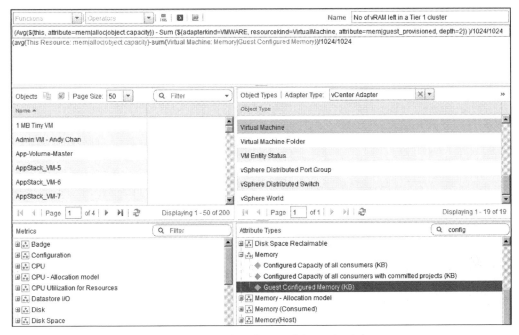

Super metric – Number of vRAM left in a tier-1 cluster

The actual formula is as follows:

```
(Avg(${this, attribute=mem|alloc|object.capacity}) -
Sum (${adapterkind=VMWARE, resourcekind=VirtualMachine,
attribute=mem|guest_provisioned, depth=2}) )/1000/1000
```

Tier 1 compute – VM

The third line chart we need to display shows the total number of VMs left in the cluster. While the first two line charts come from the **Performance Policy**, this comes from the **Availability Policy**.

Normally, availability is associated with the ESXi host. For example, you keep the maximum number of VMs in a given ESXi host. The logic here is that if any ESXi goes down, you're capping the number of affected VMs.

We apply the **Availability Policy** at the cluster level since it makes more sense. Applying it at the ESXi host level is less relevant due to HA. Yes, the chance of a host going down is higher than that of the entire cluster going down. However, HA will reboot the VMs, and VM owners may not notice. On the other hand, if a cluster goes down, it's a major issue.

The supply and demand can be defined as follows:

- Supply = The maximum number of allowed VMs in one cluster (taking into account the HA buffer)
- Demand = The total number of VMs in the cluster

Can you notice a limitation in the formula?

It assumes that your tier-1 cluster size does not vary. This is a fair assumption as you should keep things consistent in tier 1. If, for some reason, you have multiple cluster sizes (for example, 8, 10, or 12), then you have one super metric per size.

The following screenshot shows the super metric formula for the total number of VMs left in the cluster:

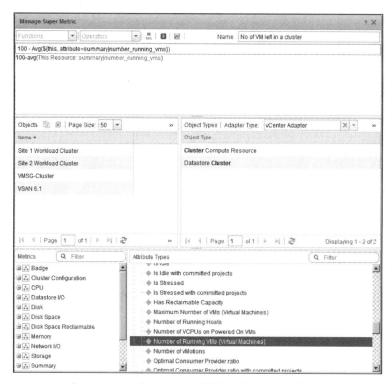

Super metric – the number of VMs left in a tier-1 cluster

We have hardcoded the maximum number that we allow. While you can do away with hardcoding to some extent, it is acceptable as policy changes require agreement from the business.

The actual formula is this:

```
100 - Avg(${this, attribute=summary|number_running_vms})
```

Tier 1 compute – summary

In the beginning of this chapter, we recapped that we needed to produce three line charts. Look at the line charts in the previous three subsections as one group. Take the one with the lowest number as the determining factor that you're running out of capacity.

You've got the supply and demand. You know when the number will reach zero.

The question is: when do you buy new hardware?

Because this is tier 1 and you promise identical specifications, this could mean a new cluster. Buying a cluster can be a substantial commitment, so it has to be planned properly.

If you manage a very large environment and are buying clusters quarterly, you can set a threshold. For example, when you are down to the 10 percent capacity, you can trigger a new cluster purchase.

You do not have to build your threshold (which is your buffer, actually) into the super metric formula as it is dynamic. Once it's hard-coded in the super metric, changing it does not change the history.

It is dynamic because it depends on the business situation. If there is a large project going live in a few weeks, then your buffer needs to cater to it. This is why we need to stay close to the business. It's also something you should know, based on your actual experience in your company. You have that gut feeling and estimate.

For an emergency, temporary solution, you can still deploy VMs while waiting for your new cluster to arrive. This is because you have an HA buffer. ESXi hosts are known for their high uptime.

Tier 2 and 3 compute

Let's recap what we need to produce in order to monitor capacity in tier-2 and tier-3 compute:

- A line chart showing the maximum and average CPU contention experienced by any VM in the cluster
- A line chart showing the maximum and average RAM contention experienced by any VM in the cluster
- A line chart showing the total number of VMs left in the cluster

You will need five super metrics, which are as follows:

- Maximum (VM CPU contention) in the cluster
- Average (VM CPU contention) in the cluster
- Maximum (VM RAM contention) in the cluster
- Average (VM RAM contention) in the cluster
- The total number of VMs left in the cluster. See tier 1, as it is the same formula with a different threshold.

These super metrics are the same ones you created for performance monitoring. You are just adding two more because capacity monitoring is a superset of performance monitoring.

We are adding the average line chart to complement the maximum line chart. To create the average super metric, you just need to replace the string max with avg in the formula. The following diagram provides an example:

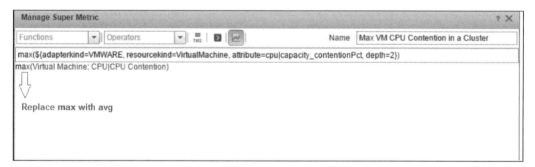

Super metric – editing a formula

The actual formulas for the two additional super metrics are as follows:

```
avg(${adaptertype=VMWARE, objecttype=VirtualMachine,
attribute=cpu|capacity_contentionPct, depth=2})
avg(${adaptertype=VMWARE, objecttype=VirtualMachine,
attribute=mem|host_contentionPct, depth=2})
```

This concludes the discussion about compute. Let's cover storage now.

Storage

Let's recap what we need to produce in order to monitor storage capacity:

- A line chart showing the maximum and average storage latency experienced by any VM in the datastore cluster
- A line chart showing the datastore disk capacity left in the datastore cluster

The first line chart tracks performance, while the second one tracks utilization.

Storage – performance

Just like compute, we just need to add the average super metric. The actual formula is as follows:

```
avg(${adaptertype=VMWARE, objecttype=VirtualMachine,
attribute=virtualDisk|totalLatency, depth=2})
```

Storage – utilization

Storage disk capacity should be tied with your actual, physical capacity. If you are using **thin provisioning** at the storage layer, then you need to measure it at this level. I prefer to use thin on VMware and thick on physical arrays, as management is easier from the VMware administrator's viewpoint.

Just like compute, we are using the supply-demand approach, where:

- Supply = The total datastore space capacity in the datastore cluster
- Demand = The total storage consumed by all VMs in the datastore cluster

The total storage consumed by VMs naturally depends on whether you are using thin provisioning or thick provisioning:

- If you are using thick provisioning, then it is simple. Just total all the storage consumed by all VMs. This is what you use for tier 1, as the VMDK is thick-provisioned.

- If you are using thin provisioning, you will have two numbers: one for **Configured** and one for **Utilized**. The number you need is unfortunately somewhere in between. You need to make a business call about where you want to take it, as it depends on your environment. If the disk growth is relatively modest, then you can take a value closer to Utilized. If not, take one closer to Configured.

Because of these factors, we need different super metrics for thick and thin provisioning.

By the way, ensure that your datastores are clean. They should not be littered with orphaned VMDKs, ghost VMs (they are not registered), and non-VM files (for example, ISO files). We cover in *Chapter 14, Storage Counters*, how they impact the metrics. You can create super metrics to track the existence of these objects.

The following screenshot shows the super metric formula to get the total amount of disk capacity left in the cluster:

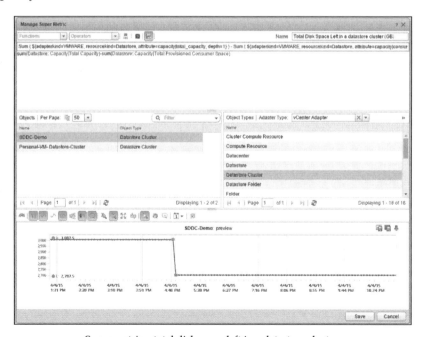

Super metric – total disk space left in a datastore cluster

The actual formula is this:

```
sum(${adaptertype=VMWARE, objecttype=Datastore,
attribute=capacity|total_capacity, depth=1}) -
Sum(${adaptertype=VMWARE, objecttype=Datastore,
attribute=capacity|provisioned, depth=1})
```

If you use thick provisioning, this is all you need.

If you use thin provisioning, the formula gives your "low" number, as your consumption is certainly not as high. You have more disk capacity than what the number is telling you. In other words, the number is too low.

You need to complement the number with your "high" number. The following screenshot shows the super metric formula to get the space left based on actual utilization:

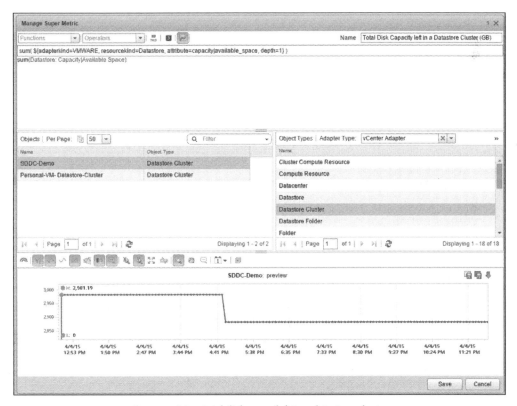

Super metric – total disk space left in a datastore cluster

The actual formula is this:

```
Sum(${adaptertype=VMWARE, objecttype=Datastore,
attribute=capacity|used_space, depth=1})
```

Can you spot a missing component in the logic?

It's something that you normally do before making changes to a VM. It's also used during backup.

Yes—snapshots. You need to include a buffer for snapshots. This can be 20 percent, depending on your environment. This super metric actually does take into account snapshots if the snapshot has not been released. I am referring to the time when a snapshot is taken at night as part of the daily backup.

Snapshots are a weak point of small datastores, as you have pockets of unusable capacity. This does not have to be hardcoded in your super metric, but you have to be mentally aware of it.

Network

Let's recap what we need to produce in order to monitor network capacity:

- A line chart showing the maximum network dropped packets at the physical data center level. We use a physical data center and not vSphere cluster, as they eventually share the same core switches.

- A line chart showing the maximum and average ESXi vmnic at the same level as per the previous point. This will tell you whether any of your vmnics are saturated.

In the first line chart, notice it only has the maximum line. We're not tracking the average dropped packets. The reason is that we're not expecting any packet loss, so the average is irrelevant.

We covered the first line chart in the performance chapter. So we just need to add the utilization line chart.

Dropped packets are much easier to track, as you expect 0 everywhere. Utilization is harder. If your ESXi has mixed 10 GE and 1 GE vmnics, you would expect the 10 GE vmnic to dominate the data. This is where consistent design and standards matter. Without it, you need to apply a different formula for different configurations of ESXi hosts.

You want to ensure that not a single vmnic is saturated. This means you need to track it at the vmnic level, not ESXi host level. Tracking at the ESXi host level can hide the data at the vmnic level.

Let's take an example to illustrate:

Your ESXi has 10 1-Gigabit NICs. You are seeing a throughput of 4 Gbps.

At the ESXi host level, it's only 40 percent utilized. But that 4 Gbps is unlikely to be spread evenly. There is a chance that a single vmnic is saturated while others are hardly utilized.

The following screenshot shows the super metric formula to get the maximum vmnic utilization on a single ESXi host. Notice the use of the **THIS** functionality in the formula, as the formula is being applied to the object itself.

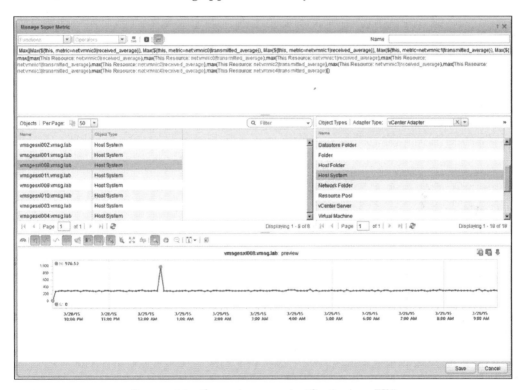

Super metric – the maximum vmnic utilization in an ESXi

One habit you should have when it comes to creating super metrics is to always verify the formula. In the following screenshot, we manually plot each vmnic's TX and RX. We have eight lines. Notice that the maximum of these eight lines matches the super metric we created. With this, we have proof that it works as expected.

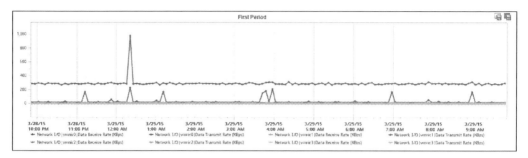

Super metric – manual validation

We are tracking received and transmit separately as either can hit the physical limit. Some workloads, such as VDI, are transmit-heavy. **PCoIP** will maximize the bandwidth whenever possible so that it can deliver the best user experience.

The formula line in the screenshot may not be clear, so here is the actual formula:

```
Max ([
Max(${this, metric=net:vmnic0|received_average}),
Max(${this, metric=net:vmnic0|transmitted_average}),
Max(${this, metric=net:vmnic1|received_average}),
Max(${this, metric=net:vmnic1|transmitted_average}),
Max(${this, metric=net:vmnic2|received_average}),
Max(${this, metric=net:vmnic2|transmitted_average}),
Max(${this, metric=net:vmnic3|received_average}),
Max(${this, metric=net:vmnic3|transmitted_average})
]) * 8 / 1000
```

This is based on four vmnics per ESXi. If you have two 10-Gigabit NICs, then you just need vmnic0 and vmnic1. If you have six vmnics, then you have to add vmnic4 and vmnic5.

We've got the maximum utilization. For the average, vRealize Operations already provides the metric. There is no need to create a super metric.

By the way, there is a physical NIC that is not monitored. Can you guess which one?

Yes, it's the iLO NIC.

That does not show up as a vmnic. The good thing is that generally, there is very little traffic in an `iLO` network, and certainly no data traffic.

The previous two metrics work for a single ESXi host. You can enable alerts, and since you have visibility at the ESXi level, you can know for sure which ESXi was affected.

You may say that with DRS and HA, you should also apply it at the cluster level. We just need to create another super metric. Since we already have the data for each host, all we need to do is apply `Max` to the ESXi super metric. Yes, vRealize Operations allows a super metric on top of another:

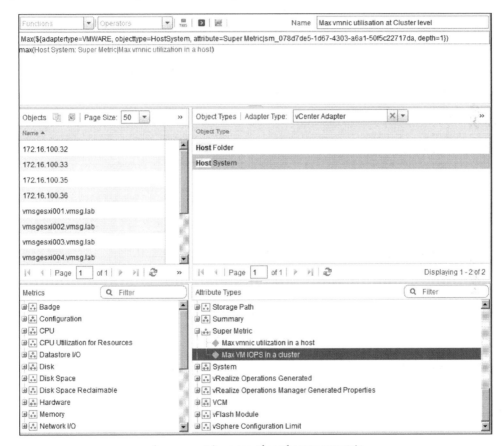

A super metric on top of another super metric

As usual, we preview the formula and then verify it manually on the following screen.

Here is the preview screenshot:

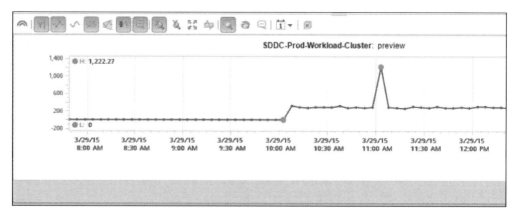

Super metric – the preview portion of the dialog box

And here is the manual validation from each member ESXi of the cluster:

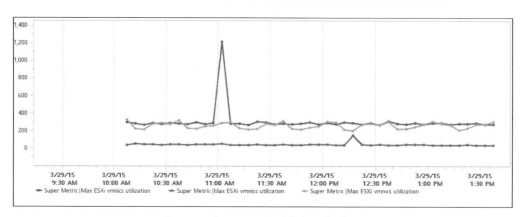

Super metric – manual validation of values

The preceding formula works at the cluster level. What if you need to apply it at higher levels?

You need to adjust the depth parameter. In the following example, we use the `World` object:

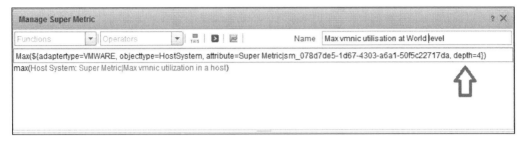

Super metric – adjusting the depth parameter

We manually set `depth=4` as the hierarchy from World to ESXi host is as follows:

- World
- vCenter data center
- vCenter
- Cluster
- ESXi

Putting it all together

We have seen all the super metrics required to monitor performance. Let's put them together and see the actual dashboards. The following example is for a tier-2 cluster:

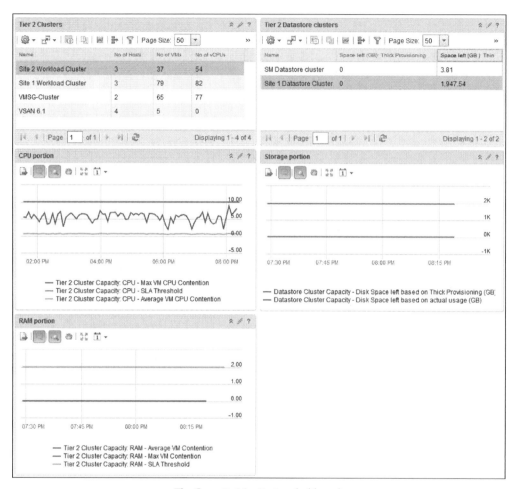

The Capacity Monitoring dashboard

The reason you need to have separate dashboards for each tier is the SLA. Each tier has its own metric. The **View** widget cannot show different metrics based on certain conditions.

Enhancements to the dashboard

The preceding dashboards should be sufficient. However, if you think you need additional visibility to help you understand your environment, you can:

- Use the percentile chart
- Add utilization information

We will use compute as an example. It should be relatively straightforward to apply the idea to storage and network.

The percentile chart

The maximum value can be too aggressive. All it takes is one VM experiencing high contention, and you have to consider the cluster full already. This is fine if your IaaS is indeed unable to meet the business demand. What if the demand is not from the business but IT's own generated workload?

An example is a full AV scan or full backup that was performed during non-business hours. They may impact the VMs, making them suffer from contention. You may consider that acceptable if business is not affected.

This is where standard deviation and percentile come in. You can find out the value at, say, the 95th percentile, giving you better insight.

In addition, the chart can be difficult to read if you are plotting a long period of time.

The **Forensics** widget allows you to plot the value of the 75th and 95th percentiles. In the following example, the maximum CPU utilization at more than 18 percent was a one-time occurrence. In fact, we can easily see that it is actually below 10 percent for more than 95 percent of the time.

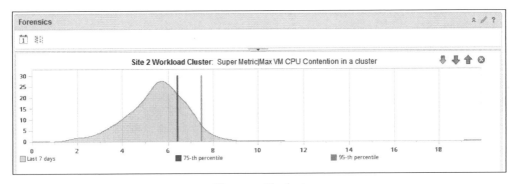

The percentile chart

Utilization information

The dashboard we created so far is based on VM CPU contention. While it is the right thing to do, we are all accustomed to seeing cluster or ESXi utilization. "Old habits die hard" is certainly true in the virtual world.

You can get insight into ESXi utilization with the following line charts:

- A line chart showing the maximum CPU demand and average CPU demand of all ESXi hosts in the cluster per service tier. So, you will have two lines per service tier. Notice that we use host, not cluster. It is more granular this way.

- A line chart showing the maximum RAM consumed and the maximum RAM demand for all hosts per tier. We have to use both consumed and demand due to the two-level memory hierarchy.

We did not mix different service tiers in the previous line charts. Can you figure out why?

Tier-3 hosts have higher utilization due to higher oversubscription. Therefore, they will dominate the result!

We are using the maximum for both as we are tracking peak utilization here. We are not tracking the average utilization. The following screenshot shows an example of the super metric:

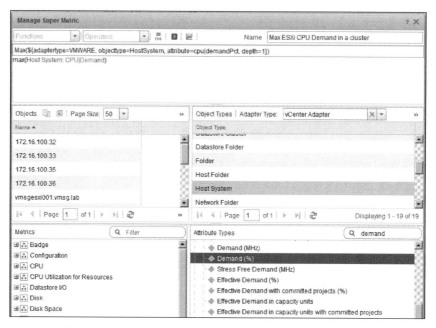

Super metric – the maximum CPU demand of all hosts in a cluster

As Utilization is optional information, we will cover it in *Chapter 8, Specific-Purpose Dashboards*.

Rightsizing VMs

There are three factors to consider when rightsizing VMs:

- Downsize or upsize
- Server workload or VDI workload
- CPU or RAM

While the concept is similar, the solution and implementation are not. As a result, there are eight combinations of solutions in all. We will cover the more popular ones. Downsize typically applies to server workload, while upsize applies to VDI workload.

Upsize is generally not your concern for server workload. Your business offering is IaaS, meaning your scope does not cover the VM. The VM owner will be the one to tell you whether their VM needs more resources. In addition, adding resources costs her money (you should have proper chargeback operationalized), so she will only do it when it makes business sense.

From your viewpoint, as someone looking after all the VMs, you can use Log Insight to quickly tell which VM hit high CPU usage and when. It plots from the vCenter alarm. The following screenshot shows you how to do it:

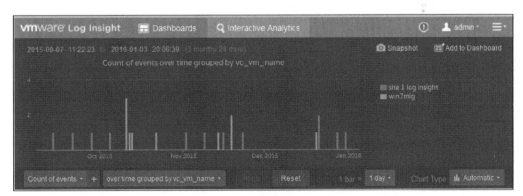

Log Insight – the count of events over time by VM name

The previous screenshot shows a healthy environment as only two VMs hit high CPU usage for almost 4 months. The entire query is only driven by two filters, and both are provided out of the box by Log Insight:

Log Insight – filtering with out-of-the-box variables

The following screenshot shows the opposite example. A lot of VMs hit high CPU usage in just 1 week. This is a severe case of underprovisioned VMs.

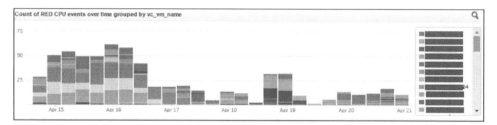

Log Insight – the count of VMs hitting high CPU utilization

In addition to a chart, Log Insight can also display the information in table format. This is useful if you want to have other information, such as the host where the VM was running at that point in time and the cluster and vCenter servers.

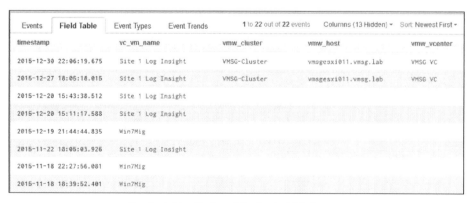

Log Insight – display of the log in table format

Downsize does not apply to VDI workload as you give everyone the minimum configuration. Typically, this means two vCPUs and 4 GB of RAM for the 64-bit version of Windows 7 or Windows 10. Upsize is important in VDI because you need to know which users need more resources. There are bound to be users who need more than two vCPUs and 4 GB of RAM.

This chapter covers the server workload. We will cover upsizing VDI workload in *Chapter 8, Specific-Purpose Dashboards*, as this chapter focuses on IaaS.

Rightsizing large VMs

Rightsizing large VMs is a very popular request from VMware administrators, as it is common for VMs to be sized conservatively by the application team. The root cause of this stems from physical servers, where it is common for the servers to have excess RAM and CPU. Physical servers come with standard configurations. If an application only needs 17 GB of RAM and three cores, the physical server will likely have 32 GB of RAM and eight cores.

The result is that many VMs have too many vCPUs and vRAM. If you want a healthy environment, you need to eradicate, or at least minimize, this bad practice.

The question from your CIO is how many VMs are overprovisioned, and for each oversized VM, what the degree of overprovisioning is.

Reducing someone's VM is a lengthy process that involves downtime, so you want to focus on the largest VM. Reducing one 16-vCPU VM to a 4-vCPU one gives you better returns than reducing three 8-vCPU VMs to 4-vCPU ones. The actual total vCPU reduction is the same (12 vCPUs in this example), but the ESXi vmkernel scheduler will have an easier task of juggling the VMs as the 16-vCPU VM needs 16 physical cores eventually (even though it's not using it most of the time).

The solutions for CPU and RAM differ, so we will cover them separately. As explained in *Chapter 5, Capacity Monitoring*, you should not change both CPU and RAM at the same time.

Rightsizing vCPUs

The dashboard in this subsection visually tells you how deep and widespread the overprovisioning problem is. You get to see all the large VMs, and from here, you can drill down into an individual VM and see whether it's really using all those allocated resources.

Step 1 – create a group

The first step is to create a group that contains all the large VMs. This should be a dynamic group so that VMs are added or removed as they change their configuration. You can start with VMs that have eight or more vCPUs, because those with just four vCPUs have less room to be adjusted.

Use the following screenshot as an example of how to create the group. The group dynamically grabs all the VMs with four vCPUs or more. You should get eight vCPUs or more in your environment.

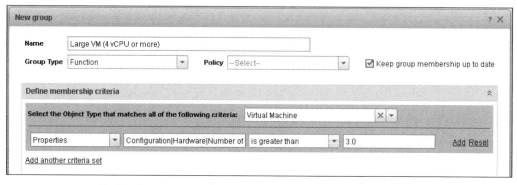

vRealize Operations – a dynamic group of VMs with large vCPU counts

We do not specify RAM as RAM should be dealt with separately.

We use **Function** as the **Group Type**. You can use any other type, as it's just a tag.

Once we have the group, we can analyze it.

Step 2 – create super metrics

We want to see what the group maximum CPU utilization is across a period of time. We plot the value for the last month. If the values are low, the large VMs are way overprovisioned. Remember, it only takes one VM among all the large VMs for the line chart to spike.

If the large VMs are properly sized, the line chart should be hovering around 80% almost all of the time. If you have many large VMs, one of them will tend to have high utilization at any given time.

To get that maximum CPU utilization, we need to create a super metric that tracks the maximum CPU demand among all the large VMs. The following diagram shows how you do it:

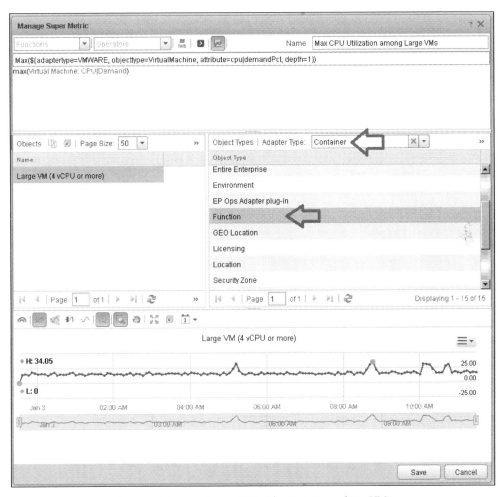

Super metric – maximum CPU utilization among large VMs

To preview the super metric, choose the **Container** adapter type. A group is considered a container in vRealize Operations. After that, click on **Function**. This is the group type we chose earlier.

In the preceding graph, **Large VM** as a group is only using 34 percent at its peak. This means that not a single one of them used more than 35 percent CPU over the chosen period. This is an example of overprovisioning.

Click on **Save** to create the super metric. As usual, don't forget to associate it with the correct object type:

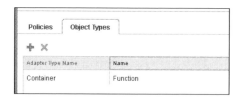

The strength of the maximum super metric is that it can show a severe case of overprovisioning across many VMs over a long period of time.

The limitation of maximum is its value is defined by a single VM at any given time. If the VMs take turns to hit high utilization, the line chart will show a high value. To see whether many VMs are correctly sized, we need to show the average CPU demand, considering the following:

- If this chart is hovering around 40-60 percent most of the time, then the VMs are correctly sized
- If this chart is below 25 percent all the time for entire month, then the large VMs are oversized

You do not need to create the **minimum**. There are bound to be VMs that are idle at any given time.

Your two line charts should look like the following:

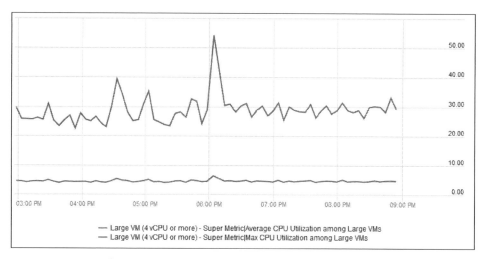

Super metric – maximum and average VM CPU utilization

Step 3 – create a heatmap

Now, these charts are good as overall metrics. But they're missing something. Can you guess what?

Yes, they're missing the VMs themselves. What if upper management wants to see at a glance all the large VMs' utilization?

For that, we can create a heatmap. It will show all the VMs. We can group them by ESXi host so that we can see where they run. You want to see them well spread in your clusters and not concentrated in just one host. The following considerations apply:

- The VMs in the heatmap are sized by vCPU. So it's easy to see which VMs are the biggest among the large VMs. A 32-vCPU VM will have a box that is four times larger than what an 8-vCPU VM has, so it will stand out.
- The VMs in the heatmap are colored by CPU workload.

Now, this is where we can be creative. A heatmap is visually easy to interpret, as it is color coded. We can visually show the degree of overprovisioning by choosing the right color. Keep these points in mind:

- The ideal utilization value is 50 percent, indicating rightsizing. We will associate 50 percent with green.
- A VM that is oversized will have low utilization. So we will set 0 percent as black. If the heatmap is mostly a dark color, we know we have an issue of overprovisioning. The degree of the darkness visually tell us the degree of the overprovisioning.
- A VM that is undersized will have high utilization. We do not want this issue either, so we will set 100 percent as red.

We expect to see mostly green, as most VMs should be within 40-60 percent.

The following screenshot shows how you configure it:

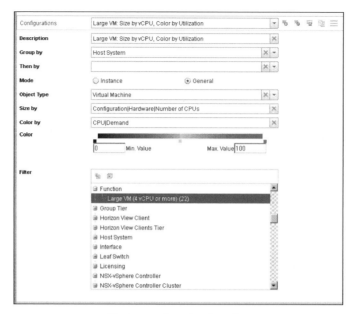

Heatmap – changing the color

We've created this heatmap several times. It's a powerful visualization. The following dark heatmap is a typical result:

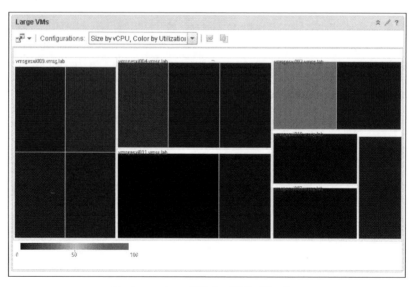

Heatmap – large VMs by CPU utilization

Step 4 – create a list

The heatmap is great, but it does not sort the VMs. This is where the **Top-N** widget comes in. It lists all the large VMs in the environment. So choose the group instead of the entire VM population. You will find the group under **Function**, as that's what you classified it as earlier.

For the counter, choose **Virtual Machine** as the object. Choose the **VM CPU Demand** metric, as shown here:

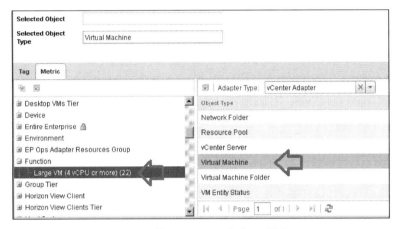

Top-N – filtering to just the large VMs

Once done, you will get a **Top-N** widget, as shown in the following screenshot:

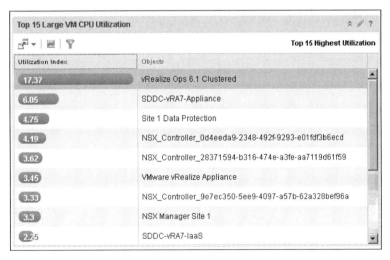

Top-N – top 15 VMs in terms of CPU utilization

Step 5 – create a detailed vCPU line chart

Can we show the preceding **Top-N** to a VM owner who happens to own only one VM?

The answer is obviously no. It is not convincing enough.

We know that the application team wants to see the actual utilization of each vCPU in the past month. It is insufficient to show the overall VM CPU utilization.

Each line chart shows the utilization of a vCPU in the past month. Hence, if you have eight vCPUs, there will be eight lines. If the number shows a low utilization for some of the vCPUs, it means that you should reduce the vCPU count. I have provided an example of four vCPUs in the following screenshot. We can see that they move in tandem and only hit above 50 percent for a short period. In the line chart, 20,000 equals 100-percent utilization.

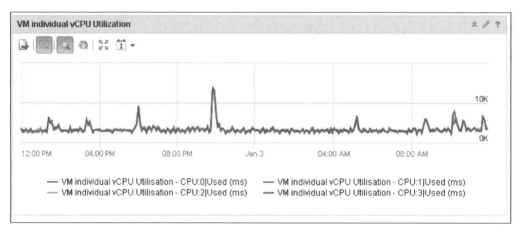

Line chart – selected VM CPU utilization

Step 6 – add a percentile chart

The preceding line chart provides detailed and convincing information. However, it does not answer quickly where the utilization is according to the 95th percentile. Knowing what the utilization is 95 percent of the time in the past month gives VM owners the confidence to rightsized.

Let's use two examples to highlight the usefulness of this information:

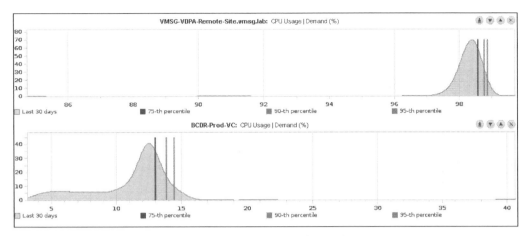

The Forensics widget – distribution chart

In the first example, the VM has a very high CPU demand. It has an average of more than 98 percent in the past 30 days, as you can see the curve peaks above the 98-percent point. You should upsize the vCPU as it's spending most of its time above 98 percent.

In the second example, the VM has low CPU demand. It has an average of about 12 to 13 percent in the past 30 days. If you take the top 5-percent utilization (that is, the 95th percentile), it is still below 15 percent. This means that 95 percent of the time, the CPU demand is below 15 percent. It is relatively safe to reduce the vCPU by four times, as the VM never demands beyond 25 percent.

Step 7 – configure interaction

Remember to configure the interaction. The Top-N widget drives the line chart widget. Here's how you configure it:

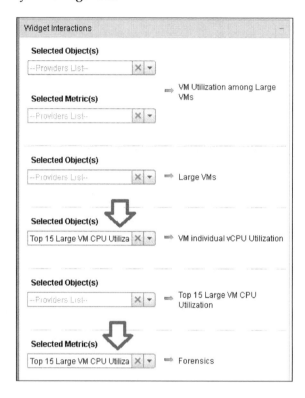

The resultant dashboard

The following screenshots show what the dashboard looks like once done. It has two parts, the overall part and the detailed part:

- The overall part shows all the large VMs
- The detail part zooms into a single VM

This is the overall part:

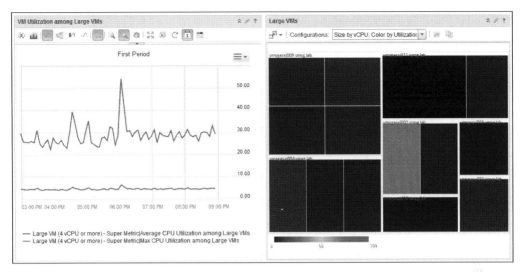

Large VMs – the CPU utilization dashboard

And here is the detailed part. There is no interaction among them, as the **View** widget is not able to drive the **Top-N** widget yet.

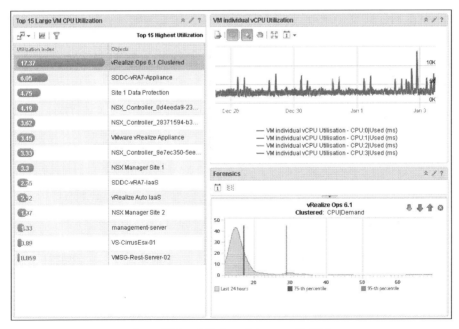

Large VMs – drill down into a specific VM

I understand that the proposed VM rightsizing is a manual process, and you need to check the VMs one by one and discuss them with the VM owners. On the other hand, a VM owner will certainly want a detailed discussion and proof before agreeing to reduce the size of a VM.

Rightsizing memory

As shared in *Chapter 5*, *Capacity Monitoring*, rightsizing RAM is harder. Different applications use memory differently. *Chapter 13*, *Memory Counters*, explains why Windows has complex memory management. As a result, it's actually difficult to determine the actual memory required by applications.

While it is not perfect, we can have good memory monitoring by tracking Windows memory using these three metrics:

- The **available memory**: If it is less 1 GB, the VM needs more RAM.
- The **committed memory**: If it is more than 80 percent, the VM needs more RAM.
- The size of `pagefile.sys`: By default, Windows sets the pagefile size to the size of the physical memory. If it is bigger than the physical memory, the VM needs more memory.

Now, these points lend themselves to the upsizing use case, not downsizing. To turn it into downsizing, use the first two counters. The reason you do not need the third counter is that `pagefile.sys` does not normally shrink below the size of the physical RAM.

All the three counters use in-Guest information. This likely means that an agent is required. If you do not have the visibility, you have two choices:

- If downsizing memory is not a pressing matter, leave it and focus on other projects.
- If downsizing memory is a pressing matter, use **memory consumed** and **memory active** as the proxies. Focus on the biggest VMs and ignore the smaller ones.

Large VM groups

Just like the case with CPU, the first step is to create a group that consists of large VMs. We are using 8 GB or more here, while you should probably use 24 GB.

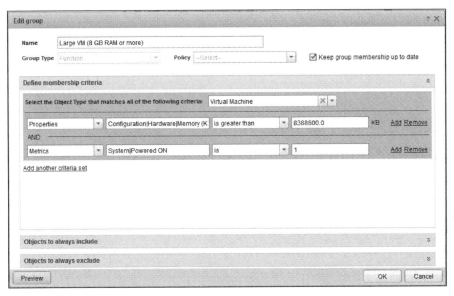

vRealize Operations – a VM with a large amount of RAM

If you want to exclude the powered-off VMs, you can add the **Powered ON** metric, as shown in the preceding screenshot. Notice that it is a metric, not a property.

Standard deviation

We use the **View** widget and standard deviation to help us size more confidently. If you are not sure how standard deviation can be used as a tool, Michael Ryom explains at `https://michaelryom.dk/troubleshooting-with-vrops-part-4-standard-deviation`.

You enable standard deviation using the **Transformation** feature of the **View** widget. The following example shows how it is applied:

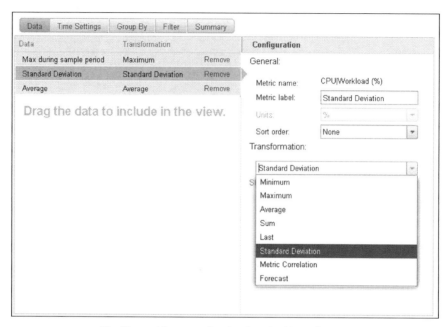

The View widget – configuring Standard Distribution

Let's take a few minutes to ensure we are on the same page on standard deviation. We will use a simple example.

Say a VM's memory workload average is 50 percent in the past day. The standard deviation is 10 percent. That means that in the past 24 hours, 95 percent of its workload fell between 30-70 percent. The standard deviation formula states that 95 percent of the data falls within two standard deviations. If the maximum is 95 percent, it means that the VM only hits that workload for 5 percent of the time in the past day. That's still 72 minutes, a long time from a VM owner's viewpoint. Three standard deviations takes us to 99.7 percent. This means that 99.7 percent of the time, the workload falls between 20-80 percent. That 0.3 percent translates to 4 minutes in the last 24 hours.

Let's now take a real example. Notice the first one has an average of 21.52 percent. The standard deviation is only 2.24 percent. The maximum is however a whopping 96 percent. So it is off the range. We can quickly tell that this not normal. Since the sample period below is 24 hours (1440 minutes), it means that this is a one-off data sample in vRealize Operations.

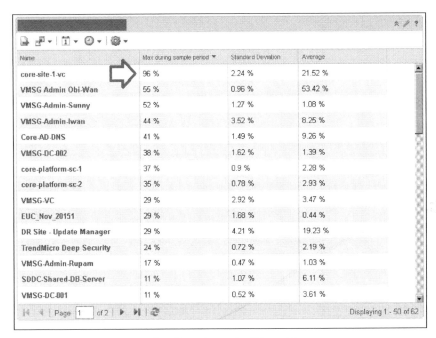

vRealize Operations – the View widget

Zooming into the VM to plot the entire 24 hours, we can see that it's indeed a one-off. Bingo!

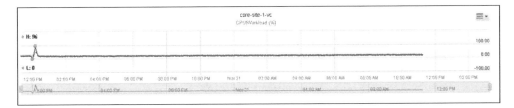

The View object

We are now ready to create our **View** object. Create a new one and use the following as a guide:

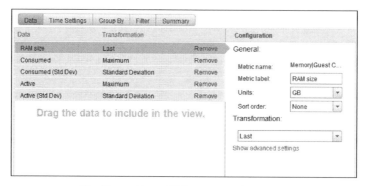

The View widget – VM memory information

To filter the View widget so that it only displays the large VMs, set **Self Provider** to **On**.

It will give you a list of objects to choose from. Choose **Function**, and then click on the group you created earlier. Use the following screenshot to guide you:

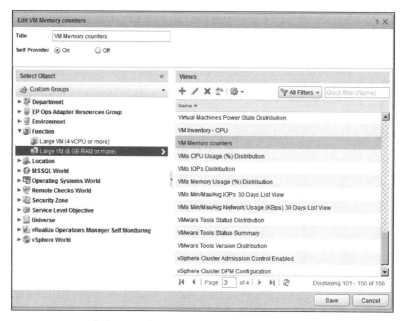

The View widget – filtering to the large VM group

The resultant dashboard looks like this:

Name	RAM size ▼	Consumed	Consumed (Std Dev)	Active	Active (Std Dev)
SDDC-vRA7-Appliance	18 GB	17.97 GB	270.43 MB	5.74 GB	323.83 MB
vRealize Auto IaaS	16 GB	10.89 GB	3.01 GB	13.36 GB	432.45 MB
NSX Manager Site 1	16 GB	13.1 GB	100.72 MB	2.38 GB	240.91 MB
NSX Manager Site 2	16 GB	15.66 GB	15.54 MB	2.63 GB	224.61 MB
vRealize Ops 6.1 Clustered	16 GB	15.2 GB	342.48 MB	9.85 GB	771.54 MB
VMware vRealize Appliance	16 GB	9.16 GB	182.89 MB	4.52 GB	341.51 MB
SDDC-vRA7-IaaS	16 GB	11.85 GB	794.08 MB	5.06 GB	198.4 MB
Site 2 Log Insight	12 GB	11.89 GB	22.23 MB	8.76 GB	912.21 MB
management-server	8 GB	2.09 GB	176.57 KB	0.4 GB	51.66 MB
VMSG-App-Volume-Manager	8 GB	8 GB	0 KB	1 GB	105.99 MB
vDemo-Prod-Site-ESXi-02	8 GB	0.96 GB	9.62 MB	0.31 GB	48.92 MB
core-site-1-vc	8 GB	7.61 GB	35.47 MB	5.19 GB	208.67 MB
vRealize Operations 6.1	8 GB	7.93 GB	22.07 MB	5.32 GB	213.91 MB
VS-CirrusEsx-01	8 GB	1.3 GB	12.99 MB	0.34 GB	51.41 MB
vDemo-Prod-Site-ESXi-03	8 GB	1.12 GB	11.67 MB	0.31 GB	50.63 MB
VMSG-VC	8 GB	7.36 GB	72.21 MB	3.5 GB	359.36 MB
VS-CirrusDem-03	8 GB	1.58 GB	14.95 MB	0.39 GB	50.15 MB
vDemo-Prod-Site-ESXi-04	8 GB	1.13 GB	13.3 MB	0.31 GB	46.54 MB
vDemo-vCenter-01	8 GB	7.92 GB	2.24 MB	3.61 GB	152.52 MB
Site 1 SRM Server	8 GB	1.61 GB	137.4 MB	0.37 GB	59.84 MB
vDemo-Prod-Site-ESXi-01	8 GB	0.82 GB	5.04 MB	0.3 GB	47.41 MB

Large VMs: Memory Usage

Page 1 of 1 — Displaying 1 - 24 of 24

A list of VMs with large RAM size

We now have a list of all running VMs that are larger than a certain size. We can sort them by any column. By default, we have configured it so that it is sorted by RAM size in descending order. This allows you to focus on the largest VMs.

Yes, that's all you need to downsize memory if you do not have visibility into the Guest OS. A simple approach, made possible by standard deviation.

Summary

We covered how you should approach capacity management in a virtual data center. Once you split capacity management into the two distinct layers, it will become natural and will transition you into the service-provider model. You need to see the application team as a customer who needs to know about the detailed specifications of your infrastructure. You provide them as a service. To achieve this, you need to unify the three components (compute, network, and storage) as one integrated capacity planning component. It is no longer sufficient to look at them as three separate components managed by three different teams.

In the next chapter, we will cover use cases beyond the core performance and capacity management use cases. It will also provide examples of how you can be creative with dashboards and super metrics.

8

Specific-Purpose Dashboards

We covered general-purpose dashboards in the previous two chapters. They are your primary dashboards. This chapter complements those chapters by covering specific use cases. They are often used by specific roles (for example, the network team, storage team, and senior management). As a result, they may cut across performance, capacity, availability, and configuration. They may also cover both the VM layer and the infrastructure layer.

In this chapter, we will cover the following topics:

- Dashboards for the operations team
- Dashboards for the storage team
- Dashboards for the network team
- Dashboards for the VDI team

Dashboards for the big screen

It is common to see critical information about the environment being projected on the big screen in the office or **network operating center** (NOC). Such dashboards take up prime real estate. They have high visibility. They should quickly tell the health of the environment and how customers are being served.

The challenge is this: how effectively is the information presented?

An effective dashboard will make viewers take action if the information presented shows a problem. If it does not, then it defeats the purpose of having it in the first place.

To make an effective big-screen dashboard, keep in mind these guidelines:

- The content is chosen so that it drives the viewer into action. If it displays something that is red most of the time, after a while, viewers will ignore it. When something on the big screen is red, you want action to be taken. Thus, the color changes in vRealize Operations should be chosen such that if everything is functioning normally, the entire screen is essentially green.

- There is no human interaction, as there is no user clicking on any part of the dashboard. As a result, remove any buttons whenever possible. Also, there is no need for widget interaction.

- The information maintains the target audience's attention. If you display the same information for 15 minutes, and it is static information, people will lose interest. The dashboards should automatically cycle every minute. You can modify this time period, add more dashboards, and change the order. This also prevents burned pixels on the screen.

- The dashboards show minimal information, typically with large numbers. They do not show detailed charts as those are hard to read from afar. Ideally, all the numbers are percentages, with 0 being bad and 100 being perfect.

- The dashboards use color to classify information. Color is easier to digest from afar and at a glance. A good approach is to use the vRealize Operations key colors (green, yellow, amber, and red).

- The screen is simplified and the browser is set to full-screen.

- Have white space so that the overall visual is not cluttered.

You should categorize the information presented. Here is one way to do it: look at the three main areas of monitoring, and cycle the dashboards.

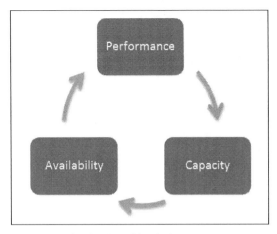

The dashboard for the big screen

You can have more than one dashboard per category, as you want to keep each dashboard minimal. One way to keep the information minimal while enhancing readability is to zoom in in the browser.

Add configuration and security if you think it makes sense. Just follow the previous guidelines.

You can also split your dashboards into these two categories to reinforce the message that there are two distinct layers and that your team should focus on the customers' first:

- VM
- Infrastructure

Tomas Baublys explains how you can keep the vRealize Operations UI simple at `https://communities.vmware.com/people/tbaublys/blog/2015/12/12/how-to-create-a-user-and-assign-a-dashboard-in-vr-ops-and-hide-everything-else`. Follow it to have unnecessary components hidden from the screen.

The NOC availability dashboard

Let's look at our first dashboard. Availability is probably the most common requirement. You should show the three main components: compute, storage, and network.

Compute availability

For compute, ensure you pick the right counter to check ESXi host uptime. Do this by checking the metrics. For example, we can see that there are two metrics provided for ESXi status. However, one of them is only updated daily, as shown by the red arrows:

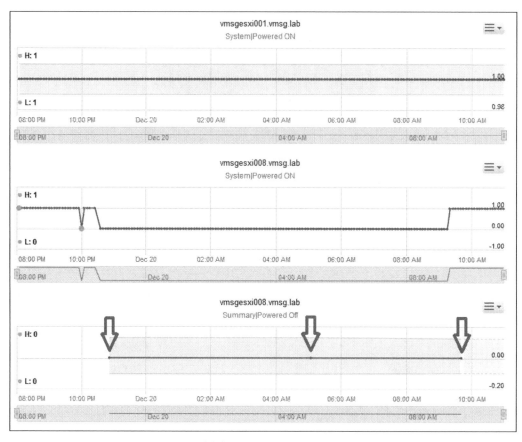

ESXi availability – picking the right counters

From this, it is clear that the metric you need is **System | Powered On**.

Once you confirm the metric, it's a matter of building the heatmap. Heatmaps are more suitable than line charts if you have many objects. On the projected screen, you can probably only displays 10 line charts at a time before they get too small. With heatmaps, you can display more, as each object takes up less real estate on the screen.

Heatmaps also let you group the objects. Use the following screenshot as a guide to configuring the heatmap:

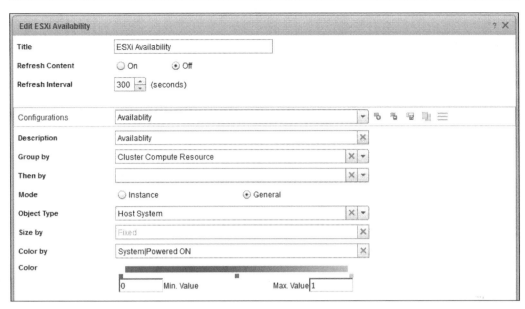

Tracking ESXi availability – configuring the heatmap

The reason we use a fixed size for this heatmap is to get viewers to focus on the uptime. Once it is configured, you will have something like this:

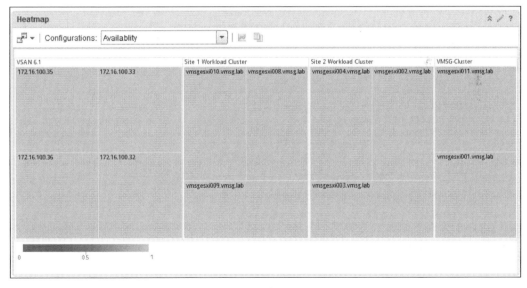

The ESXi availability heatmap

It's easier to see when each ESXi is the same size. You can see we have four clusters, and each cluster has two to four hosts.

However, if you want to focus on your newer clusters (which are probably bigger), you can include the size dimension. This is useful if your clusters and ESXi hosts are not uniform, which is the case we have in the following screenshot:

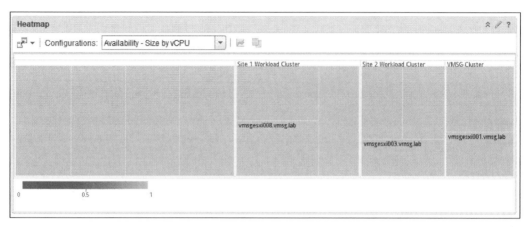

The ESXi availability heatmap – with cluster sizes shown

You'll notice that one of the clusters is much larger than the rest. It has more physical cores. To include this size dimension, choose **CPU | Provisioned vCPU** from the **Availability - Size by vCPU** options list. Yes, we are sizing it based on the total number of physical cores.

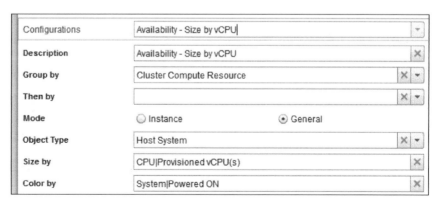

ESXi availability – heatmap configuration

Storage availability

Monitoring storage availability is best done by the specific adapter for that storage model. EMC has developed their own adapter, and Blue Medora provides them for a variety of brands.

We will cover VSAN as an example here. You can monitor any of the SSDs or magnetic disks for soft errors. They are the leading indicators of a hard error.

Use the storage adapter to give you visibility. In the following example, we use the magnetic disk object. It has a metric that tracks errors.

We can size the widget so that it matches the physical setup. The VSAN cluster has four nodes, and each node has four magnetic disks. As you can see, each row corresponds to a host. They are sorted by name, so the first host takes up the first row.

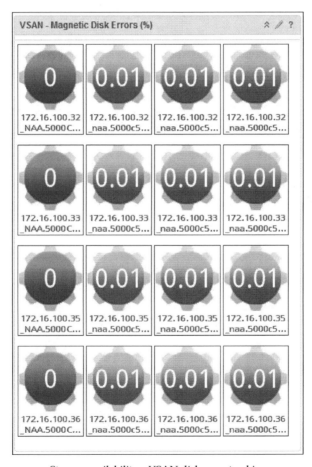

Storage availability – VSAN disk error tracking

Since we saw some errors in the example, let's find out what they are. We can search on the log, but which log files should we search, and what should we search for?

This is where **vRealize Log Insight** integration comes in. In the following example, we have searched on one of the disks and it has returned the errors from the log. This speeds up troubleshooting with VMware Support as you know the exact messages in the log.

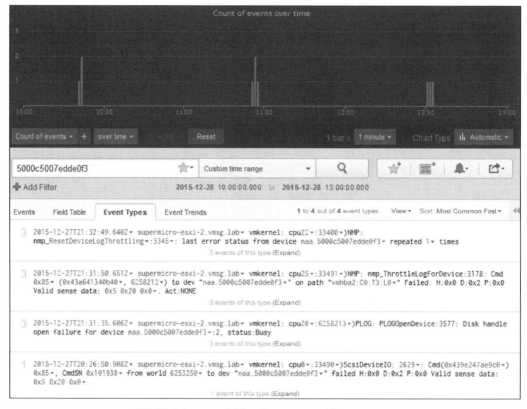

VSAN disk error – drilling down to actual log messages

Network availability

You can also monitor the uptime of the physical switch used in your SDDC. Install the management pack for network devices and configure SNMP for each switch.

The uptime metric is in one-hundredths of a second, so we need to convert it to something easier to understand. We use **day** in the following super metric:

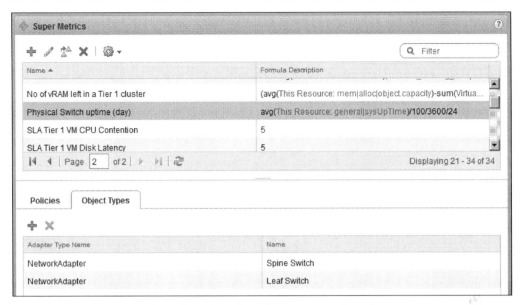

Physical switch uptime – the super metric formula

Apply the super metric to both **Spine Switch** and **Leaf Switch** objects so that any physical switch will have this metric. Here is an example of what the dashboard looks like. It has three switches. We can see that each of them has been up for over 200 days.

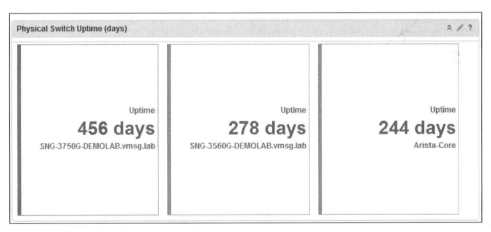

Network availability – physical switch uptime

There are a few things you need to do to achieve this widget. The first is to specify the basic settings, such as the number of columns, rounding of decimals, and font size. We use the following settings:

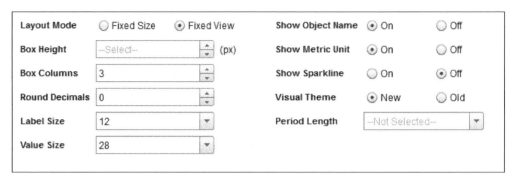

Physical switch uptime – widget configuration

The next thing is to specify the object and metric to use. For each metric, ensure you give it a label and specify the unit of measurement.

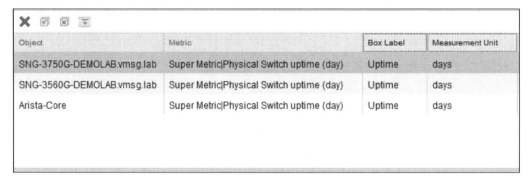

Physical switch uptime – widget configuration

You can color code the switch based on the uptime. For example, if you specify 1 as the **Red Bound**, then any switch whose uptime is less than 1 day will be shown in red. We specify 200, 300, and 400 in our example to show the color coding in action. In practice, you will set a much lower number.

The default order is **Red Bound**, **Orange Bound**, and **Yellow Bound**. It expects the range to increase (a higher number means a worse situation). To change it, simply drag and drop to change the order, as the hint says!

			Drag And Drop To Change Order
Color Method	Yellow Bound	Orange Bound	Red Bound
Custom	400	300	200
Custom	400	300	200
Custom	400	300	200

Physical switch uptime – widget configuration

The NOC performance dashboard

We covered performance in *Chapter 6, Performance-Monitoring Dashboards*, so it's a matter of tailoring the same information for big-screen use cases. We need to present less information, as it has to be visible from a distance. It also has to be visual, so color coding will increase the dashboard's usability. The viewer needs to be able to make sense of the information at a glance.

Recall that the IaaS business provides four basic components: CPU, RAM, disk, and network. We use the contention metrics to define the IaaS performance, and we measure it against the promised performance SLA.

The following screenshot provides an example for CPU performance. We use the **Health Chart** widget as it can display information in different colors based on multiple thresholds. This enables you to quickly see whether you are close to your performance SLA.

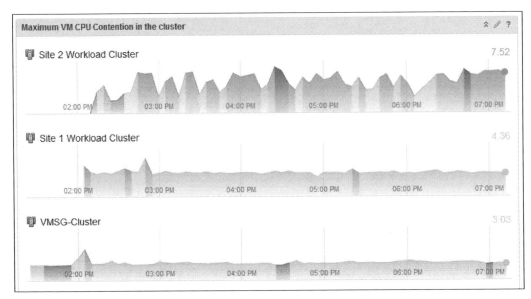

The performance dashboard – cluster performance chart (CPU)

We have three clusters in the previous example. We can quickly tell that the first cluster is close to its performance SLA threshold. In fact, it has breached it a couple of times, as you can see two periods of red. It has plenty of orange periods, meaning it was near its capacity.

The second cluster is coping better. It has not breached any CPU performance SLA. Every VM is being served well from the CPU point of view.

The third cluster has the most capacity. It is sustaining a lower contention.

In general, your tier-1 (most expensive) cluster should mostly be displaying green, as you are bound by availability. Your tier-3 (cheapest) cluster should be mostly displaying orange. None should be showing red.

Let's move to memory performance SLA:

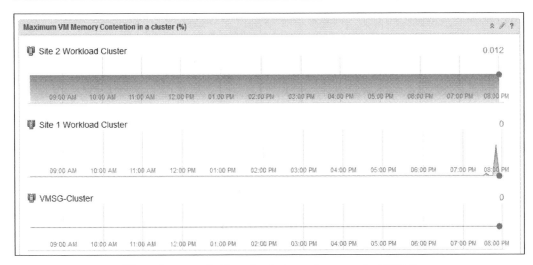

The performance dashboard – cluster performance chart (RAM)

In this example, assuming your performance SLA for memory is less than 0.02 percent, you are delivering that SLA. All clusters have either zero or near-zero contention.

To complete the dashboard, add the **Disk Latency** and **Network Dropped Packet** metrics. All the metrics are from the super metrics you created in *Chapter 6, Performance-Monitoring Dashboards*. You are just showing them differently as the use case is different.

The following is the example for disk:

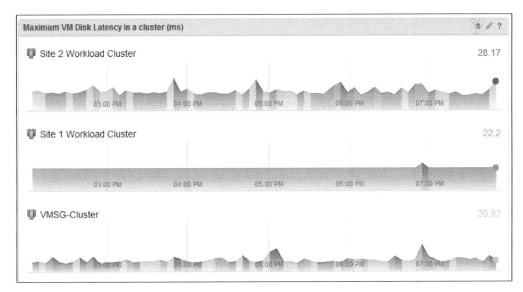

The performance dashboard – cluster performance chart (disk)

To configure a **Health Chart** widget, there are three parts you need to work on.

Use the next figure as a guide. I've put red arrows to mark the areas you need to configure. Ensure **Self Provider** is set to **On**, as there is no interaction in the big screen use case.

You control how much information is shown in **Period Length**. As this is shown on "live TV", a period of 1 – 24 hours makes sense. Choose the type of object you want to display. If you have a single tier, you can choose the cluster object. If you have multiple tiers, you choose the group for that tier.

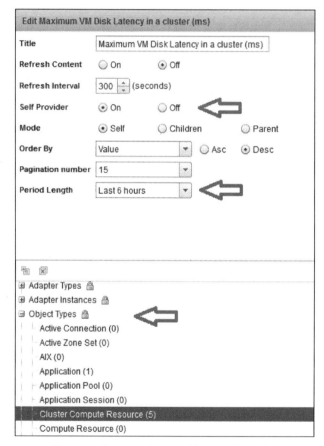

Cluster performance chart – widget configuration

The second part you need to configure is the metric itself. If you have multiple tiers, you need to create one widget per tier. The reason is you can only have one set of thresholds, as can be seen in the following screenshot:

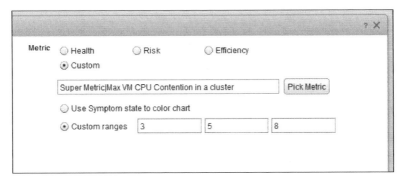

Cluster performance chart – widget configuration

Click on the **Pick Metric** button to specify the metric you want. It will bring up the following dialog box. Choose the object and the metric.

Can you guess why we need to specify the object again? Didn't we just choose the cluster in the previous screenshot?

Cluster performance chart – widget configuration

The reason is the relationship. The **Health Chart** allows you to display either the objects themselves, their children, or their parents.

The NOC capacity dashboard

In the previous chapter, we talked about complementing contention-based data with utilization-based data. So, let's see an example. The following widget shows the maximum ESXi CPU utilization in a cluster:

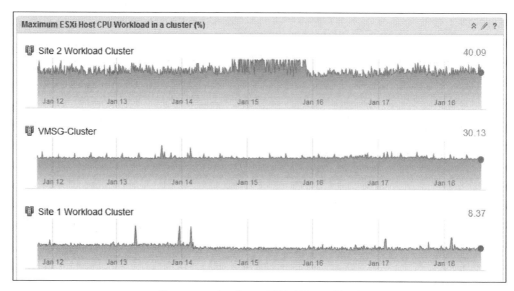

Cluster capacity chart – ESXi CPU workload

We show 1 week of data instead of 1 day as capacity monitoring is not something that you need to do on a daily basis. It takes weeks to add physical capacity, and you also want to see the bigger picture before adding capacity.

For memory, you need to be aware of the two-level memory hierarchies with virtualization. Note that all the counters are called **workload** in vRealize Operations, so choose carefully.

The following is based on **Memory Consumed**:

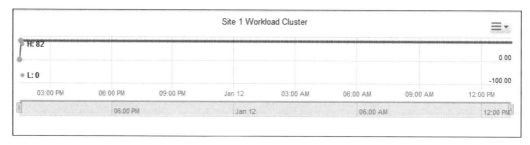

Cluster memory – consumed RAM

The following is based on **Memory Active**. As you might expect, the active memory is lower than the consumed memory. It is 33 percent versus 82 percent.

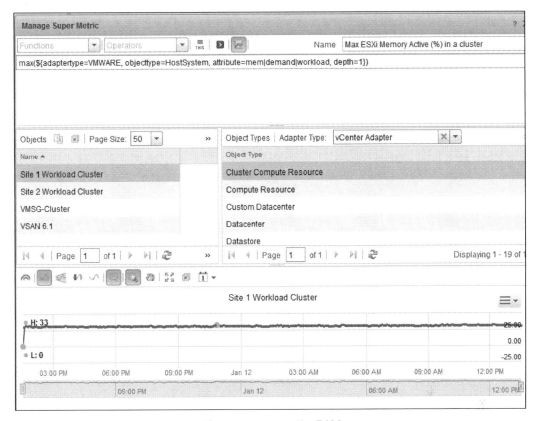

Cluster memory – active RAM

Once you configure it, create a new **Health Chart** widget for each metric.

The following shows an example of the **Memory Consumed**. The range is expected to be high. The first cluster has a maximum ESXi memory consumed of 97 percent. If you are basing your analysis on this counter alone, you will conclude that you need more RAM.

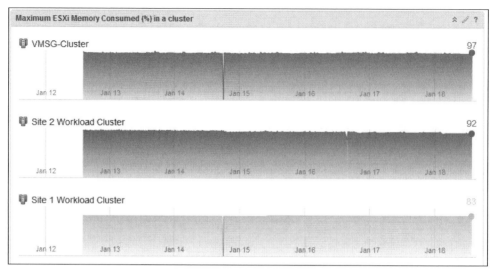

Cluster capacity – the consumed memory chart

And here is the chart for **Memory Active**. Notice that the number is much lower. Even if you set it to 50 percent, the graphs will still be green.

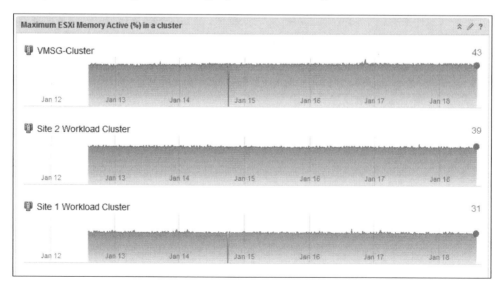

Cluster capacity – the active memory chart

This tells you that you need to use both counters. Using one will result in a an incorrect capacity decision. You should show the two widgets side by side for ease of comparison. *Chapter 13*, *Memory Counters*, provides the explanation.

The NOC configuration dashboard

vRealize comes with three default dashboards for configuration, covering the VM, host, and cluster. They are useful for checking the consistency of your configuration across many objects.

For the purpose of the big screen, we will see two examples of configuration items that you want to check daily. The first one is snapshots, and the second one is low disk space inside the Guest OS.

vRealize Operations can generate an alert when a VM has large disk snapshots, disk I/O latency problems caused by snapshots, or high CPU co-stop due to snapshots. Since we already have the alert, this dashboard provides additional visibility so that you can prevent the alert. It tells us how many VMs have large snapshots. We use the **View** widget and create a bar chart:

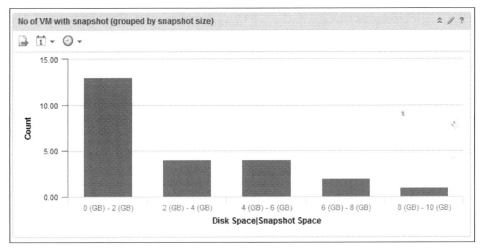

VM snapshots – grouped by snapshot size

In an ideal environment, this bar chart will be empty. This means that no VM has a snapshot.

You can certainly complement the above with the actual list of VMs with the biggest snapshots. Just be mindful that the text might be too small on the projector screen.

In the following screenshot, we have a dozen VMs with large snapshots:

Top 25 VMs with the largest snapshots

The second example I want to provide is disk utilization inside the Guest OS. If the disk availability is less than 10 percent, you can proactively inform your customer to archive or add another disk.

We use the same bar chart again, as it's easier to see on the projector screen:

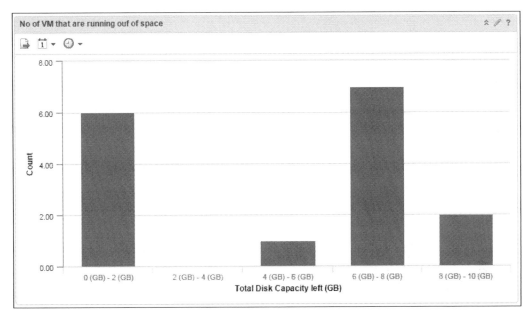

VM disk capacity left (inside Guest OS)

In a healthy environment, where no VM is running out of space, this bar chart will be empty.

Monitoring ESXi host temperature

It is common for customers to monitor the fan speed and temperature of hardware equipment. Rising fan speed or temperature can be a good warning indicator of failure or high utilization.

If you have many ESXis, tracking them one by one is tedious. It also makes more sense to track at the cluster level due to HA, DRS, and VSAN. The following screenshot shows an example of four clusters:

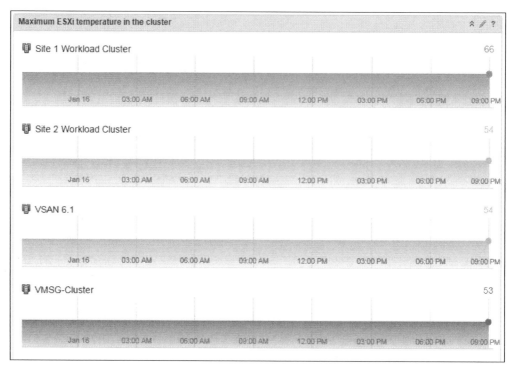

Tracking ESXi temperature

From this, viewers can easily see whether the cluster utilizations are in the healthy range or not. I have adjusted the threshold accordingly so that they display different thresholds. In your environment, they should mostly be green, as they should be within the range you deem healthy.

The blog at `http://virtual-red-dot.info/is-any-of-your-esxi-hosts-in-any-of-your-data-centers-overheating/` has the implementation details.

Dashboards for the storage team

Chapter 11, SDDC Key Counters, explains how distributed storage, such as VSAN, differs fundamentally from centralized storage. *Chapter 14, Storage Counters*, shows that this results in different objects and counters. This chapter shows an example of how we monitor them.

LUN performance monitoring

A common requirement of storage monitoring is to see the data at the physical storage level. The data at this level eliminates the information at VM level. If the performance is good at this level but poor at the VM level, you should check the disk queue length inside the Guest OS.

ESXi tracks the latency on each device it sees; this means LUNs (in central storage) or physical disks (in distributed storage). For central storage, this means VMFS datastores. There are no devices in NFS datastores.

For distributed storage, ESXi has to be able to see the physical disk. If the disk is directly passed through to the VM, it is no longer visible by the vmkernel. The vmkernel does not have visibility into distributed storage products that use direct pass-through.

For the overall picture, plot the maximum and average latency across all devices and hosts. The average is useful as the maximum can be a one-off event with no real business impact.

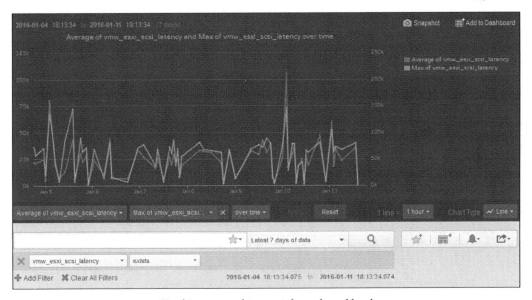

Tracking storage latency at the vmkernel level

If the number is not good, you can zoom in. For example, group them by the LUN or device ID so that you can see whether the issue impacts a few or many LUNs.

Since VSAN integrates into the vmkernel, you get visibility into each VSAN disk. This means you are getting visibility at the lowest level.

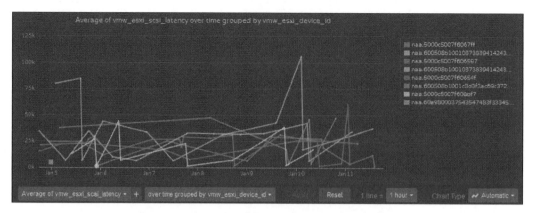

Storage latency at the vmkernel level – grouped by LUN

You can also zoom in to a specific ESXi host. This is more useful in VSAN than in a centralized array, as the device actually resides on the ESXi host. It is also a single piece of physical disk, not a RAID volume presented by the array.

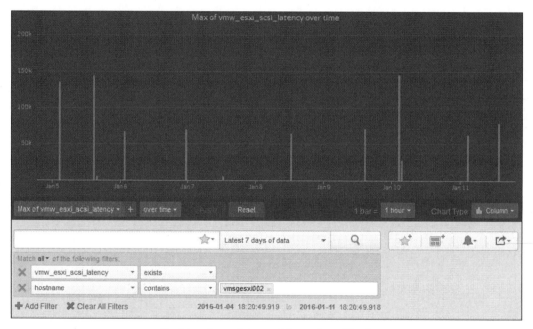

Tracking storage latency at the vmkernel level

For more details, review `http://virtual-red-dot.info/vsphere-storage-latency-view-from-the-vmkernel/`.

VSAN performance monitoring

Lenin Singaravelu and Sankaran Sivathanu presented the *Virtual SAN Performance Deep-Dive* session at VMworld 2015. The session ID is **STO4949**. In their session, they shared the common problem sources for VSAN performance:

- CPU bottlenecks
- Network issues
- Hotspots in clusters
- VSAN overhead (for example, re-sync operations, flush timer, and snapshots)

Let's consider an example to show how you can monitor VSAN performance. vRealize Operations have built-in dashboards for VSAN, and you can easily extend and customize them.

In this example, we will extend the dashboard by adding visibility into the SSD read cache hit rate. We know that read performance is optimal when the data is read from the cache. A cache miss will have a performance penalty, as the data has to be read from a slower disk (SSD or magnetic).

Tracking each SSD one by one is tedious. Create a super metric to track the minimum hit rate among all the SSDs in the cluster. If the number is near 100%, it means you have a high hit rate for all SSDs.

To create the super metric, use **Solid State Device** under the **Storage Devices** adapter, not under **vCenter** adapter. The next screenshot shows how to do it.

The **vCenter** adapter does not recognize VSAN objects. If you do not have the **Storage Devices** adapter yet, get it from the **VMware Solutions Exchange** and install it.

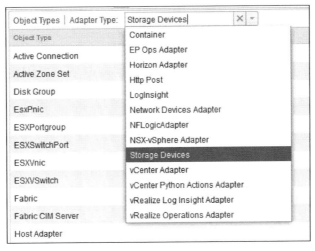

vRealize Operations – Choosing an adapter

Not all vSphere clusters are VSAN clusters. To make it easier to recognize which one they are, **Storage Devices** has its own object for VSAN clusters. This object is four levels above the SSD object, so don't forget to set `depth=4` in the formula.

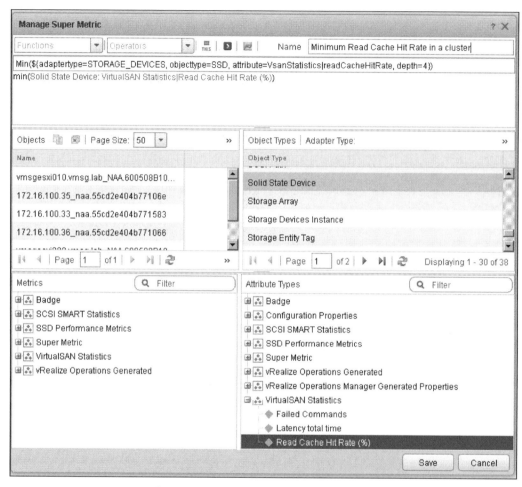

Super metric – VSAN Read Cache Hit Rate (%)

Remember to choose the correct object to apply it to. It is a VSAN cluster object, not a vSphere cluster object.

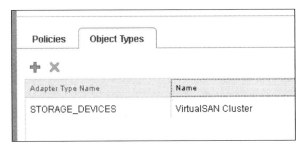

vRealize Operations – Applying a super metric to an object

Once you have it, it is a matter of displaying it. We use the health chart widget as it is color coded. This makes it easy to see at a glance whether your VSAN cluster is performing well. If all the read operations are coming from the SSD, you should see a green chart such as this:

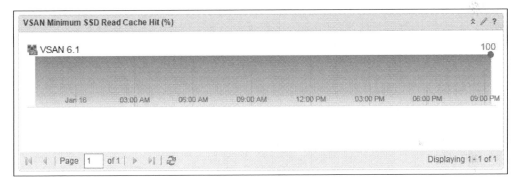

VSAN Read Cache Hit – summary

This chart is good for overall data. If you have multiple VSAN clusters, you can show all of them in a dashboard.

If there is a performance issue, you need to drill down to each SSD. You can plot each of the SSDs together so that you can see a pattern. The following example shows four SSDs in a VSAN cluster:

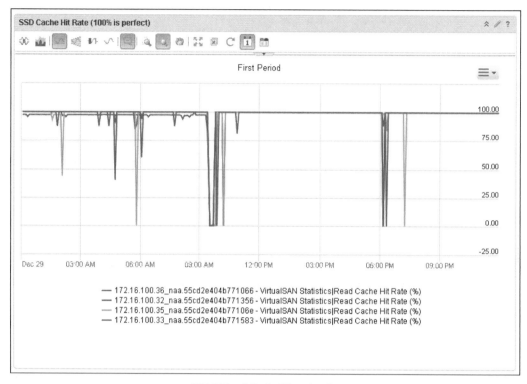

VSAN Read Cache Hit – details

You will notice that there are times when the read operations did not come from the SSD at all. The hit rate dropped to **0** percent at some points. I did some performance tests during that day, with a working set that was deliberately set to exceed the SSD capacity.

We've got SSDs covered. What about magnetic disks?

In general, a hybrid VSAN cluster will have more magnetic disks than SSD disks. For example, you may have one SSD for every four magnetic disks. Displaying many objects in a single line chart can make the line chart hard to read.

You can use the **Scoreboard** or **Scoreboard Health** widget to display each physical magnetic disk. Here is an example using the **Scoreboard** widget:

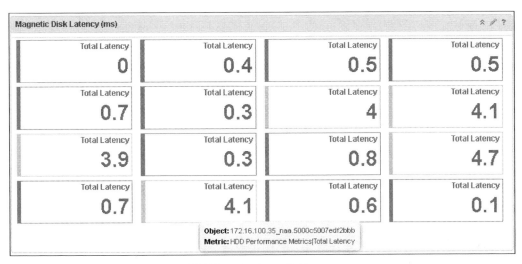

VSAN monitoring – disk latency

This may not be visual as the disks are all performing well. The next screenshot shows an example where the threshold has been configured to show colors other than green.

This time around, we are using the **Scoreboard Health** widget, and this cluster has a lot more magnetic disks.

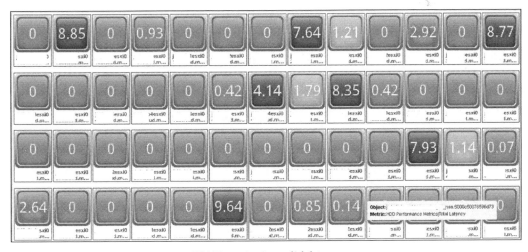

VSAN monitoring – disk latency

In an environment with a lot of disks, you might want to group the magnetic disks by disk groups. This lets you see whether there is a hot spot. If you use a heatmap, you can also add an **IOPS** dimension. The higher the workload, the bigger the box representing that magnetic disk. Here is what the resultant heatmap looks like:

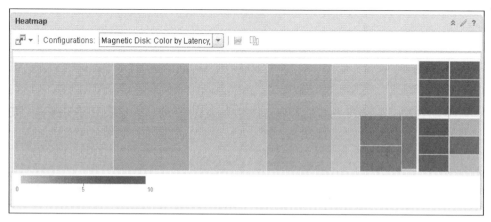

VSAN monitoring – disk latency grouped by disk groups

To configure this, use the following configuration as an example:

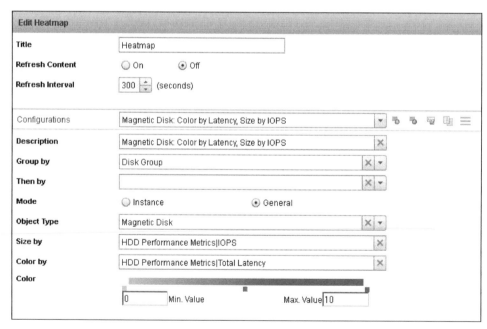

VSAN monitoring – heatmap configuration

Once you have both SSDs and magnetic disks analyzed, it is time to work on the performance at the **Disk Group** level. The disk groups in a VSAN cluster will not have identical workloads. So, it's wise to plot them individually. You can see in the following example that the four disk groups (in a cluster of four hosts) do not perform equally. Their latency values are different.

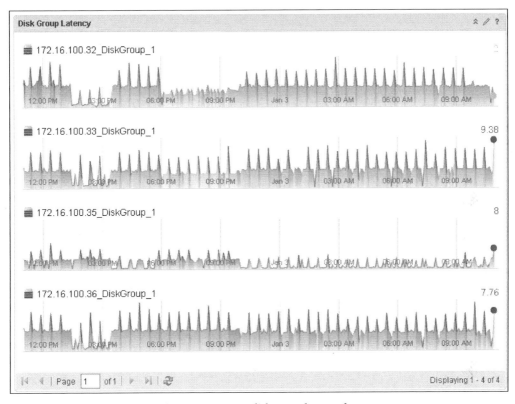

VSAN monitoring – disk group latency chart

Do not forget to configure the widget. For instructions, refer to the big screen dashboard covered earlier in this chapter, and the following diagram:

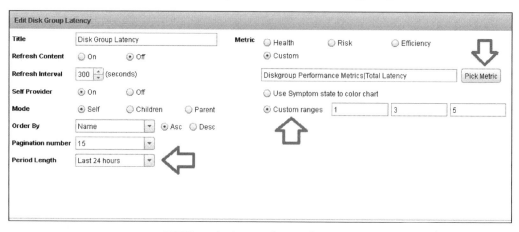

VSAN monitoring – widget configuration

The latency value you set in the **Custom ranges** field depends on the architecture. All flash devices will have lower values, such as the one shown in the preceding diagram.

VM performance monitoring

Chapter 6, Performance-Monitoring Dashboards, shows how you can quickly identify whether any VM is abusing your shared storage. We also covered how you can monitor the performance of your infrastructure.

The dashboards are good enough for overall monitoring. But if you are a storage specialist, you want to know more detailed information. For example, you want to know the following:

- What's the demand like? Are the IOPS distributed relatively well among VMs, or do you have 10 percent of VMs dominating 90 percent of the IOPS?
- Which datastores are having a hard time meeting the VMs' IOPS demand?
- Given a VM, what's the breakdown of its demand per virtual disk?

Let's see how we can answer the first question. We need a heatmap showing how the infrastructure is coping with the demand. It should show the latency and IOPS for all VMs. The heatmap should have these features:

- **Color by latency**: So that all the high-latency VMs will be easily visible.
- **Size by IOPS**: So that you can see whether you have highly demanding VMs dominating your array. This lets you quickly find those VMs that generate the bulk of the IOPS.

Here is an example where a single VM dominates the entire shared storage. It is doing more IOPS than all other VMs combined! With a heatmap, relative information such as this is easily spotted.

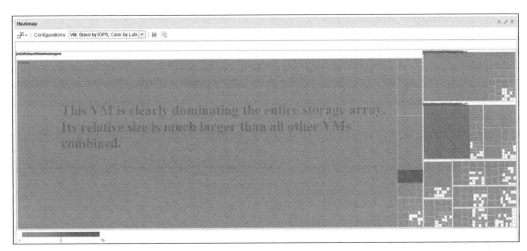

VM monitoring – relative IOPS among VMs

In a normal environment, you will have a more balanced distribution.

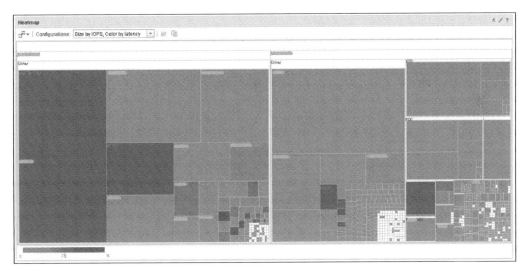

VM monitoring – relative IOPS among VMs

Because this is for all tiers, you want to group the information per tier in the heatmap. If you have many VMs, you can create separate heatmaps for each tier in the same widget. Using separate heatmaps allows you to set different thresholds. Showing a different threshold is useful as you have a different SLA.

Datastore capacity monitoring

The target user for the datastore capacity monitoring use case is someone who is doing capacity planning for storage. This is also useful for the storage administrator or storage architect.

This particular dashboard demonstrates how you can be creative with super metrics. This dashboard is courtesy of Yuval Tenenbaum, who was the Europe Lead SE for Cloud Management, based in the UK.

As a storage administrator, you may have a policy of not placing more than 30 VMs per datastore. You also want to keep 20 percent free space to cater to snapshots and growth. In a large environment, this can be difficult to enforce and track. If you have hundreds of datastores, it can be cumbersome to show the degree of compliance on a single screen.

Ideally, you would like to see a heatmap showing all datastores; the higher the number of VMs or the lesser the capacity left in percentage, the more the datastore should be highlighted (in red). So, the heatmap would show the information at a glance; if the boxes in the heatmap are closer to green, it means all of your datastores have a good buffer in terms of both the number of VMs and the capacity remaining. Achieving this requires a super metric that tracks the maximum of both the high number of VMs and the capacity remaining.

Let's explain the preceding section with an example.

The following table addresses the capacity portion. In this example, the size of the datastore is 4 TB, and you have set 80 percent as the threshold.

Consumed	Provisioned	Threshold	Ratio
1.6 TB	4 TB	3.2 TB	0.50
2.2 TB	4 TB	3.2 TB	0.69
2.8 TB	4 TB	3.2 TB	0.88
3.6 TB	4 TB	3.2 TB	1.13

If the consumed space is **1.6 TB**, the ratio is **1.6/3.2**, or 50 percent. As the consumed space grows, so does the ratio. At **3.6 TB**, which is still below the **4 TB** configured space, the ratio is already above 1. If you set 1 as red and 0 as green in the heatmap, you will get a full red box since **1.13** is above 1, even though you still have some room to react (in this example, 400 GB remains).

The following table addresses the **Number of VMs** dimension. In this example, the policy is to not have more than 30 VMs per datastore. You decide to set the threshold at 80 percent, which equals 24.

Number of VMs deployed	Threshold	Ratio
16	24	0.67
20	24	0.83
24	24	1.00
28	24	1.17

If a datastore has **24** VMs, the ratio will be **24/24** or **1.00**. If you set 1 as red and 0 as green in the heatmap, you will get a full red box even if you have a buffer of six more VMs. We now need to combine the two dimensions into a single super metric. We will take the maximum of their values, so we get a full red box when either threshold is reached. The super metric needs to use the `This Resource` function as you need to point to the resource itself. The actual formula is shown in this screenshot:

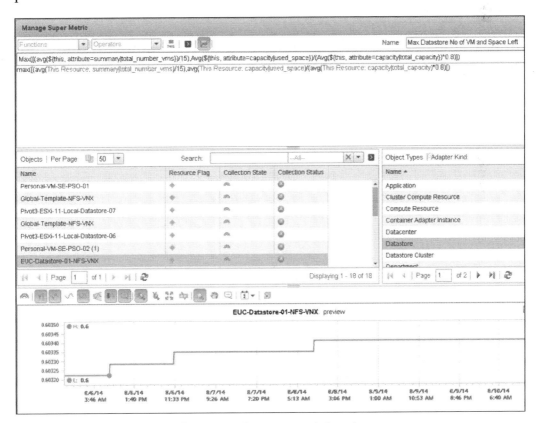

Storage capacity - super metric formula

This is the formula mentioned in the screenshot:

```
Max([(avg(${this, attribute=summary|total_number_vms})/30),
Avg(${this, attribute=capacity|used_space})/(Avg(${this,
attribute=capacity|total_capacity})*0.8)])
```

Once you have it, you can show the information in a `heatmap`.

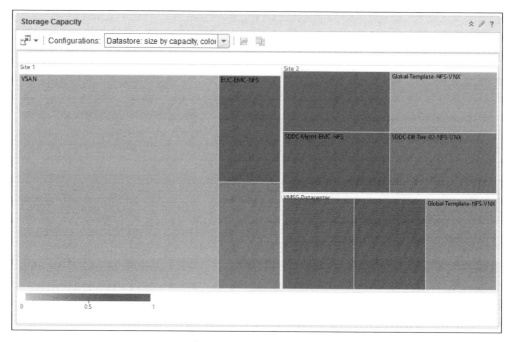

Storage capacity – heatmap

You've probably noticed that we have excluded the local datastores.

There are a few techniques to do this.

The one that we use here is using the vCenter `Datastore Folder` object. In vCenter, simply create folders, and place the shared datastores in those folders. They will appear in vRealize Operations automatically, because it recognizes vSphere folders as objects.

The following screenshot shows an example:

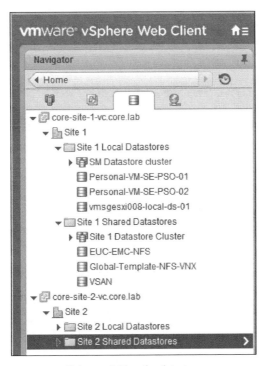

vSphere – folders for datastores

In the following screenshot, we have filtered the list so it only displays datastores that belong to the three folders selected:

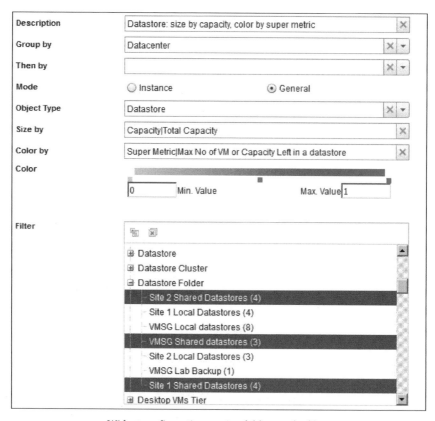

Widget configuration – using folders as the filter

Dashboards for the network team

We cover in *Chapter 11, SDDC Key Counters*, that SDDC network monitoring can be divided into three layers:

- The first layer is the VM, which typically has only one vNIC. From a performance-monitoring point of view, this is relatively the simplest layer.

- The second layer is the hypervisor and NSX. Together, they provide virtual switches, often distributed across many hosts. With NSX, the hypervisor has a distributed router, a distributed firewall, an edge gateway, and a load balancer.

- The third layer is made up of the physical switches and routers in the data center. This also includes the WAN link and Internet connectivity.

To prove that the network is performing well, you need to do a few things:

- Show that there is no error
- Show that the network latency is low
- Show that utilization is below physical capacity
- Keep special packets, such as broadcast and multicast, to a minimum

We can deliver the preceding points, except latency. *Chapter 15, Network Counters,* explains the limitations in latency monitoring.

Errors in the network

To show that there is no error in the network, you need to check whether:

- Any VM has dropped packets
- Any ESXi has errors or dropped packets

Let's show them in two separate charts so that it's easier to see whether the problem is at the VM or ESXi level. This means that we need to create two super metrics that track the maximum of dropped packets. The first one will track all VMs in the data center; the second one will track all ESXi hosts. For ESXi hosts, you can also track error packets.

The other reason why we need to track at the ESXi level is that not all traffic is VM traffic. There are vmkernel traffics such as vMotion and VSAN.

This can be done with a line chart, which shows that not a single ESXi or VM has experienced dropped packets. For the ESXi host, you need to get the data from all vmnics.

If your network is healthy, the charts will show flat lines at **0**. This means not a single ESXi host or VM in the entire data center is experiencing packet drops in any of its NICs.

The following screenshot shows the super metric formula to check whether any ESXi has packets dropped in a cluster. The preview shows that the **VSAN 6.1** cluster does not have any packets dropped.

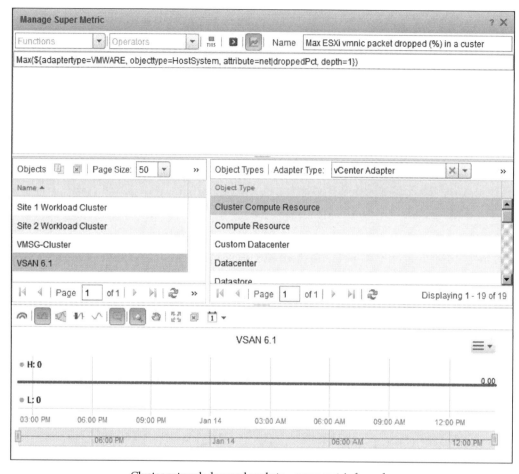

Cluster network dropped packets – super metric formula

You may not see the metric when you try to perform the super metric for the VM. That's because it is not enabled by default. You need to enable the collection of that metric first. Modify the policy and enable the metrics.

In the event that you have a dropped or error packet, you can show it with a **Top-N** widget. The line chart will show the time the problem occurred, and the **Top-N** timeline can be changed to match it. You need to have three **Top-N** widgets. Assuming you just need to show the top 20, you will have:

- The top 20 VMs with dropped packets
- The top 20 ESXi hosts with dropped packets
- The top 20 ESXi hosts with error packets (receive)
- The top 20 ESXi hosts with error packets (transmit)

The counters you can display obviously depend on what vRealize Operations provides.

The following screenshot shows what you can display for ESXi hosts. It has error packets, which a VM object does not have.

The VM object does not have it because vCenter itself does not collect it.

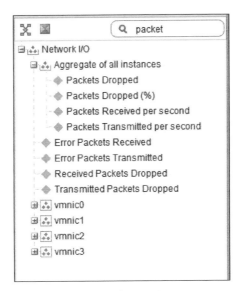

Error packet metrics

It is easier to show four widgets than combine the counters as this means that you do not have to create a super metric. It also means that you get to see more detail, which is the objective here.

The following are two of the **Top-N** widgets that you need to build:

Top 20 VMs and Top 20 ESXi hosts with packet drops

The data displayed by the ESXi is actually what you want to see. Not a single ESXi has experienced packet drops. They are all showing 0, not 100, percent.

If you need to see the distribution by network, you can create a heatmap. Group the VMs by distributed port group, not by ESXi host. This lets you quickly see the data per network.

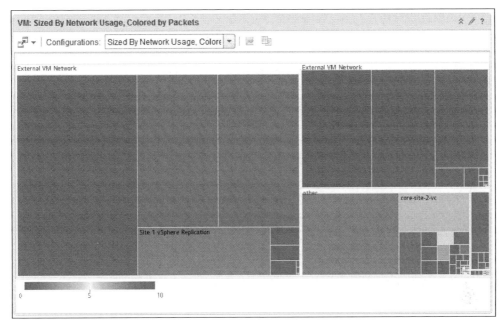

VM network heatmap – sized by usage and colored by dropped packets

To group the VMs by distributed port group, choose **vSphere Distributed Port Group** from the drop-down menu, as shown in the following screenshot:

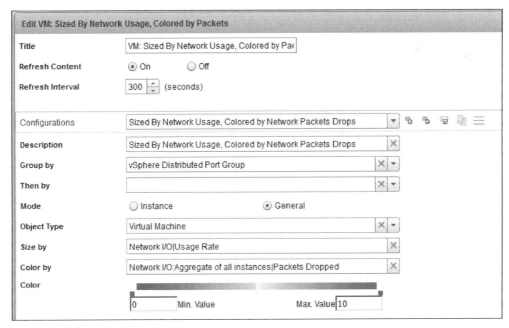

VM network heatmap configuration

Utilization of the network

To show utilization, you apply the same concept, which is using a super metric that tracks the maximum value of network utilization. Keep the following in mind:

- For a VM, you should expect the value to be less than 1 Gbps. If your ESXi uses 10 gigabits and your VM sees this, it is possible that a network-intensive VM will sustain 1 Gbps for 5 minutes. You need to know this because it impacts the performance of other VMs or the host.

- For ESXi, you should expect the value to be below 1 Gbps or 10 Gbps per vmnic, depending upon whether you are using 1-gigabit or 10-gigabit Ethernet.

If the value is too close to the physical wire speed, you need to dig deeper to see whether it is caused by a VM or non-VM workload.

This is the super metric for VM. You can take the maximum in a cluster or distributed port group.

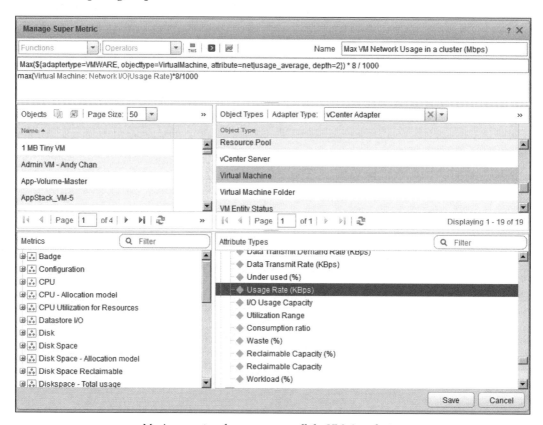

Maximum network usage among all the VMs in a cluster

If you choose to group by distributed port group, there is no need to change the depth=1 value. The port group is an object just one level higher than the VMs. Once created, apply the super metric to the **Distributed Port Group** object, not the cluster object.

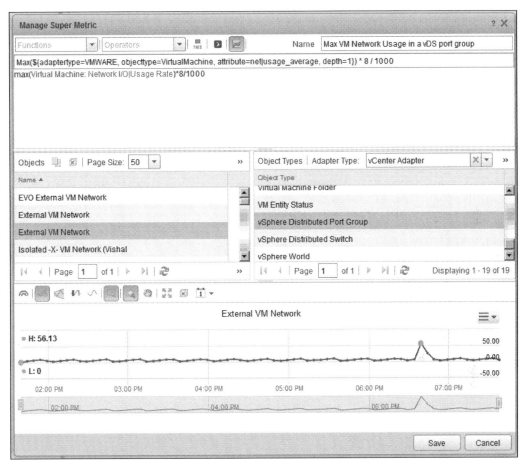

Maximum network usage among all VMs in a distributed vSwitch port group

You can complement the line chart with a **Top-N** widget, for example, show the top 30 VMs in terms of network utilization.

A small percentage of your VMs may have their backup via the LAN. You can track them separately if you standardize them to use the second vNIC. You are probably using a second vNIC since your backup network should be on a different network.

Tracking ESXi network utilization is harder as an ESXi host has multiple vmnics, and features such as load-based teaming can move workloads from one vmnic to another. The blog at `http://virtual-red-dot.info/is-any-of-your-esxi-vmnics-saturated/` explains how you monitor whether any of your ESXi vmnics are saturated.

Special packets in the network

For special packets (broadcast and multicast), we expect them to exist from time to time, so the value will not be zero all the time. We do, however, expect them to be minimal and remain low. They should not be trending upwards. We can track them by plotting a line chart that shows the sums of broadcast traffic from all ESXi hosts in the entire data center, expressed in the number of packets. It is enough to just plot TX as we are only concerned about whether any VM generates broadcast traffic.

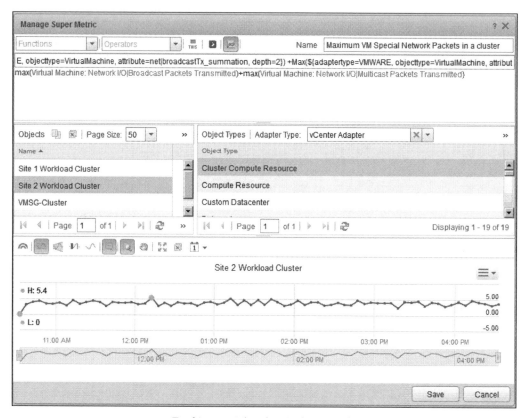

Tracking special packets in the network

We do not expect a VM to send regular broadcast and multicast packets, so their values should be zero most of the time. It is sufficient to use **Top-N**, as we can go back to any moment in time.

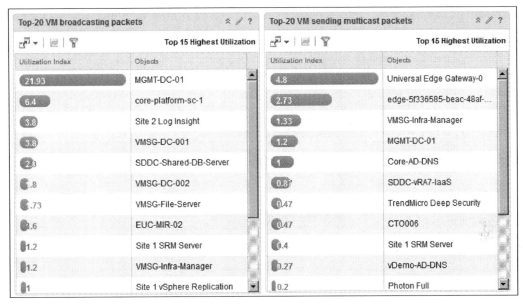

Top 10 VMs sending special packets

Dashboards for the VDI team

Chapter 5, Capacity Monitoring, explains that VDI scope is wider than server workload. Besides the IaaS component, you need to monitor Windows VMs and the VDI servers. VDI is more than *vSphere + Horizon.* Here are the common areas that you need to monitor:

VMware VDI Data	Tools
vSphere	vRealize Operations
vSphere Tasks, Events, Alarms	Log Insight
ESXi logs	Log Insight
vCenter Server, vCenter Database	vRealize Operations for vCenter, Log Insight
Horizon Servers	vRealize Operations with EP Agent, Log Insight
View Event Database	Log Insight
F5 (Load Balancer)	vRealize Operations (Blue Medora)
F5 logs	Log Insight
Storage (e.g. VSAN, EMC)	vRealize Operations
Storage logs	Log Insight
TrendMicro Deep Security appliance	vRealize Operations
TrendMicro logs	Log Insight
Horizon View	vRealize Operations (for View)
Zero Client logs	Log Insight
Physical switches	vRealize Operations (Network MP), Log Insight

Components to monitor in VMware Horizon

This results in more dashboards and the need for additional monitoring tools and adapters. Let's look at two common use cases in this book.

Is the DaaS serving the user well?

vRealize Operations provides in-Guest visibility and application-specific counters for VDI. This enables you to track performance at more points. In fact, there are 12 metrics you can check to ensure that your DaaS platform is indeed serving the VDI user well.

The article at http://virtual-red-dot.info/12-kpis-for-high-performance-vdi covers the details, so we will summarize them here.

The 12 metrics used as KPIs are as follows:

Component	Metric	Threshold
CPU	Contention	2%
CPU	Workload	70%
CPU	Run Queue	<3
RAM	Available RAM	500 MB
RAM	Committed RAM	70%
RAM	Contention	0%
Network	PCoIP latency	200 ms
Network	PCoIP TX packet loss	1%
	PCoIP RX packet loss	
Network	PCoIP latency variance	50 ms
Disk	Read latency	15 ms
	Write latency	
Disk	Queue length	2

You are right to say that the table has 13 counters. vRealize Operations is not able to measure the **Disk Queue Length** yet.

Let's discuss some of the counters so that you know how they are used.

Let's look at the VM CPU workload. The pattern matches a typical office pattern. CPU was low from before 6:30 am until around 8 am.

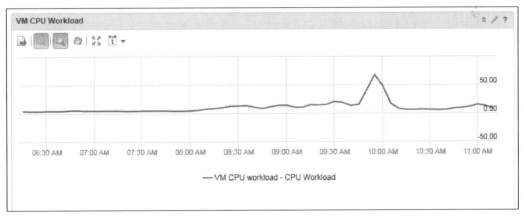

VM CPU workload

At around 8 am, the CPU usage started to rise. A typical conclusion is that the user has logged in to the desktop and started doing some work. The CPU usage then had a short spike to less than 50 percent before 10 am. The user never demands a lot of CPU. The capacity we give to the user is sufficient.

But what about performance? Did we deliver the capacity that was asked?

We need to turn to **VM CPU Contention** to answer the question. The following screenshot shows the **VM CPU Contention** counter:

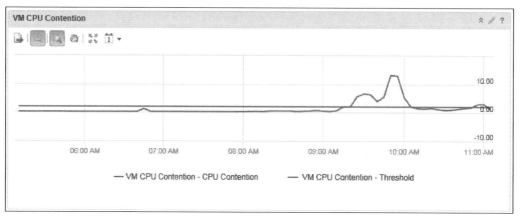

VM CPU Contention

The counter was low from around 6 am to around 9 am, as the user was not using the desktop yet. At around 9 am, the **CPU Contention** started to rise. It actually breached the performance SLA that you promised. Looking at this counter alone, you know that the VM was not served well in terms of CPU. At around 9:45 am, the VM was only asking for about 60% CPU, and yet, the **Desktop as a Service (DaaS)** was not able to deliver it. You need to reduce demand or increase physical capacity, as there is obviously a performance gap.

Let's now see an example where the DaaS is delivering its promised SLA. We will use memory in this example. The following screenshot shows the VM **Memory Contention** counter:

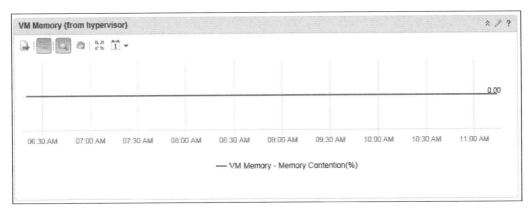

VM Memory Contention

The value is **0**, indicating no contention. This is what we expect in an environment where the ESXi host is not under memory pressure. If you do not overcommit memory, the ESXi host will never have memory contention as there is enough for every VM.

It's a good thing that the DaaS platform is able to deliver its promise to the VM. But does the VM itself need more? We need to look inside Windows for that. One of the Windows counters is **Committed RAM**.

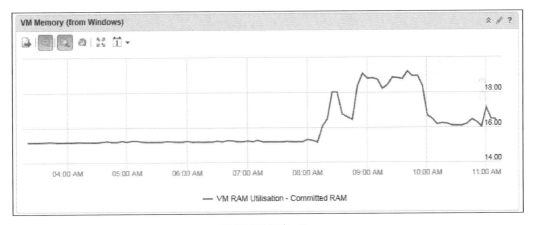

VM RAM Utilization

As we can see from the preceding graph, Windows did not need more than what was configured. We expected the number to hover around 50 to 70 percent, indicating that the configured RAM was sufficient.

Let's turn to storage now. Again, we see a similar usage pattern. We probably can conclude by now that the user started to use the VDI around 8 am. The disk latency was low before 8 am and started to rise afterwards. The good news is it remains healthy. It did exceed 10 milliseconds for 5 minutes for write latency, but the read was much lower at that time. So the overall latency is still below 10 milliseconds.

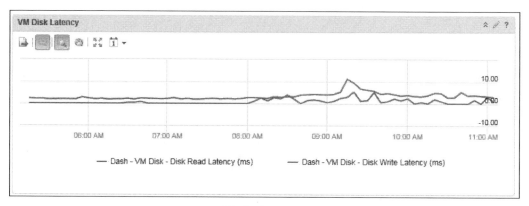

VM Disk Latency

Lastly, let's look at network. *Chapter 4, Performance Monitoring,* explains that we should monitor at the application layer (PCoIP in VDI case) and not the infrastructure layer (Windows or vSphere).

The following chart shows that both PCoIP **Received** and **Transmit** packet loss are within the healthy range. Healthy data at the application layer means there is no need to look at the infrastructure layer:

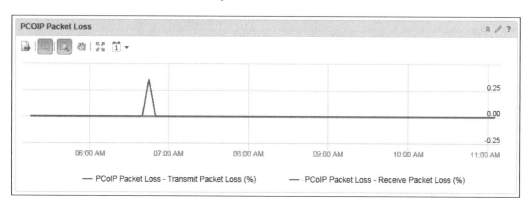

VM PCoIP packet loss

To complete the check, we should also look at the PCoIP latency. The number is again within the healthy range.

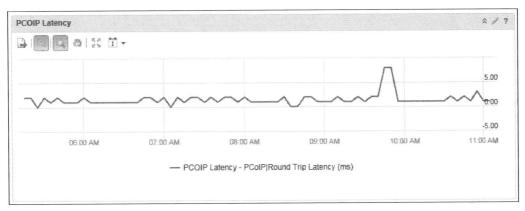

VM PCoIP latency

If there is a performance issue, the above 12-point check should give you the ability to narrow down where the issue is.

Which VDI users need bigger VMs?

Chapter 7, Capacity-Monitoring Dashboards, explains how you can downsize large VMs that are overprovisioned. Let's now look at the opposite use case. We will also use VDI workload, as VDI starts with the minimum configuration and upsizes accordingly. VDI workload also differs from server workload.

Chapter 5, Capacity Monitoring, explains that RAM has different behavior than CPU. As a result, we need different counters for CPU and RAM.

 For CPU, we should use the data from outside the Guest.
For RAM, we should use the data from inside the Guest.

Horizon View gives you visibility inside the Guest as it comes with an agent out of the box. The vRealize Operations agent for Horizon has been integrated into the base Horizon View agent.

The article at `http://virtual-red-dot.info/which-vdi-user-needs-more-cpu-or-ram/` has the details for both CPU and RAM. The following is an example of the result. The **View** widget shows the users along with the key RAM metrics.

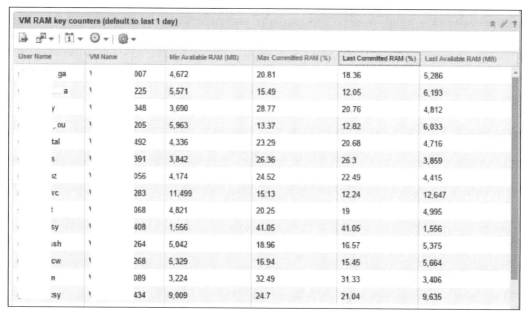

User Name	VM Name		Min Available RAM (MB)	Max Committed RAM (%)	Last Committed RAM (%)	Last Available RAM (MB)
ga	\	007	4,672	20.81	18.36	5,286
a	\	225	5,571	15.49	12.05	6,193
y	\	348	3,690	28.77	20.76	4,812
ou	\	205	5,963	13.37	12.82	6,033
tal	\	492	4,336	23.29	20.68	4,716
s	\	391	3,842	26.36	26.3	3,859
iz	\	056	4,174	24.52	22.49	4,415
vc	\	283	11,499	15.13	12.24	12,647
t	\	068	4,821	20.25	19	4,995
sy	\	408	1,556	41.05	41.05	1,556
ish	\	264	5,042	18.96	16.57	5,375
cw	\	268	5,329	16.94	15.45	5,664
n	\	089	3,224	32.49	31.33	3,406
sy	\	434	9,009	24.7	21.04	9,635

VM memory usage

You need to know when to use this **View** widget. In a VDI environment, there are regular non-user-generated workloads that impact all users. Examples are full AV scans and Windows patches. You should manually exclude the time, as it impacts the result. For example, you typically run the full scans and perform Windows patches on weekends. If you run the preceding list on a Friday, you can go back 5 days but no longer than that.

Summary

We covered quite a number of dashboards and use cases in this chapter. It complements your effort to operationalize performance and capacity monitoring. All in all, they should be sufficient to monitor your VMware environment.

In the next two chapters, we will tap into the expertise of Blue Medora to show you how you can complete your SDDC monitoring by monitoring non-VMware products.

9
Infrastructure Monitoring Using Blue Medora

I have worked with the Blue Medora team for quite some time. Hence, it is not a surprise to me that they have produced many complementary management packs. Customers can also buy their products through VMware and hence benefit from a single contract and support. As a result, I have asked the Blue Medora team to contribute this and the following chapter, as I think it best that it's written by the makers themselves. Mike Langdon and Cameron Jones from Blue Medora are the authors of this chapter and the next one, respectively.

From here onwards, you are getting the information straight from the Blue Medora team.

We will cover the following topics:

- NetApp
- F5 BIG-IP
- Cisco Nexus
- Cisco UCS
- Lenovo Compute
- Dell PowerEdge Servers

Overview

In order not to repeat the material that we've already produced and made available at http://www.bluemedora.com/, we are approaching the product from a different angle.

For each product, we will answer one question.

How healthy is the system?

Broadly speaking, there are three aspects that determine the health of an infrastructure product:

- **Availability**
- **Performance**
- **Configuration**: Suboptimal or wrong configuration can impact performance

Not all three aspects play an equal role. For example, with a server, health is predominantly about availability and configuration. Performance is already covered by ESXi. On the other hand, for storage, health is predominantly driven by performance.

NetApp storage

Storage is often visualized as the bottom of the enterprise hardware stack — and with good reason. Storage resource performance is paramount to a high-performance data center. It underpins the viability of your entire operation. The management pack for NetApp storage brings the machine-learning powers of vRealize to your controllers, LUNs, volumes, aggregates, clusters, and disks, letting you proactively monitor your storage layer.

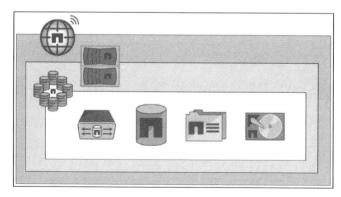

The NetApp logical architecture

Information is collected by way of NetApp's API services, an HTTP REST interface that allows access to NetApp performance data *without affecting performance.*

The key indicators for NetApp performance are latency and IOPS. These metrics are front and center in the **NetApp Overview** dashboard. Heat maps are presented for each piece of a NetApp array, from a high-level roll-up view of the system down to individual volumes. The color of each object gives an immediate reading of its performance:

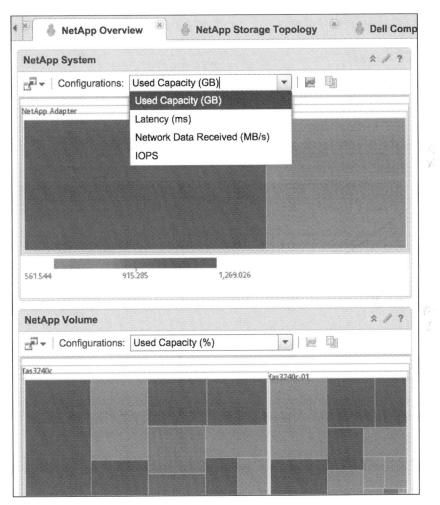

The NetApp Overview dashboard showing problem areas in red

While performance is key for storage, it doesn't mean much without availability. For that, we turn to the **NetApp Storage Topology** dashboard. In this dashboard, the relationships within the NetApp system and out to the virtual layer are highlighted. In this view, interdependencies are revealed and areas of concern can be identified based on these connections. One troubled Virtual Machine may indicate a larger problem for other Virtual Machines using the same NetApp volume:

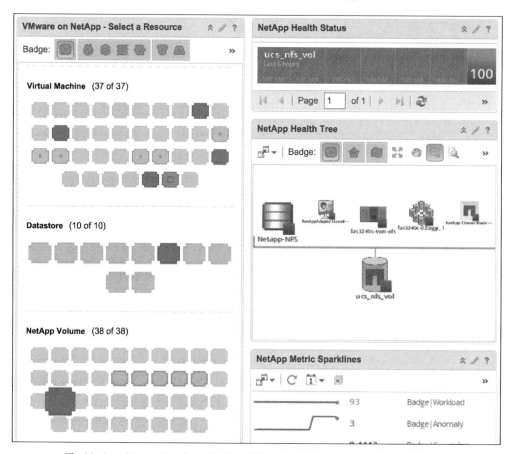

The NetApp Storage Topology dashboard showing the interconnectedness of things

Finally, for NetApp, we can find configuration details in the NetApp Systems dashboard. This dashboard gives us configuration basics, such as the IP of the NetApp system, but it also gives us pressing alerts. These alerts can include outages, out-of-norm metrics, and warnings directly from NetApp's On **Command Unified Manager**:

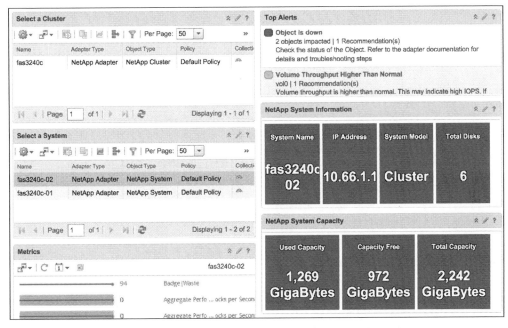

Configuration and alerts with the NetApp Systems dashboard

F5 BIG-IP

F5 BIG-IP is the 500-pound gorilla of **Application Delivery Controllers** (ADCs). BIG-IP's reputation for performance and configurability is unparalleled.

However, the native options for monitoring are limited to a few dashboards or to using SNMP calls and the iControl API manually:

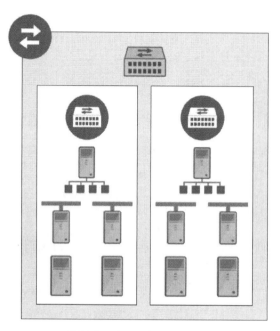

F5 Big IP – Logical architecture

The Blue Medora management pack for BIG-IP does the heavy lifting, going directly to the iControl API. We bring back metrics and configuration data on physical and virtual systems; iApps and application services; and virtual servers, pools, pool members, and nodes.

From there, the management pack connects BIG-IP components—both nodes and virtual systems—to VMs. This gives you a holistic view of BIG-IP that goes beyond the system itself and out to the VMs that make up the apps:

The F5 BIG-IP World Overview dashboard

The F5 BIG-IP **World Overview** dashboard provides easy access to performance and availability for the BIG-IP system as a whole. Scoreboards provide the status on pools, pool members, and virtual servers. Meanwhile, heat maps show performance for systems and nodes:

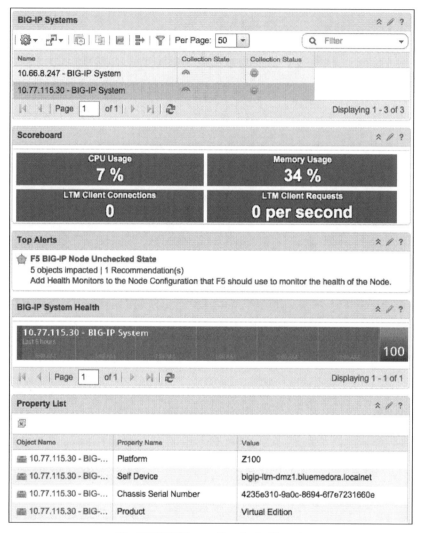

The F5 BIG-IP System Details dashboard

When it comes to configuration, the **F5 BIG-IP System Details** dashboard is the first place to look. Recommendations for best practices can be found here. For example, you will receive a friendly reminder if you have not configured the F5 health monitors on a node.

Cisco Nexus switches

Cisco has long been a major player in enterprise infrastructure. As the workloads running on Cisco servers and through Cisco switches are becoming increasingly virtualized, the necessity of bringing them into a combined view with the virtual layer has heightened.

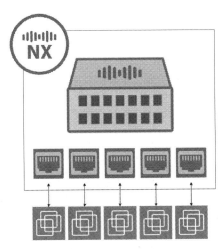

A Cisco Nexus switch

The management pack for Cisco Nexus corrals Nexus series switches via SNMP and associates them with VMs:

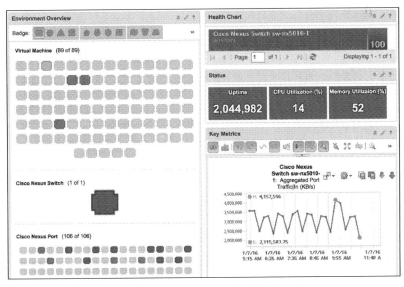

The Cisco Nexus Relationship dashboard

The **Cisco Nexus Relationship** dashboard gets down to business, showing you the status of the ports and the Virtual Machines reliant on those ports. Here, we can see performance data such as port traffic aggregated for the switch, or we can dig into port-level metrics:

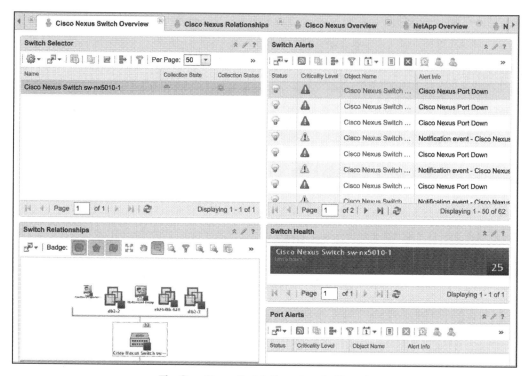

The Cisco Nexus Switch Overview dashboard

For configuration, the **Cisco Nexus Switch Overview** dashboard is the answer. Here, we find alerts for outages and misconfigurations. Port throughput statistics are also available below the folds.

Cisco UCS

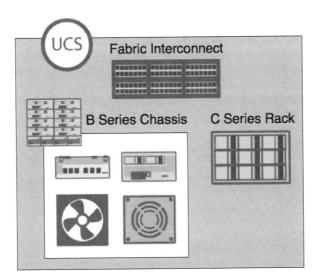

Cisco UCS

Cisco **Unified Computing System (UCS)** is Cisco's scalable, stateless solution for the compute layer with an integrated switch called a fabric interconnect. Our management pack uses the UCS Manager REST API to pull metrics, configuration details, and alerts for the chassis, blades (or servers), fabric interconnects, IO modules (also known as fabric extenders), fans, and power supplies. A common use of Cisco UCS is in the FlexPod converged system, alongside NetApp and Cisco Nexus.

We also provide specialized dashboards to view FlexPod as a whole.

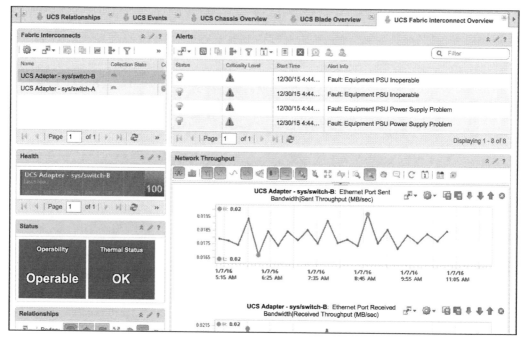

The UCS Fabric Interconnect Overview dashboard

A major performance concern for UCS administrators is throughput for blades and fabric interconnects. The **UCS Fabric Interconnect Overview** and **UCS Blade Overview** dashboards provide throughput metrics over time.

Alerts and key performance indicators for related resources, such as hypervisors for blades, are also provided.

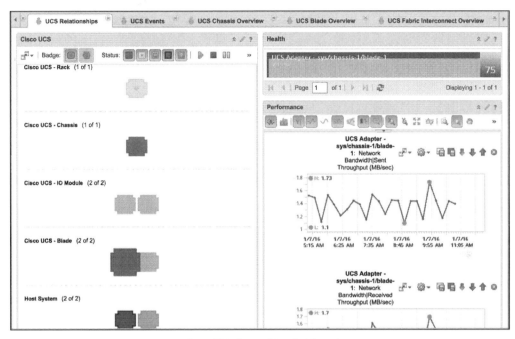

The UCS Relationships dashboard

Meanwhile, the **UCS Relationships** dashboard gives a quick view of problem areas in the entire UCS landscape. Beyond that, you can see hosts and VMs that are affected by UCS availability issues.

Lenovo Compute

Next comes our management pack for Lenovo compute. We support both chassis and blade configurations and standalone racks. This management pack gives you the option of connecting via Lenovo's XClarity REST API or via SNMP. With this solution, we have focused on availability, configuration, and the connection to the virtual layer. For a more comprehensive view of your Lenovo deployments, we also offer a management pack for Lenovo Network:

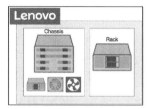

Lenovo Compute

The **Lenovo Compute Overview** dashboard allows you to have an at-a-glance appraisal of server and chassis health. A red or yellow rectangle means trouble is around the corner.

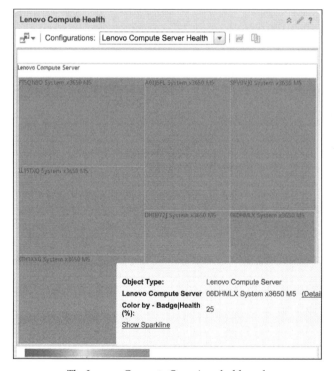

The Lenovo Compute Overview dashboard

If we identify an issue with a rack on the general overview dashboard, we can then progress to the **Lenovo Compute Rack Overview** dashboard, where we can dig into the details. Here, we will find any alerts for the rack and see the affected hypervisors.

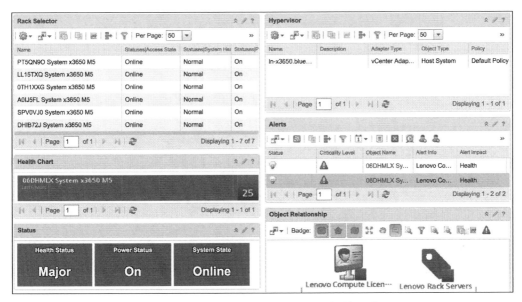

The Lenovo Compute Rack Overview dashboard

For the status of all your Lenovo compute elements, the **Lenovo Compute Relationships** dashboard provides a complete view. Here, we can immediately understand which VMs are endangered by a possible outage on a particular server.

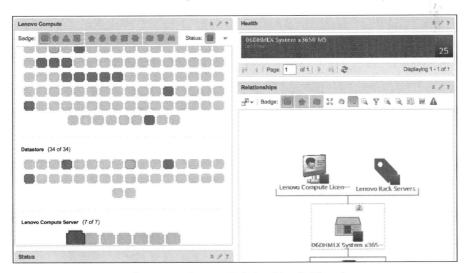

The Lenovo Compute Relationships dashboard

Dell PowerEdge servers

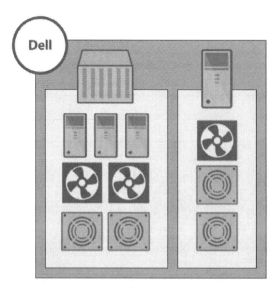

A Dell PowerEdge server

We will end this chapter with a discussion of our management pack for Dell PowerEdge servers. Once again, this solution covers both scalable-chassis and standalone server configurations. On the availability side of things, we'll look at mundane objects—power supplies and fans—that can conspire to ruin your day. We'll also alert you to misconfiguration, such as a disabled BIOS.

This management pack connects to your Dell servers via SNMP.

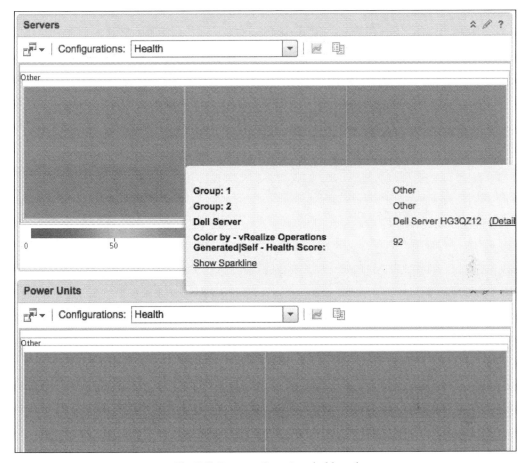

The Dell Compute Overview dashboard

The **Dell Compute Overview** dashboard presents health states for servers, power units, and fans (or cooling units, as Dell would have you call them). This is your morning-coffee view of your Dell PowerEdge systems.

A big red rectangle here probably means a trip to the racks, but at least you caught it before operations were hindered.

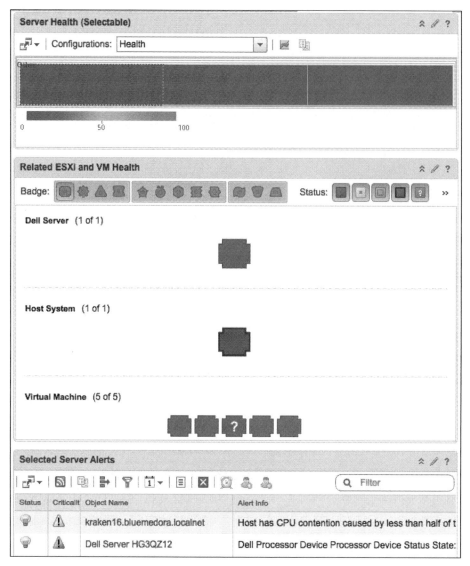

The Dell Compute Health Investigation dashboard

Before trudging off to the data center, a look at the **Dell Compute Health Investigation** dashboard is warranted. Here, you will notice the VMs relying on your Dell server, and you can track down the top alerts affecting your system.

Summary

We covered how you can complete your SDDC infrastructure monitoring by monitoring the non-VMware components of your SDDC. You should have the dashboards you need to quickly identify the health of these components. At Blue Medora, we regularly release new products to complement vRealize Operations and vRealize Log Insight.

In the next chapter, we will cover the application layer. This makes your investment in vRealize Operations more complete, as you can see end to end from application to infrastructure.

10
Application Monitoring Using Blue Medora

In *Chapter 9, Infrastructure Monitoring Using Blue Medora*, we showed you how you can ensure the health of your infrastructure using Blue Medora's management packs. However, our management packs do not end there. We cover the entire stack, from hardware to applications. In this chapter, we will talk about only a few of our many application and database management packs available through Blue Medora. This list is constantly growing. To see a full list of our products at any time, visit us at `http://www.bluemedora.com/`.

In this chapter, we will cover the following topics:

- Microsoft SQL Server
- Oracle EM
- Citrix XenDesktop and XenApp
- IBM Tivoli
- IBM DB2
- SAP HANA

Overview

As shared in the previous chapter, we are approaching the product from a different angle.

For each product, we will answer one question:

How healthy is the system?

Broadly speaking, there are three aspects that determine the health of a software product:

- **Availability**
- **Performance**
- **Configuration**: Suboptimal or wrong configuration can impact performance

Microsoft SQL Server

Microsoft SQL Server (MS SQL) is one of the most deployed databases in the enterprise world. It is not surprising that many of our vRealize customers request top-of-the-line monitoring for this database. Using the management pack for Microsoft SQL Server, the VMware administrator can quickly identify whether any performance degradation is a result of poor database performance or whether the root cause is actually the underlying virtual infrastructure. The management pack has hundreds of in-depth performance and capacity metrics that allow the VMware administrator and the DBA to quickly identify the root cause of any performance issue.

First, let's take a look at performance. At Blue Medora, we provide in-depth dashboards that give the administrator the information they need to solve any problem. These dashboards may seem complicated; however, they are actually very simple and easy to use. While looking at performance, let's take a look at two specific dashboards:

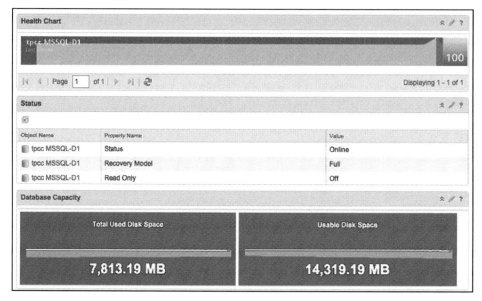

The MS SQL Database dashboard

The first dashboard we are going to look at is called the **MS SQL Database** dashboard. This dashboard shows an in-depth view of any database that the administrator has promoted. In the top-left corner of the dashboard, we can see two selectors. One of them is for selecting any MS SQL server we have configured in our instance of **vRealize Operations** (**vROps**). The following selector is for choosing the specific database we wish to monitor.

Once we have selected a database, the rest of our page will load with metrics about that resource. Next to the selectors, we will show the most pertinent information first: health and availability. By default, we can see the health over time for the past 6 hours. This allows us to not only ensure that our database is healthy now, but has been healthy while we were away. If the health is below 100, there will be a related alert that we can investigate.

These alerts come from two separate sources. The first type of alert comes from vRealize Operations. We call these native alerts. Our management packs get all the backend benefits from vROps that the VMware resources get. What do I mean by that? Any metric that we collect and store in vROps is subject to vROps' machine-learning algorithms. This means that on top of learning the VMware environment, vROps will learn the MS SQL environment as well. vROps will then set dynamic thresholds, allowing us to be alerted when those thresholds are breached. These alerts allow us to see problems before they occur, following trends to give us warnings before there is performance degradation. The second source of alerts comes straight from MS SQL. Any alert that would normally be raised in an MS SQL instance is now also shown in vRealize Operations. These alerts will also affect the health score of the database, allowing us to quickly identify any current issues that may be happening. Both types of alerts will be prominently displayed in the **Alerts** widget to the right of our selectors. From there, we can double-click on any of these alerts to get more information on what is really going on in our environment.

If we need to dig deeper into any issues, we can now look at the performance metrics provided by our management pack. This dashboard includes information on the database size, disk operations, log sizes, and index performance. We can quickly scroll through the dashboard to see whether anything is out of place. Of course, if there are any key metrics that the administrator would like to add to this dashboard, all of our dashboards are completely customizable. Our dashboards are built to serve as many people as possible, but we know that every environment is unique. If there is a key metric that a team finds important and is not displayed in the dashboard, it is easy to add. We collect hundreds of metrics for the administrator to choose from.

The next dashboard that is important to look at while diagnosing issues is the **MS SQL Server VM Relationship** dashboard. Although our management pack allows the administrator to monitor any MS SQL instance (virtualized or not), this dashboard allows us to diagnose issues faced by the MS SQL server running on VMware. Let's take a quick look at it.

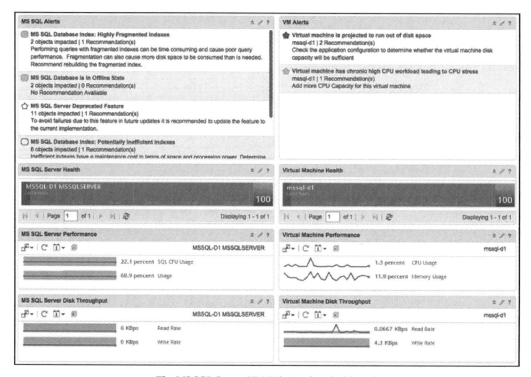

The MS SQL Server VM Relationship dashboard

On the left-hand side of the screen, we can see our two selectors again. This time, they are for the MS SQL server and the virtual hosts, or VMs. Once we have selected both our objects, we can see a relationship tree that shows us all the objects related to our MS SQL server.

In the middle column, we will get important data about the MS SQL server. Once again, we start with alerts and health, immediately showing us whether anything is wrong with our database. Once we have identified whether something is wrong, we can see **Key Performance Indicators** (**KPIs**) focused around CPU, memory, and disk.

In the final column, we can see key metrics around the Virtual Machine, very much in the same order. We can see whether there are any alerts or health issues, and then CPU, memory and disk metrics are also displayed for the Virtual Machine.

As we take in this dashboard in as a whole, we can quickly identify where an issue may lie. If we have an alert on the MS SQL server, is it contained just to that resource, or is the issue being caused by the underlying virtual infrastructure? In this case, we can see that our Virtual Machine has resource contention, leading to it being stressed. This will inevitably cause issues for the MS SQL server. To prevent any performance issues, we will need to provision our VM with more resources.

Now that we have covered performance, we will also want to look at availability. Availability is naturally a very important thing when monitoring our applications and databases. At Blue Medora, we try to make it clear immediately when we notice that we cannot collect data on any of the instances that are configured. When we find this to be the case, we do two things: first, we create an alert and then, we drop the health score to critical. But how does the administrator identify where these issues are? We have two places to quickly investigate them. The first is the **Alerts** page provided by **vROps**. The second is our **MS SQL Server Overview** dashboard:

Criticality ▼	▼	Alert	Alert Type	Alert Subtype	Status
●		MS SQL Database Is In Offline State	Application	Configuration	💡
●		MS SQL Database Index: Highly Fragmented Indexes	Application	Configuration	💡
●		MS SQL Database Index: Highly Fragmented Indexes	Application	Configuration	💡
⬠		MS SQL Server Deprecated Feature	Application	Configuration	💡
○		MS SQL Database Index: Unused Maintained Indexes	Application	Configuration	💡

MS SQL Alerts

On the alerts page provided by vROps, we can quickly see any alert in our environment. These alerts can come from VMware, MS SQL, or any other management pack that is installed. To make this easier to filter though, we have allowed our users to filter by object type. We can see a filter in the previous screenshot of MS SQL Alerts. This allows us to see alerts only for our MS SQL management pack. Here, we can see a few critical alerts, which show that we cannot connect to some of our MS SQL instances. When we identify an issue such as this, it usually means one of two things. The first is that the credentials have changed or expired.

The second is that we are no longer able to reach the instance because it has been taken down, moved, or deleted. At this point, we should check the VM it is hosted on as well as our credentials that we use to connect:

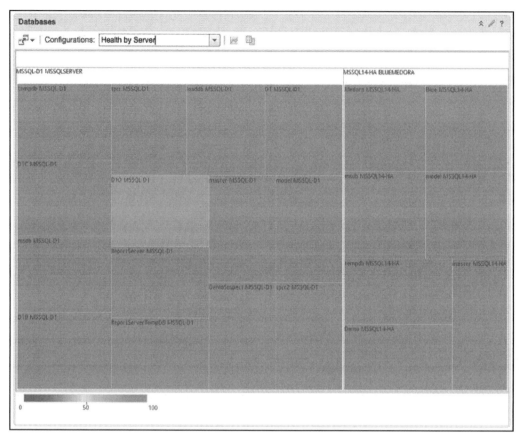

The MS SQL Server Overview dashboard

We have also provided an **easy-to-use** dashboard that shows the health of all the MS SQL objects in vROps. Here, we can see the health of our MS SQL servers, MS SQL databases, and MS SQL always-on Availability Groups. If any of these are red, it means there is a critical alert on them. From here, we can click on the Show Detail button after selecting the red object in order to investigate the alert. Most often, these alerts occur because the objects are unavailable. This dashboard makes it easy to quickly identify when we are no longer able to access an object.

The last part of ensuring our database is healthy is to look at configuration. The MS SQL management pack is easy to configure, agentless, and requires read-only permissions. We have a one-to-one relationship between configured instances and MS SQL servers, so it is impossible to flood the vROps environment. However, there are some things the administrator should look for when monitoring their environment:

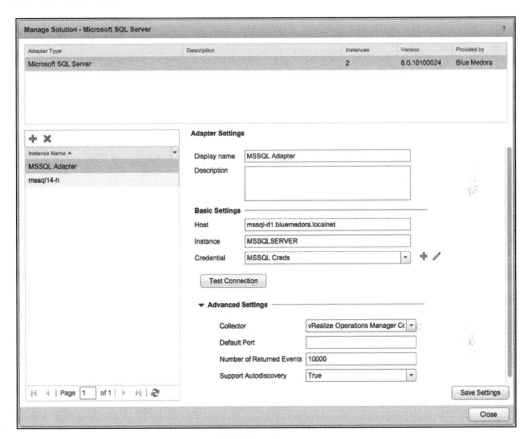

MS SQL configuration

First, under the **Advanced Configuration**, the default setting is to collect 10,000 MS SQL events. These are events in MS SQL that can be turned into alerts in vROps. 10,000 is a safe default, but in larger environments, the administrator may want to add more. It is important that they ensure that their environment can handle adding more events.

Events count as metrics, so use the VMware Sizing Guide to ensure there is enough room to collect more events before changing the default:

MS SQL Discovery Action

We also realize that it may be hard to always use the one-to-one configuration. So, we have added in an action that allows the administrator to discover all MS SQL instances on a given domain. Although it is unlikely that the administrator floods their environment, if they do have a large MS SQL installation and a small vROps installation, it may be wise to use the Sizing Guide before running this action.

The management pack for Microsoft SQL Server allows the administrator a quick glance as well as an in-depth look at performance, availability, and configuration, which allows them to quickly see any health issues that may arise in their environment.

Oracle Enterprise Manager

The management pack for **Oracle Enterprise Manager** (OEM) works differently from our other database and application management packs. This is because OEM is an enterprise-monitoring tool itself. OEM allows Oracle DBAs to monitor their Oracle Database instance, Oracle RAC, ASM, and any other Oracle workload. Our management pack will bring that data from OEM into vRealize Operations. Whether the administrator is looking to move from OEM to vROps or just wants the same data their DBAs are looking at, the management pack for Oracle Enterprise Manager works great for seeing these workloads.

Because an Oracle DBA can have many different types of workloads running in OEM, our configuration allows the vROps admin to choose specifically what they want to see. If a brand new plugin is added to an OEM system, we can bring that data straight into vROps as well. This allows us to collect data from any Oracle workload that a DBA may monitor:

The management pack for Oracle Enterprise Manager comes with many dashboards that allow the user to monitor the performance of their Oracle workloads. One of the most important workloads is Oracle Database. Here is an screenshot of the **Oracle DB VM Mashup** dashboard:

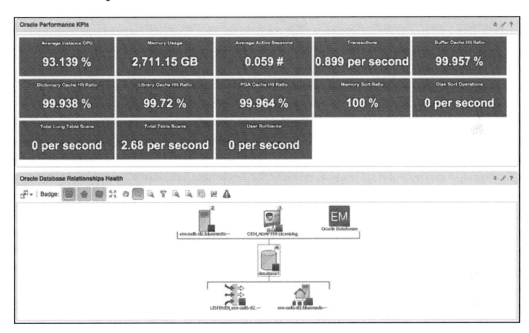

The Oracle DB VM Mashup dashboard

In the top-left corner, there is a selector that allows us to look at any Oracle Database instance in our OEM instances. Once a database is selected, the dashboard will show key data about it. One of the primary widgets, shown in the top-left corner, shows data about alerts. Any current issues with the database will be brought to the administrator's attention immediately. Just like the management pack for Microsoft SQL Server, we have native vROps alerts as well as alerts straight from Oracle Enterprise Manager:

When an alert comes in from OEM, vROps will give the user more information about the issue and provide a link back to OEM. In OEM, we will be provided with more details about that alert and be able clear it once the issue is taken care of:

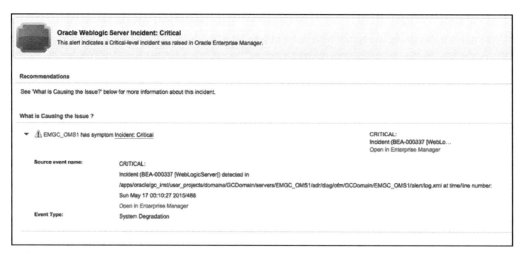

An alert that links back to Oracle Enterprise Manager

This feature comes in handy when moving from OEM to vROps or just troubleshooting an issue with a DBA.

As we continue to move down the **Oracle DB VM Mashup** dashboard, we will be provided with KPIs. These KPIs are available for both Oracle Database as well as the virtual machine. Oracle Database metrics consist of information based on the sessions, SGA settings, hits, sorts, transactions, memory, and CPU. While metrics related to the Virtual Machine consist of CPU, memory, swap, and disk latency. This data is shown primarily through scoreboards, allowing us to quickly identify whether there is an issue in the database or the Virtual Machine hosting it.

Towards the bottom of the dashboard, there are two more widgets that continue to give us a better view of the performance of our Oracle Database instance. The first widget shows us the relationships between this database and any other OEM target it is related to. For example, an Oracle Database instance may be related to a listener or OEM host. These relationships help us quickly identify whether an issue we see in the database target has propagated to any other target in OEM. The second widget shows configuration information related to the database. Examples of this can be the version of the database or the CPU counts on the Virtual Machine. Once we find the root cause of the problem, we can ensure that these configuration settings are valid for this Oracle Database instance.

Availability is the next area we will want to investigate. This management pack pulls each OEM object's availability straight from OEM. If we cannot connect to the OEM box, we will automatically know that none of our objects are available. To display this data, we use the **Oracle EM Overview** dashboard, which can display data for every OEM resource type:

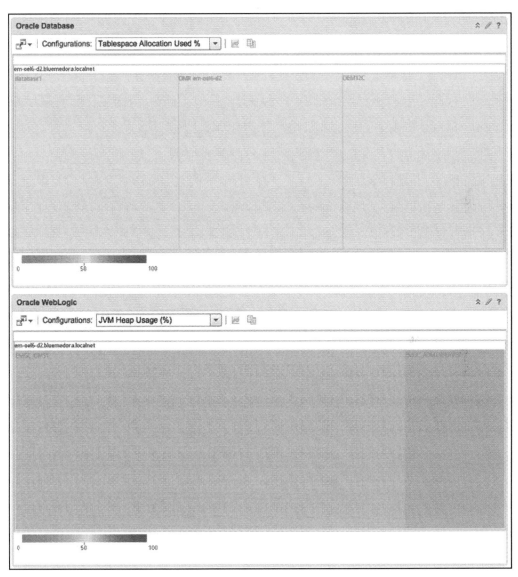

Some resources monitored by the Oracle EM Overview dashboard

In this dashboard, we show the health of all objects in our OEM environment. These objects are shown using **heatmaps** that allow an at-a-glance view of the health of each object. When an object is red, it often means it is unavailable. Using this dashboard, we can quickly ensure that all of our OEM resources are healthy and available:

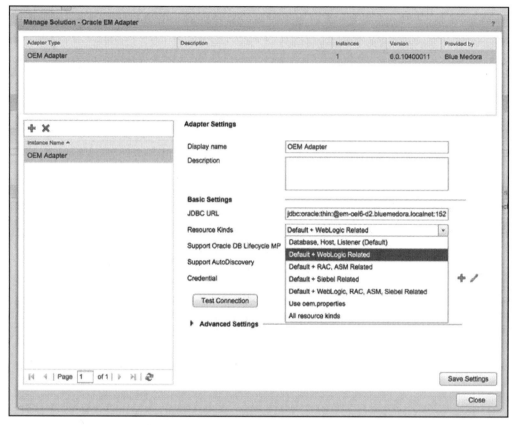

Default configurations for the OEM management pack

Configuration in the management pack for OEM can be tricky. Because the management pack can pull in so many different resources from OEM, it is important that we do not flood our vROps environment. To ensure there aren't too many resources, we have created a number of options to help the administrator quickly add the resources most important to them. In the previous screenshot, we can see that we have created quick configuration of the database, host, listener, RAC, ASM, Siebel, and Weblogic objects. However, if the administrator would like to customize this list, they can select the **Use oem.properties** option.

This selection allows the administrator to use two configuration files to monitor any resource type available in OEM. These configuration files also allow the user to select individual metrics they want to collect on these resource kinds. This allows complete customization of the OEM management pack:

```
#minimum trailing time (from 'now') to query in minutes, default is 1min
minQueryWindow=1

#allowedResourceKinds  Oracle EM Target Types to collect
allowedResourceKinds=host,oracle_database,oracle_listener

#resourceUpStatuses
resourceUpStatuses=Target Up

#schema that contains OEM objects
schema=SYSMAN

#number of records to fetch at a time when reading data
mainFetchSize=500
```

Advanced OEM configuration

The management pack for OEM is extremely powerful. It allows the user to pull in hundreds of different resources and metrics. However, it is important to use these configuration files to ensure that the environment does not get flooded. The management pack for OEM is perfect for viewing any Oracle workload in vRealize Operations.

Citrix XenDesktop and XenApp

We have many customers who run Citrix workloads on VMware. The first part of our Citrix solution is the management pack for Citrix XenDesktop and XenApp. This management pack allows VMware administrators to see all their Citrix workloads inside of vROps. The management pack also creates relationships between Citrix components, the underlying database (using the management pack for MS SQL), and any related Virtual Machine. This allows the administrator to get a complete view of their Citrix workloads.

To help you diagnose an issue, we have dozens of dashboards that look at the specific details of any Citrix resource in vROps. From the site to the VDA, you can see data on each resource type, allowing you to find the exact location of any performance issue in the user's Citrix environment. Our **User and Session Details** dashboard is one of the most powerful:

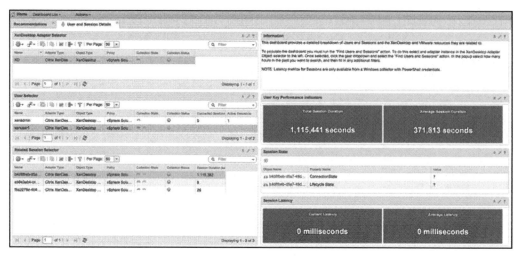

The User and Session Details dashboard

The previous screenshot shows the **User and Session Details** dashboard. This dashboard allows us to monitor the session and login times of individual Citrix users. This dashboard is key for a Citrix administrator. When a user informs the administrator that their session is slow or that it took them a long time to log in, this management pack can locate that session using vROps' powerful Action Framework. When the user runs the out-of-the-box action, they will get data on those specific sessions.

Using the selectors at the top, the user can find the session that is having trouble. Then, the rest of this dashboard will be populated with data. Not only will the administrator see more data on a specific session (such as time, state, and latency), but they will also see any other vROps objects that are related to that session. For example, the dashboard will show exactly which application or desktop the user was using as well as important KPIs for that object.

The dashboard also shows the related VMware objects, such as the Virtual Machine, ESXi host, and datastore. This allows the administrator to go all the way from the user's session to the underlying virtual infrastructure to diagnose the latency problem:

The XenDesktop Overview dashboard

Handling availability in this management pack is very similar to the previous two. We primarily use two functions: the alerts and overview dashboards. The management pack will throw an alert anytime it cannot access a specific Citrix component. If that alert is thrown, details will be given on why the management pack cannot access the Citrix object and turn the health red. The management pack comes with a **XenDesktop Overview** dashboard, which will show these health statuses for any Citrix component. In this view, we can see that there is a red **Machine Catalog**, indicating that it is most likely unreachable.

Using the alerts and this dashboard allows us to quickly identify any Citrix availability problems we may have:

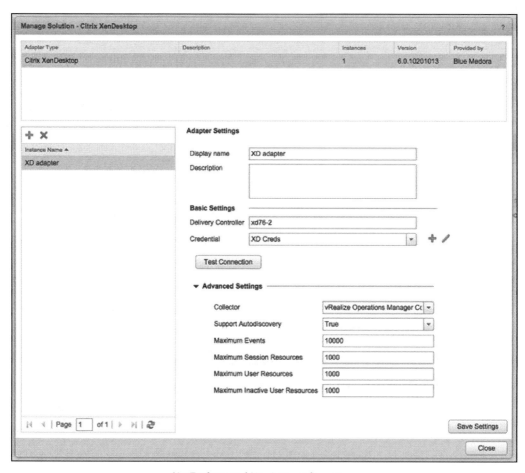

XenDesktop and XenApp configuration

The management pack for Citrix XenDesktop and XenApp allows the administrator to quickly see user and session information using the Action Framework. However, the administrator needs to be careful of how many sessions they bring back at a given time. Configuration is extremely important for this. In the advanced settings of the management pack, the configuration allows the user to set how many sessions they want to pull back with every collection. In this case, we see that we have it set to 1,000. 1,000 is a safe number in many environments. However, it may be possible to increase this number to provide more session data. Make sure to consult the **Sizing Guide** and look at what other objects are bringing pulled into vRealize Operations before increasing the number of objects brought back.

The management pack for Citrix XenDesktop and XenApp is just the first step of Blue Medora's Citrix solution. It allows Citrix and VMware administrators alike to monitor their workloads quickly inside of vROps. Unlike any other monitoring solution, Citrix administrators now get the predictive analysis and machine learning that vRealize provides, creating the most powerful monitoring solution to date.

IBM Tivoli

IBM Tivoli has been a key infrastructure solution for many administrators for years. It can be hard to make the move to vRealize as the primary monitoring tool when there is years of information still on Tivoli. Fortunately, the management pack for IBM Tivoli can bring back all the data that has been collected in IBM Tivoli straight into vRealize Operations.

There are many scenarios that may lead an administrator to bring data from Tivoli to vROps. The one mentioned in the previous paragraph is just one example. Another reason to use the management pack for IBM Tivoli is to support a technology that is not supported by a vRealize management pack but is supported by an agent in Tivoli. Either way, the administrator can bring any workload monitored by IBM Tivoli and display it in vRealize Operations.

Once these workloads are inside of vROps, the administrator can monitor them like they would any other management pack. The first thing we will want to investigate is performance. Let's take a look at one resource kind we often see promoted: the Linux OS. Although OS monitoring is already supported by EP Ops (or Hyperic), it can be a pain to redeploy all the agents that are already deployed for Tivoli. Instead of redeploying all these agents, just use the management pack for IBM Tivoli:

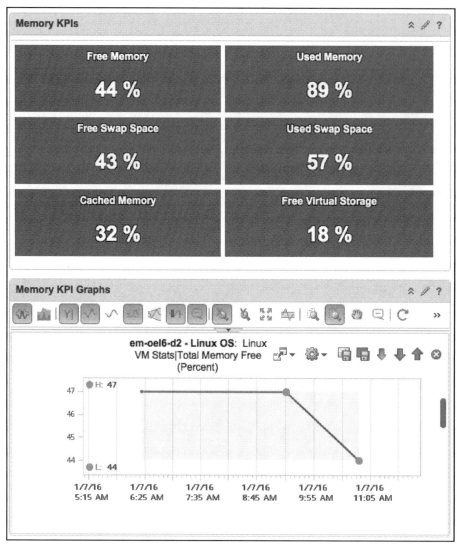

The Linux OS dashboard

The **Linux OS** dashboard will give us a deeper look at performance. This dashboard allows us to see KPIs of any selected Linux OS. In this dashboard, the top row is full of selectors for the OS, processors, and physical disks. Once each of these resources is selected, the second row will display KPIs for each specific component. Some of these KPIs consist of metrics that show memory, CPU, and disk space. Finally, in the third row, some of these KPIs are displayed over time, so that the administrator can truly see the health of the Linux box.

The management pack provides many dashboards to be able to quickly identify performance of key objects inside of Tivoli. Besides the **Linux OS** dashboard previously mentioned, dashboards for DB2, Websphere, and Windows OS are provided. Since any Tivoli workload can be monitored in vROps using the management pack, these dashboards are highly customizable for displaying these workloads:

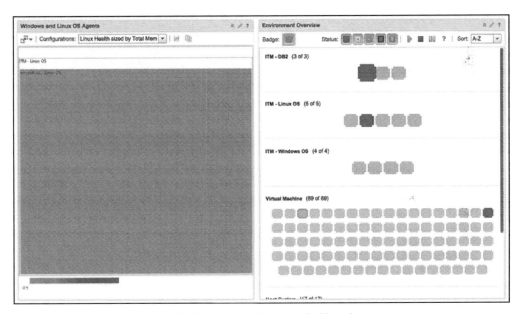

The Environment Overview dashboard

To take a closer look at availability, the **Environment Overview** dashboard should be used. This dashboard shows availability a little differently than previous management packs. In the left-hand side column, we have specialized widgets that show us the health of any OS (Linux or Windows) that we are monitoring. In the right-hand side column, we also have widgets that show all our **Least Healthy** OS agents. This allows us to quickly identify whether any of our OS agents need to be fixed. In the center however, we have an environment overview dashboard that brings in a number of Tivoli-monitored workloads and displays their health. When the administrator selects an object, they will see its health based on the color-coding of the object. It will also display any other object that the selected object is related to. That includes the VM, ESXi host, and datastore. At a glance, we can quickly identify whether any of these objects are available:

```
#
Linux OS | Linux CPU        | P | 5
Linux OS | Linux Disk       | P | 5
Linux OS | Linux VM Stats | X | 5
#
Summarization and Pruning Agent | KSY CONNECTIVITY              | X | 5
Summarization and Pruning Agent | KSY NODE FAILURES            |   | 5
Summarization and Pruning Agent | KSY SUMMARIZATION CONFIG     | X | 5
Summarization and Pruning Agent | KSY SUMMARIZATION STATISTICS | X | 5
Summarization and Pruning Agent | KSY TABLE STATISTICS         |   | 5
#
```

Advanced configuration

Because **IBM Tivoli Monitoring (ITM)** can have so many aggregate groups that get turned into resources in vROps, configuration is extremely important. We ship our product with a configuration file that brings in key aggregate groups automatically. However, this file allows the administrator to add as many different aggregate groups as they want. If too many aggregate groups get added, it could lead to environment flooding. To prevent this from happening, it is important to size the environment before adding too much customization to the file. This file will allow the administrator to bring in any new aggregate group they wish to.

Like the management pack for OEM, the management pack for ITM is extremely powerful. It can bring in any resource from the infrastructure built on ITM. These metrics are more powerful than ever before, taking advantage of the vROps machine-learning backend. This new power will take the ITM experience to a whole new level.

IBM DB2

The management pack for IBM DB2 is one of the major databases represented in our **vROps Database Solution**. This management pack is key for any VMware administrator who wants to ensure their databases are healthy, available, and unaffected by performance degradation. It also provides in-depth metrics down to the query level, which allow users to ensure the actual database's health as well as the underlying infrastructure's:

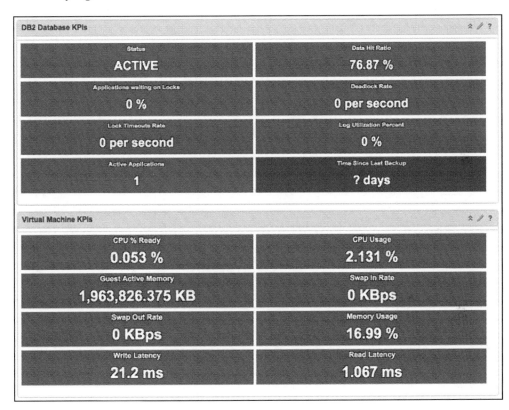

The DB2 on VM dashboard

When looking at performance, there are two primary dashboards that the administrator can use. The first is the **DB2 on VM** dashboard. This dashboard helps give the administrator a view of any DB2 database that they are virtualizing. Like the dashboard shown in the management pack for MS SQL, this dashboard's primary feature is that it shows this product and how it relates to VMware. The ability to see both these metrics side by side allows us to quickly diagnose the root cause of any issue.

In the left-hand side of this dashboard, we have two selectors. When we select a DB2 database from the top, the Virtual Machine it is running on will automatically get selected below. Once these objects are selected, the widgets on the right will immediately start to be populated with key metrics about each. For the database, metrics about locks, deadlocks, and hit ratios will be displayed. As for the VM, CPU, memory, swap, and write/read latency are the primary focus areas. If there is any issue with the database, we can quickly identify whether it is related to the Virtual Machine:

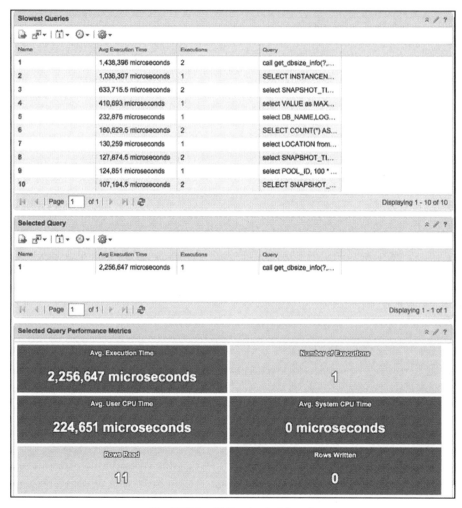

The DB2 Top-N Queries dashboard

When the administrator wants to dig in deeper and show important metrics about the database, they should start with the **DB2 Top-N Queries** dashboard. This dashboard allows the administrator to see all of the top metrics by query execution time. Let's start by looking at the top half of the dashboard. In the top left, there is a selector that allows us to select any database we have promoted. When a database is selected, the top 10 slowest queries we be populated in the widget next to it. This widget will show data about the average execution time, the number of times the query has been run, and the actual text of the query.

The bottom half gives us even more detail, focused on query information. On the left, we have a heatmap that also acts as a selector. We can select this heatmap to show data based on query execution time, user CPU time, or system CPU time. Because this data is formatted in a heatmap, it helps us quickly identify any outliers. Once the administrator selects the query in the heatmap, they can see information on that individual query on the widget to the right. We can see data such as how many times it was run, the average execution time, and how many rows were read.

The configuration of this management pack is simple. We do not need to worry about resource flooding or advanced configuration. Everything simply works! However, to ensure that all metrics are being collected, ensure the following is enabled on the DB2 side:

- The `HEALTH_MON` DB2 configuration parameter
- The switch for monitoring statements
- Permissions for the management pack to query the lock waits in the administrative view
- Table monitoring (`DFT_MON_TABLE`) for the database being monitored

This is well documented in our installation guide, which has commands on how to activate each of these properties. Once the administrator has everything set up, all of the management pack's metrics can be collected.

SAP HANA

The management pack for SAP HANA is important for two of our solutions at Blue Medora. Firstly, it is our first NoSQL database in our Database Solution. It is also one of our two management packs that allow full monitoring for SAP (the other being our management pack for SAP):

One of the key dashboards to use when monitoring SAP HANA is the **SAP HANA on VMware Layer View** dashboard. Like many of our other dashboards, it focuses on the concept of showing SAP HANA on VMware. This helps us quickly identify whether the underlying infrastructure will cause any issues to our SAP HANA installation:

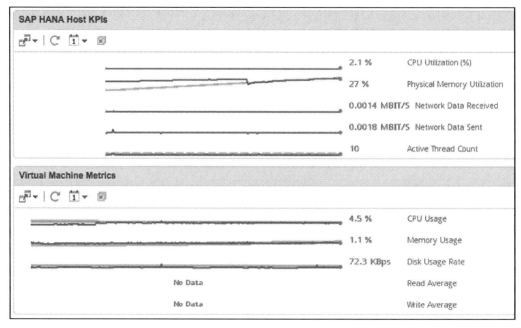

The SAP HANA on VMware Layer View dashboard

In the left-hand side, we will see all of our selectors. This dashboard has selectors for the SAP HANA System, the SAP HANA host, the Virtual Machine that the HANA host is running on, and the underlying ESXi host. In the right-hand side, we can see key metrics for SAP as well as for the virtual layer below it. These metrics will quickly show us any issues that may have occurred in the past few hours:

Another key dashboard for performance is the **SAP HANA Environment Overview** dashboard. This dashboard gives the administrator key metrics for any of their HANA environments as well as the virtual layer under it:

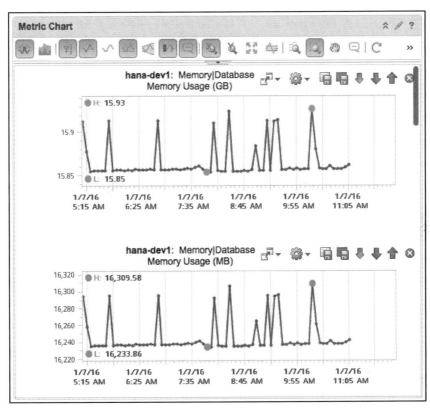

The SAP HANA Environment Overview dashboard

In the left-hand side, there is a heatmap that displays any SAP HANA host based on selectable metrics, such as CPU percent, table growth, or disk utilization. Under the heatmap, the dashboard displays data about the top five least healthy hosts by CPU percent, SELECT statements per second, and memory used. In the next two columns, we have an **Environment View** that acts as a selector. We can select any HANA or VMware object, and in the two columns on the right-hand side, any metric available to that object will be displayed. This helps the administrator dig in and see any metric the management pack collects. This dashboard is key when the administrator really needs to see metrics that are not always in the forefront.

This dashboard is also important when looking at availability. In this middle column, we can always see the health of any HANA component. If one of these components is red, we know it is possible that it is because the object is unavailable. We can select the component and navigate to the **Selected Resource Metrics** widget. Using this widget, the administrator can select the vRealize Operations Generated and find availability. Once availability is selected, it will be loaded into the **Metric Chart** widget. If the metric's value is 0, the HANA resource is unavailable:

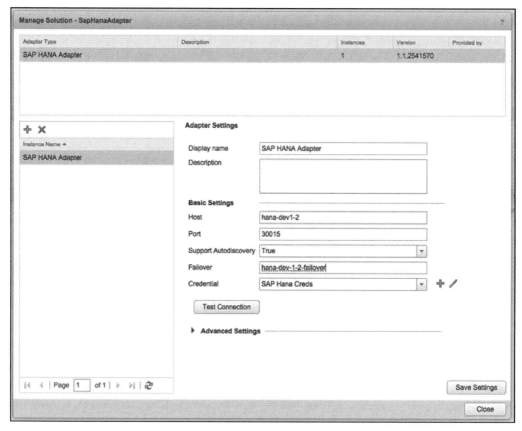

SAP HANA configuration

The SAP HANA management pack is simple to configure. However, if the administrator is using failover in their HANA environment (and wants to monitor it in vROps), there will be an additional field to fill out in the SAP HANA configuration panel. The **Failover** field will need to be filled with a comma-separated list of any backup HANA hosts that may be set up. Now, if failover happens in the HANA environment, vROps will immediately start to monitor the backed-up HANA host.

Summary

We covered how you can complete your SDDC monitoring by monitoring non-VMware components of your SDDC. With Blue Medora, you can monitor both the infrastructure and application layers. This complete visibility enables you to have better insight into your SDDC.

This chapter takes us to the end of Part 2 of the book. You should have enough dashboards to operationalize your SDDC monitoring. Part 3 of the book is more of a reference. We will take a tour of all the counters in vCenter and vRealize Operations. At over 100 pages of explanation, this tour is going to take a while, so sit back and enjoy!

Part 3
Counters

Part 3 acts as a reference section. It documents in depth all the counters in vCenter and vRealize Operations. It covers the metrics from 2 dimensions, so you get a more complete perspective.

- The first dimension is by vSphere objects. We cover all the metrics from VM to World objects. You will be able to see what metrics are available, or not available, as we move from VM to World.

- The second dimension is by the 4 elements of infrastructure: CPU, RAM, Disk and Network. You will be able to see what each metric means for each element.

vRealize Operations does not simply regurgitate the counters that vCenter has. It starts by understanding the unique behavior of vSphere, then simplifying it by consolidating and standardizing the counters. For example, vRealize Operations creates derived counters such as Contention and Workload, then applies them to CPU, RAM, disk, and network.

Not all vSphere-specific characteristics are properly understood by management tools that are not designed for SDDC. Partial understanding can lead to misunderstanding as wrong interpretation of counters can result in wrong action taken.

Part 3 consists of 5 chapters

- Chapter 11 covers the counters by vSphere objects.
- Chapter 12 covers CPU in depth.
- Chapter 13 covers Memory in depth
- Chapter 14 covers Storage in depth
- Chapter 15 covers Network in depth

11
SDDC Key Counters

I have explained what *Part 3* covers, so let's begin the journey into the wonderful world of counters.

In this chapter, we will start *Part 3* by covering the following:

- Counters related to compute (CPU and RAM)
- Counters related to storage
- Counters related to network
- All metric groups in vCenter and vRealize Operations

Compute

The following diagram shows how a VM gets its resources from ESXi. It is a pretty complex diagram, so let me walk you through it. We are using RAM as the example, although the concept applies to CPU too:

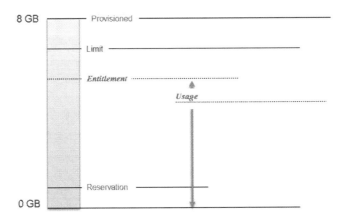

How a VM gets its resources

The tall rectangular area represents a VM. Say this VM is given **8 GB** of virtual RAM. The bottommost line represents **0 GB** and the topmost line represents **8 GB**. The VM is configured with **8 GB** of RAM. We call this **Provisioned**. This is what the Guest OS sees, so if it is running Windows, you will see **8 GB** of RAM when you log in to Windows.

Unlike a physical server, you can configure a **Limit** and a **Reservation** in a VM. This is done outside the Guest OS, so Windows or Linux does not know. You should minimize the use of **Limit** and **Reservation** as it makes SDDC operations more complex.

Entitlement means what the VM is entitled to. In this example, the hypervisor entitles the VM to a certain amount of memory. I have not shown a solid line and used an *italic* font style to mark that **Entitlement** is not a fixed value but a dynamic one determined by the hypervisor. It varies every minute, determined by the **Limit**, **Entitlement**, and **Reservation** of the VM itself and any shared allocation with other VMs running on the same host.

Obviously, a VM can only use what it is entitled to at any given point of time, so the **Usage** counter cannot go higher than the **Entitlement** counter. The green line shows that **Usage** ranges from **0** to the **Entitlement** value.

In a healthy environment, the ESXi host has enough resources to meet the demands of all the VMs on it with sufficient overhead. In this case, you will see that the **Entitlement**, **Usage**, and **Demand** counters will be similar to one another when the VM is highly utilized. This is shown by the green line, on which **Demand** stops at **Usage** and **Usage** stops at **Entitlement**.

The numerical value may not be identical, because vCenter reports **Usage** in percentage, and it is an average value of the sample period. vCenter reports **Entitlement** in MHz and it takes the latest value in the sample period. It reports **Demand** in MHz and it is an average value of the sample period. This also explains why you may see **Usage** a bit higher than **Entitlement** in highly utilized vCPUs. If the VM has low utilization, you will see that the **Entitlement** counter is much higher than **Usage**.

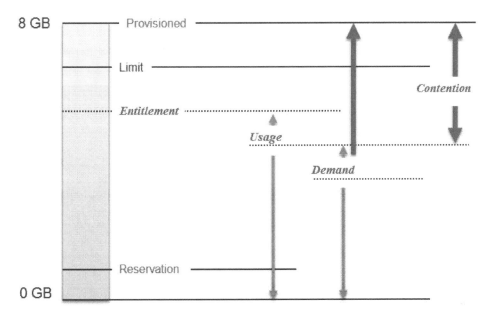

How Contention relates to Demand and Usage

An environment in which the ESXi host is resource-constrained is unhealthy. It cannot give every VM the resources they ask for. The VMs demand more than they are entitled to use, so the **Usage** and **Entitlement** counters will be lower than the **Demand** counter. The **Demand** counter can go higher than **Limit**, naturally. For example, if a VM is limited to 2 GB of RAM and it wants to use 5 GB, then **Demand** will exceed **Limit**. Obviously, **Demand** cannot exceed **Provisioned**. This is why the red line stops at **Provisioned**, because that is as high as it can go.

 The difference between what a VM demands and what it gets to use is the VM **Contention** counter.

Conceptually, **Contention** is **Demand** minus **Usage**. Mathematically, the actual formula is more complex than this.

If the Contention is zero, the VM gets to use everything it demands. This is the ideal level, as performance will match the physical world. This Contention value is required to demonstrate that the infrastructure provides a good service to the application team. If a VM owner comes to see you and says that your shared infrastructure is unable to serve her VM well, the VM Contention counter is your defense mechanism.

The Contention counter should become a part of your SLA or **Key Performance Indicator (KPI)**. It is not relevant for tracking utilization. When there is contention, it is possible that both her VM and your ESXi host have low utilization, and yet the VM performs poorly.

This typically happens when the VMs are relatively large compared to the ESXi host. Let's take a simple example to illustrate this. I will use the CPU component of compute this time around. The ESXi host has two sockets and 20 cores. Hyper-Threading is not enabled in order to keep this example simple. You run just two VMs, but each VM has 11 vCPUs. As a result, they will not be able to run concurrently. The hypervisor will schedule them sequentially as there are only 20 physical cores to serve 22 vCPUs. Here, both VMs will experience high contention.

Hold on! You might say, "There is no Contention counter in vSphere and no memory demand counter, either."

This is where vRealize Operations comes in. It doesn't just regurgitate the values in vCenter. It has implicit knowledge of vSphere and a set of derived counters with formulae that apply that knowledge.

Before we go into the metrics, you need to have an understanding of how the vSphere CPU scheduler works. The following diagram shows the various states that a VM can be in:

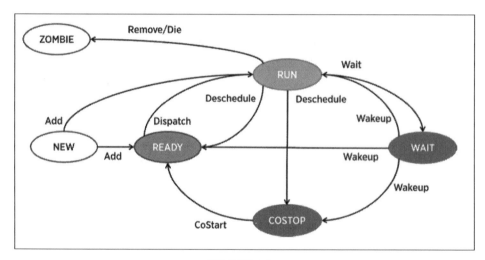

VM: CPU states

The preceding diagram is taken from a performance study called The *CPU Scheduler in VMware vSphere 5.1* (http://www.vmware.com/resources/techresources/10345). This whitepaper documents the CPU scheduler for VMware administrators. While it is written for vSphere 5.1, it is highly relevant for vSphere 6.0 Update 1. Read this paper as it will help you explain to your customers (the application team) how your shared infrastructure juggles all those VMs at the same time. It will also help you pick the right counters when you create your custom dashboards in vRealize Operations.

Storage

If you look at the ESXi and VM metric groups for storage in the vCenter performance chart, it is not clear at first glance how they relate to each other. You have many metric groups that you need to check, such as these:

- Storage network
- Storage adapter
- Storage path
- Datastore
- Virtual disk
- Disk

How do they impact one another? When do we use which metric group? How do they work in distributed storage (for example, VSAN)?

The following diagram explains the relationship. The green boxes are what you are likely to be familiar with. You have your ESXi host, and it can have an **NFS Datastore, VMFS Datastore**, or **RDM** objects. **VSAN** presents a VMFS datastore. The blue-colored boxes represent the metric groups you see in vCenter performance charts.

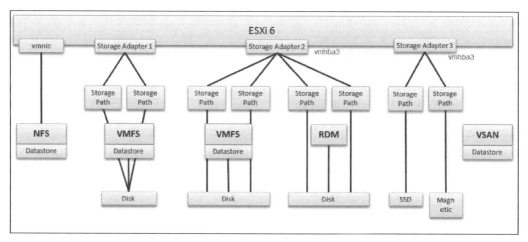

From ESXi to Disk

Can you figure out why there is no path to the **VSAN Datastore**? We'll do a comparison, and hopefully you will realize how different distributed storage and central storage are from a performance-monitoring point of view.

In the central storage architecture, NFS and VMFS datastores differ drastically in terms of counters, as NFS is file-based while VMFS is block-based Here are the differences:

- For NFS, it uses the vmnic, and so, the adapter type (FC, FCoE, or iSCSI) is not applicable. Multipathing is handled by the network, so you don't see it in the storage layer.

- For VMFS or RDM, you have more detailed visibility of the storage. To start off, each ESXi adapter is visible, and you can check the counters for each of them. In terms of relationship, one adapter can have many devices (disk or CD-ROM). One device is typically accessed via two storage adapters (for availability and load balancing), and it is also accessed via two paths per adapter, with the paths diverging at the storage switch. A single path, which will come from a specific adapter, can naturally connect one adapter to one device. The following diagram shows the four paths:

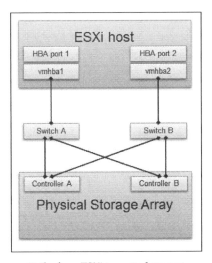

Paths from ESXi to central storage

A storage path takes data from ESXi to the LUN (the term used by vSphere is "disk"), not to the datastore. So, if the datastore has multiple extents, there are four paths per extent. This is one reason why you should not use more than one extent, as each extent adds four paths.

 If you are not familiar with **VMFS extents**, Cormac Hogan explains it here:

http://blogs.vmware.com/vsphere/2012/02/vmfs-extents-are-they-bad-or-simply-misunderstood.html

For the VMware **Virtual Machine File System (VMFS)** (non-VSAN), you can see the same counters at both the datastore level and the disk level. Their values will be identical if you follow the recommended configuration to create a 1:1 relationship between a datastore and a LUN. This means that you present an entire LUN to a datastore (use all of its capacity):

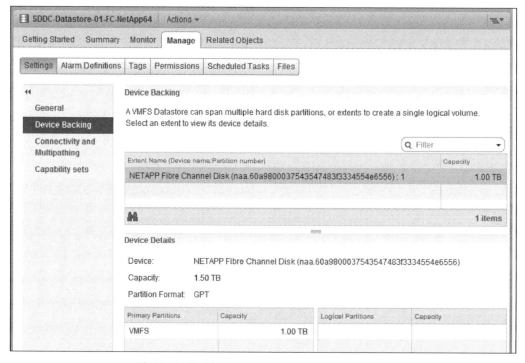

The Device Backing screen for an FC or iSCSI datastore

With VSAN, the difference in architecture is visible in the UI. The following screenshot shows the same screen (the **Device Backing** screen) but on a VSAN datastore. It is a simple VSAN datastore, but you can see that it is very different. Compare the two screenshots, and you will realize that they differ at a fundamental level.

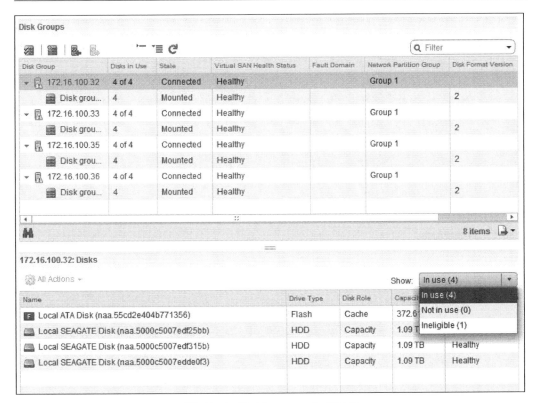

The Device Backing screen for VSAN

In VSAN, there is no **Connectivity and Multipathing** menu. There is also no **Capability Sets** menu. Neither of these is relevant in VSAN.

In VSAN, the datastore is not mapped to a LUN. It is supported by disk groups. The preceding screenshot shows a simple VSAN datastore. It only has four nodes. Each node has one disk group. Each disk group has four magnetic disks and one SSD.

ESXi and storage

The following screenshot shows how we manage ESXi storage. Click on the ESXi you need to manage, select the **Manage** tab, and then select the **Storage** sub tab. In this sub tab, we can see the adapters, devices, and the host cache. The screenshot shows an ESXi host with a list of its adapters. We have selected **vmhba2**, which is an FC HBA. Notice that it is connected to five devices. Each device has four paths, giving 20 paths in total.

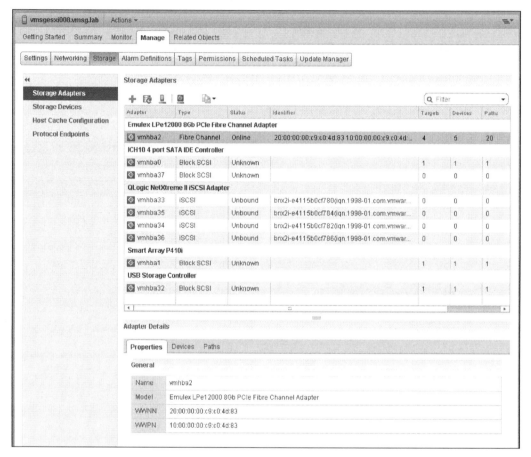

The ESXi Storage Adapter screen

What do you think it will look like on VSAN? The following screenshot shows a storage adapter on VSAN 6.1. It is an **LSI Logic** card.

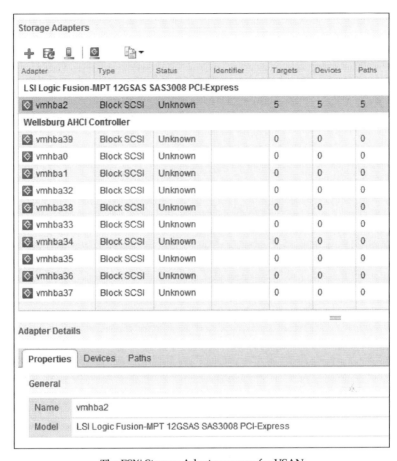

The ESXi Storage Adapters screen for VSAN

This VSAN storage adapter has **5 Targets**, **5 Devices**, and **5 Paths**. If you guessed that it is a 1:1 mapping among targets, devices, and paths, you are right.

We know that VSAN is not part of the storage fabric, so there is no need for an **Identifier**, which is made up of a **World Wide Node Name (WWNN)** and **World Wide Port Name (WWPN)**.

Let's expand the **Devices** tab. The details of the five devices are shown. The device capacity, operational state, and type are shown. We can see that we have one SSD (**Flash**).

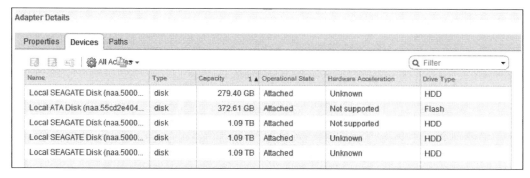

ESXi Storage Adapters – the Devices tab for VSAN

Let's expand the **Path** tab. We can see the **LUN ID** here. *This is important.* Every SSD has an **LUN ID** that begins with **55**, while the ones for mechanical drives begin with **5000**:

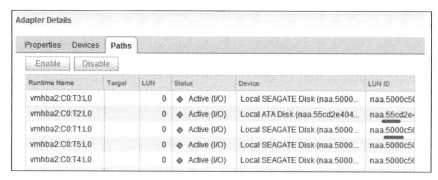

ESXi Storage Adapters – the Paths tab for VSAN

The fact that the hypervisor can see the device is important. That means the vmkernel can report if there is an issue, be it performance or availability. This is different if the disk is directly passed through to the VM. The hypervisor loses visibility. We cover in *Chapter 8, Specific-Purpose Dashboards*, how you can get visibility into each VSAN physical disk because it is transparent to ESXi.

Continuing our comparison between central and distributed arrays, we will move on to the **Storage Devices** tab in a central array. The following screenshot shows the list of devices. Because NFS is not a device (disk), it does not appear in this list. We have selected a local disk so that we can compare with VSAN. It happens to be a flash disk.

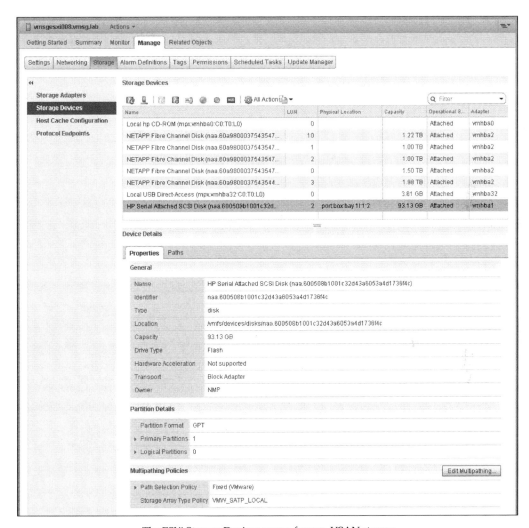

The ESXi Storage Devices screen for non-VSAN storage

Now, let's look at a VSAN device. We expect similarity as it is also a local physical disk.

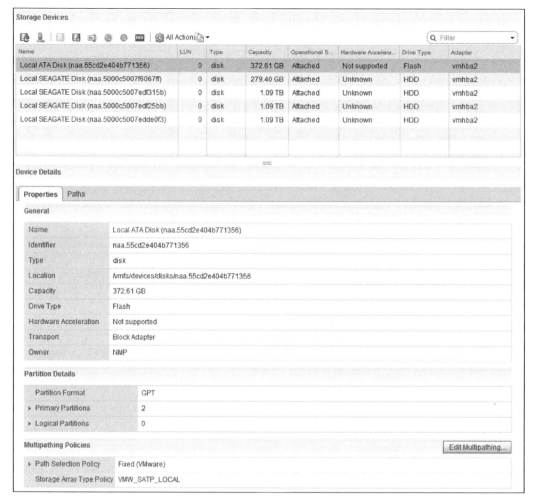

The ESXi Storage Devices screen for VSAN

In fact, everything looks pretty much the same. This is because both are local disks, and both are SSD. The difference is in the partitions. If you expand the **Partition Details** section, you will not see VMFS, because VSAN's underlying file system is not VMFS. In fact, you will see VSAN and Virsto. If you remember, VSAN incorporates technology from Virsto, a company that VMware acquired.

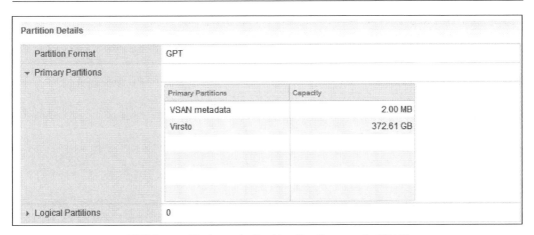

ESXi Storage Devices – the Partition Details screen for VSAN

Continuing our comparison, let's now click on the device path. For an FC device, you will be presented with the information shown in the next figure, including whether a path is active or not:

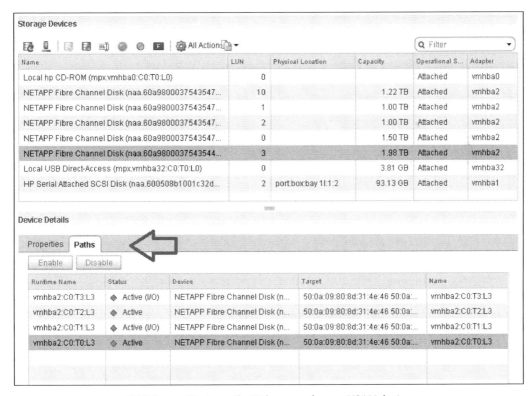

ESXi Storage Devices – the Paths screen for non-VSAN devices

Notice that not all paths carry I/O; it depends on your configuration and multipathing software. Because each LUN typically has four paths, path management can be complicated if you have many LUNs.

What does a path look like in VSAN? As we saw earlier, there is only one path.

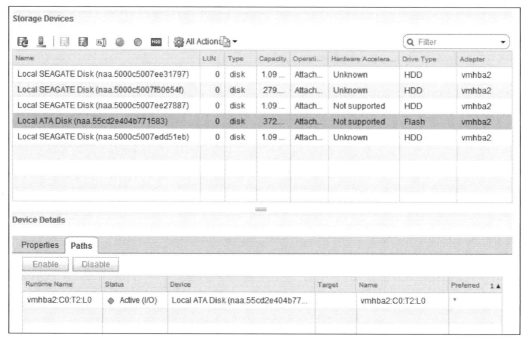

ESXi Storage Devices – The Paths screen for VSAN

We have covered how ESXi sees storage. It is good to know that VSAN is transparent to ESXi. Not all local storage is visible to the hypervisor.

VMs and storage

Compared to ESXi, the story is quite different on the VM layer. A VM does not see the underlying shared storage. It sees local SCSI disks only. So, regardless of whether the underlying storage is NFS, VMFS, VSAN, or RDM, it sees all of them as virtual disks. You lose visibility in the physical adapter (for example, you cannot tell how many IOPS on **vmhba2** are coming from a particular VM) and physical paths (for example, how many disk commands travelling on that path are coming from a particular VM).

On non-VSAN systems, you can see the impact at the datastore and the physical disk level. The datastore counter is especially useful. For example, if you notice that your IOPS is higher at the datastore level than at the virtual disk level, this means you have a snapshot. The snapshot I/O is not visible at the virtual disk level as the snapshot is stored on a different virtual disk.

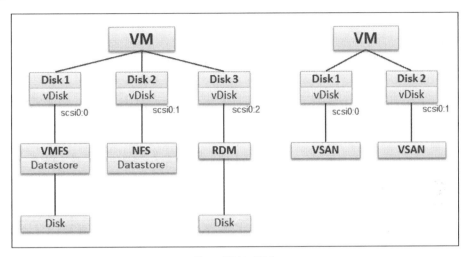

From VM to Disk

We saw earlier in this chapter that VSAN is different. The datastore and disk behave differently as a result. From performance monitoring, you cannot monitor VSAN by looking at the **VM Datastore** and **VM Disk** counters.

Network

From the point of view of performance and capacity management, network has different fundamental characteristics than compute or storage. The key differences are summarized in the following table:

Compute or storage	Network
A relatively high amount of resources available to the VM	A low amount of resources available
Granular resource allocation at the VM level	Coarse allocation
Single-purpose hardware	Multi-purpose hardware
A node	An interconnect

Let's understand these differences in more detail, starting from the first one:

At the end of the day, the net resources available to the VMs is what we care about. What the ESXi and IaaS platform use is considered an overhead.

An ESXi host has a fixed specification (for example, two CPUs, 36 cores, 256 GB of RAM, two 10 GE NICs). This means that we know the upper physical limit. How much of that it available to the VMs? Let's take a look:

- For compute, the hypervisor consumes a relatively low proportion of resources. Even if you add a software-defined storage such as VSAN, you are looking at around 10 percent total utilization, but this depends on many factors.

- The same cannot be said about network. Mass vMotion (for example, when the host enters maintenance mode), storage vMotion (in IP storage case), VM provisioning or cloning (for IP storage), and VSAN all take up significant network bandwidth. In fact, the non-VM network takes up the majority of the ESXi resources. If you have two 10 GE NICs, the majority of it is not used by the VMs.

The second difference with network is the resources that are given to a VM itself:

- For compute, we can configure a granular size of CPU and RAM. For the CPU, we can assign one vCPU or two, three, four, and so on.

- With network, we cannot specify the vNIC speed. It takes the speed of the ESXi vmnic assigned to the VM port group. So each VM will either see 1 GE or 10 GE (you need to have the right vNIC driver, obviously). You cannot allocate a different amount, such as 500 Mbps or 250 Mbps, to the Guest OS. In the physical world, we tend to assume that each server has 1 GE and the network has sufficient bandwidth. You cannot assume this in a virtual data center as you no longer have 1 GE for every VM at the physical level. It is shared and typically oversubscribed. While you can use **Network I/O Control** and **vSphere Traffic Shaping**, they are not configuration properties of a VM.

The third difference is that the hardware itself can provide different functionalities. Here's how:

- For compute, you have servers. While they may have different form factors or specifications, they all serve the same purpose — to provide processing power and working memory for the hypervisor or VM.

- For network, you have a variety of network services (firewall and load balancer) in addition to the basic network functionalities (switch, router, and gateway). You need to monitor all of them to get the complete picture. These functionalities can take the form of software or hardware.

The fourth difference is the nature of network:

- Compute and storage are nodes. When you have a CPU or RAM performance issue on one host, it doesn't typically impact another host on a different cluster. The same thing happens with storage. When a physical array has a performance issue, generally speaking, it does not impact other arrays in the data center.
- Network is different. A local performance issue can easily be a data center-wide problem.

Because of all these differences, the way you approach network monitoring should also be different. If you are not the network expert in your data center, the first step is to partner with experts. This is why I have asked the NetFlow Logic team to contribute a chapter to this book.

SDDC and network monitoring

The arrival of software-defined infrastructure services also changes the way you monitor your network. The following diagram shows a simplified setup of an ESXi host:

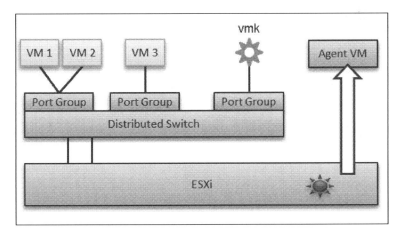

A simplified setup of an ESXi

In a single ESXi host, there are four areas that need to be monitored for complete network monitoring:

- VM network
- The vmkernel network
- ESXi kernel modules
- Agent VMs

In the preceding example, we have three VMs running in the host. **VM 1** and **VM 2** are connected to the same **Virtual Extensible LAN (VXLAN or VLAN)**. **VM 3** is on a different VXLAN, hence it is on a different port group. Monitoring at the **Port Group** level complements monitoring at the **VM** level and **ESXi** level.

Traffic at the **Distributed Switch** level is more than VM traffic. It also carries vmkernel traffic, such as vMotion and VSAN. Both the vmkernel and VM networks tend to share the same physical uplinks (ESXi vmnic). As a result, it's easier to monitor at the Port Group level.

Sounds good so far. What is the limitation to monitoring at the distributed port group level?

The hint is in the word "distributed".

Yes, the data is the aggregate of all the ESXi hosts using that distributed port group!

By default, **VM 1** and **VM 2** can talk to each other. The traffic will not leave the ESXi. Network monitoring tools that are not aware of this will miss it. Traffic from **VM 3** can also reach **VM 1** or **VM 2** if an **NSX Distributed Logical Router** is in place. It is a vmkernel module, just like the **NSX Distributed Firewall**. As a result, monitoring these kernel modules, and the host overall performance, becomes an integral part of network monitoring.

The fourth area we need to monitor is **Agent VMs**. An Agent VM is mapped to one ESXi host. It does not need HA protection as every ESXi host has one. It also does not need to reside on a network datastore.

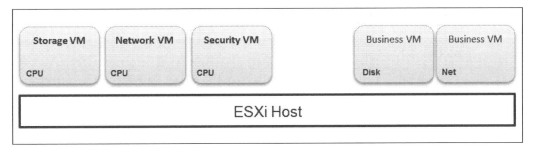

An ESXi Host, Agent VMs, and Business VMs

The diagram shows an ESXi host with three agent VMs. The first VM provides a storage service (an example is Nutanix **Controller VM (CVM)**), the second VM provides the **Network** service, and the third VM provides a **Security** VM.

Let's use the **Security** service as an example. A popular example here is the Trend Micro Deep Security virtual appliance. It is in the data path. If the business VMs are accessing files on a fileserver on another network, the files have to be checked by the security virtual appliance first. If the agent VM is slow (and it could be due to factors that are not network-related), it will look like a network or storage issue as far as the business VMs are concerned. The business VMs do not know that their files have been intercepted for security clearance, as it is not done at the network level. It is done at the hypervisor level.

The source of the data

A complete monitoring of the network requires you to get the data from five different sources, not just from vSphere. In SDDC, you should also get data from the application, Guest OS, NSX, and NetFlow/sFlow/IPFIX from VDS and physical network devices. For VDI, you need to get data at the application level. I have seen dropped packets at the application layer (PCoIP) when Windows sees no dropped packets. The reason is that the packet arrives out of order and hence is unusable from a PCoIP viewpoint.

The following diagram shows a simplified stack. It shows the five sources of data and the four tools to get the data. It includes a **Physical Switch** as we can no longer ignore the physical network once we move from just vSphere to complete SDDC.

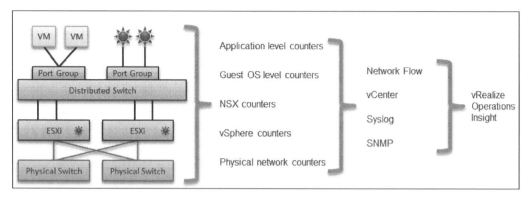

From source to dashboard

Network packet analysis has two main approaches: header analysis and full-packet analysis. Header analysis is certainly much lighter but lacks the depth of full analysis. You use this to provide overall visibility as it does not impose a heavy load on your environment.

vRealize Operations and Log Insight, when coupled with Blue Medora and NetFlow Logic solutions, provides visibility into the physical network and virtual network (NSX).

The impact of virtualization on network monitoring goes beyond what we have covered. Let's add NSX Edge to the mix so that you can see the traffic flow when the edge services are also virtualized. You will see that a network problem experienced by a VM on **ESXi A** could be caused by another VM running on **ESXi B**. The following diagram is a simplified setup, showing a single **NSX Edge** VM residing in another cluster:

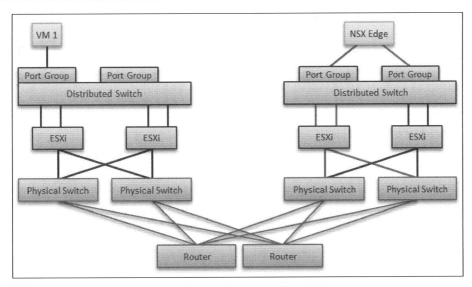

Routing with NSX Edge on a dedicated cluster

In the previous example, let's say **VM 1** needs to talk to the outside world. An **NSX Edge** VM provides that connectivity, so every TCP/IP packet has to go through it. The Edge VM has two virtual NICs, one for each network. If the **NSX Edge** VM has a CPU issue or the underlying ESXi has a RAM issue, it can impact the network performance of **VM 1**.

You may be wondering whether an Edge VM does a lot of processing. Let's look at a real-world example. How much traffic do you think this Edge VM is handling?

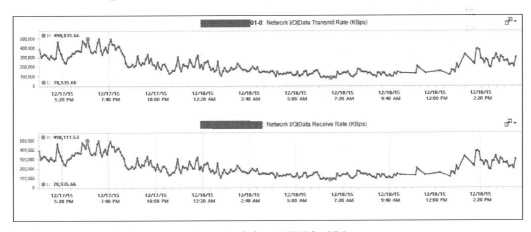

Example of a busy NSX Edge VM

At near 1 million KBPS, the VM is driving nearly eight Gbps' worth of data! This number is the sum of **Receive** and **Transmit**, so the theoretical limit is 20 Gbps as this VM uses a 10-Gbps NIC. Notice that the pattern for both **Receive** and **Transmit** is identical, as **NSX Edge** is practically a gateway.

This NSX Edge happens to be the only VM on the host. This means we can expect the data at the host level to mimic that. The host does not run distributed storage (for example, VSAN), so there is no traffic other than this VM. The chart in the following figure confirms this:

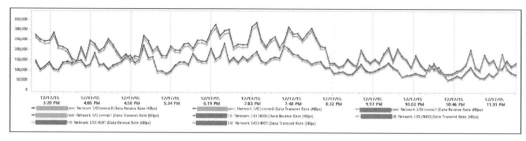

Network utilization at the Edge and ESXi levels

There are practically two lines, even though we've actually plotted eight line charts. What do the two lines map to?

Yes, they map to North-South and South-North traffic. An end user requesting data from a web server would be South-North, while the web server's response would be North-South.

"Wait," you might say, "there should only be four lines! Why do we have eight lines?"

Can you figure it out from the following diagram?

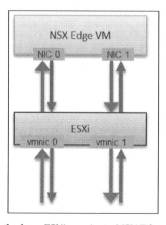

Traffic paths from ESXi vmnics to NSX Edge and back

These eight arrows map to the eight lines. There is one line chart for every arrow. There are four NICs, and each has receive and transmit.

If you use NSX, there is a good chance that you will have multiple NSX Edge VMs. I have a customer with less than 100 VMs. On the same host, you may also run distributed storage (for example, VSAN), as an Edge cluster is typically isolated. I have customers with multiple Edge VMs, and monitoring the health of those Edge VMs becomes an integral part of network monitoring.

vSphere does not provide protocol analysis functionality, which is instead available through a packet analyzer or sniffer program, such as Wireshark and NetFlow Logic's Netflow Integrator. With vSphere alone, you will not know, for example, which VMs are talking to which VMs, the latency they experience, and what protocols are travelling in your network.

NetFlow Logic has developed products that extend both vRealize Operations and Log Insight. Their products also complement the network monitoring solutions from VMware. We will cover this later on in the book.

Good network management is about understanding the application. In a way, we should treat vCloud Suite as an application. There are now two layers of applications in SDDC:

- Infrastructure applications (for example, Virtual SAN, NSX, F5, and Trend Micro)
- Business applications (for example, your company intranet or website)

This is consistent with the fact that you will have two layers of network when it is virtualized. You will use VXLAN for your VM and VLAN for your infrastructure.

When you virtualize your network with NSX, vRealize Operations provides visibility via its management pack for NSX. You can download this complementary product from **VMware Solution Exchange** at `https://solutionexchange.vmware.com`.

As of early 2016, most companies have implemented 10 GE technology in their data centers. Network monitoring is both simpler and harder in a 10-Gb environment versus a 1-Gb environment. It is simpler as you have a lot fewer cables and more bandwidth. It is harder as you cannot easily differentiate between traffic types as the physical capacity is now shared.

In 10 GE, you should enable vSphere **Network I/O Control (NIOC)** because the non-VM network can spike and consume a large bandwidth. The following screenshot shows the default configuration for network I/O control. As you can see, the VM network takes up a small portion. The default value is 100 shares at high priority, with no reservation.

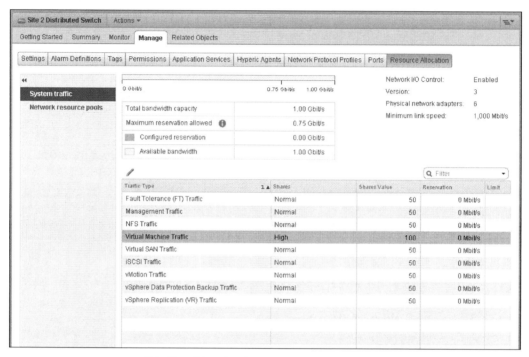

Distributed Switch – the Resource Allocation screen

Relying on load-based teaming to balance the load for performance needs may not provide enough sensitivity to meet SLAs, as it kicks in every 30 seconds. For a discussion about NIOC, review Frank's blog at `http://frankdenneman.nl/2013/01/17/a-primer-on-network-io-control` and Duncan's blog at `http://www.yellow-bricks.com/2013/10/29/virtual-san-network-io-control` so that you can configure your settings correctly.

Incorrect configuration will make both performance management and capacity management difficult.

Because the physical capacity of the network is shared, you have a dynamic upper limit for each workload. The VM network port group will have more bandwidth when there is no vMotion happening. Furthermore, each VM has a dynamic upper limit as it shares the VM network port group with other VMs.

In the previous screenshot, we have created a network resource pool and mapped the VM network port group to it. Even if you dedicate a physical NIC to the VM network port group, that NIC is still shared among all the VMs. You do not have a constant number of VMs on a host due to vMotion and DRS, so the upper threshold is dynamic.

The resources available to a VM also vary from host to host. Within the same host, the limit changes as time progresses. Unlike **Storage I/O Control** (**SIOC**), NIOC does not provide any counters that tell you that it has capped the bandwidth.

NIOC can help limit the network throughput for a particular workload or VM. If you are using 10 GE, you would want to enable NIOC so that a burst in one network workload does not impact your VM. For example, a mass vMotion operation can saturate the 10-Gb link if you do not implement NIOC. In vCenter 6, there is no counter that tracks when NIOC caps the network throughput. As a result, vRealize Operations will not tell you that NIOC has taken action.

Determining network workload

Determining CPU or RAM workload is easy: there is a physical limit. While network has a physical limit, it can be misleading to assume it is available to all VMs all the time.

In some situations, the bandwidth within the ESXi host may not be the smallest pipe between the originating VM and its destination. Within the data center, there could be firewalls, load balancers, routers, and other hops that the packet has to go through. Once it leaves the data center, the WAN and Internet are likely to be a *bottleneck*. This dynamic nature means every VM has its own practical limit.

Because of this practical consideration, vRealize Operations does not make the assumption that the physical vmnic is the bandwidth available. It is certainly the physical limit, but in most cases, it is not represent the actual bandwidth available. vRealize Operations observes the peak utilized bandwidth and sets this as the upper limit.

The following chart shows that a vCenter 5.5 VM network's usage varies between 18,000 KBPS and 25,772 KBPS during the three days for which the usage has been tracked. vRealize Operations observes the range and sets the maximum network usage to near the peak (25,772 KBPS). This counter is useful in that it tells you that the utilization never exceeds this amount.

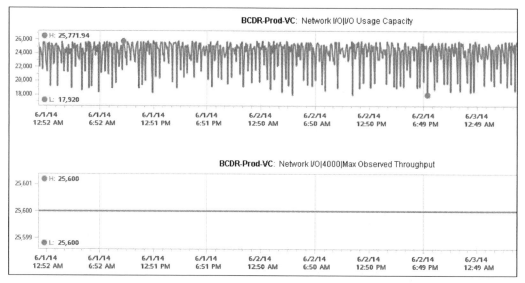

The network workload counter

The **Max Observed Throughput** number is adjusted dynamically. The following screenshot shows two ESXi hosts in the same cluster. The spike could be due to a mass vMotion in that cluster.

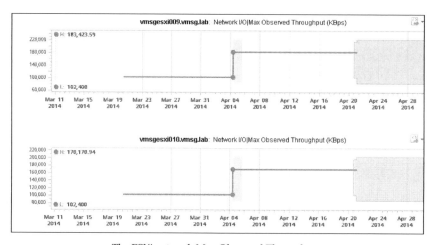

The ESXi network Max Observed Throughput

vRealize Operations does not track the vmnic speed at the individual vmnic level since that's considered a configuration element. It can track at the aggregate level only. Because you normally set the network to auto negotiate, the speed can sometimes drop (for example, from 1 Gbps to 100 Mbps). This is something you need to check manually if you encounter network slowness while your network utilization is below 100 Mbps. In this case, the **Max Observed** counter can give a clue.

Based on all the preceding factors, the **Max Observed** counter is a more practical indicator of the network resources available to a VM than the physical configuration of the ESXi vmnic. You should use this counter as your VM maximum bandwidth. For ESXi, you should also use the physical vmnic as a guideline.

vRealize Operations provides the **Workload** (in percent) counter or **Demand** (in percent) counter, which are based on this maximum observed value. For example, if the VM **Usage** counter shows 100 KBPS, and **Max Observed Throughput** shows 200 KBPS, then the **Demand** (in percent) counter will be at 50 percent.

Metric groups

So far, we have covered the concepts of compute, storage, and network monitoring. Now we are ready to dive into the counters. The counters are accessible via GUI from these three tools: **esxtop**, **vCenter**, and **vRealize Operations**.

They serve different purposes, as follows:

- **esxtop**: It operates at an individual host level, providing the deepest and most granular detail. It can go down to a granularity of 2 seconds. This is useful when you already know which ESXi host and VM you want to troubleshoot. This book does not cover the counters in esxtop.

- **vCenter Server**: It complements esxtop by providing a view across hosts and other objects in vSphere. However, its granularity is at an interval of 20 seconds.

- **vRealize Operations**: It complements vCenter by extending the coverage beyond vSphere. It can go up to the application level or down to the physical infrastructure. It also allows you to slice and dice the combined data. However, its default granularity is at an interval of 5 minutes.

The terms "counter" and "metric" are interchangeable, and vCenter 6.0 uses both terms. You can see that the next screenshot in the *VM metric groups* section has the terms **Chart Metrics** and **Select counters** for this chart. We call metrics and counters grouped together a **metric group**.

You will notice that vRealize Operations has many more metric groups than vCenter. Pick the right metric as the same metric name can have different values in different metric groups.

VM metric groups

The following screenshot shows the vCenter metric groups for a VM. They are listed on the left-hand side under the **Chart Metrics** heading. We have selected **Virtual disk** in the following screenshot and the details for it are shown. Notice that the two virtual disks of the VM are shown on the right-hand side.

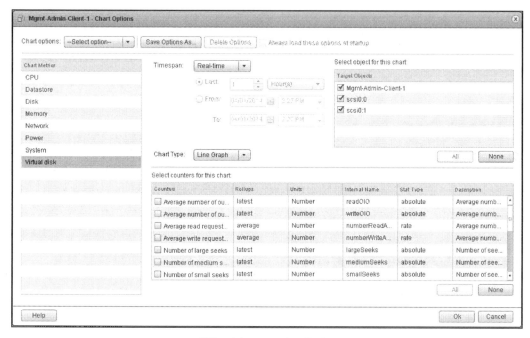

VM metric groups in vCenter

From the list in the preceding screenshot, you may notice that there is no metric group for **Virtual Flash** and **vSphere Replication**. They are only available at the ESXi level. This means that you will not be able to know the metric for a given VM. You have to go to the ESXi to see it. At the host level, you can choose **Stacked Graph** (per VM) to see the data per VM.

vRealize Operations provides more metric groups for VMs, and the next table shows the comparison. These additional metric groups, and their associated metrics, are valuable in both performance and capacity management. I'm not listing them in alphabetical order, but according to the following types: CPU, RAM, network, storage, and others.

I have left values under the **vCenter 6.0** column blank so that you can easily see which metric groups are unique to vRealize Operations.

Scope	vCenter 6.0	vRealize Operations
CPU	CPU	CPU
CPU		CPU - Allocation model
CPU		CPU Utilization for Resources
RAM	Memory	Memory
RAM		Memory (Host)
RAM		Memory - Allocation model
Network	Network	Network I/O
Network		Network I/O (Host)
Storage	Datastore	Datastore I/O
Storage	Disk	Disk
Storage		Disk Space - Allocation model
Storage		Disk Space Reclaimable
Storage		Guest File System statistics (visible only with VMware Tools installed on the VM)
Storage	Virtual Disk	Virtual Disk
Others	Power	Power (not shown by default)
Others	System	System

ESXi metric groups

The next screenshot shows the vCenter metric groups for a host. For some of the counters, you can get the information at the individual component level, for example, CPU core and individual vmnic. For others, the values are only available at the host level. The value of the individual components can be useful during troubleshooting.

In the following screenshot, we have selected the **CPU** metric group. The individual cores are shown on the right-hand side. Knowing the data at the CPU core level is useful because a typical ESXi host has many cores (for example, two sockets, 36 cores, and 72 threads). Plotting a chart at the core level can reveal whether the utilization is balanced or not. If you have many large VMs in the host, you may notice that some cores are highly utilized while others are idle.

Note that **vSphere Replication** and **Virtual flash** are given their own groups. This makes it easier to monitor the environment. In a large environment where you have many VMs protected, you can track the total TX and RX to see the patterns.

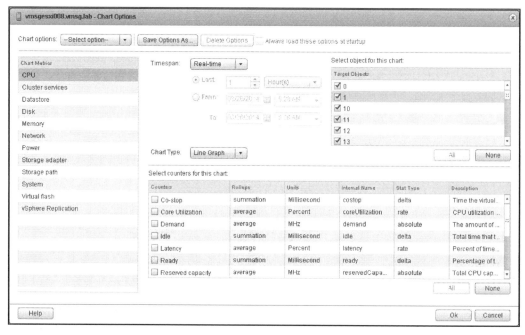

ESXi metric groups

As you may guess by now, vRealize Operations provides additional metric groups, and the following table shows the comparison. Just like the comparison for VMs, we have excluded standard vRealize Operations metric groups. You will see later that vRealize Operations also provides more at the individual core and vmnic level.

Scope	vCenter 6.0	vRealize Operations
CPU	CPU	CPU
CPU		CPU Utilization for Resources
RAM	Memory	Memory
Network	Network	Network I/O
Storage	Datastore	Datastore I/O
Storage	Storage adapter	Storage adapter
Storage	Storage path	
Storage	Disk	Disk
Storage		Disk Space

Scope	vCenter 6.0	vRealize Operations
Storage		Disk Space Reclaimable
Storage		Storage
Storage	Virtual flash	vFlash Module
Storage	vSphere Replication	vSphere Replication (only appears if the host has vSphere Replication)
Others	Cluster services	
Others	Power	Power (not shown by default)
Others	System	System
Others		Hardware

You may notice that there is a metric group called **Cluster services** in vCenter. This is applicable if the host is part of a DRS cluster. It only has two components— **CPU** and **Memory fairness**. It calculates the *fairness* of distribution among members of the cluster.

It is not necessary to actively track the cluster services, as an unbalanced cluster does not mean you have a performance issue. For example, assume that you have an eight-node cluster. Host 1 is running at 90 percent utilization, while Host 2 to Host 8 are running at 0 percent utilization. So long as Host 1 does not experience contention, balancing the cluster does not give you increased performance. In fact, if your workload is network-intensive between VMs (for example, in a three-tier application), the VMs are better off running in the same host as the traffic between VMs never needs to travel on the physical network. The cluster services are shown in the following screenshot. Notice that the **Rollup** is latest. This makes sense as you want to know the latest data, not the average.

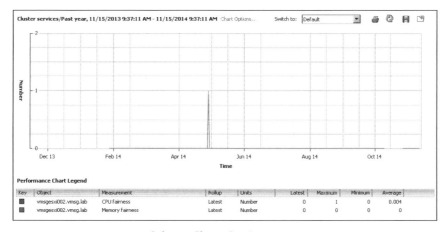

vSphere – Cluster Services counters

Cluster metric groups

The next screenshot shows the vCenter metric groups for a cluster. As you can see, it has a lot less information than the host metric groups. For example, information related to storage and network do not appear in the cluster metrics. As a result, monitoring and troubleshooting become tedious at the cluster level in vCenter. You need to check individual hosts one by one.

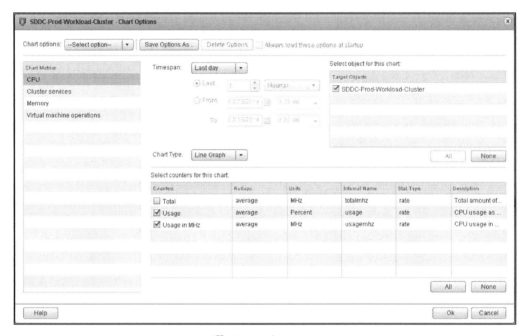

Cluster metric groups

This is where vRealize Operations comes in. It provides more metric groups at the cluster level, as shown in following screenshot:

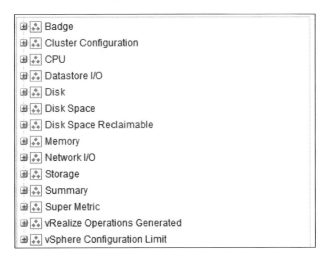

You can see that it provides network and storage counters that are missing in vCenter. Because of these additional metrics, you can now do performance and capacity management at the cluster level. In the dashboards that are provided in *Part 2* of this book, you will notice that the cluster is the object where we create a majority of the super metrics. The reason for this is that a cluster is the smallest logical building block due to HA and DRS.

Datastore metric groups

The screenshots of the vCenter metric groups for the other objects (VM, host, and cluster) shared earlier were shown in the **Advanced** option of the **Performance** tab. vCenter does not have this **Advanced** option for datastore objects. Instead, it presents you with a fixed list of charts, as can be seen in the next screenshot. Therefore, we cannot list the vCenter metric groups for datastores as we did for the other objects.

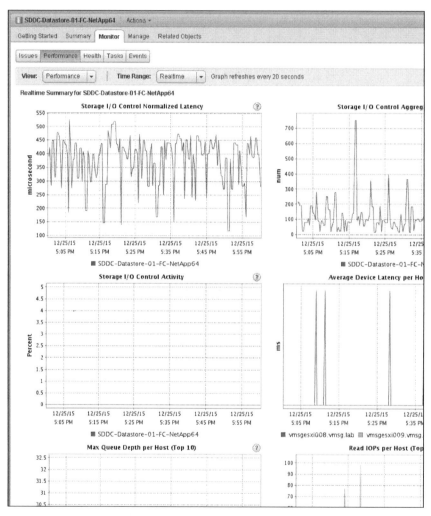

vCenter datastore metric groups

vRealize Operations again complements vCenter by providing an extensive list of metric groups, as shown in the following screenshot. This enables us to see the key storage counters (IOPS, throughput, latency, and capacity).

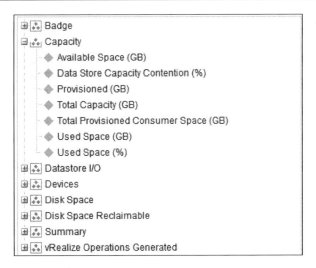

Datastore metrics provided by vRealize Operations:

In addition to the metrics, vRealize Operations also shows the relationship. This is useful in analysis, when you need to plot metrics from different objects. We can see from the following screenshot the relationship between a datastore cluster, datastore, and VMs:

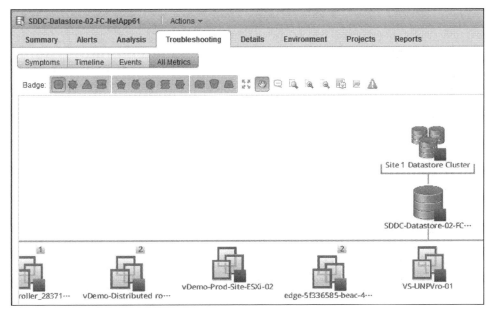

The datastore relationship diagram provided by vRealize Operations

Datastore cluster metric groups

As for individual datastores, vCenter does not have the **Advanced** option for the datastore cluster **Performance** tab. It presents you with a fixed list of charts, as can be seen in this screenshot:

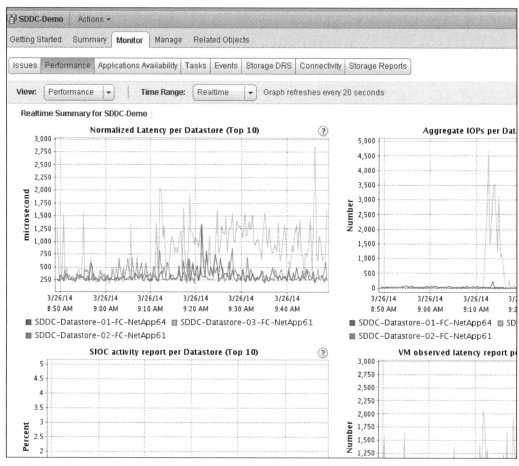

vCenter datastore cluster metric groups

vRealize Operations provides both performance counters and disk capacity counters.

For performance, the datastore metric group provides all the key metrics (IOPS, latency, and throughput). It provides the breakdown for read, write, and total, as can be seen in the following screenshot:

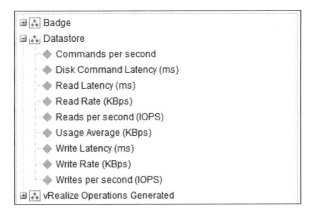

The disk space metric group provides capacity information, including the space used for snapshots. The capacity counter is not enabled by default. You can enable them in the **policy**.

Distributed switch metric groups

The following screenshot shows that vCenter does not provide performance counters for a distributed switch. In fact, there is no **Performance** tab.

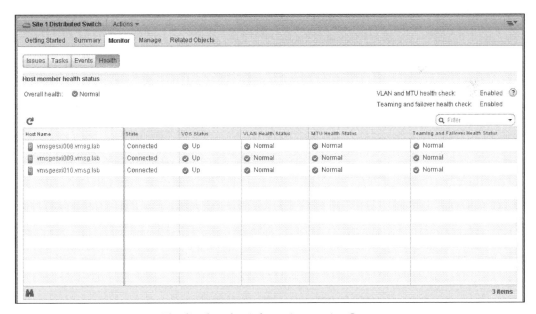

The distributed switch metric group in vCenter

This means you need to monitor the switch at the individual ESXi level. This can make correlation difficult, as there are types of traffic that are inter-ESXi in nature, for example, vMotion, storage vMotion, and distributed storage. Being able to see how much bandwidth they consume on the shared physical NICs can be useful for both performance troubleshooting and capacity planning.

vRealize Operations provides this visibility across the distributed switch. It also introduces a new object for the distributed port group. With these two objects, you can check the network performance from the network point of view. You can check both the ingress and egress traffic at either the switch level or port group level. We will cover them in *Chapter 15*, *Network Counters*.

For a standard switch, the counters are provided as part of the ESXi host as it is not an object that resides outside the host. While all standard switches are completely independent of each other, all virtual switches that communicate with each other over the physical network are related from the performance point of view. There is a value in being able to view a summary of the switches across hosts at a higher level. With ESXi moving from 1 GE NIC to 10 GE NIC, the reason for choosing a distributed switch becomes stronger.

Data center metric groups

The next screenshot shows the vCenter metric groups for a data center. As you can see, there is even less information than for a cluster object. We lost all the information on CPU, RAM, network, and storage. It provides only VM operations, such as power on and reboot.

Information at the data center level is actually useful, as both distributed switches and datastores can go across clusters. Viewing data at the data center level means you know for sure you are not getting partial data.

In a small environment, where one data center has only one cluster, the information at the data center level is logically redundant.

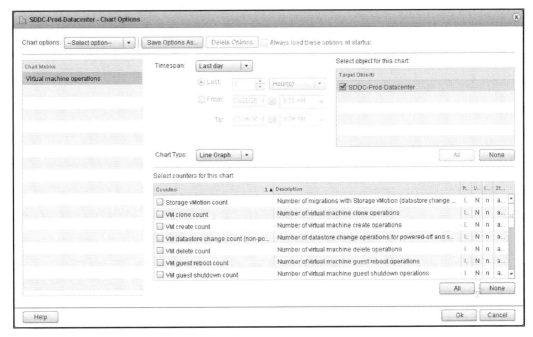

The vSphere datacenter metric group

vRealize Operations, on the other hand, provides a more complete list of metric groups, as shown in the following screenshot:

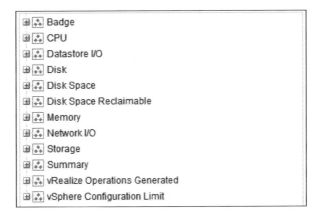

In most deployments, a single vCenter will only manage one vCenter data center. So, viewing the information at either level is sufficient as both will provide identical data. There are situations where you may decide to have multiple data center objects in a single vCenter. The following are some examples:

- Your vCenter manages multiple physical data centers. In this case, you create one data center object for each physical data center. In situations where you need long-distance vMotion, you create a single data center spanning two physical data centers.

- You have many remote branches, with limited WAN bandwidth back to headquarters. You prefer to have one vCenter to make management easier and optimize vCenter licenses.

- You have a very large data center spanning multiple floors, with each floor having its own independent network and rows of racks.

- You want to have tighter control, both from a security and an operations point of view. Having a separate data center increases the logical separation.

Let me know if you have other use cases in which you need a separate vCenter data center. In my opinion, vCenter data centers are typically associated with a physical location or boundary, and they have a 1:1 relationship.

vCenter metric groups

The next screenshot shows that vCenter does not provide performance counters at the vCenter level. There is no **Performance** tab. The **Health** tab in fact comes from vRealize Operations integration.

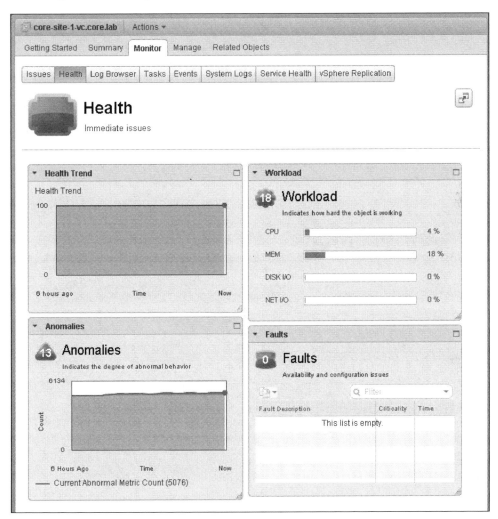

The vCenter Health tab

vRealize Operations, on the other hand, provides a list of metric groups, as shown in the following screenshot. They are useful when you need to see the big picture.

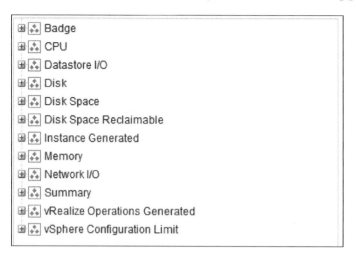

World metric groups

In addition to the vCenter level, vRealize Operations goes up even higher, introducing an object called **World**. It recognizes that most customers deploy multiple vCenter Servers. The following are the use cases in which you may deploy multiple vCenter Servers:

- There are two vCenter Servers for the server VMs (**Virtual Server Infrastructure** or **VSI**), one in each physical data center. They are paired by **VMware Site Recovery Manager**. The vCenter Servers manage both the production and non-production VMs.

- There are two vCenter Servers for the desktop VMs (**Virtual Desktop Infrastructure** or **VDI**), one in each physical data center. They are fronted by **VMware Horizon Servers**, which create a logical desktop pool spanning both physical data centers in an Active/Active configuration.

- Some customers have a very large number of VMs. I work with customers with 45,000 server VMs and more than 50,000 desktop VMs. These customers may want to have a separate pod in which each vCenter Server manages, say, 10,000 VMs.

- For customers who operate in multiple continents or geographical areas where network latency and stability become an issue, there is a need to deploy a vCenter Server near that continent or area.

- Customers typically have branches that need servers, too. Depending on the number of branches, latency, bandwidth, and local IT capability, a vCenter may be required on the remote branch.

- For business workload that is highly confidential, where the business workload has its own physical infrastructure (storage, network, server, rack, UPS, KVM, and so on), and resides on a separate namespace (that is, not a part of an Active Directory), a separate vCenter is logically required. The environment is also typically managed by a different administrator.

- One vCenter Server is provisioned for non-production usage, as the preceding vCenter Servers are all production servers. This allows you to test patches and updates and upgrade the vCenter Server in the non-production environment first. vCenter has many components (web client server, inventory, database, and so on), and having a test environment lets you test them confidently.

Information at the World level covers all the vCenter Servers, so it provides a bird's-eye view of the entire infrastructure. The increased scalability in vRealize Operations 6 means that this can be a global view covering tens of thousands of VMs. vRealize Operations provides the following metric groups at the World level:

```
⊞ ⚬ Anomaly
⊞ ⚬ Badge
⊞ ⚬ Capacity Remaining
⊞ ⚬ Compliance
⊞ ⚬ CPU
⊞ ⚬ Density
⊞ ⚬ Disk
⊞ ⚬ Efficiency
⊞ ⚬ Faults
⊞ ⚬ Health
⊞ ⚬ Memory
⊞ ⚬ Network
⊞ ⚬ Risk
⊞ ⚬ Stress
⊞ ⚬ Summary
⊞ ⚬ Time Remaining
⊞ ⚬ vRealize Operations Generated
⊞ ⚬ Waste
⊞ ⚬ Workload
```

Counters in vSphere and vRealize

You should spend time understanding vCenter and esxtop counters. *Part 3* of the book is not meant to replace vSphere manuals. Read the vSphere documentation on this topic, as it gives you the required foundation for mastering vRealize Operations.

vSphere and vRealize Operations manuals are freely available. Just Google vSphere documentation and Google will have it readily available for you. The exact chapter you need to review is shown in the following screenshot:

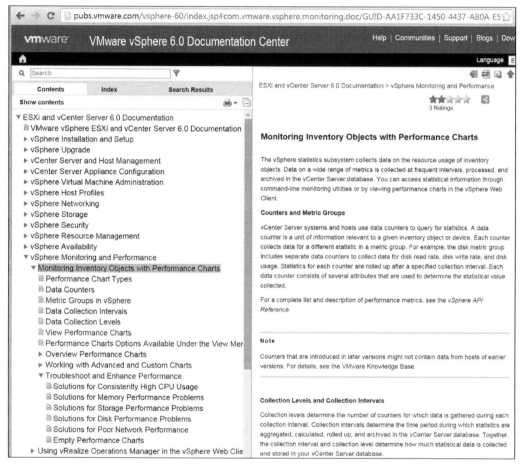

The vSphere 6 Monitoring and Performance manual

The counters are also documented in the **vSphere API/SDK Documentation**, as shown in the following figure:

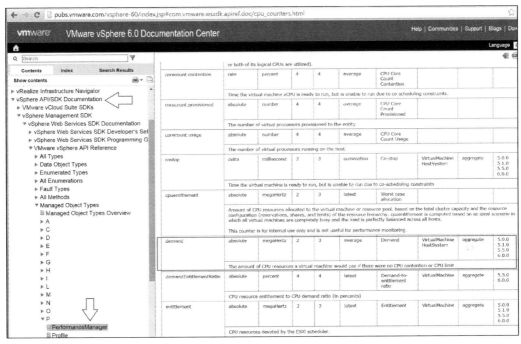

The vSphere 6 manual – the Performance Manager section

Follow the path shown, and choose **Performance Manager** from the list under the letter **P**. It lists the metrics. I have highlighted the **Demand** metric. As you can see, it applies to VM and ESXi, and has been available since vSphere 5.0. From the definition, you can see that this is the counter you want to track for IaaS performance as it takes into account **Contention** and **Limit**.

The third part of the vSphere manual you need to review is the **esxtop** manual. It provides good information on the counters. In the following diagram, I have shown the two metrics used heavily in the book:

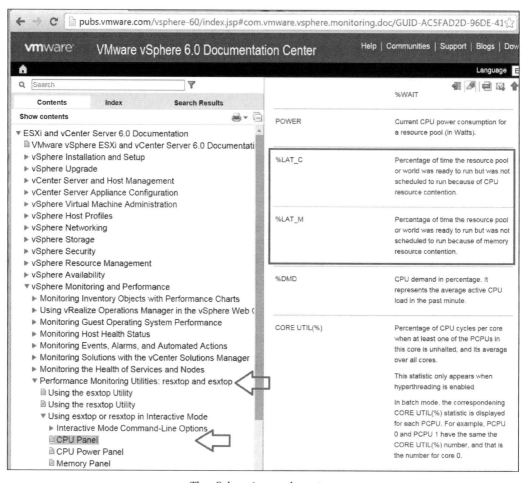

The vSphere 6 manual – esxtop

You should also be familiar with the architecture of ESXi, especially how the scheduler works.

vCenter has a different collection interval (sampling period) depending on the timeline you are looking at. Most of the time, you are looking at the real-time statistic (chart), as other timelines do not have enough counters. You will notice right away that most of the counters become unavailable once you choose a timeline. In the real-time chart, each data point has 20 seconds' worth of data. That is as accurate as it gets in vCenter. Because all other performance management tools (including vRealize Operations) get their data from vCenter, they are not getting anything more granular than this. As mentioned previously, esxtop allows you to sample down to a minimum of 2 seconds.

Speaking of esxtop, you should be aware that not all counters are exposed in vCenter. For example, if you turn on 3D graphics, there is a separate SVGA thread created for that VM. This can consume CPU and it will not show up in vCenter. The **Mouse**, **Keyboard**, **Screen** (MKS) threads, which give you the console, also do not show up in vCenter.

The next screenshot shows how you lose most of your counters if you choose a timespan other than real time. In the case of CPU, you are basically left with two counters, as **Usage** and **Usage in MHz** cover the same thing. You also lose the ability to monitor per core, as the target objects now only list the host and not the individual cores.

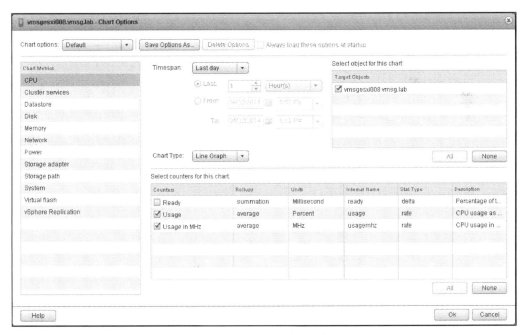

vCenter counters are lost beyond 1 hour

Because the real-time timespan only lasts for 1 hour, the performance troubleshooting has to be done at the present moment. If the performance issue cannot be recreated, there is no way to troubleshoot in vCenter. This is where vRealize Operations comes in, as it keeps your data for a much longer period. I was able to perform troubleshooting for a client on a problem that occurred more than a month ago!

vRealize Operations takes data every 5 minutes. This means it is not suitable for troubleshooting performance that does not last for 5 minutes. In fact, if the performance issue only lasts for 5 minutes, you may not get any alert, because the collection may happen exactly in the middle of those 5 minutes. For example, let's assume the CPU is idle from 08:00:00 to 08:02:30, spikes from 08:02:30 to 08:07:30, and then again is idle from 08:07:30 to 08:10:00. If vRealize Operations is collecting at exactly 08:00, 08:05, and 08:10, you will not see the spike as they are spread over two data points. This means that for vRealize Operations to pick up the spike in its entirety without any idle data, the spike may have to last for 10 minutes.

The **Rollups** column is important. An entry of **average** means the average of 5 minutes in the case of vRealize Operations. What about **summation**?

It is actually the average for those counters where accumulation makes more sense. Let's take an example. **CPU Ready Time** gets accumulated over the sampling period. vCenter reports performance every 20 seconds, which is 20000 milliseconds. The following table shows a VM has different **CPU Ready Time** at each second. It had 900 milliseconds **CPU Ready Time** for the fifth and sixth seconds, but had a lower number for the remaining 18 seconds.

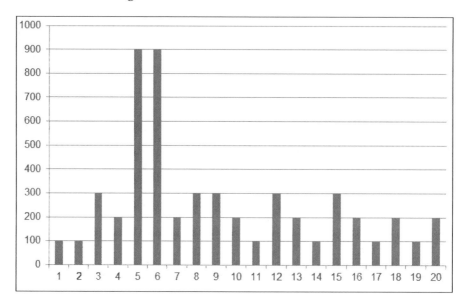

Over a period of 20 seconds, a VM may accumulate different **CPU Ready Time** values for each second. vCenter sums up all these numbers and then divides it by 20,0000. This is actually an average, as you lose the peak.

Latest, on the other hand, is different. It takes the last value of the sampling period. For example, in this 20-second sampling, it takes the value between 19 and 20 seconds. This value could be lower or higher than the average of the entire 20-second period.

So what is missing here is the peak of the sampling period. In the 5-minute period, vRealize Operations does not collect low, average, and high from vCenter. It takes average only.

Let's talk about the **Units** column now. Some common units are milliseconds, MHz, percent, KBPS, and KB. Some counters are shown in MHz, which means you need to know your ESXi physical CPU frequency. This can be difficult due to CPU power-saving features, which lower the CPU frequency when the demand is low. In large environments, this can be operationally difficult since you will have different ESXi hosts from different generations (and are hence likely to sport different GHz processors). This is also the reason why a cluster is the smallest logical building block. If your cluster has ESXi hosts with different frequencies, these MHz-based counters can be difficult to use, as the VMs get vMotioned by DRS.

Summary

In this chapter, we covered the world of counters in vCenter and vRealize Operations. The counters were analyzed based on their four main groupings (CPU, RAM, disk, and network). We also covered each of the metric groups, which map to the corresponding objects in vCenter. For the counters, we also shared how they are related and how they differ.

In the next four chapters, we will dive deeper into each of these four main groupings, dedicating a chapter to each group. To give us a two-dimensional analysis, we would not approach it from the vSphere objects' point of view. Instead, we will examine the four key types of metrics (CPU, RAM, network, and storage).

12
CPU Counters

We will continue our venture into the world of counters by focusing on CPU counters in this chapter. We will cover both performance counters and capacity counters. The topics that will be covered in this chapter are as follows:

- VM CPU counters
- ESXi CPU counters
- Cluster CPU counters
- CPU counters for higher-level objects, such as vCenter

CPU counters at the VM level

The following screenshot shows the VM CPU counters in vCenter 6.0, taken from the C# client:

Description	Rollup	Units	Internal Name	Collection Level
☐ Swap wait	Summation	Millisecond	swapwait	3
☐ Idle	Summation	Millisecond	idle	2
☐ Run	Summation	Millisecond	run	2
☐ Used	Summation	Millisecond	used	3
☐ Max limited	Summation	Millisecond	maxlimited	2
☐ Co-stop	Summation	Millisecond	costop	2
☐ Ready	Summation	Millisecond	ready	1
☐ Readiness	Average	Percent	readiness	4
☐ Wait	Summation	Millisecond	wait	3
☐ System	Summation	Millisecond	system	3
☐ Demand-to-entitlement ratio	Latest	Percent	demandEntitlemen…	4
☑ Usage in MHz	Average	MHz	usagemhz	1
☐ Overlap	Summation	Millisecond	overlap	3
☐ Demand	Average	MHz	demand	2
☐ Latency	Average	Percent	latency	2
☐ Entitlement	Latest	MHz	entitlement	2
☑ Usage	Average	Percent	usage	1

VM CPU counters

The **Collection Level** column does not apply to vRealize Operations. Changing **Collection Level** does not impact which counters get collected by vRealize Operations. It collects all counters from vCenter using its own filter, which you can customize.

In vCenter, there are 17 counters available at the VM level, and 12 of them are available at the virtual core level too. This means that a VM with two vCPUs (or two virtual cores) will have 40 counters (*2 x 12 + 16*). A vSphere environment with 1,000 VMs with two vCPUs as the average VM size will have 40,000 counters!

In vCenter, you can only look at two types of counters at the same time. Because VMs can impact each other's performance, you need a management tool that can cut across all of these 40 counters across many VMs in all vCenter Servers. vRealize Operations allows you to slice and dice all of these counters across VMs. Ronald Buder, a VMware vExpert in Singapore and an expert in vRealize Operations, succinctly describes vRealize Operations as "big data".

Back to the 17 counters — the five counters that are not available at the virtual core level are:

- Usage
- Entitlement
- Latency
- Demand-to-entitlement ratio
- Demand

Out of these, what can't you track at the vCPU core level?

You cannot track the CPU latency on a per-core basis. Also, you cannot use **Demand** and **Usage**, and therefore, you have to use **Used** (which is in milliseconds) or **Usage in MHz** when looking at metrics at the core level. Counters that provide values in the percentage format are easier to understand than counters that provide values in milliseconds or MHz, as the percentage format takes into account the context of what is available to the VM. Values in MHz can in fact be misleading if the VM is moved to another host running at a different frequency.

vSphere understands virtual sockets and virtual cores. However, in the vCenter performance chart, it does not distinguish between them.

Read the post by Mark Achtemichuk at `http://blogs.vmware.com/vsphere/2013/10/does-corespersocket-affect-performance.html` for a deeper understanding of virtual sockets and cores.

A virtual socket can have many virtual cores. From configuration point of view, there is a difference between a socket with eight cores and eight sockets with one core each. From a performance point of view, as long as the entire VM vCPU fits into a single physical socket, there will be little difference.

There are three reasons why you should use single-socket multi-core for VM configurations:

- It is easier operationally as it's the default setting.
- In the performance counters, vCenter 6.0 does not distinguish between virtual sockets and virtual cores. A VM with two dual-core virtual sockets or one quad-core virtual socket will be shown as one socket and four cores.
- You must consider software licensing benefits. Some software products are licensed on a per-socket basis with unlimited cores.

Because there are a lot of counters provided by vSphere, it is easier to start by discussing what is *not* provided.

All the VM CPU counters provided are at the vSphere layer. Because the hypervisor does not have visibility into the Guest OS, you will not see counters inside the VM without an agent (for example, **VMware Tools, vRealize Operations End Point Operations**, or **Horizon View Agent**).

From a CPU point of view, the main missing counter is the CPU run queue. This is useful when determining whether the allocated vCPU is enough or not. Generally, the CPU run queue will be low if the CPU utilization is low, as the queue only develops when the CPU is used.

If you can monitor the CPU run queue, you should create a super metric in vRealize Operations that divides the run queue by the number of vCPUs. This gives you a standardized comparison across VMs with different vCPU sizes. If the value is three or higher and CPU utilization is high, this is a sign of insufficient vCPUs for the VM.

Contention counters

vCenter does not have a contention counter, but it does have raw counters that signal contention, which are leveraged by vRealize Operations to derive CPU contention. The main ones are:

- Ready
- Co-stop
- Latency

Ready is the amount of time a VM waits for a thread to be scheduled. **Ready** includes **Limit**, but not **Co-stop**. Many VMware administrators simply look at the **Ready** counter and assume that a value below 5 percent is good. This needs to stop as you need to consider more than just CPU Ready.

vSphere 6 introduces a new counter called **Readiness**. It is the Ready counter in percentage.

Co-stop is the amount of time a multi-vCPU (symmetrical multiprocessing) VM was ready to run but incurred a delay while waiting for parallel threads to be scheduled simultaneously. It is the percentage of time the VM spent in a ready, co-descheduled state. Roughly speaking, the vmkernel CPU scheduler deliberately puts a vCPU in this state if this vCPU advances much further than other vCPUs of the VM.

Co-stop means a VM vCPU is being paused by the vmkernel scheduler to allow its sibling vCPUs to catch up (a feature of relaxed co-scheduling). This naturally happens if the VM has more than 1 vCPU. The waiting happens because ESXi does not have enough physical CPUs to serve all the virtual CPUs. This is why you need to adjust the size of the VM. In *Chapter 7, Capacity-Monitoring Dashboards*, we covered the use case of adjusting the size of the VM with confidence, using individual virtual core information.

Latency is the `%LAT_C` counter in esxtop. It includes Ready and Co-stop and is also impacted by the **Hyper-Threading** (HT) busy time and the hardware CPU power state (dynamic voltage frequency scaling). Because of this, vRealize Operations uses Latency as its primary source for CPU contention data.

The contention counter and power management

The Latency counter is greatly affected by the CPU power management. It can spike if you do not set the CPU power management to maximum. The following screenshot shows the power meter on a HP Proliant server, a popular ESXi host. In the **20-Minute History Graph**, notice how the power consumption spiked and then went down. We changed the power management from balanced to maximum and then back to balanced.

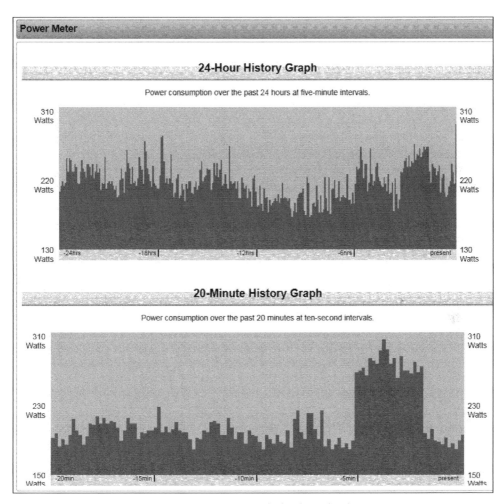

Power management at the hardware level

What do you expect we will see at the ESXi level? Specifically, what do you think the CPU latency will be during the spike? Do you think it will go down to near 0 percent?

If your answer is yes, you are right.

The next diagram shows the latency, which was hovering around 6.4 percent and dropped to 0 percent. It then went up after we changed the power management back to balanced.

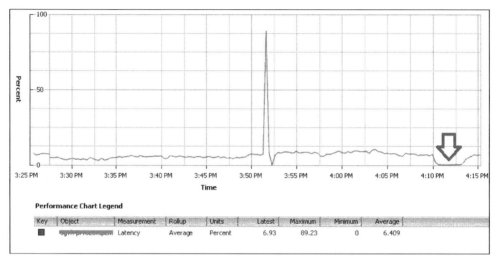

The CPU Latency counter is affected by power management

Now, the Latency counter impacts the Contention counter. You will see that Contention hovers around 6.4 percent (in this case), even though the reality is actually closer to **0**. Since we are setting SLA based on contention, you need to take this into account.

There are two options for setting the maximum CPU performance:

- At the hardware level (BIOS)
- At the ESXi level

The following diagram shows the settings on an HP Proliant DL 380 G7. The first three choices manage power at the hardware level. The *Performance Best Practices for VMware vSphere 6.0* whitepaper recommends that you configure your BIOS settings to allow ESXi the most flexibility in using (or not using) the power management features offered by your hardware and then make your power-management choices within ESXi.

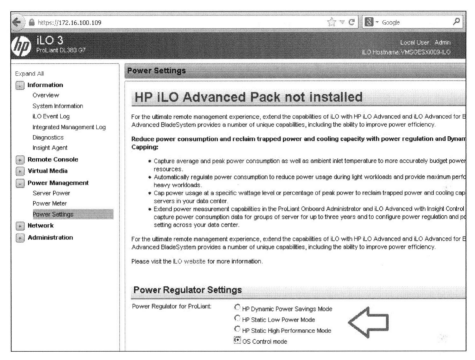

Power management settings at the hardware level

An example of how to pass the control to ESXi is shown in the following screenshot. Changing from the hardware level to software level usually requires a reboot of the host.

Once **Power Policy Settings** are enabled at the ESXi level, you can control them via vCenter, as shown in the following screenshot. None of these changes require a reboot. The default setting is **Balanced**, which you should change to **High performance** if you have workload that is sensitive to CPU latency (for example, VDI or tier-1 applications).

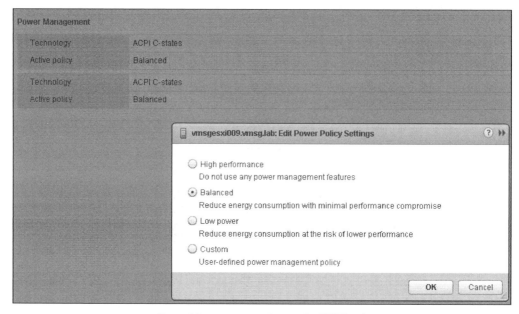

Power Management settings at the ESXi level

You can track the actual power consumption from vCenter Server or vRealize Operations.

The next screenshot shows the power consumption. This is an HP DL 380 G7 machine with two sockets containing Xeon processors and 64 GB of RAM. We changed the power policy from **Balanced** to **Low power** at around 5:50 p.m. You can see that the power consumption drops from around **150 W** to **144 W**. The spike in the chart at around 5:10 p.m. is due to vMotion. We vMotioned all the VMs from one host to another host.

The power consumption remains at around **145 W**, which means this is as low as it gets.

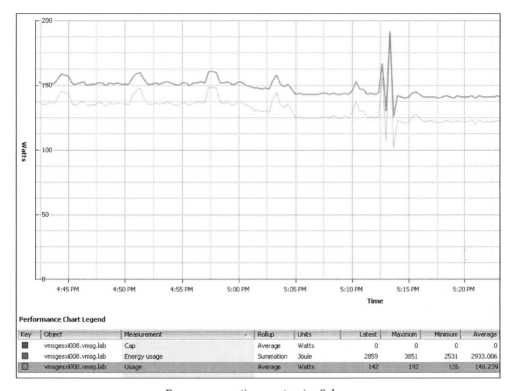

Key	Object	Measurement	Rollup	Units	Latest	Maximum	Minimum	Average
▨	vmsgesxi008.vmsg.lab	Cap	Average	Watts	0	0	0	0
▨	vmsgesxi008.vmsg.lab	Energy usage	Summation	Joule	2859	3851	2531	2933.006
▢	vmsgesxi008.vmsg.lab	Usage	Average	Watts	142	192	126	146.239

Power consumption counters in vSphere

 More information about power management can be found at `http://kb.vmware.com/kb/1018206` and `https://www.vmware.com/resources/techresources/10416`. The **Knowledge Base (KB)** article provides settings for other hardware, and the technical paper goes deeper in explaining the concepts. Rebecca Grider shows that performance impact is minimal in `http://blogs.vmware.com/performance/2013/05/power-management-and-performance-in-esxi-5-1.html`. This is reassuring because the default setting in ESXi is **balanced**.

If you do not change the CPU power management to maximum performance, you should see Latency higher than Ready, because Latency is affected by change in CPU frequency. In addition, Latency also goes up if the VM does not run on its preferred core (which is where it ran previously). Ready only goes up if the VM is unable to run at all.

The following screenshot shows that **Latency** is higher than **Ready**, because the ESXi host is set to the default CPU power management setting:

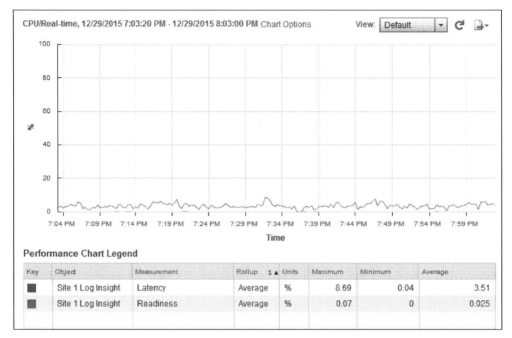

The CPU Latency versus CPU Ready counters

The **Ready** value is the flat red line near 0. It barely fluctuates between 0 and 0.07 percent. The **Latency** counter, however, spikes to 8.69 percent—an amount many times bigger!

The contention counter – why ready is not enough

vRealize Operations simplifies the tracking of contention by providing a CPU Contention counter. The next chart shows that the **CPU Contention** spikes to 10.65 percent when the Co-stop value hits 7,391 on 14 March at around 1:45 p.m. It is so much easier to think in percentage than in milliseconds. It is hard to remember whether the value 7,391 is considered good or bad, as you must multiply 20,000 by the number of virtual cores in the VM.

Note that the CPU Ready value did not spike even though Co-stop spiked, as Ready does not include Co-stop. Compared to CPU Ready, CPU Contention also tends to correlate better to CPU Usage. The following chart demonstrates that closer correlation. Note that CPU Usage and CPU Contention have a similar pattern.

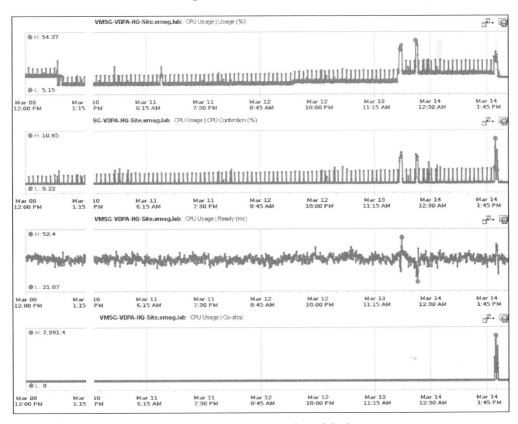

CPU Usage, Contention, Ready, and Co-Stop

In the preceding chart, CPU Ready shows very little movement. It varies from 21 milliseconds to 52 milliseconds. Since the range is 80,000, this means that the CPU Ready counter barely moves—as 50 out of 80,000 is around just 0.06%. Compare this with CPU Contention, which spikes to 10%!

Because of this higher sensitivity, you would only set the SLA on CPU Contention to the same level as CPU Ready if you configure the maximum CPU power.

Let's take another example. This time, we will focus on the correlation between utilization (Usage) and performance (co-stop, ready, contention).

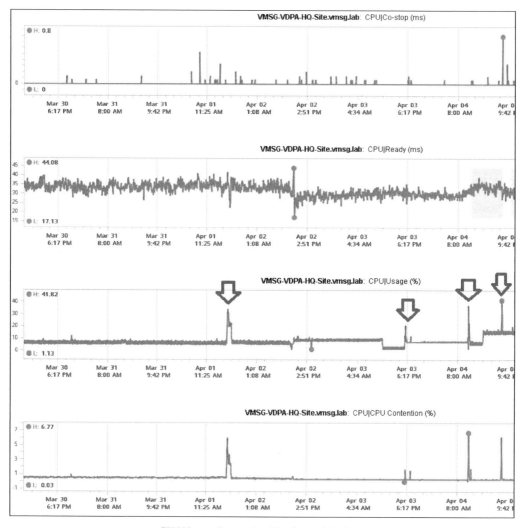

CPU Usage, Contention, Ready, and Co-Stop

From the previous chart, we can see that CPU Contention spikes when CPU Usage spikes (see the red arrows), whereas CPU Co-stop does not. We also see that CPU Ready barely moves. If you set your SLA at 5 percent for CPU Ready, you are safe. If you set your SLA to the same 5 percent for CPU Contention, you fail to deliver it on three different occasions as there are three spikes in the previous chart that passed 5%.

Your SLA value depends on your CPU power management.

If the CPU power management is set to maximum, the CPU Contention counter will show a more realistic number, which is a much lower value. The two examples in the following screenshot show that it can go down to well below 1%:

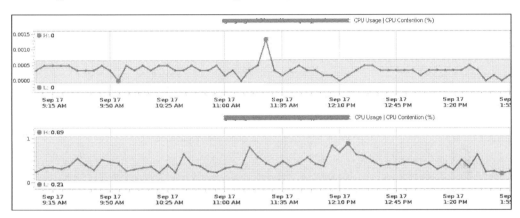

Good CPU Contention values

The Contention counter has a correlation with the Utilization counter. This is logical in a fair-share scheduler. If ESXi is unable to satisfy all demands, the VM with the highest demand will naturally experience highest contention. The more you ask, the higher the chance you're experiencing contention.

The following screenshot shows **VM CPU Demand** and **VM CPU Contention**. Both metrics move in tandem. Their pattern will not be identical as there are other VMs running in the host.

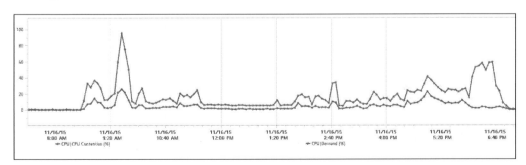

VM CPU Demand correlated with VM CPU Contention

The difference between CPU Contention among VMs in the same ESXi can be large. The following screenshot shows two VMs with essentially the same configuration. They are part of the VDI environment, so they have the same Windows 7 64-bit image and both have two vCPUs. Notice how one VM has barely any contention. That's because the utilization is also low.

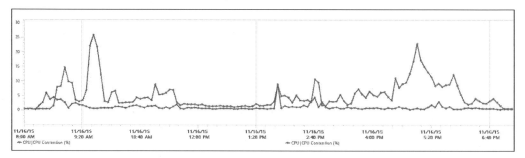

VM CPU Contention variation

Utilization counters

Once you are satisfied that there is no contention, it is time to check utilization. If it is high and the CPU run queue inside the VM is high, there is a good chance that the VM needs to be given more vCPUs. If it is low but performance is slow, you need to check whether the CPU is waiting for RAM, disk, or network.

For utilization, vCenter provides four counters:

- Demand (MHz)
- Usage (%) and Usage (MHz)
- Used (ms)
- Run (ms)

They are shown in the following screenshot. While they have similar values, they are not identical.

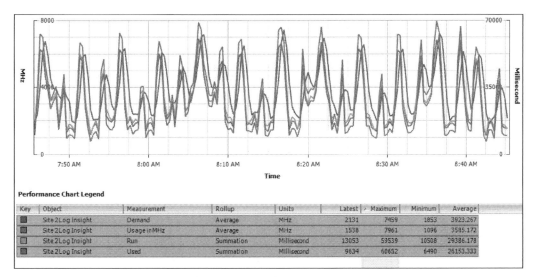

The main CPU Utilization counters

The counters have different units too. The easiest one is **Usage**, since it is also given in percentage. However, it does not take into account contention. CPU Demand takes this into account.

Another limitation with **Usage** is that it is not available at the virtual CPU level.

If you have a big VM, you need to look at individual core performance to ensure it is not oversized. A low usage at the VM level does not mean balanced utilization across all cores. If the utilization is not balanced and you see a consistent pattern for weeks, you should consider reducing the vCPUs to improve performance. Adjusting the size gives better performance than relying on relaxed co-scheduling, as the gap between the leading vCPU and the idle vCPU cannot exceed a certain threshold. Refer to the *The CPU Scheduler in VMware vSphere 5.1* whitepaper (`https://www.vmware.com/files/pdf/techpaper/VMware-vSphere-CPU-Sched-Perf.pdf`).

CPU **Run** is not enabled by default in vRealize Operations. You can enable it via the **Policy** dialog box.

Usage in MHz, Demand, and **Used** should have similar patterns in a healthy environment. Can you figure out why the value of **Demand** is higher than **Usage**? **Demand** has indeed exceeded 100 percent at one point. CPU **Demand** and CPU **Used** happen to be identical in this example:

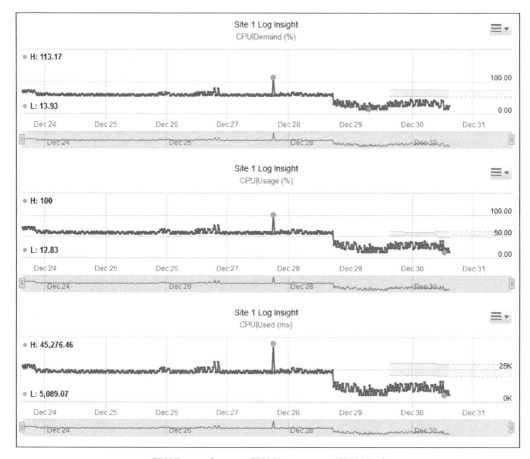

CPU Demand versus CPU Usage versus CPU Used

To convert CPU **Used** from milliseconds to percentage, divide it by 40,000. The preceding VM has two vCPUs, so the maximum value (equivalent to 100 percent) is 40,000 milliseconds. Refer to *Chapter 11, SDDC Key Counters*, if you are not sure why 20,000 milliseconds equals 100 percent.

You might think that since the sampling period is based on 5 minutes, 100 percent means 300 seconds, or 300,000 milliseconds. It is not. vRealize Operations takes the real-time chart (which is 20 seconds), and takes the average of these 20-second intervals. It does not sum them up.

Let's plot another example. In this case, all the counters are lower. The VM is not as busy as the VM in the previous example.

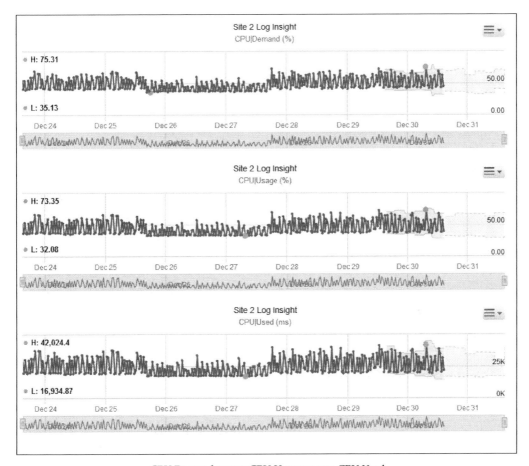

CPU Demand versus CPU Usage versus CPU Used

The CPU **Usage** is lower than CPU **Demand** again, although it is not so obvious. **Usage** peaked at 73% while **Demand** hit 75%. The CPU **Used**, however, is lower than both CPU **Usage** and CPU **Demand**. It peaked at 42,024. Since the VM has three vCPUs, we divide by 60,000 and get 70%.

The reason for the differences among these counters is they use different formulas and are affected differently by power management and Hyper-Threading.

The formulas for CPU **Used** and CPU **Run** are as follows:

- *Used = Run + System – Overlap*
- *100% = Run + Ready + Co-Stop + Wait*

CPU Used is aware that Hyper-Threading is not a full core. In Hyper-Threading, two threads share the same physical core, so there is an efficiency loss. Prior to vSphere 5.0, the efficiency loss was valued at 50 percent. This was lowered to 37.5% in vSphere 5.0 as the HT technology improved. Each physical thread is assumed to be doing 62.5% of a non-HT core. So, the total from both threads is 125%.

CPU Run does not account for Hyper-Threading and simply takes each thread as a full core. As a result, the value can be twice as large as that of CPU Used.

CPU Used also takes into account power management. When the physical CPU frequency is lowered by power management, it uses that reduced value. In this case, CPU Used will be lower than CPU Run.

On the other hand, if you have a CPU that supports Turbo mode, the CPU frequency can be higher than the nominal (rated) frequency. In this case, CPU Used can be higher than CPU Run.

The System counter tracks the amount of time spent on system processes on each vCPU in the VM. This includes the time spent by vmkernel doing storage or network I/O on behalf of the VM. The hypervisor knows whether the VM is accessing ring zero or not and whether it is executing a privileged instruction or not.

The Overlap counter counts the time vmkernel interrupts a VM to perform system services on behalf of another VM.

System and Overlap are related at the ESXi level, as the hypervisor juggles multiple VMs. If VM number 1 is currently being scheduled on core number 1 and a network packet for VM number 2 is processed by the ESXi vmkernel on the same core, the time spent appears as Overlap for VM number 1 and System for VM number 2.

The System and Overlap counters are not captured by default in vRealize Operations. You can enable it in the policy if you need to.

In an environment where the utilization is low and the VMs do not generate a lot of I/O, the value of System and Overlap will be near-zero. You can track the behavior of these two counters in your data center by creating super metrics in vRealize Operations. The super metric tracks the maximum value of each counter. A change in the pattern of the line chart is worth investigating.

The Utilization counter – CPU workload

Let's recap. We have four counters for CPU: Demand, Usage, Run and Used. The counter that I recommend is Demand.

The main reason why you should choose CPU Demand is it takes into account contention. In an environment where the ESXi is unable to meet the demand of its VMs, you will see CPU Demand to be higher than CPU Usage. The CPU Demand counter shows the utilization that would have happened if there were no contention. The charts in the following screenshot shows that the VM **Site 1 Log Insight** demands more CPU that the hypervisor was able to provide:

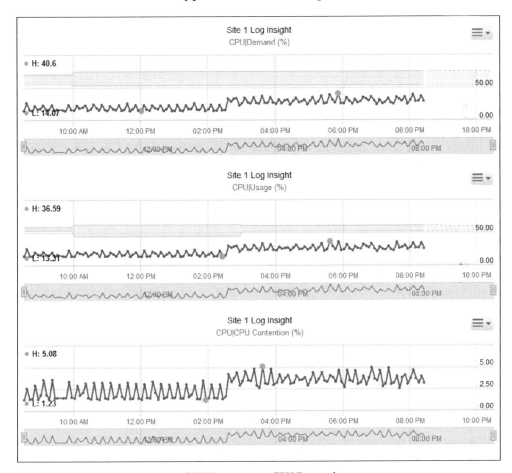

CPU Usage versus CPU Demand

Another reason for choosing Demand is it takes into account I/O operations. A VM that does heavy I/O will have higher CPU Demand. Both network I/O and storage I/O are performed by vmkernel on the VM behalf. This work can be done on another core. The time spent doing the work is charged to Demand.

vRealize Operations also provides the Workload (%) counter. It is the Demand (%) counter, but rounded to the nearest whole number. The following screenshot shows that the **Workload** chart is simplified, which makes it easier to read. The **Workload (%)** counter is even easier to read in an idle VM, because it will show a flat line.

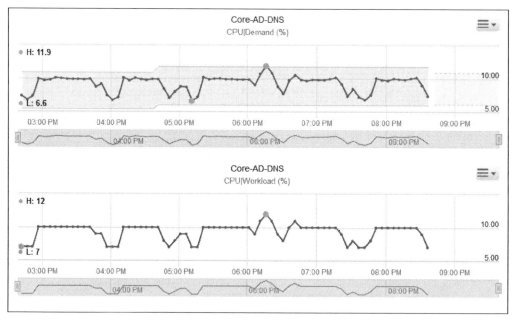

CPU Demand and CPU Workload

What should the values of CPU Workload and CPU Contention be in a healthy environment when Usage is very high? If the Usage is flat at 100%, and ESXi is able to meet all the demands, what do you expect the value of CPU Workload and CPU Contention to be?

The following chart shows a VM with 100-percent utilization. The CPU Workload counter is slightly higher as it is based on Demand, and we expect it to be a bit higher. The CPU Contention is low, as the VM is not contending with other VMs for resources.

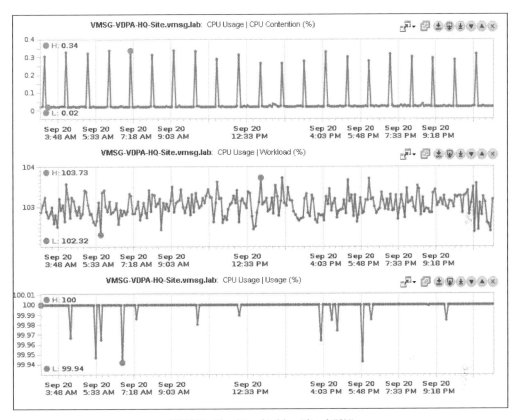

CPU Workload in a highly utilized ESXi

Other counters

The Entitlement counter tracks the CPU entitlement of the VM. If there is no contention, this value can be relatively flat (as shown in the chart in the following diagram). The red line at the top is the Entitlement. Notice that it is practically a straight line, even though the Demand and Usage fluctuate.

The value is also much higher than both Demand and Usage, showing a healthy ESXi host.

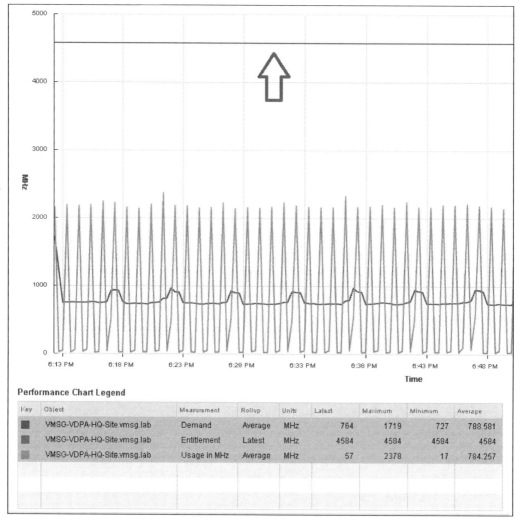

CPU Demand versus Usage

The Demand-to-Entitlement Ratio is a useful counter as you do not have to track **Demand** and **Entitlement**. Whenever the value shoots above 100 percent, the VM is experiencing CPU contention. It is not getting what it is asking for.

CPU Idle tracks the time the VM is not doing any work. A majority of VMs in test and development environments are likely to be idle most of the time.

CPU Wait includes CPU Idle, Swap Wait, and CPU I/O Wait states. Because it includes Idle time, it can be confusing initially. CPU Swap Wait tracks the time an ESXi world (this normally means a VM) is waiting for the vmkernel to swap memory. The value of CPU Wait, CPU Idle, and Swap Wait indicate there is an I/O bound. It means that the VM is being blocked, waiting for an I/O operation. This is shown in vRealize Operations with the CPU I/O Wait metric. If your VM does not experience an I/O issue, then CPU Wait and CPU Idle will be nearly identical.

The following screenshot shows such a scenario. This is a VDPA VM with four vCPUs. As a backup appliance, it does perform some I/O, but the hypervisor is serving it well.

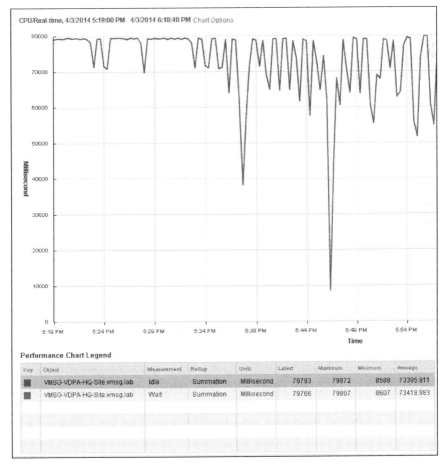

CPU Wait versus Idle

Let's look at another example. This is a two-vCPU VM, so we expect the total to not exceed 40,000 milliseconds. Again, the values of **Idle** and **Wait** are very similar, indicating I/O is not a bottleneck. This particular VM is a vCenter Appliance 5.5 Update 1.

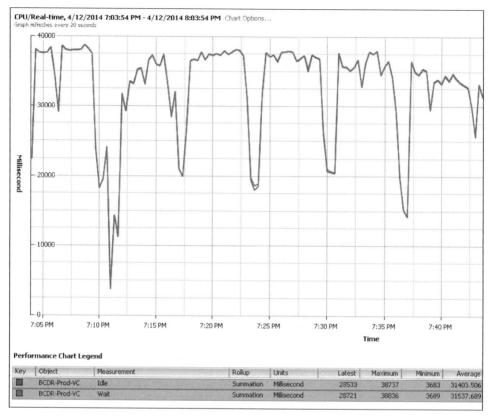

CPU Wait and CPU Idle

In a healthy environment, the value of **Swap Wait** should be zero. This counter tracks the CPU time spent waiting for memory to be swapped in from disk to DIMM. This counter is actually being used by vRealize Operations to derive the memory Contention (%) counter.

Certain counters, such as **Max Limited**, should always be zero, because you do not want to artificially place a **Limit**. With vRealize Operations, you can create a super metric that tracks the maximum value of **Max Limited** across all VMs in your entire data center. You should end up with a perfectly flat chart as the value for every VM should be zero all the time. You can then create an alert if the value is not zero, which informs you that someone has placed a limit on a VM.

VM CPU key counters

We talked about contention and utilization being the main areas that you check. The following tables summarize the recommendations on what to monitor at the core level or at the overall level (VM level in this case).

The following table shows the key CPU counter at the virtual core level:

Purpose	vCenter	vRealize Operations
Contention	Ready (ms). Co-stop (ms). Latency does not exist at the core-level.	Ready (%). Co-Stop (ms). There is no Contention counter at the core level.
Utilization	Used (ms).	Used (ms). There is no Demand counter at the core level.

vRealize Operations provides the **Ready** counter in percentage at the core level, which is easier to interpret than milliseconds.

The following table shows the key CPU counter at the VM level:

Purpose	vCenter	vRealize Operations
Contention	Limit (ms), if applicable Latency (%)	Contention (%)
Utilization	Usage (%)	Workload (%)

CPU counters at the ESXi level

The counters at the ESXi level are naturally similar to the ones at the VM level, as the hypervisor is also an OS. The key difference is that there are counters that are not applicable to ESXi hosts, such as **Entitlement**, **Max Limited**, and **System**.

The values at the hypervisor level reflect the aggregate value of all VMs in the host plus the hypervisor's own workload. The hypervisor generates its own workload, for example, vMotion, cloning, and other tasks. Kernel modules such as Virtual SAN and NSX also take up CPU resources.

Unlike VMs, which have 17 counters for CPU, ESXi comes with 15 counters for CPU. Also, unlike VMs, which provide 11 counters at the CPU core level, ESXi only provides five counters at the CPU core level. The remaining nine counters that are not available at the core level are as follows:

- Usage in MHz
- Total capacity
- Wait
- Demand
- Ready
- Readiness
- Reserved capacity
- Latency
- Swap Wait
- Co-stop

This means you will not be able to track contention at the physical core level by looking at the ESXi host metrics, as all the three counters (Ready, Latency, and Co-stop) are not available. **Reserved Capacity** and **Total Capacity** are obviously not applicable at the physical core level. You cannot use **Demand** and **Usage in MHz**; you have to use **CPU Used** (milliseconds) or **Usage (%)**.

At the physical core level, you have one counter to track **Wait** and four counters to track usage (Core Utilization, Utilization, Usage, and Used).

If you recall, at the VM level, you cannot use **Usage (%)** to track individual virtual CPU cores, but you can use **Usage in MHz**. The opposite happens for ESXi. At the ESXi level, you cannot use **Usage in MHz** to track individual physical CPU cores, but you can use **Usage (%)**:

Description	Rollup	Units	Internal Name	Collection Level
☐ Utilization	Average	Percent	utilization	2
☐ Used	Summation	Millisecond	used	3
☐ Idle	Summation	Millisecond	idle	2
☐ Core Utilization	Average	Percent	coreUtilization	2
☑ Usage	Average	Percent	usage	1
☐ Co-stop	Summation	Millisecond	costop	2
☐ Readiness	Average	Percent	readiness	4
☐ Latency	Average	Percent	latency	2
☐ Demand	Average	MHz	demand	2
☐ Swap wait	Summation	Millisecond	swapwait	3
☐ Total capacity	Average	MHz	totalCapacity	2
☑ Usage in MHz	Average	MHz	usagemhz	1
☐ Reserved capacity	Average	MHz	reservedCapacity	2
☐ Wait	Summation	Millisecond	wait	3
☐ Ready	Summation	Millisecond	ready	1

ESXi: CPU counters

Contention counters

As usual, we will focus on performance first, then capacity.

Similar to the limitation we saw with VM, there is no counter for contention in vCenter. You need to look at **Ready**, **Latency**, and **Co-stop**. These three counters are shown in the next screenshot. The **Ready** value looks healthy in this example. Notice that it was hovering around 200 milliseconds. As the graph refreshes every 20 seconds, each data point represents 20,000 milliseconds per virtual core.

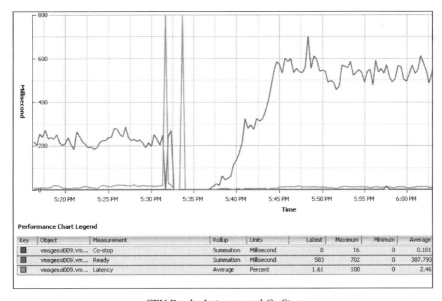

CPU Ready, Latency, and Co-Stop

The graph does not show the number of virtual cores (a VM with two vCPUs has two virtual cores). Even if there is only one VM on the host and that VM only has one vCPU, the 200 milliseconds translates to 1 percent, which is a healthy value. The value drops to near-zero when the ESXi host has some activity. The action performed resulting in this graph was executing vMotion for a number of VMs concurrently. When the ESXi has more VMs, it settles for a higher CPU Ready level, hovering around 600. This is because we have moved VMs after the mass vMotion operation, and each VM does have Ready time. The aggregate is reflected here. It is interesting to see that the Latency counter spikes twice, and it spikes to 100 percent!

Perhaps work was done on a different physical core, which means Latency would go up. Notice that each spike lasted for 20 seconds, so it will not show up in vRealize Operations, as each data point is of 5 minutes. During the entire 1-hour period, the Co-stop counter barely moved. It only moved once and only reached the value of 16 out of a maximum of 20,000.

Tracking multiple counters with different units is certainly complex. That is why it is easier to track the CPU Contention counter, available in vRealize Operations.

CPU Contention at the ESXi level is the sum of all its VM CPU Contention (in ms) divided by 20,000 milliseconds times the number of running VMs' vCPUs. Continuing with the same scenario, the equivalent chart for vRealize Operations is shown next. This is a longer timeline, so we can see the relationship between Ready and Contention and how those metrics relate to CPU Demand. There is a correlation between CPU Demand and CPU Contention. Similar to what we observed for VMs, CPU Contention is more sensitive than CPU Ready on an ESXi host. 26,213 in ms translates to 1.3%.

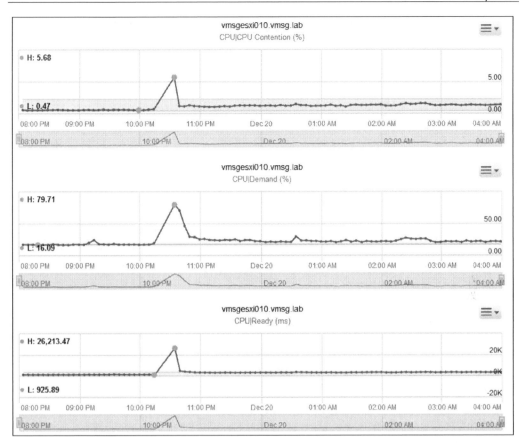

CPU Ready, Contention, and Demand

Here is another example that shows the sensitivity of CPU Contention. Notice that it hovers around 10 percent for more than 24 hours. The following chart spans March 16, 3:00 a.m. to March 18, 12:00 a.m. The portion of the chart that was cropped was showing values similar to what you see, so you're not missing any information.

CPU Contention also correlates with CPU Demand, and CPU Ready barely moves during the entire period.

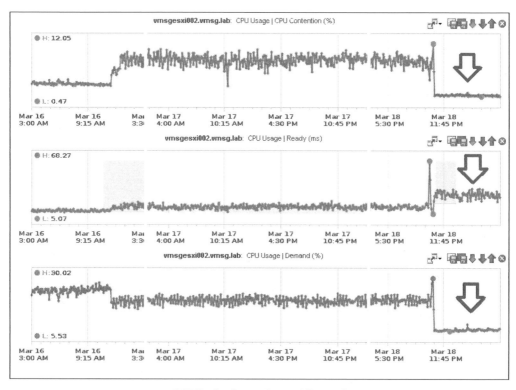

CPU Ready, Contention, and Demand

Can CPU Ready go up while CPU Contention remains the same?

Yes, it can.

The following chart is from the same ESXi host, with the view zoomed in to a later time. In this chart, CPU Ready goes up a little to 567 milliseconds. CPU Contention, however, does not react to it. In fact, the value drops a little. This happens when you have a lot of idle VMs in the ESXi host. Each idle VM has Ready time, and the aggregate is reflected in the ESXi host. Since they are idle, there is no contention.

This is yet another reason why you should use CPU Contention over CPU Ready.

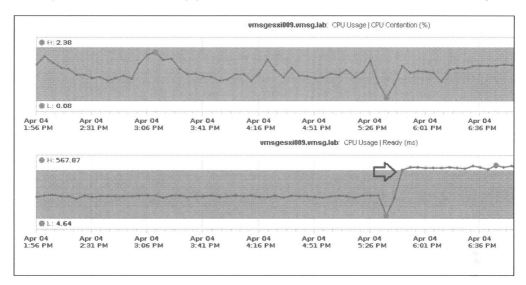

CPU Contention versus Ready

CPU Contention provides a more reliable value than CPU Ready. The following screenshot spans 30 days, which is long enough for a comparison. Notice that CPU Ready spikes to a very high number around March 14, yet it does not move at all during the remaining period.

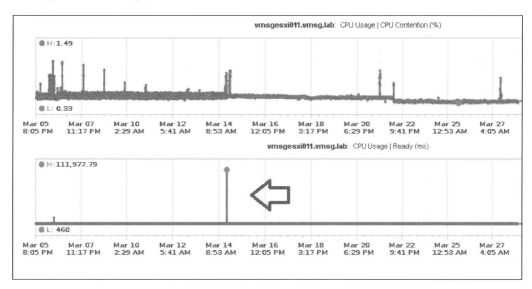

A CPU Ready spike – example 1

Here is another example where CPU Ready shoots to a high value, whereas CPU Contention remains constant. The CPU Ready spike actually lasts 10 minutes, as we see two values when we zoom into the chart.

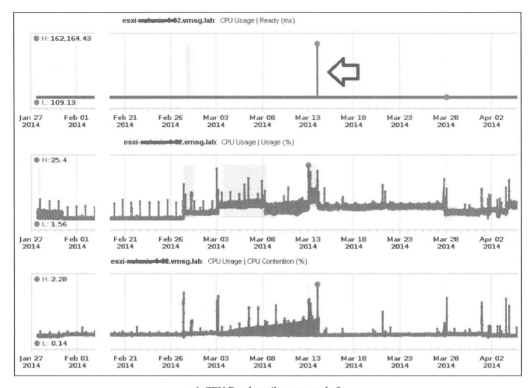

A CPU Ready spike – example 2

Notice that **CPU Usage | CPU Contention (%)** shows no spike. All the values are below 25%. There is also no contention. We do not expect Contention in general as the labs consist of small VMs and they are mostly idle.

Utilization counters – key counters

For utilization, the counters differ from those of VMs. You still have **Usage (%)**, **Usage in MHz**, **Demand (MHz)**, and **Used (ms)**. But instead of **Run**, you have **Utilization (%)** and **Core Utilization (%)**.

Let's compare the values to study them. The following chart shows Usage versus Demand. Based on the chart we saw at the VM level, we expect them to be similar but not identical in the real-time chart. This chart shows that we can rely on this assumption.

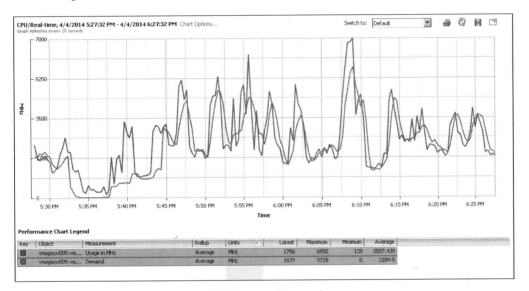

CPU Usage and Demand

We have also come to expect that although Usage and Demand in vRealize Operations will be on a different scale, their pattern will be identical when there is no contention. The following chart confirms this:

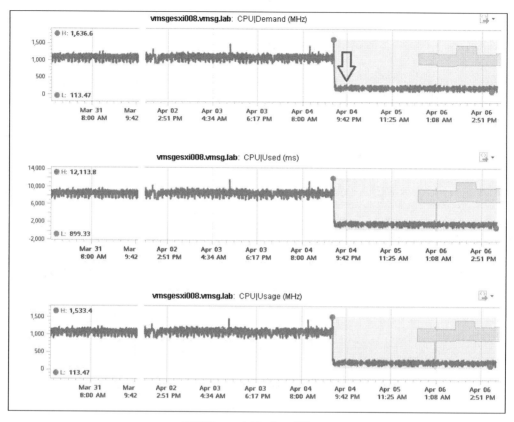

CPU Demand, Used, and Usage

As a side note, you can see the dynamic threshold in action in the preceding chart. vRealize Operations was not expecting a drop in the CPU utilization because it has been stable for days. The yellow area shows the period where the value is not within the range of vRealize Operations' predictive analysis. The light gray area is the range that vRealize Operations expected the metrics to fall within. The value drops in this example because all the VMs were moved from this host using vMotion. That is certainly not a normal operation in production.

In an environment where there is contention, CPU Demand will be higher. The following example shows an ESXi that experienced a spike in demand and was unable to fulfill all the demands:

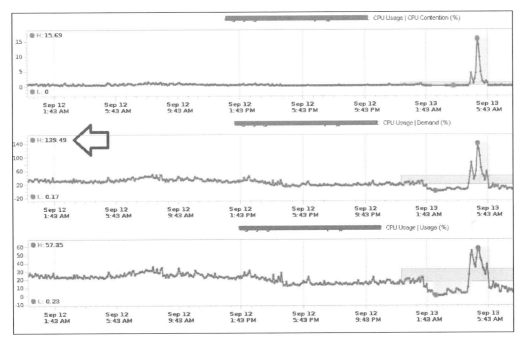

CPU Contention, Demand, and Usage

During the period it was able to meet the demands, the CPU Demand and CPU Usage counters were similar (it's hard to see due to the scale), and the CPU Contention counter was low. However, during that sharp spike, both CPU Demand and CPU Contention rose to reveal the issue. CPU Usage only rose to 57 percent. If you were using CPU Usage as an alert, you would not get one! This is why you should not use CPU Usage in the environment.

Just like in the case for VMs, vRealize Operations also provides the Workload (%) counter for the ESXi host. The next screenshot shows why you should use Workload over Demand. It is easier to read as the value is rounded.

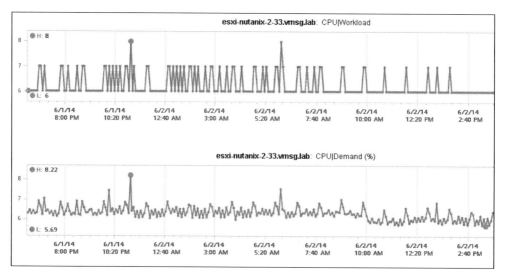

CPU Workload and Demand

At individual core levels, vRealize Operations retains two metrics to track: **Usage (%)** and **Used (ms)**. The two values are identical, as you can see from the following chart. If you take the peak value of CPU Used (which is around 8,314) and divide it by 20,000, you get the peak value of Usage (which is around 42%).

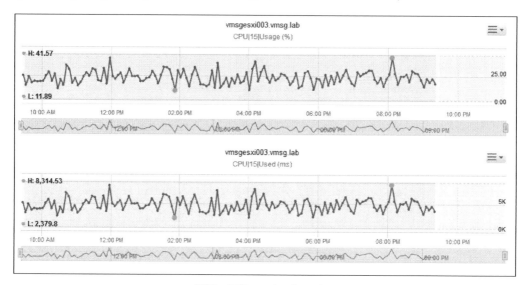

ESXi – CPU core-level metrics

Utilization counters – secondary counters

We mentioned previously that some counters in ESXi are the sum of the associated counters of all the VMs running in the host. CPU **Wait** is such an example. The next diagram shows CPU **Wait** hovering around 220,000. The sharp drop to around 170,000 was caused by moving a VM off the host using vMotion. The remaining VMs on the host were then moved using vMotion, causing the counter to drop to zero.

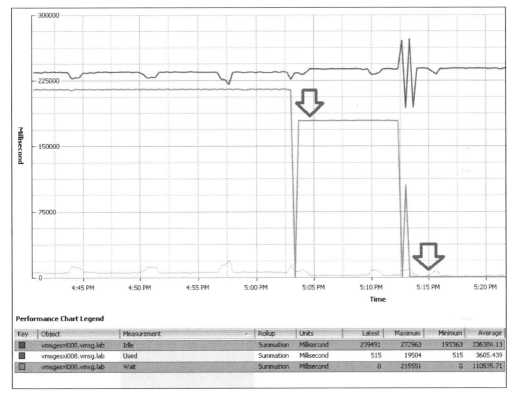

Performance Chart Legend

Key	Object	Measurement	Rollup	Units	Latest	Maximum	Minimum	Average
■	vmsgesxi008.vmsg.lab	Idle	Summation	Millisecond	239491	272963	193363	236386.13
■	vmsgesxi008.vmsg.lab	Used	Summation	Millisecond	515	19504	515	3605.439
■	vmsgesxi008.vmsg.lab	Wait	Summation	Millisecond	0	215551	0	110535.71

CPU Idle, Used, and Wait

Now, let's look at **Core Utilization** and **Utilization**. These counters are not available at the VM level. They are also not included in vRealize Operations by default. Core Utilization includes Hyper-Threading, as the value is twice as much. I verified with a few other ESXi hosts (a different model and on a different cluster).

The value of **Core Utilization** is higher than the values of **Utilization** and **Usage**, although it is not always double because it takes into account Hyper-Threading.

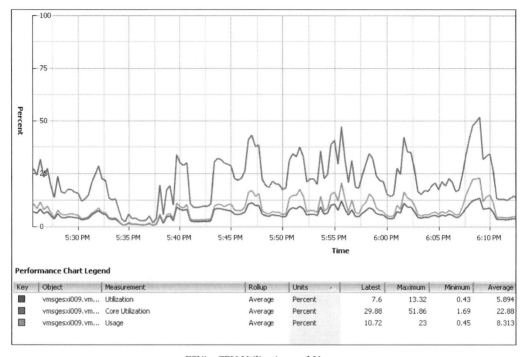

Key	Object	Measurement	Rollup	Units	Latest	Maximum	Minimum	Average
■	vmsgesxi009.vm...	Utilization	Average	Percent	7.6	13.32	0.43	5.894
■	vmsgesxi009.vm...	Core Utilization	Average	Percent	29.88	51.86	1.69	22.88
■	vmsgesxi009.vm...	Usage	Average	Percent	10.72	23	0.45	8.313

ESXi – CPU Utilization and Usage

The preceding screenshot shows **Utilization** at the ESXi host level. Now, let's look at a single core. The value of **Core Utilization** is around double that of **Utilization**.

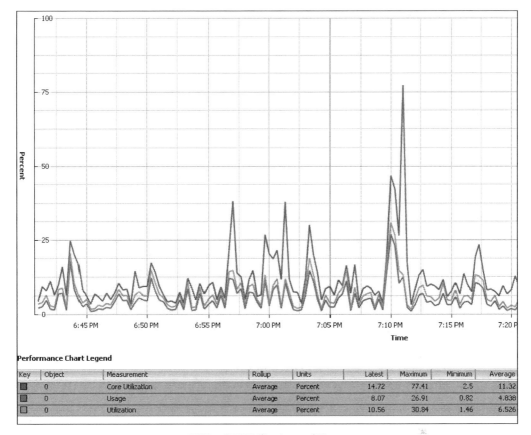

Key	Object	Measurement	Rollup	Units	Latest	Maximum	Minimum	Average
■	0	Core Utilization	Average	Percent	14.72	77.41	2.5	11.32
■	0	Usage	Average	Percent	8.07	26.91	0.82	4.838
□	0	Utilization	Average	Percent	10.56	30.84	1.46	6.526

ESXi – CPU Utilization and Usage

As we already have enough counters for utilization, we do not see a use case to use the **Core Utilization** and **Utilization** counters. Considering they are not included in vRealize Operations, they are considered a corner-case situation. For such troubleshooting, esxtop might be a better tool.

ESXi provides the following two capacity-related counters that are not available at the VM level:

- **Total capacity**: This is the sum of all the physical cores in MHz. It does not take into account Hyper-Threading. It does take into account CPU power management, as the value is around 11 percent to 18 percent—lower than the stated CPU frequency.

Reserved capacity: This counter tracks any reservation made for VMs. In the example shown in the following chart, a reservation of 5,000 MHz is set for a VM. Capacity management should be done at the cluster level and not at the host level. As such, I do not see a use case for this counter. If you do, let me know.

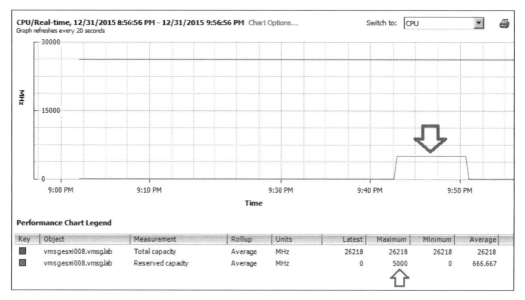

ESXi – Total Capacity and Reserved Capacity

If your cluster uses a lot of VM-level reservations, you can create a super metric that calculates the capacity remaining from a reservation point of view. You do this by using the following formula:

(Reserved Capacity / Total Capacity) * (100) percent

CPU Wait, Swap Wait, and Idle behave the same way in ESXi as they do in VMs. So, you should expect Swap Wait to be zero all the time during business as usual, indicating that your ESXi is not accessing memory from the disk. None of these three counters are captured in vRealize Operations by default, where there are other counters that can tell us the same information. For example, there are storage and memory counters to indicate issues caused by storage or memory.

You can also get visibility into the vmkernel daemons and processes. I've listed some of them in the following diagram. How many can you recognize?

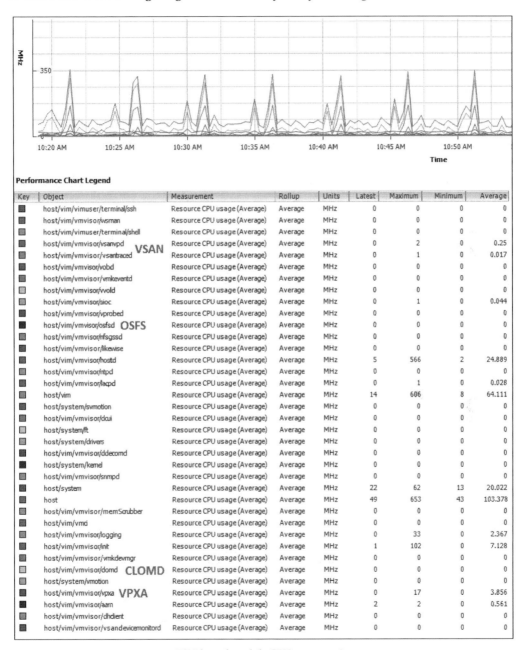

ESXi kernel module CPU consumption

In general, the total CPU utilization of vmkernel is not something you need to include in your capacity planning. The previous chart shows the utilization of each process. It gives you the latest, maximum, minimum, and average utilization of each.

I have highlighted some of them. As VSAN is a kernel module, its components appear alongside other vmkernel components. They are explained in the *VMware Virtual SAN Diagnostics and Troubleshooting Reference Manual* by Cormac Hogan.

We have also highlighted VPXA. That process should be familiar to you.

ESXi CPU key counters

We talked about **Contention** and **Utilization** being the main metrics to check for. The following tables summarize what you should monitor at the core level or at the overall object (host) level.

This table shows the ESXi CPU core level counters:

Purpose	vCenter	vRealize Operations
Contention	None	None (as it is derived from vCenter)
Utilization	Usage (%)	Usage (%)

This table shows the ESXi-level CPU counters:

Purpose	vCenter	vRealize Operations
Contention	Ready (ms) Co-stop (ms) Latency (%)	Contention (%)
Utilization	Usage (%)	Workload (%)

CPU counters at the cluster level

vCenter 6.0 only provides three CPU counters at the cluster level (as shown in the next screenshot):

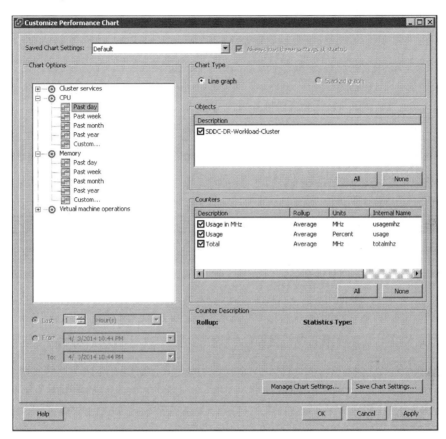

Cluster CPU counters provided by vCenter

These are the three counters:

- CPU Usage (MHz)
- CPU Usage (Percent)
- Total (MHz)There is no storage or network metric group provided. Also, the data is not available in real time, meaning that the data granularity is in intervals of 5 minutes, not 20 seconds.

Let's look at an example of the values of the two usage counters. I've excluded the **Total** metric from the next screenshot, as you would not be able to see the fluctuation in the **Usage in MHz** counter if it were included.

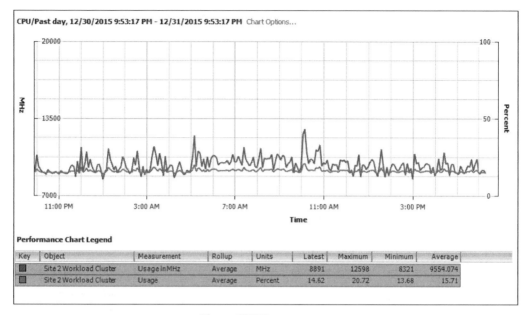

Cluster CPU Usage counters

The Total counter is a relatively static counter. It does not take into account vSphere HA. Changing the cluster HA setting does not impact this value. However, it does seem to take into account CPU power management. For example, we are getting a total value of 56 GHz, whereas the actual total is 63 GHz. I checked with a cluster with identical configuration (hardware and CPU power management), and the values differed slightly.

vRealize Operations provides a richer set of CPU counters at the cluster level. They are useful as performance and capacity management should be done at cluster level. A majority of the counters are an average or a sum of all host members. There are no peak counters. This makes sense, as DRS will balance your cluster. However, in situations where the overall cluster has low utilization, you can have an unbalanced distribution. This also makes sense, as balancing it does not necessarily result in improved performance. Having a peak counter in this case is useful, as the average will not tell the full story.

As a result, you should track both average and peak. In addition, you should track both the contention and the utilization. This means that you are tracking four data points. Together, the four points should give you good insight into the performance of your environment. The next table lists the key counters that give you these four data points. It shows you the vRealize Operations and cluster counters.

Purpose	Counters	Roll up	Description
Contention	Contention (%)	Average	Use a super metric to get the peak.
Utilization	Workload (%)	Average	Use a super metric to get the peak. This does not take into account HA. The workload will be higher if an HA event occurs.

We perform capacity management at the vSphere Cluster level. vRealize Operations provides metrics that help you in determining the cluster capacity.

For example, you normally exclude the HA buffer in your capacity calculation. This can be a challenge if you have more than one HA policy. vRealize Operations provides a counter that tracks the usable CPU after taking into account HA. The counter is named **Usable Capacity (vCPU)**, and can be found as shown here:

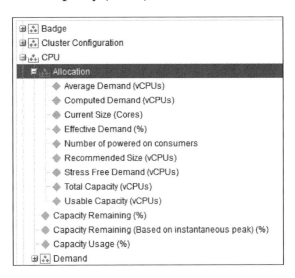

vRealize Operations also provides the total capacity available. In the following example, we have plotted both counters. This is a four-node cluster, where each host has 16 cores and 32 threads. We have set the cluster HA settings to the popular 1-host setting:

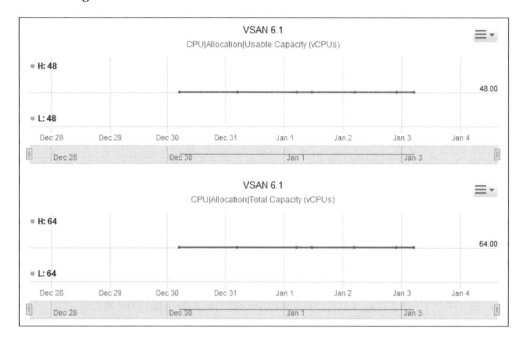

As you can see from the graphs, the counters count the cores, not the threads. They do not take into account HT.

The same functionality is also provided for memory.

CPU counters at higher levels

By higher levels, I mean data center, vCenter, and World objects. Measuring at this level is useful in a large environment where you have many clusters. In a small environment with fewer than five clusters, it makes more sense to manage at the cluster level.

By now, we know that vCenter provides very little information at these levels. It does not provide information about CPU, RAM, disk, or network. vRealize Operations provides a set of key counters, which are useful in overall management. For example, the following two counters quickly tell us the state of CPU demand and contention for the entire infrastructure managed by a vCenter:

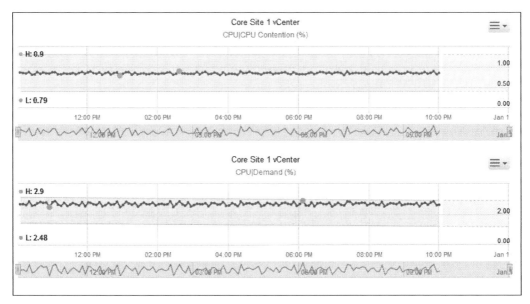

vRealize Operations provides more counters for higher-level objects

When looking at an object higher than the cluster level, there is no more automatic load balancing. If you have 10 clusters in a single vCenter data center and the workload is not balanced among the 10 clusters, vSphere will not load balance for you.

Capturing the peak by taking the highest value of the data center utilization in a given time period will give a lower value, as the data center utilization is the average of all clusters. I call this Approach 2, and it was covered earlier.

As a result, it makes more sense to capture the peak by taking the highest value from the members of the group. In this example, the cluster with the highest peak will determine the peak value. I call this Approach 1, and it was explained in *Chapter 5, Capacity Monitoring*.

You then complement the peak counter with the average counter. These two counters will serve as your upper and lower thresholds in your performance or capacity management. Plot them on a single line chart so that you can see the trends. If there is a big gap, it means you have unbalanced deployment. Some clusters are busier than others. You should expect your tier-1 clusters to have lower utilization than your tier-3 clusters.

Because there are three levels above clusters, you need to decide which method of determining the peak makes sense for your environment. How you roll up the peak information will impact the results. You do not have to worry about how you roll up the average information, as vRealize Operations does it for you already. An average of a large group tends to be low, so you need to complement it with the peak.

Let's use an example to make it clearer. Imagine you manage a global environment spread over three continents. You have 10 vCenter Servers managing 6 global data centers and 100 remote branches. There are a total of 100,000 VMs in 5,000 hosts in 500 clusters. You can use the following approaches:

- **Approach 1**: For all the three levels, you could have a single host giving you the peak of all of your 5,000 hosts. This would be misleading.

- **Approach 2**: For all the three levels, you could flatten the peak and you would end up with a number that is close to your average (which is already given by vRealize Operations out of the box).

So you need to apply some combination. For example, at the World level, the peak could be the peak from a single vCenter (Approach 1). At the vCenter level, the peak could be the peak at a certain time (Approach 2).

This table lists the key counters you should be using at these levels. Notice how vRealize Operations has provided you with a consistent set of metrics.

The following table shows the vRealize Operations and cluster counters:

Object	Purpose	Counters	Roll up
Datacenter	Contention	Contention (%)	Average
Datacenter	Utilization	Workload (%)	Average
vCenter	Contention	Contention (%)	Average
vCenter	Utilization	Workload (%)	Average
World	Contention	Contention (%)	Average
World	Utilization	Workload (%)	Average

Summary

In this chapter, we discussed CPU counters in both vCenter and vRealize Operations. We covered what they mean and what values you should expect for a healthy environment. The relationship between metrics was also explained. I provided screenshots to make the learning easier and added real-world examples.

Let's take a journey down memory lane (pun intended) in the next chapter.

13
Memory Counters

We covered CPU in depth in the previous chapter. Let's now take a trip down memory lane. We will take the same approach we did with CPU. The following topics will be covered in this chapter:

- VM memory counters
- ESXi memory counters
- Cluster memory counters
- Memory counters for higher-level objects

Memory – not such a simple matter

Memory differs from CPU as it is a form of storage. Unlike CPU, which executes instructions as they enter it, memory keeps information for a much longer period of time. We are comparing nanoseconds to seconds (or longer, up to months, depending on the uptime of your VM). Information is stored in memory in standard block sizes, typically 4 KB or 2 MB. Each block is called a page. At the lowest level, the memory pages are just a series of zeroes and ones.

Keeping this concept in mind is useful as you review the memory counters. Memory has a very different nature compared to CPU, and the storage nature of memory is the reason why memory monitoring is more challenging than CPU monitoring.

Before you proceed with this section, you need to be familiar with vSphere memory management. The whitepaper at https://www.vmware.com/resources/techresources/10206 provides a good explanation. It is based on vSphere 5.0, but is still relevant in vSphere 6.0 Update 1. The only difference is the introduction of reliable memory technology in vSphere 5.5, which does not consume a lot of RAM because it is only for the vmkernel.

Many useful things about monitoring are shared in the paper, especially the fact that the hypervisor does not have direct visibility inside the Guest OS. When a Guest OS frees up a memory page, it normally just updates its list of free memory; it does not release it. This list is not exposed to the hypervisor, and so the physical page remains claimed by the VM. This is why the Consumed counter in vCenter remains high when the Active counter has long dropped. Because the hypervisor has no visibility into the Guest OS, you may need to deploy an agent to get visibility into your application. You should monitor both at the Guest OS level (for example, Windows and Red Hat) and at the application level (for example, MS SQL Server and Oracle). Check whether there is excessive paging or the Guest OS experiences a hard page fault. For Windows, you can use tools such as *pfmon*, a page fault monitor.

pfmon is not to be confused with `perfmon`. See the KB article *Excessive Page Faults Generated By Windows Applications May Impact the Performance of Virtual Machines (1687)* at `http://kb.vmware.com/kb/1687`.

It is acceptable for an application to release memory that it does not use, and a well-behaved application will listen to the requests of the Guest OS to release inactive pages. It is advisable to discuss the performance impact of releasing unused memory with the application architect.

Another reason for deploying an agent is the Active counter itself. The vSphere manual says that it tracks the amount of memory that is actively used, as estimated by vmkernel based on recently-touched memory pages. In summary, the ESXi host periodically checks a sample of all the consumed pages of the VM and determines the Active counter's percentage. ESXi will assume that the sample is representative and derive the Active value for the VM as a whole. As a result, using Active in isolation can lead to sizing that is too aggressive or too conservative.

This is covered in detail by Mark Achtemichuk at `http://blogs.vmware.com/vsphere/2013/10/understanding-vsphere-active-memory.html`.

We will cover the metrics in more detail when we cover VM memory utilization counters later in this chapter.

There are certainly situations where you cannot deploy an agent. For example, in a large environment, it is common that the infrastructure team does not even have read access to the Guest OS, let alone permission to install an agent. You do not know what is running inside the Guest OS and yet you get a call if there is an issue.

In this situation, you can get some visibility if you put the pagefile into a virtual disk by itself. The entire VMDK only contains the swap partition with no temporary directory or other purpose. You can then use the virtual disk I/O counters to track swap activity, as memory read/write becomes disk read/write.

You should also check out the following sections in the **VMware vSphere 6.0 Documentation Center**:

- **Memory Virtualization Basics** (shown in the following screenshot)
- **Administering Memory Resources**

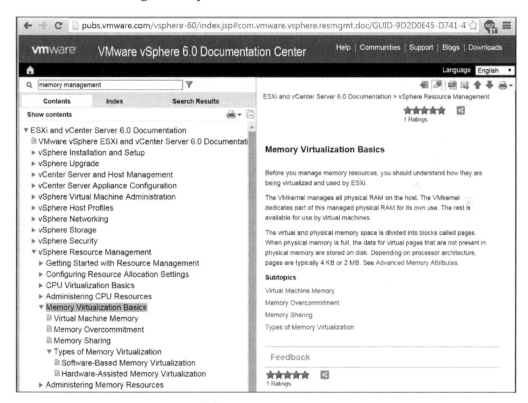

vSphere memory management

As of early 2016, 256 GB of RAM on a two-socket ESXi host is becoming common. Assuming 16 GB is being used by the hypervisor and hypervisor-based services (antivirus, firewall, load balancer, distributed router, and Virtual SAN), that still leaves plenty of RAM for around 25-50 VMs per host (depending upon the size of the VMs). 50 VMs per host is probably the upper limit you want to place for server VMs before concentration consolidation risk becomes a real issue that you will need to answer for to your customer.

In tier 1 (the highest tier), the number of VMs per host is likely a lot lower. For VDI, the number can be higher because each desktop VM is likely configured with just 6 GB vRAM, they have many common pages (**transparent page sharing**), and users are not active most of the time.

Memory counters at the Guest OS level

Memory rightsizing is best done with metrics from inside the Guest OS. You can use data from Linux or Windows for this. vRealize Operations 6.1 provides an agent that you can deploy on the Guest OS. We covered the deployment in this article: `http://virtual-red-dot.info/vrealize-operations-6-1-end-point-operations/`. With the agent, you can compare the data from inside the Guest and outside the Guest side by side.

We will cover Windows in this book as Windows memory management is not something that is well explained. Ed Bott sums it up the article at `http://www.zdnet.com/article/windows-7-memory-usage-whats-the-best-way-to-measure/` by saying, "Windows memory management is rocket science." Like Ed has experienced, there is conflicting information, including that given by Microsoft. Mark Russinovich explains the situation in this TechNet post: `https://blogs.technet.microsoft.com/markrussinovich/2008/11/17/pushing-the-limits-of-windows-virtual-memory/`.

As shared in *Chapter 5, Capacity Monitoring*, the server workload and desktop workload differ. The net effect is that server workload tends to be stable, while VDI workload has wide fluctuation. As vRealize Operations monitors every 5 minutes, the peak can be hidden in the VDI workload.

Both Windows for desktops (7, 8, 10) and Windows Server (2008, 2012, 2016) take advantage of the physical memory well. It's aware that caching data on RAM speeds up performance. The more RAM you give, the more it caches.

The following screenshot is taken from a Windows 7 laptop, so there is no element of hypervisor at play here. As you can see, the **Committed Memory** is only 3 GB, but **Free Memory** is down to 16 MB. Windows is caching heavily: more than 200% of used memory. If you simply look at *Free*, you would conclude that we need more RAM.

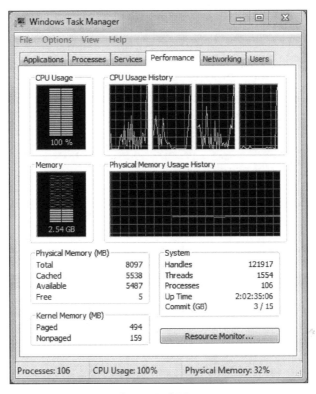

Windows 7 Task Manager

The counters you use to monitor Windows 2008 R2 are the same that you use to monitor Windows 7. While their memory management is not identical, you can use the same tool to monitor both. Windows in fact provides three tools for both OSes, which are as follows:

- Resource Monitor
- Task Manager
- Performance Monitor

While Resource Monitor is the easiest to check and understand, **Performance Monitor** gives you flexibility to choose the metrics.

With Windows providing three built-in tools, you may wonder whether we need vRealize Operations as the fourth. Windows tools report every second, while vRealize Operations reports every 5 minutes. 5 minutes is 300 seconds, and it is an average. So you can expect the data to be different as the sampling length is different.

The vRealize Operations use case is for monitoring, while tools that can go down to a more granular level (Log Insight, Windows tools, esxtop) are for troubleshooting. They are not so suitable for overall monitoring, as you will incur a performance penalty while monitoring performance. In addition, you really do not want to react to every spike that lasts for only a few seconds. There is a good chance it does not impact the business.

Let's go back to our Windows tools. From **Resource Monitor**, you can clearly see that there are five regions in the physical memory.

I am showing two examples in the following screenshots. One is a physical machine, while the other is a VM. Can you tell which one is a VM?

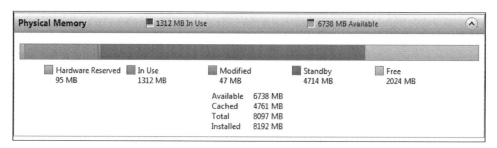

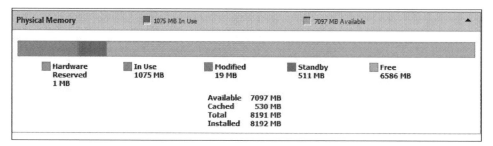

Windows 7 Resource Monitor

Yes, the VM is the one with negligible **Hardware Reserved**.

The Windows title is **Physical Memory** as it does not include the `pagefile.sys`. Counters that include virtual memory, such as committed memory, are not shown as a result.

The five regions are:

- **Hardware Reserved**: This is typically less than 10 MB on a VM, so you can ignore it.
- **In Use**: These are the pages that are used at present.
- **Modified** and **Standby**: These act as cache. In most cases, the **Modified** page will have a relatively smaller value than **Standby**.
- **Free**: This is actually free and zero. Unlike Linux, Windows zeroes pages upon boot.

These five regions are clear, as they do not overlap. But what about **Available** and **Cached**?

Available means exactly what the word means. It is the amount of physical memory immediately available for use. Immediately means Windows does not need to copy the existing page before it can be reused.

In formula, here are their definitions:

- *Cached = Standby + Modified*
- *Available = Standby + Free*

It is easier to visualize this, so here it is:

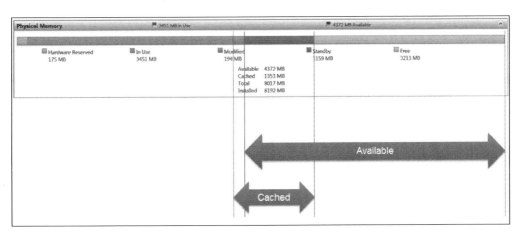

Windows memory: Available and Cached

We have seen that Windows takes advantage of physical RAM and uses it as cache. So if you want to size for optimized performance, you need to include the cached memory. If you want to be cost effective, exclude the cache. This sounds logical and reasonable. Let's refine a little bit since **Modified** is not immediately available. So here is the recommendation for memory rightsizing:

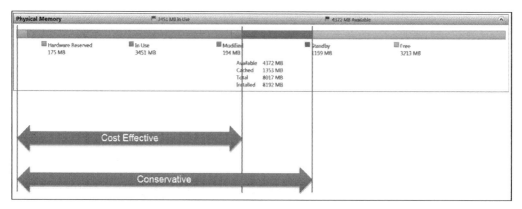

Windows memory: sizing approach

There are two ways we can determine when a VM needs more RAM:

- RAM usage is high
- Available RAM is low

I'm using the second one as it's easier for you to see. If I show **RAM Usage** at 13,574 MB, you still need to know the total configured RAM (for example, 16 GB RAM), and then subtract the number. Well, that will take you to the **Available RAM**.

I prefer an absolute number instead of percentage. Unlike CPU, the range of values for RAM varies widely. You may have VMs from 2 GB of RAM to 128 GB of RAM. At 90% utilization, a VM with 4 GB RAM has only 400 MB available RAM, while a VM with 128 GB RAM has plenty of memory available.

Use the following formulas to rightsized VM memory:

- *For best performance, use Total - Free*
- *For cheapest cost, use Total - Free - Standby*

Obviously, the cheapest option has performance impact as the **Standby Memory** is excluded.

While this is good enough, you can enhance it by considering the virtual memory. All we have done until now has just been on the physical memory.

Windows uses both the physical and virtual memory concurrently. It does not wait until the physical memory is full before using the virtual memory. The `pagefile.sys` file is not something you can ignore.

The following example shows that Windows 2012 R2 uses virtual memory even though it has plenty of physical RAM. **System Information** shows it has 8 GB of **Physical Memory** and 1.25 GB of pagefile, giving it 9.5 GB of **Virtual Memory**. For a small **Microsoft Active Directory** server doing just DNS and AD, 8 GB is more than enough.

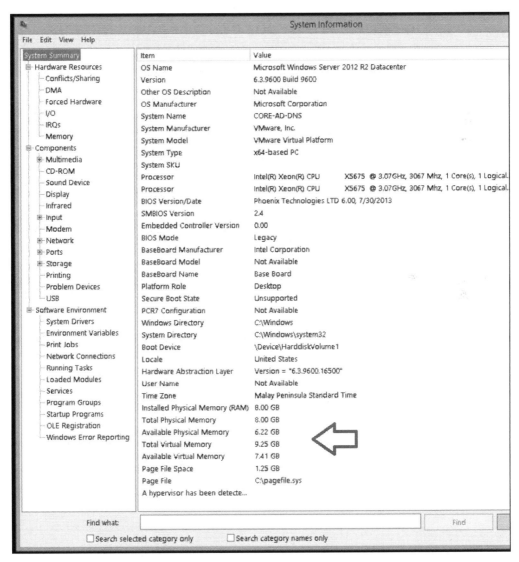

Windows 2012 System Information

Microsoft recommends that you do not delete or disable the pagefile. See this for reference: `http://windows.microsoft.com/en-us/windows/change-virtual-memory-size`.

Let Windows manage the pagefile size. This is the default setting, so you likely have it already. By default, Windows sets the pagefile size to the same size as the physical memory. So if the VM has 8 GB of RAM, the pagefile is an 8-GB file. Anything above 8 GB indicates that Windows is under memory pressure.

The pagefile is an integral part of Windows' total memory. Mark Russinovich explains this at `https://blogs.technet.microsoft.com/markrussinovich/2008/11/17/pushing-the-limits-of-windows-virtual-memory/`. There is **Reserved Memory** and then there is **Committed Memory**. Some applications like to have their committed memory in one long contiguous block, so they reserve a large chunk upfront. Databases and the JVM belong to this category. This reserved memory does not actually store meaningful application data or executables. It is only when the application commits the page that it is used. Mark explains, "When a process commits a region of virtual memory, the OS guarantees that it can maintain all the data the process stores in the memory either in physical memory or on disk."

Notice the phrase "on disk". Yes, that's where `pagefile.sys` comes in. Windows will either use the physical memory or `pagefile.sys`.

So, how do we track this committed memory?

The metric you need to track is the committed byte. The percent committed metric should not hit 80. Performance drops when it hits 90%, as if this were a hard threshold used by Windows. I disabled the pagefile to verify the impact on Windows. I noticed a visibly slower performance even though Windows 7 was showing less than 1 GB of free memory. In fact, Windows gave an error message, and some applications crashed. If you use a pagefile, you will not hit this limit.

We have covered **free memory** and **committed memory**. Do they always move in tandem? If memory is committed by Windows, does it mean it's no longer free and available?

The answer is no. Brandon Paddock demonstrated at `http://brandonlive.com/2010/02/21/measuring-memory-usage-in-windows-7/` that you can increase the committed page without increasing memory usage. He wrote a small program and explained how it's done. The result is that Windows committed page size is double that of memory usage. The Free Memory and Cached Memory did not change.

We have covered the metrics provided by the Guest OS (Windows, in this example). How does it compare with the metrics from outside the Guest?

Since the vantage point is different, it is possible that the value differs. In most cases, the difference is acceptable.

I'll show you an example where the difference was big enough to have resulted in a false alarm by the hypervisor. I use the word "hypervisor", as it should apply to all hypervisors, not just vSphere.

In the following chart, vRealize Operations show three values, marked as **A, B,** and **C**.

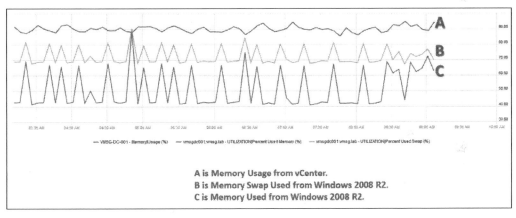

VM memory counter comparison

A is the memory usage counter from the hypervisor. **C** is the memory used counter from inside the Guest OS. The delta is quite significant. The pattern is also different. **B** is plotted for completeness, just in case you're curious about the value of swap.

The value in vCenter was hovering around 90 percent, and it actually triggered an alarm:

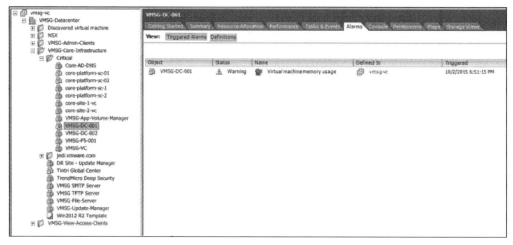

False alarm from outside the Guest OS

Let's check the other counters of this VM, just in case we're missing something. As you can see in the following chart, there is no ballooning, swapping, or compression. Memory latency is also zero. In other words, there is no hypervisor-related factor that can impact the VM internal memory usage and all that can be provided is an irrelevant alarm—hence the need to monitor in-Guest.

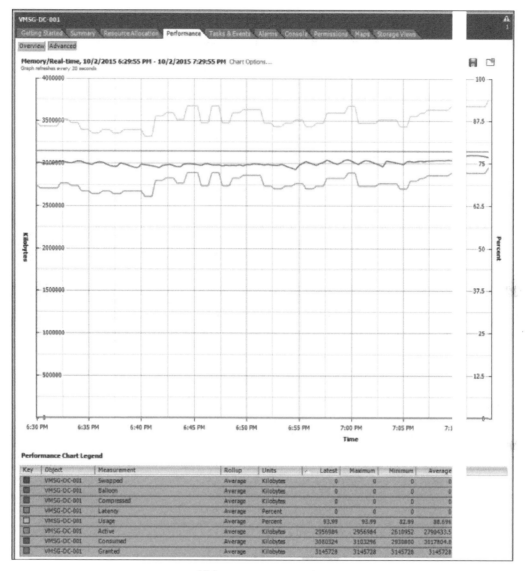

VM memory usage counters

I have given you only a summary of Windows memory management. For details on Windows 2008 memory management, review this: `http://virtual-red-dot.info/how-to-measure-windows-2008-memory-usage`. For details on Windows 7 x64, review this: `http://virtual-red-dot.info/how-to-measure-windows-7-memory-usage/`.

Memory counters at the VM level

vCenter 6.0 Update 1 provides 28 counters for RAM in order to track the various features of VM memory management. Compared to physical servers, where you normally just monitor the memory utilization and swapping, these are a lot counters. All the counters are shown in the next screenshot. With 28 counters per VM, a vSphere environment with 1,000 VMs will have 28,000 counters just for VM RAM!

It is certainly too many to be monitored as part of overall management. The latter part of this chapter will share the three key counters you need to track to manage performance and capacity.

Description	Rollup	Units	Internal Name	Collection Level
☐ Memory saved by zipping	Latest	Kilobytes	zipSaved	2
☐ Decompression rate	Average	KBps	decompressionRate	2
☐ Swapped	Average	Kilobytes	swapped	2
☐ Overhead touched	Average	Kilobytes	overheadTouched	4
☑ Balloon	Average	Kilobytes	vmmemctl	1
☑ Active	Average	Kilobytes	active	2
☐ Shared	Average	Kilobytes	shared	2
☐ Entitlement	Average	Kilobytes	entitlement	2
☐ Host cache used for swapping	Average	Kilobytes	llSwapUsed	4
☐ Active write	Average	Kilobytes	activewrite	2
☐ Reserved overhead	Average	Kilobytes	overheadMax	2
☐ Zipped memory	Latest	Kilobytes	zipped	2
☐ Swap out	Average	Kilobytes	swapout	2
☐ Compressed	Average	Kilobytes	compressed	2
☐ Balloon target	Average	Kilobytes	vmmemctltarget	2
☐ Latency	Average	Percent	latency	2
☐ Swap in rate	Average	KBps	swapinRate	1
☐ Swap in rate from host cache	Average	KBps	llSwapInRate	2
☐ Overhead	Average	Kilobytes	overhead	1
☑ Consumed	Average	Kilobytes	consumed	1
☐ Zero	Average	Kilobytes	zero	2
☐ Swap in	Average	Kilobytes	swapin	2
☐ Compression rate	Average	KBps	compressionRate	2
☐ Swap target	Average	Kilobytes	swaptarget	2
☐ Swap out rate to host cache	Average	KBps	llSwapOutRate	2
☐ Swap out rate	Average	KBps	swapoutRate	1
☑ Granted	Average	Kilobytes	granted	2
☐ Usage	Average	Percent	usage	1

VM – RAM counters

At the ESXi level, vCenter provides 33 counters. As you can expect, some of the counters at the ESXi level are essentially the sum of associated counters of all VMs running in the host, plus vmkernel's own memory counters (since it also consumes memory). This aggregation is useful as VMs do move around within the cluster. Since there are a lot of counters, let's compare the differences first.

The following counters are unique to VM monitoring and they do not exist at the ESXi level:

- **Entitlement**: This makes sense, since entitlement is a property of a VM.
- **Overhead touched**
- **Reserved overhead**
- **Zipped memory**
- **Memory saved by zipping (KB)**: The compression ratio is either 2x or 4x, so this counter tracks the total memory saved. With the availability of other counters, we have yet to find a use case for it.
- **Balloon target**: If you see a nonzero value in this counter, it means that the hypervisor has asked this VM to give back memory via the VM balloon driver. This does not necessarily indicate a reduction of performance, as it depends upon whether the memory page released by the balloon driver is a free one or not. If it is from the free memory, then the Guest OS does not need to perform a page out to meet the request of its balloon driver. If it is not, then the Guest OS will page out, and this can impact performance. A page out happens when the Guest OS is running high on memory. This means that it is acceptable to see some ballooning so long as both the **Consumed** and **Active** counters are low.
- **Swap target**: This is different from ballooning, as the hypervisor has no knowledge of the free memory inside the Guest OS. It is important to note that this is a target, meaning it may not be achieved. The hypervisor is clever enough to do compression instead, if it can compress at least 2x (meaning a 4-KB block becomes less than 2 KB). If it cannot, logically, the choice is to swap out. As a result, any value in this counter indicates that the host is unable to satisfy the VM memory requirement. Use vMotion on one or more VMs out of the host until the **Swap** target counter hits zero.

You may notice that there is no compression target. We have a balloon target and swap target, so we should expect a compression target too. Does this sound logical?

Not really. Because both swap and compression work together to meet the swap target counter, the counter should actually be called **Compression** or **Swap target**.

We looked at counters that do not exist on ESXi. Let's now look at counters that exist so that you can make a comparison. The following counters exist in ESXi but do not exist at the VM level:

- Used by vmkernel
- Heap
- State
- Low free threshold
- Reserved capacity
- Unreserved
- Total capacity
- Swap in from host cache
- Swap out from host cache
- Shared common

The Used by vmkernel counter is obviously not applicable to a VM. With ESXi sporting around 256 GB of RAM these days, the memory consumed by the hypervisor is very small compared to the total RAM. This is even after kernel-module functionalities from NSX and VSAN.

Before we dive into the details of key counters, let's quickly cover what is not available. There is no counter for large pages. This means that you cannot tell whether VM memory is being backed by large pages or not. At the ESXi level, you cannot tell how many gigabytes of the RAM is made up of large pages. A topic on large pages merits a discussion by itself, as there are many levels to check (ESXi, Guest OS, and application) and factors to consider (performance, cost, and manageability). You should enable a large page in use cases where performance matters the most (that is, in clusters where there will be no oversubscription) and disable it where cost matters the most (that is, where you want to have heavy oversubscription). There is also another useful counter that is missing. It exists for CPU but not for RAM.

Go back and look at the list. Can you spot it?

That counter is **Demand**.

We will talk about it when we cover utilization. Right now, we need to cover contention. We will use the same approach we used for CPU counters, which is starting with contention, followed by utilization, and ending with other counters.

Contention counters

As expected, vCenter Server does not provide a counter for memory contention. You can certainly check for signs of contention, such as the existence of balloon, swapped, or compressed memory. A nonzero value in any of these counters indicates ESXi had or has memory pressure and it may impact this VM.

Can you guess why I use the word "may" instead of "will"?

It's because it does not always mean that the VM performance is affected. If the page being swapped out is a free page and the VM does not use it, then there is no performance hit. The performance issue happens when the Guest OS wants to access that page, because the hypervisor has to bring the page back to the physical DIMM first. Certainly, the higher the value is for balloon, swapped, and compressed, the higher the chance of a performance hit happening in the future if the data is requested. The severity of the impact depends on the VM memory shares, reservation, and limit. It also depends upon the size of the VM's configured RAM. A 10-MB ballooning will likely have more impact on a VM with 0.5 GB of RAM than on one with 128 GB.

It is also possible to have balloon showing a zero value while compressed or swapped are showing nonzero values—even though in the order of ESXi memory reclamation techniques, ballooning occurs before compression. This indicates that the VM did have memory pressure in the past that caused ballooning, compression, and swapping then, but it no longer has the memory pressure. Data that was compressed or swapped out is not retrieved unless requested, because doing so takes CPU cycles. The balloon driver, on the other hand, will be proactively deflated when memory pressure is relieved.

Without an SSD as a cache, swapped memory would mean severe memory performance degradation. If your use case requires high ESXi memory utilization and regular swapping is likely, then you should consider implementing SSDs as a cache. For a VM, retrieving swapped pages from a host-side SSD is much faster than from a spinning disk.

 Check out the write-up by Duncan Epping at `http://www.yellow-bricks.com/2011/08/18/swap-to-host-cache-aka-swap-to-ssd/`.

Once you enable the host cache, you should also track the host cache used for swapping, the swap out rate to host cache, and the swap in rate to host cache counters.

There is also a counter called **Latency (%)** that tracks the percentage of time for which the VM is waiting as it is accessing swapped or compressed memory.

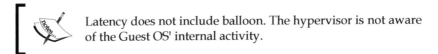 Latency does not include balloon. The hypervisor is not aware of the Guest OS' internal activity.

This is certainly useful. Just because a VM has a portion of its memory compressed does not mean that it is accessing that compressed memory. Therefore, it is acceptable to see Balloon or Compressed or Swap as long as Latency is 0.

You should also check Entitlement and make sure it is not capping the Demand value or Consumed value. It is possible for a VM to not have its memory swapped, compressed, or ballooned, but still not get what it demands. Check whether there are reservations on other VMs and limits on this VM. This is why you should not set these two counters (Reservation and Limit) and use Share instead.

The following chart shows a healthy environment. This VM's **Consumed Memory** is consistently lower than its **Entitlement Memory**.

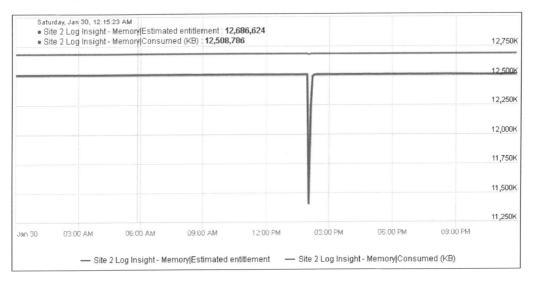

It is tedious to check every VM one by one. With vRealize Operations, you can create a super metric that tracks Entitlement/Demand or Entitlement/Consumed. You need to use the **This Resource** icon, so the formula is applied to the VM itself:

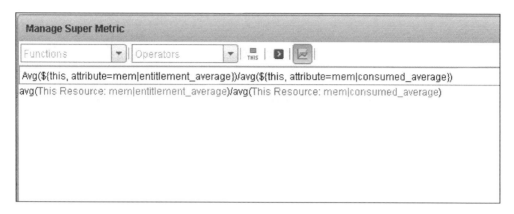

You should expect a value of 1 or higher. A value between 0 and 1 means Demand is greater than Entitlement, which is not what you want. In a healthy environment, all your VMs will give you a value greater than 1. You can create a heatmap that shows all VMs. If you choose a range between 0.8 and 1.0, where 0.8 is red and 1.0 is green, then a small percentage of contention will result in a color change, making it visible. For a test/dev cluster where you deliberately drive for a higher utilization, adjust the range beyond 1.

As you can tell from the preceding part, it is difficult to check contention as there are many counters and factors to consider.

This is where the **Contention (%)** metric in vRealize Operations is useful. It is actually derived from the CPU **Swap Wait (ms)** counter, as shown in the next screenshot. The following VM has four vCPUs. If you divide 16,539 by 4, you will get 4,134. Then, 4,134 ms over 20,000 ms is 20.67 percent.

Chapter 4, Performance Monitoring, provides an example of the threshold you should set.

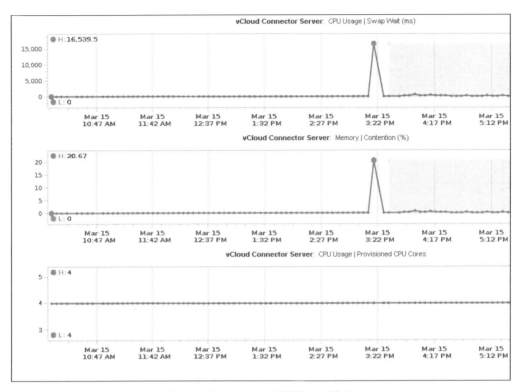

Memory Contention is CPU Swap Wait

Let's look at another example of **Memory | Contention (%)** in action. This time, there were no VMware tools in the VM (the balloon driver relies on VM tools being installed). The VM experienced both **Swapped** and **Compression**. About 33 MB was swapped and 24 MB was zipped, which are low amounts of contention as the VM has 6 GB of RAM. The **Contention (%)** went up to around 0.2 percent, reflecting the low amount of contention. The counter then dropped even though the swapped and zipped counters remained where they were.

Can you figure out why Contention dropped?

The answer is CPU **Swap Wait**. The CPU Swap Wait went down, because the VM did not access those pages anymore:

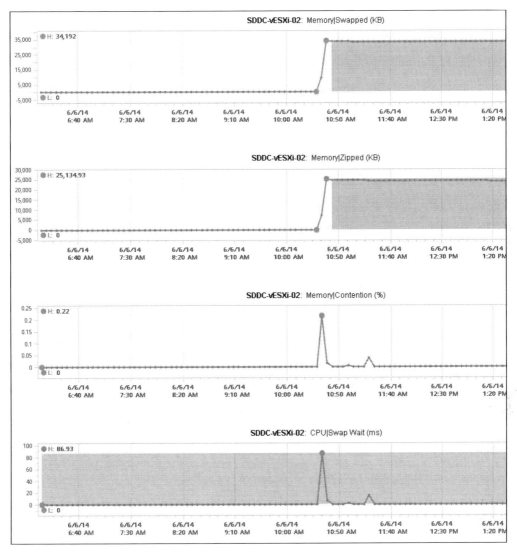

Memory Contention is CPU Swap Wait

Utilization counters

For utilization, vCenter provides **Active (KB)**, **Active Write (KB)**, **Consumed (KB)**, **Granted (KB)**, and **Usage (%)**. Because you will have VMs with different vRAM sizes, it is easier to use the **Usage (%)** counter.

Pay special attention to the **Usage** counter. It has different formulas depending on the object:

- For VMs, it is mapped to Active
- For ESXi, it is mapped to Consumed
- For clusters, it is mapped to Consumed and Memory overhead

The effect of this formula is that you will see ESXi usage as much higher than your VM usage. For example, if all the VMs have the same size of RAM and their usage is about the same, you will notice your ESXi usage is higher than VM usage.

Technically speaking, mapping usage to active for VM and consumed for ESXi makes sense, due to the two-level memory hierarchy in virtualization. Operationally, this can create some confusion, as it is not a consistent mapping.

At the VM level, we use active as it shows what the VM is actually consuming (related to performance). At the host and cluster levels, we use consumed because it is related to what the Guest OS has claimed (related to capacity management).

The blog post by Mark Achtemichuk shared earlier explains that using Active (KB) alone will normally result in aggressive sizing. For an application that manages its own memory (for example, JVM and database), this can result in poor performance for the application. These applications have their own sets of working memory and the Guest OS does not understand this. Performing ballooning in this situation may result in a hard page fault as far as the application is concerned, because the Guest OS does not know how the application uses memory. In some situations, it might be better for the application to be given less memory to begin with.

You should use consumed as a guide for such applications. Because it is application dependent, you should consider deploying vRealize Infrastructure Navigator, which is a component of vRealize Operations. As shown in *Chapter 2*, *Software-Defined Data Centers*, it can tell you whether you have databases and application servers.

Does this mean we can just give a VM whatever resources the VM owner asks? This is not a wise policy. From experience, I know that applications tend to be oversized if I do not apply a sanity check. This is a common practice for physical servers, as the server comes with a standard RAM configuration. We also know that there are cases where applications simply ask for memory and then never use it again.

Oversizing, as you probably have experienced first-hand, can lead to poorer performance. It also takes longer to boot and to use vMotion for a larger VM—more does not always mean better when the underlying platform is virtualized.

Reducing a VM's memory requires both the application developer and infrastructure engineer to discuss and agree upon the sizing. However, this is not always possible: in a global organization with thousands of VMs, it may not be practical to install agents. What metric do you use then?

As a workaround in such a scenario, vRealize Operations provides the Demand metric. It uses Active as a starting point. The Demand counter takes into account that an OS needs a minimum amount of RAM to function properly. The range is typically 64 MB to 512 MB, depending upon the size of configured RAM and active memory. It also takes into account memory contention.

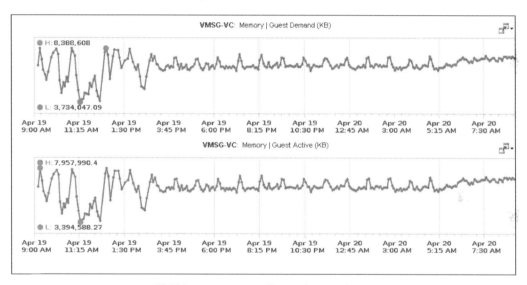

VM Memory counters – Demand versus Active

In an environment where there is little memory contention, you will see a pattern like the one shown in the preceding screenshot. Without checking the Consumed and Configured counters, you cannot tell whether Demand is high enough. This is because the Demand metric is not shown as a percentage. This is where Workload (%) comes in. Because it is a percentage, you can also make a relative comparison among VMs of different sizes.

The **Demand (KB)** counter, because the unit is an absolute amount (instead of a percentage), can be useful when combined with the use of a dynamic group. Let's say your environment has a lot of large VMs mixing with many small VMs in the same cluster. In this situation, you want to know the impact that these large VMs have in your cluster. For that, you need to know whether they are using the memory given to them, as large VMs tend to be over-configured. A VM may be configured with 128 GB of RAM, but does it actually use that much RAM?

You can create a dynamic group in vRealize Operations whose members are VMs with more than 24 GB of vRAM, then create a super metric that is applied to that dynamic group and tracks the maximum value of **Demand (KB)** memory. You divide the number by 1,024 x 1,024 to get the value in terms of GB.

If the super metric shows a small number most of the time, then you know that these large VMs are over-configured and not really impacting your cluster. You can then start looking from the biggest VMs, as they provide the biggest downsizing potential.

If the super metric shows a large number, then you need to check for signs of contention in your cluster, hosts, and VMs.

Other counters

The shared memory counter is not applicable at the VM level, as each VM believes it is alone with the underlying physical resources to match its configured size. The shared memory counter is naturally read-only, as a write from any VM will make the page different and therefore no longer shared. If you have a uniform set of VMs and yet the shared memory counter is low, it could be that the Guest OS writes a lot to its pages.

The **Overhead touched, Reserved overhead,** and **Overhead counters** can generally be ignored as their values are low. The following screenshot shows that their values are barely visible. The following VM has 10 GB of RAM. I rebooted the VM towards the middle of the timeline (see the red arrow), just to be sure the counters were behaving properly.

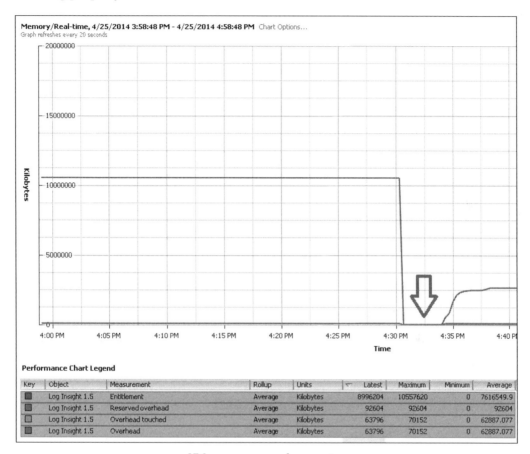

VM memory – secondary counters

Putting it together

Let's now take an example to see how all the VM-level counters relate, using a vCenter 5.5 Linux appliance as an example. Logically, there are differences in memory behavior between the Linux appliance and vCenter installed on Windows.

For this example, the VM is configured with 3 GB of vRAM and rebooted to ensure we have a clean start. The recommended size for a vCenter appliance is 8 GB, so this is well below the default value.

The following chart shows that it has hit a steady state after the initial boot. The highest line is the **Entitlement** line, as it is **Granted** + **Overhead**. The hypervisor has entitled the VM to the entire 3 GB of RAM as the host has plenty of memory. The Granted and Consumed counters are practically identical. The lines are in fact overlapping, with the Consumed line overwriting the Granted line. It is a flat line, meaning all the pages the VM asked for are backed by physical DIMMs.

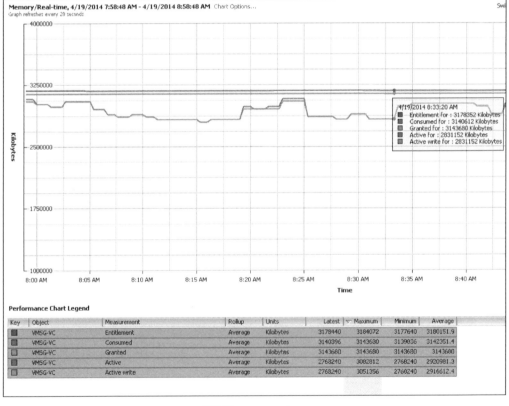

VM Memory counters

It is good to see that the **Consumed** value is both high and flat. As we know, **Consumed** goes up when the Guest OS asks for the memory, which means the Guest OS is writing to its physical memory pages (which in turn are backed by hypervisor physical memory). If the VM no longer needs it but ESXi does not use the page, ESXi keeps the pages just in case they are required in the future.

You probably noticed that both the **Active** and **Active Write** counters are high. These values are close to the **Consumed** value. This indicates the Guest OS is actively using most of its consumed memory. In fact, the value of Active write is almost identical to the value of **Active**. The green line is practically covering the gray line. This behavior is specific to vCenter, meaning not all VMs will have **Active** write identical to **Active**.

If we look at the vRealize Operations 5.8 appliance, for example, the pattern is very different. As you can see in the next screenshot, **Active write** is definitely lower than **Active**, and both are much lower than **Consumed**:

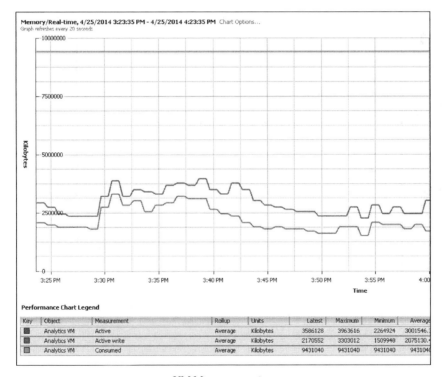

VM Memory counters

Let's now add the **Usage** counter as follows. I have removed some counters to make the following chart easier to interpret and added the **Balloon** counter. The **Usage** counter tracks the Active counter closely. The **Usage** counter shows that the VM has very high memory utilization, averaging at 93 percent in the past hour, which triggers a vCenter alert.

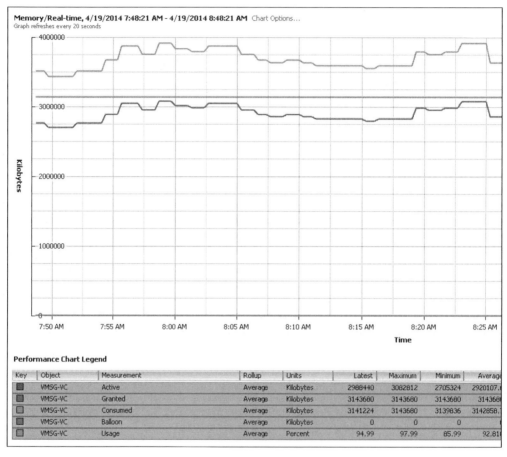

VM Memory counters

The **Balloon** counter is 0 for the entire duration, indicating there is no memory pressure at all. Let's look at the remaining counters that measure contention. As you can see from the following chart, they are all zeroes. We can deduce that latency should be zero too.

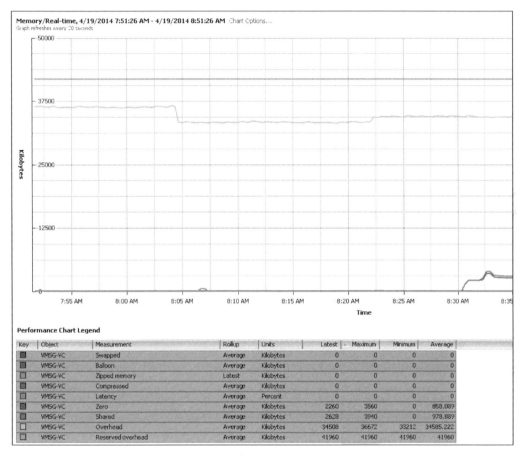

VM Memory counters

You can also see the **Overhead** and **Reserved overhead** counters. As expected, their value is insignificant as the memory overhead in vSphere is low. The **Reserved overhead** is the thin and flat gray line at the top, while the yellow line below it is the **Overhead** counter.

The **Zero** counter tracks all pages with just zeroes on them (unused pages). As expected, the value is low as this is a Linux OS—Linux does not touch any pages until they are actively used. In Windows 2008, you will see a high spike during boot, as Windows initializes all the pages available to it on startup. After a while, it will taper off as this is just part of the initial boot. The next screenshot shows that. The **Active write** counter is identical to **Active** as this is the period where Windows was writing zeroes.

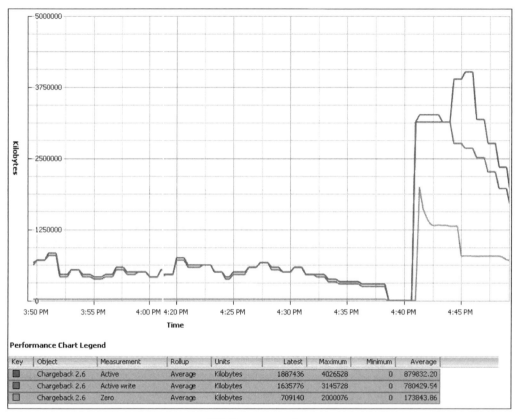

VM Memory counters

I was curious to see how the VM memory utilization counter, as reported by the hypervisor, would change if I give the VM more RAM. I shut down the VM and increased the RAM to 8 GB. You can see from the following chart that **Usage** went up. The **Usage** counter will look different if you are using the metric from inside the Guest OS.

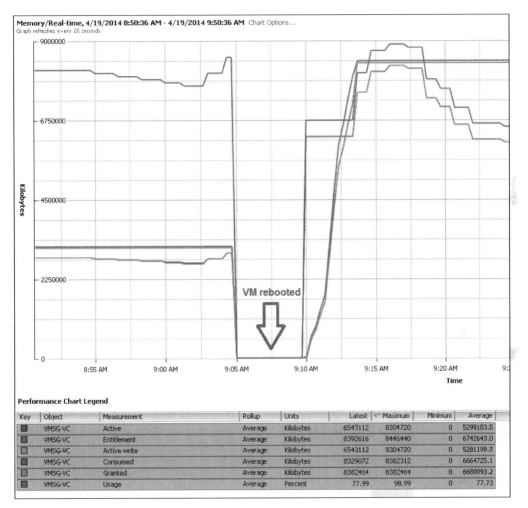

VM Memory counters

It is interesting to note that **Active** and **Active write** shoots up ahead of **Entitlement** and **Granted** during boot. Testing with another VM (VMware Log Insight 1.5, which is also based on SuSE Linux) led to the same behavior. This is not due to writing to the VM swap file, as the VM RAM reservation was set to maximum. This is normal behavior during VM boot, as the values drop after that to below **Entitlement** and **Granted**.

For Windows, you may see that **Consumed** shoots up ahead of **Granted**. As mentioned previously, Windows writes zeroes as it initializes the pages and vmkernel is smart enough to do a copy-on-write, so all the pages are pointing to the same physical page. This can result in the **Consumed** counter being higher than the **Granted** counter, as **Granted** only counts the physical page once. After a while, as the pages are replaced with actual data, the **Granted** counter will go up as each of the new pages is backed by large pages (common in Windows 2008 and Windows 7). The **Granted** counter tends to have a stable value as it only goes down if the host is under memory pressure.

VM memory key counters

We have talked about contention and utilization being the main areas you need to check. The following table summarizes the counters you should monitor:

Purpose	vCenter	vRealize Operations	Description
Contention	CPU Swap Wait	Contention (%)	Memory Contention is based on CPU Swap Wait.
Utilization (Cost Effective)	Usage (%)	In Use	If you do not have EP Agent, use Workload (%) as the "lower" threshold and Consumed (KB) as the "upper" threshold.
Utilization (Performance Optimized)	Consumed (KB)	In Use + Cache	For the "upper" threshold. There is no Usage/Usable (%) metric at the VM level.

Memory counters at the ESXi level

vCenter 6.0 Update 1 provides even more counters at the ESXi level: 38 counters for RAM plus 11 for vmkernel RAM. The vmkernel has around 50 processes that are tracked. As a result, a cluster of 8 ESXi can have over 800 counters just for ESXi RAM!

The counters are shown in the next screenshot. Most of them are not shown as a percentage, making it difficult to compare across ESXi hosts with different memory sizes.

Description	Rollup	Units	Internal Name	Collection Level
☐ VMFS Working Set	Latest	TB	vmfs.pbc.workingSet	4
☐ Swap in from host cache	Average	Kilobytes	llSwapIn	4
☐ Latency	Average	Percent	latency	2
☐ Swap out to host cache	Average	Kilobytes	llSwapOut	4
☑ Swap used	Average	Kilobytes	swapused	2
☐ Maximum VMFS Working Set	Latest	TB	vmfs.pbc.workingSetMax	4
☐ VMFS PB Cache Size	Latest	Megabytes	vmfs.pbc.size	4
☐ Maximum VMFS PB Cache Size	Latest	Megabytes	vmfs.pbc.sizeMax	4
☐ Reserved capacity	Average	Megabytes	reservedCapacity	2
☐ Swap out rate to host cache	Average	KBps	llSwapOutRate	2
☐ Shared	Average	Kilobytes	shared	2
☐ Swap in rate from host cache	Average	KBps	llSwapInRate	2
☑ Active	Average	Kilobytes	active	2
☐ VMFS PB Cache Capacity Miss Ratio	Latest	Percent	vmfs.pbc.capMissRatio	4
☐ Overhead	Average	Kilobytes	overhead	1
☐ VMFS PB Cache Overhead	Latest	Kilobytes	vmfs.pbc.overhead	4
☐ Total capacity	Average	Megabytes	totalCapacity	2
☐ Zero	Average	Kilobytes	zero	2
☐ State	Latest	Number	state	2
☐ Heap free	Average	Kilobytes	heapfree	4
☑ Consumed	Average	Kilobytes	consumed	1
☐ Used by VMkernel	Average	Kilobytes	sysUsage	2
☑ Shared common	Average	Kilobytes	sharedcommon	2
☐ Low free threshold	Average	Kilobytes	lowfreethreshold	2
☐ Swap out rate	Average	KBps	swapoutRate	1
☐ Swap in	Average	Kilobytes	swapin	2
☐ Host cache used for swapping	Average	Kilobytes	llSwapUsed	4
☐ Compression rate	Average	KBps	compressionRate	2
☐ Decompression rate	Average	KBps	decompressionRate	2
☐ Compressed	Average	Kilobytes	compressed	2
☑ Granted	Average	Kilobytes	granted	2
☐ Swap out	Average	Kilobytes	swapout	2
☐ Swap in rate	Average	KBps	swapinRate	1
☐ Heap	Average	Kilobytes	heap	4
☐ Unreserved	Average	Kilobytes	unreserved	2
☐ Usage	Average	Percent	usage	1
☑ Balloon	Average	Kilobytes	vmmemctl	1
☐ Active write	Average	Kilobytes	activewrite	2

ESXi – RAM counters

As for the vmkernel processes, they are not shown under the **Memory** group, but under the **System** group. In most cases, you do not need to track the CPU or RAM consumed by the kernel processes. We have covered them in *Chapter 13, Memory Counters*, so we will not repeat that here. From the following chart, you can see that the vmkernel takes up negligible memory:

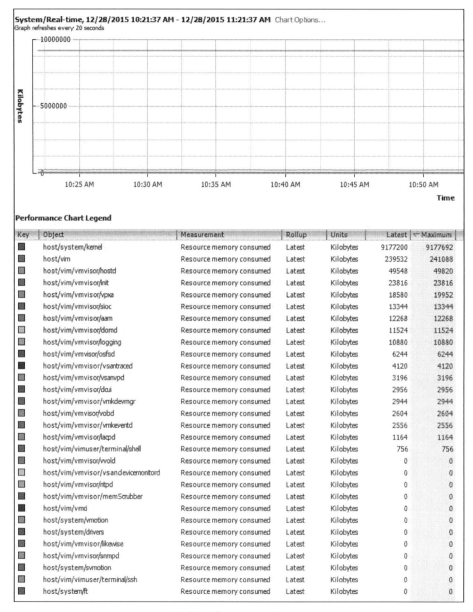

ESXi kernel memory utilization

If you need to track the memory consumption of vmkernel, vRealize Operations provides two counters, as shown next:

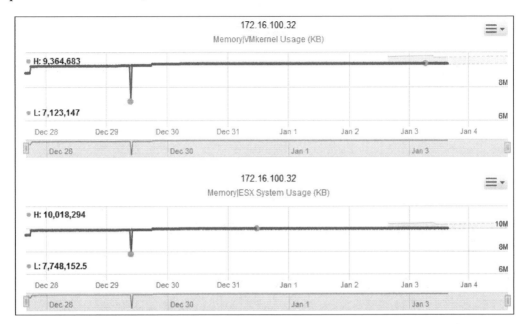

VMkernel Usage and **ESX System Usage** track kernel utilization.

Contention counters

Just like in the case of VM, vCenter Server does not provide a counter for Contention for ESXi. You check the same set of counters for a sign of contention, which are **Balloon, Swapped, Compression**, and **Latency**. You should also check for **CPU Swap Wait**, as that counter tracks when the CPU is waiting for memory.

We know that contention happens at the hypervisor level, not at the VM level. The VM is feeling the side effects of the contention, and the degree of contention depends on each VM's shares, reservation, and utilization. ESXi begins taking action if it is running low on free memory. This is tracked by a counter called **State**. The State counter has five states:

- High
- Clear
- Soft
- Hard
- Low

ESXi uses this to trigger when it reclaims memory from VM. Unless you are deliberately aiming for high utilization, all the ESXi hosts should be in the high state. The spare host you add to cater for HA or maintenance mode will help in lowering the overall ESXi utilization. The value of the high state is **0**, so you can create a super metric that tracks the maximum value of all the hosts across your entire data center.

Having said that, just because the host is low on free physical RAM does not mean that the VMs are performing poorly. Even the presence of swapping out does not mean VMs are performing poorly when the swapped memory is not being accessed by the OS.

Poor VM performance only happens when the VM experiences swap in or decompression. The State counter indicates that free memory is running low on the host, and the host is proactively making free more physical RAM to reallocate as requested by the VMs.

The **Low free threshold** (KB) counter provides information on the actual level below which ESXi will begin reclaiming memory from VM. This value varies in hosts with different RAM configurations. Check this value only if you suspect that ESXi triggers ballooning too early. You should not be seeing this behavior with the changes in ESXi 5.0 onwards. It uses an algorithm that results in a lower threshold on ESXi hosts with large RAM configurations. Without this, an ESXi with 256 GB of RAM would see the occurrence of ballooning when 15.3 GB (6 percent) of RAM is still available. With this sliding scale, the threshold would be around 3.3 GB, a more reasonable number.

In the next screenshot, the threshold is sitting at around 1 GB for an ESXi with 48 GB of RAM.

For more information, check out this post by Frank Denneman
http://blogs.vmware.com/vsphere/2012/05/
memminfreepct-sliding-scale-function.html.

The screenshot also shows **0** ballooning, which is a sign that the ESXi host has no memory pressure. Latency is also **0**, which means it has not accessed memory that is swapped or compressed.

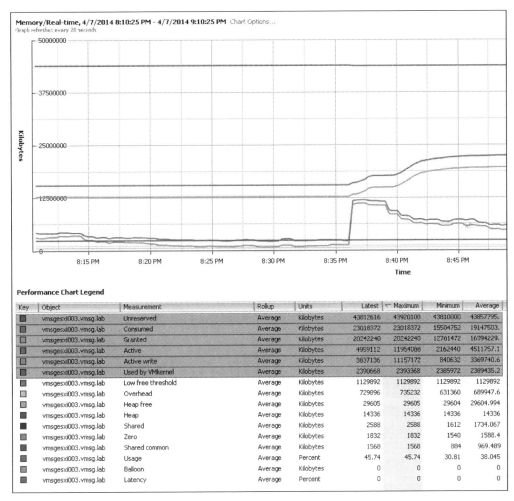

ESXi Memory counters

At the ESXi level, **Contention (%)** is the aggregate of all its VM **Contention (%)** counters. The next screenshot shows this relationship. In this ESXi host, the only VM experiencing contention is the **SDDC-vESXi-02 VM**. No other VMs are experiencing contention. So, the pattern reflects this at the ESXi level, with a much lower value at the ESXi level. To complete the picture, the contention happened because ESXi had high memory utilization. The usage suddenly went up from a stable 88 percent to 92.52 percent, triggering ESXi to free up memory:

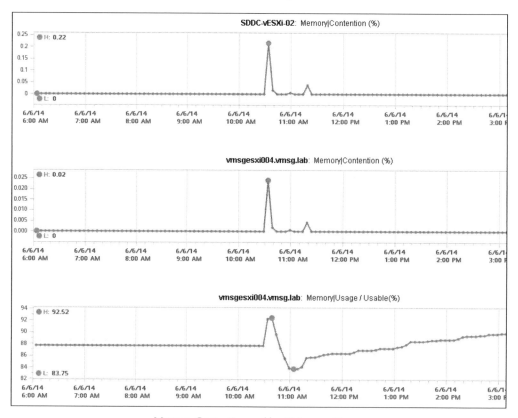

Memory Contention and host Memory Usage

Utilization counters

vCenter provides **Active (KB)**, **Active write (KB)**, **Consumed (KB)**, **Granted (KB)**, and **Usage (%)** for utilization. Granted at the host is the total of the granted counters of VMs running on the host. It includes the shared memory. Consumed is the amount of memory used on the host. It includes both VM memory and hypervisor memory, so it is slightly higher than Granted. In other words, *Consumed = Total host memory - Free host memory*.

You should check both **Active (KB)** and **Usage (%)** to give you the average and peak utilization. Active would give you the average while **Usage (%)** indicates the peak. If you have a lot of applications that need to manage their own memory (for example, JVM and database), then you would gravitate toward **Usage (%)**. If not, you would gravitate towards the **Active** counter. Just like the situation with VMs where vRealize Operations provides a new counter called **Demand**, vRealize Operations also has the Demand counter at ESXi level. It is called **Machine Demand** (KB).

The Workload counter translates Machine Demand into percentage, making it possible to compare it with **Usage (%)**. As you can see in the following chart, plotting them on the same chart gives you the range of memory utilization:

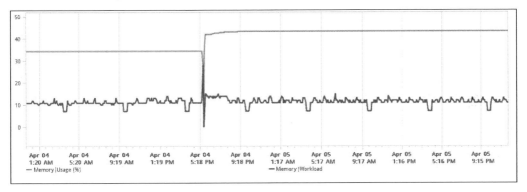

ESXi Memory – Usage versus Workload

Memory shared is the sum of all the VM memory pages that are pointing to a shared page. **Memory shared common** is the sum of all the shared pages. As a result, Memory shared common is at most half the value of Memory shared, as sharing means at least two blocks are pointing to the shared page. If the value is a lot less than half, then you are saving a lot. Today's ESXi hosts sport hardware-assisted memory virtualization from Intel or AMD. With this technology, vmkernel uses large pages to back the VM memory. As a result, the possibility of shared memory is low, unless the host memory is highly utilized. In this state, the large pages are broken down into small, shareable pages. So you can also use the **Memory shared common** counter to track for signs of host memory under pressure.

The **Heap** counter shows the memory used by the vmkernel heap and other data. This is normally a constant and small value. In some hosts with 48 to 64 GB of RAM, we see that the heap size has a constant value of 14 MB, which is negligible.

The **Total capacity** counter is not the same as the total RAM in the host. Generally speaking, we find it to be around 98 percent of the host physical RAM. For example, on a host with 64 GB of physical RAM, the **Total capacity** counter will report around 62.6 GB. vRealize Operations provides a metric called **Provisioned Memory** (KB), which will show you the actual configured RAM (64 GB in this example).

Reserved Capacity (MB) only counts reservation. Therefore, the value will be a lot lower than the total capacity, as most customers do not use reservation. It also includes memory reserved by the vmkernel, which should be less than 0.5 GB and hence negligible.

Consumed versus Active

Let's take a look at one example of how partial information can be misleading in a troubleshooting scenario. It is common for customers to invest in an ESXi host with plenty of RAM. 256 to 512 GB of RAM is becoming common. One reason behind this is the way vCenter displays information. In the following screenshot, vCenter is giving an alert. The host is running on high memory utilization. The screenshot does not show the other host, but you can see that it has a warning, as it is high too. The screenshots are all from vCenter 5.0 and vRealize Operations 5.7, but the behavior is still the same in vCenter 6 Update 1. vRealize Operations 6.1 onwards shows both **Memory Consumed** and **Active**.

I'm using vSphere 5.0 and vRealize Operations 5.x to show the screenshots in order to provide an example of the point stated earlier, which is the rapid change of SDDC.

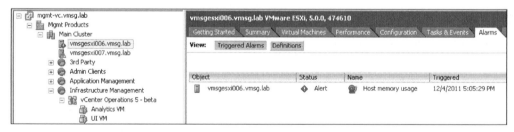

vSphere 5.0 – Memory Alarm

The first step is to check whether someone has modified the alarm by reducing the threshold. The next screenshot shows that utilization above 95 percent will trigger an alert, while utilization above 90 percent will trigger a warning. The threshold has to be breached by at least 5 minutes. The alarm is set to a suitably high configuration, so we will assume the alert is genuinely indicating a high utilization on the host.

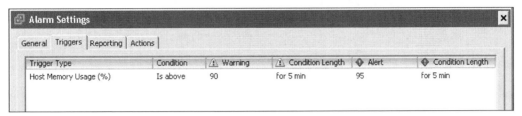

vSphere 5.0 – Alarm Settings

Let's verify the memory utilization. We need to check both the hosts as there are two of them in the cluster. Both are indeed high. The utilization for **vmsgesxi006** has gone down in the time taken to review the **Alarm Settings** tab and move to this view, so both hosts are now in the **Warning** status.

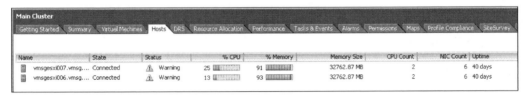

vSphere 5.0 - Hosts tab

Now, we will look at the **vmsgesxi006** specification. From the following screenshot, we can see it has 32 GB of physical RAM, and RAM usage is 30747 MB. It is at 93.8 percent utilization.

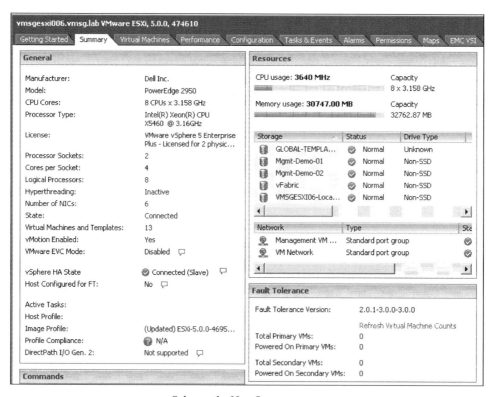

vSphere – the Host Summary page

Since all the numbers shown in the preceding screenshot are refreshed within minutes, we need to check with a longer timeline to make sure this is not a one-time spike. So, let's check for the last 24 hours. The next screenshot shows that the utilization was indeed consistently high.

For the entire 24-hour period, it was consistently above 92.5 percent, and it hit 95 percent several times. So this ESXi host was indeed in need of more RAM.

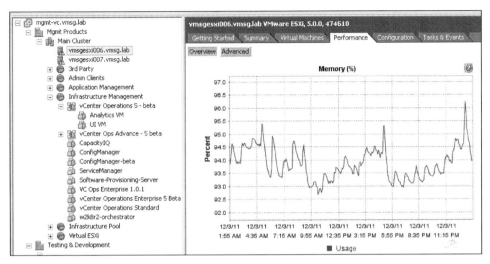

ESXi Memory – very high usage for 24 hours

Deciding whether to add more RAM is complex; there are many factors to be considered. There will be downtime on the host, and you need to do it for every host in the cluster since you need to maintain a consistent build cluster-wide. Because the ESXi is highly utilized, we should increase the RAM significantly so that it can support more or larger VMs. Buying bigger DIMMs may mean throwing away the existing DIMMs, as there are rules restricting the mixing of DIMMs. Mixing DIMMs also increases management complexity. The new DIMMs may require a BIOS update, which may trigger a change request. Alternatively, the larger DIMMs may not be compatible with the existing host, in which case we may have to buy a new box. So a RAM upgrade may trigger a host upgrade, which is a larger project.

Before jumping in to a procurement cycle to buy more RAM, let's double-check our findings. It is important to ask what the host is used for and who is using it.

In this example scenario, I know the environment well. This is the VMware ASEAN lab, which I have managed for the past few years.

Let's check out the memory utilization again, this time with the context in mind. Can you see the possibility of over-reporting here?

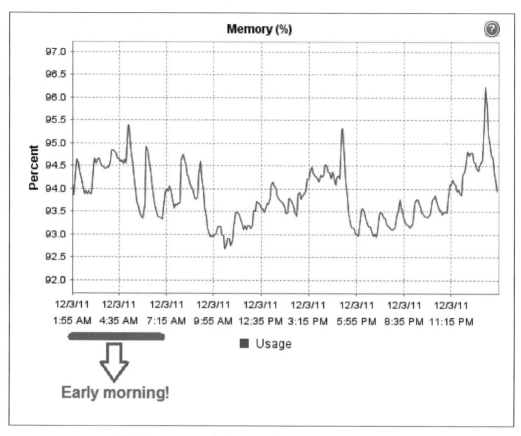

ESXi Memory – very high usage when no one was using the lab

The preceding graph shows high memory utilization over a 24-hour period, yet no one was using the lab in the early hours of the morning!

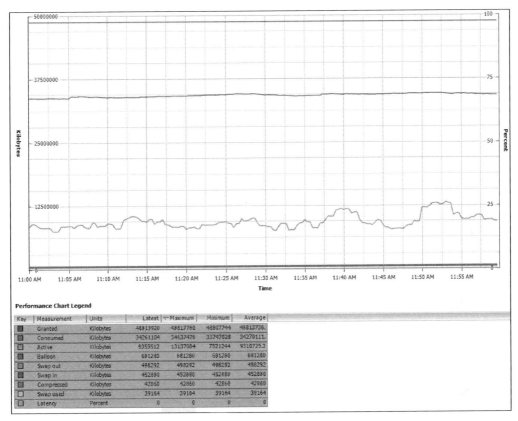

ESXi Memory counters

We will now turn to vRealize Operations for an alternative view. The following diagram from vRealize Operations 5 (not 6.1) tells a different story:

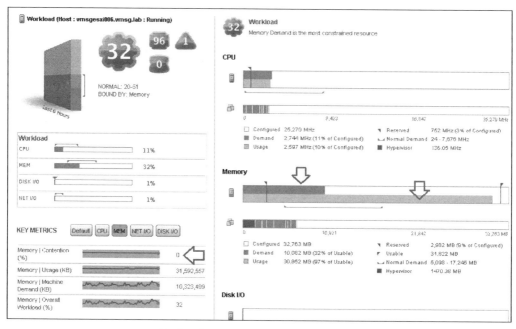

vRealize Operations 5 – the Host Details page

CPU, RAM, disk, and network are all in the healthy range, as you can see in the Workload area. Specifically for RAM, it has 97 percent Usage but 32 percent Demand. Note that the **Memory** chart is divided into two parts, as shown by the two red arrows. The upper bar shows the **Memory Demand**, while the lower bar shows the **Memory Usage** counter.

On the bottom left, note the **Key Metrics** section. vRealize Operations 5 shows that **Memory | Contention** is at 0 percent. This means none of the VMs running on the host is contending for memory. They are all being served well!

vRealize Operations 5 uses a different counter than vCenter. vRealize Operations 6.1 changes this and aligns itself with vCenter. Neither approach is wrong, actually. You need both metrics to tell you the full picture, as that's the nature of two-level memory management.

Just because a physical DIMM on the motherboard is mapped to a virtual DIMM in the VM does not mean it is actively used (read or write). You can use that DIMM for other VMs and you will not incur (for practical purposes) performance degradation. It is common for Windows to initialize pages on boot with zeroes but never use them subsequently.

Not all performance management tools understand this vCenter-specific characteristic. They would have given you a recommendation to buy more RAM.

We saw earlier that the behavior remains the same in vCenter 6.0 Update 1. The next screenshot shows the counters provided by vCenter 6.0. This is from a different ESXi host, as I want to provide you with a second example.

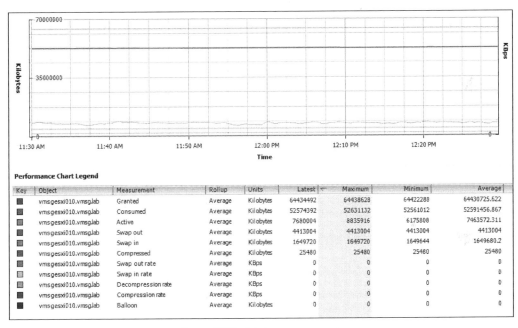

vCenter 6.0 Update 1 memory counters

This ESXi 6 host has 64 GB of RAM. Memory **Consumed** is stable at around 50 GB. **Memory Active** is much lower at 8 GB.

Notice that the ballooning is **0**, so there is no memory pressure for this host. You might notice that swap out and and swap in are not **0**. The value of **Memory Compressed** is also not **0**. But the value of Memory **Balloon** is **0**. Can you explain what's going on here?

The clue is in the rate counters. I have shown all the four rate counters (**Swap out rate**, **Swap in rate**, **Decompression rate**, and **Compression rate**). They are all 0. The memory pressure happened in the past and is no longer happens during the time of reporting.

 As you will see later in this book, vCenter uses the Active counter for utilization for VM. So the Usage counter has a different formula in vCenter, depending on the object. This makes sense as they are at different levels.

Let's take an example to see where a memory pressure issue happens. The following chart shows an ESXi 6 Update 1 system. It has 64 GB of RAM, as shown with the **Provisioned Memory** counter.

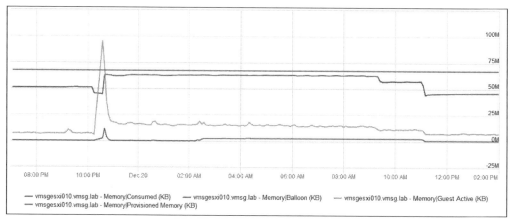

ESXi Memory counters

At around 10 pm, a lot of VMs were provisioned. The **Guest Active Memory** went above the physical resource. As you can expect, the ESXi was under memory pressure, and its memory consumed rose. ESXi certainly uses techniques such as **transparent page sharing**. As the memory consumed rose to near the provisioned RAM, ESXi activated the ballooning process.

Once the memory pressure was reduced, the ballooning process stopped. The consumed memory remained at its level as there was no need to remove pages that were mapped to physical DIMMs, as there was no new request.

For further information on this topic, review Kit Colbert's presentation on memory in vSphere at VMworld 2012. The content is still relevant for vSphere 6. The title is *Understanding Virtualized Memory Performance Management* and the session ID is **INF-VSP1729**. You can find it at http://www.vmworld.com/docs/DOC-6292.

ESXi memory key counters

We talked about contention and utilization being the main areas you should check. The following table summarizes the counters you should monitor at the host level for RAM:

Purpose	vCenter	vRealize Operations	Description
Contention	CPU Swap Wait	Contention (%)	Memory Contention is based on CPU Swap Wait
Utilization	Active (KB)	Workload (%)	For the "lower" threshold
Utilization	Usage (%)	Usage/Usable (%)	For the "upper" threshold

Memory counters at cluster level

vCenter does not provide a lot of memory counters at the cluster level. From the following performance chart dialog box, you can see that the number of counters drops to just five. Counters related to contention, such as **Compression**, **Swap**, and **Latency**, are no longer available. The Latency counter would be especially useful to track at the cluster level if you had a large environment.

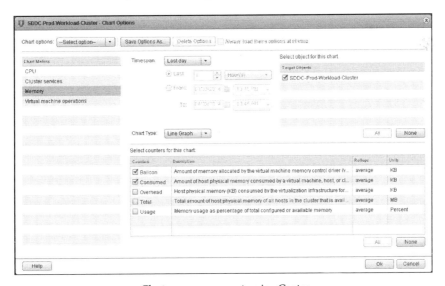

Cluster memory counters in vCenter

The data is not available in real time. This means the data granularity is at 5-minute intervals, not 20 seconds. As the rollup is an average, it means any spike within a 5-minute period may not be visible. In practice, however, most performance problems would still likely be detectable with 5-minute data points.

The counters do not take HA into account. For example, the Total counter sums all the host physical memory.

The **Consumed** memory does not take into account the host memory. So the memory used by vmkernel is not included. This is practically negligible as most ESXi hosts sport more than 128 GB of RAM.

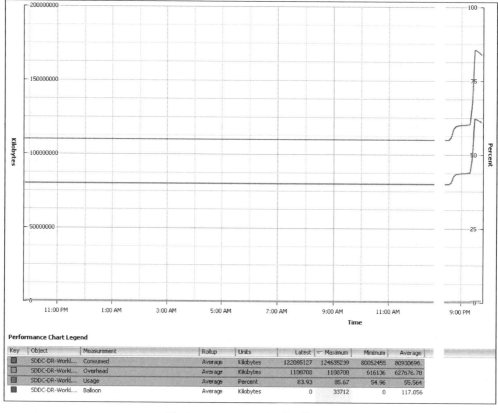

Key	Object	Measurement	Rollup	Units	Latest	Maximum	Minimum	Average
■	SDDC-DR-World...	Consumed	Average	Kilobytes	122085127	124635239	80052455	80930696
□	SDDC-DR-World...	Overhead	Average	Kilobytes	1108708	1108708	616136	627676.78
■	SDDC-DR-World...	Usage	Average	Percent	83.93	85.67	54.96	55.564
■	SDDC-DR-World...	Balloon	Average	Kilobytes	0	33712	0	117.056

Cluster memory counters in vCenter

Unlike the other counters, which just sum up each host in the cluster, the **Usage** counter is an average of all hosts. So if a large cluster (more than eight nodes) has an unbalanced RAM utilization, you may not see a high value. You can create a super metric that tracks the maximum RAM among all the hosts in the cluster. You can then plot this chart together with the **Cluster average** chart. This will give you both the average and the peak.

The **Usage (%)** and **Usage/Usable (%)** counters provide the same data. The following screenshot shows that they are identical over a period of one week:

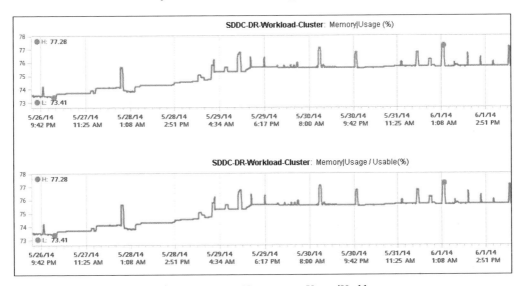

Cluster memory – Usage versus Usage/Usable

vRealize Operations provides a richer set of counters at the cluster level. Refer to *Chapter 11, SDDC Key Counters*, as the approach is similar for memory. The following table lists the key counters.

The **Workload** counter uses active memory, while the **Usage** counter uses consumed memory. Therefore, we consider them to be the lower and upper limits, respectively:

Purpose	Counters	Roll up	Description
Contention	Contention (%)	Average	As it is an average, you should complement it with a super metric that is based on the peak contention of a member host
Utilization	Workload (%)	Average	For the "lower" threshold
Utilization	Usage/Usable (%)	Average	For the "upper" threshold

We perform capacity management at the vSphere Cluster level. vRealize Operations provides metrics that help you in determining the cluster capacity. For example, you normally exclude the HA buffer in your capacity calculation. This can be a challenge if you have more than one HA policy. vRealize Operations provide a counter that tracks the usable memory after taking into account HA. The counter is named **Usable Capacity (KB)**. Its value is in KB, so you need to convert to GB.

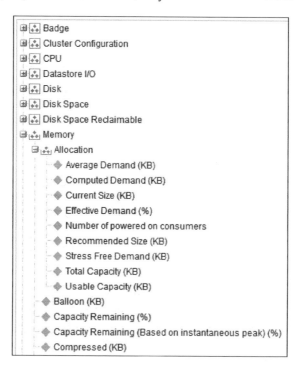

vRealize Operations also provides the total capacity available. In the following example, I have plotted both counters. This is a four-node cluster, where each host has 192 GB of RAM. We have set the cluster HA settings to the popular 1 host.

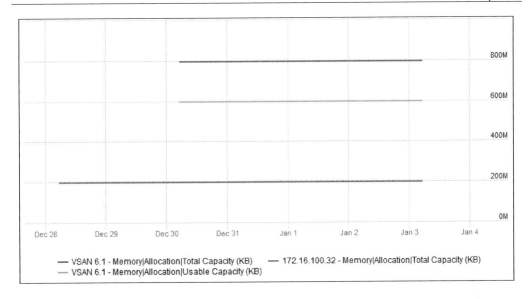

To see the actual value, we list the individual metrics. Do you notice that the numbers are a little different?

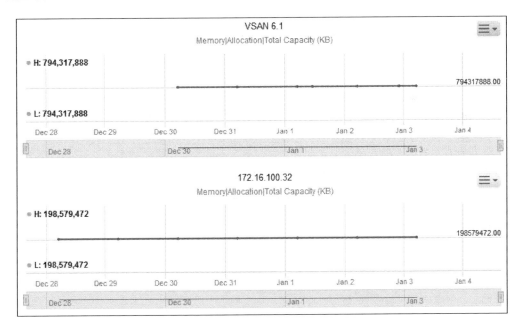

198,579,472 KB is not exactly 192 GB. It is around 189 GB. That small amount of memory is not considered. I checked the values on ESXi hosts ranging from 36 GB to 192 GB. For a small ESXi with 36 GB of RAM, the value is less than 1 GB. For a 64-GB ESXi, the value is 1.3 GB.

Memory counters at higher levels

As covered earlier in the book, vCenter does not provide information at this level. vRealize Operations provides a set of counters at the vCenter object level. There are, naturally, fewer counters for these higher-level objects, as we just need a summary:

Object	Purpose	Counters	Roll up
Datacenter	Contention	Contention (%)	Average
Datacenter	Utilization	Workload (%)	Average
vCenter	Contention	Contention (%)	Average
vCenter	Utilization	Workload (%)	Average
World	Contention	Contention (%)	Average
World	Utilization	Workload (%)	Average

The **Contention** counter is an average. As an average of a group with many members tends to be low, you should complement it with a super metric that is based on the peak contention of a member cluster.

Usage/Usable (%) is no longer relevant once you incorporate performance in your capacity management.

Summary

I hope you enjoyed the trip down memory lane. In this chapter, we discussed memory counters in both vCenter and vRealize Operations. The relationships between metrics were also explained. I provided screenshots to make the learning easier and added real-world examples.

We have now covered both CPU and memory, which means we are done with compute. Let's go through the network storage counters in the next chapter.

14
Storage Counters

We will continue our exploration of counters by covering storage counters in this chapter. We will take the same approach as we did with CPU and RAM. We will cover the following topics:

- The layers in the storage subsystem
- VM storage counters
- ESXi storage counters
- Cluster storage counters
- Datastore storage counters
- Storage counters for higher-level objects, such as datacenter, vCenter, and world
- Counters for capacity monitoring
- VMware VSAN counters

Multilayer storage

Virtualization increases the complexity of monitoring storage performance. Just like memory, where we have more than one level, we have three levels for storage. At the highest level, we have VMs. A VM typically has two to three virtual disks (or RDMs), such as an OS drive, paging file drive, and data drive. A large database VM will have even more.

We are interested in data both at the VM level and at the individual virtual disk level. If you are running a VM with a large data drive (for example, an Oracle database), the performance of the data drive is what the VM owner cares about the most. At the VM level, you get the average of all drives; hence, the performance issue could be masked out.

Below the VM level, we have the datastore level. What you can see at this level and, hence, how you monitor, depends on the storage architecture. We will cover the centralized storage architecture first as it is a more deployment. We will cover the distributed architecture separately due to major differences in monitoring.

In a typical shared storage, multiple VMs share a datastore. So, it is common to have an I/O blender effect, where sequential writes on individual VMDK files become random writes at the datastore level. This can occur either in VMFS or NFS.

Below the datastore, we have the physical storage. The datastore is normally backed one-to-one by a LUN, so what we see at the datastore level matches what we see at the LUN level. Multiple LUNs reside on a single array.

I did not include ESXi as a level in our discussion of storage counters since, in general, it is not a cause of storage bottlenecks. Yes, the vmkernel prioritizes and queues the I/O, but all these operations should last less than 1 millisecond. If the I/O is held at the kernel, there is a good chance that the physical device latency is more than 10 milliseconds.

The following table shows the level of visibility that you get from vCenter at each level. I have added VMs as you should look at this level before diving into a specific vDisk of the VM. I am assuming that the array level provides the necessary information and all of it can be presented to vRealize Operations via a management pack (for example, NetApp, HDS, EMC, and Pure Storage).

Level	Latency	IOPS	Throughput
vDisk	It can track read or write latency, but not the overall latency.	Yes. You need to add them manually.	Limited
VM	Yes. Track the highest latency at the datastore or disk counter. Track the read or write latency at the datastore counter.	Yes. Use the datastore or disk counter.	Limited
Datastore	Yes	Yes	Yes
Array	Yes	Yes	Yes

The **VM** in the table stands for a typical VM. A typical VM has multiple virtual disks but they are all in the same datastore. It does not use RDMs. If your VM has an RDM, you will notice in the **Disk** metric group that vSphere can only track the highest latency. This is not necessarily the highest latency. It is the latency at the point of collection. It cannot track the average latency on that 20,000-millisecond collection period. This means that there is no read or write latency per disk, either.

If your VM has its VMDK files residing in multiple datastores, then you can only track the highest latency among all datastores (for VMFS or NFS) or LUNs (for VMFS or RDM)—there is no breakdown. For each datastore, it can track read or write latency, but it cannot track overall latency.

The same limitation for latency applies to IOPS and throughput. This is another reason for minimizing the usage of RDMs and spreading the VMDK files of a single VM across multiple datastores.

The cells for **Datastore** are marked as **Yes** in the previous table even though vCenter only provides a limited set of values. This book assumes you use a management tool such as vRealize to complement vSphere.

We have covered what you can see at various levels of storage. Let's now move on to the actual counters. We will use the same approach we used for CPU and other counters: starting with contention, followed by utilization, and ending with other counters as required.

Contention counters

For storage, the counters for contention are clear. First, ensure that you do not have dropped packets for your **IP Storage** or **SCSI commands aborted** for your block storage. They are a sign of contention as the datastore (VMFS or NFS) is shared. SCSI lock was more common in the earlier versions of vSphere, before a more granular locking was introduced. The **Bus Resets** and **Commands Aborted** counters should be **0** all the time. As a result, it should be fine to track them at higher-level objects. Create a super metric that tracks the maximum or summation of both, and you should expect a flat line.

Once you have ensured that you do not have dropped packets on IP storage or aborted commands on block storage, you can use the latency counter for defining and measuring your performance SLA. In most cases, it is sufficient to measure the average latency, without the need to comply to both read latency and write latency.

Total latency is not **read latency** + **write latency**, because it is not a simple summation. In a given second, a VM issues many IOPS. For example, a VM may issue 100 reads and 10 writes in a second. Each of these 110 commands will have their own latencies. The "total" latency is the average of these 110 commands. In this example, the total latency will be influenced more by the read latency, as the workload is read-dominated.

If you are using **IP Storage**, take note that **Read** and **Write** do not map 1:1 to **Transmit (Tx)** and **Receive (Rx)** in **Networking** counters. **Read** and **Write** are both mapped to the **Transmit** counter as the ESXi host is issuing commands and is hence transmitting the packets.

vCenter also provides information about the number of I/Os that have been issued but not yet completed. The **Number of Outstanding I/O** counter tracks these and provides a separate counter for read and write. Certainly, the higher the number of outstanding I/Os is, the higher the latency becomes. The following chart shows that 148 outstanding write requests resulted in a write latency spike of 505 milliseconds that was sustained for 20 seconds. The level to which latency will increase for each outstanding I/O depends on many factors, such as the drive specification and the overall storage throughput.

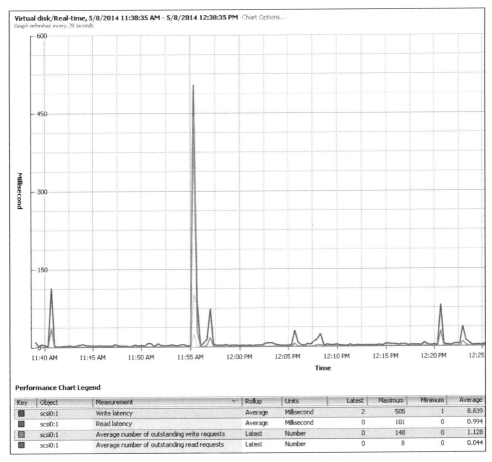

VM virtual disk – latency versus outstanding I/O

Utilization counters

For utilization, we need to look at both IOPS and throughput. You will find a number of counters that provide these data points, depending on the objects you are analyzing.

Ideally, we should be able to figure out the root cause behind the poor storage performance. These are some possibilities, handy to keep in mind while performing analysis:

- **The array**: Look into the array if the physical device latency counter is high. There are many possible causes, as an array has many layers and components. With most arrays now having SSD or pure SSD, the array causing an issue related to IOPS is becoming less likely.

- **The network**: Look into this if the fabric is saturated or you are using **IP Storage**. Even if you are on a 10-gigabit network, it is possible to have contention if you do not turn on **Network I/O Control**.

- **The ESXi host**: Look into this to determine whether the poor storage performance is caused by bad configuration, such as the wrong multipath policy being chosen or there being insufficient HBA queue depth. You should also look at non-VM workloads such as **vSphere Replication** and host-based security services.

- **The VM**: Look into this if the workload is high. The common VM-related storage performance issues are snapshots that were not removed, an antivirus update or scan, Windows patches, and backup. Backup jobs are a common performance hit, especially if they hit several related VMs at once — either on the same host or the same datastore. Another cause could be a developer running Iometer (http://www.iometer.org/) or a database test.

If all of these points are good and yet the VM has a storage issue, check whether the disk length is full inside the Guest OS filesystem.

Storage counters at the VM level

At the VM level, you can look at counters at the individual virtual disk level, datastore level, and disk level. Not all counters are available for all storage types, as explained here:

- If you look at the virtual disk counters, you can see VMFS and VMDK files, NFS VMDK files, and RDMs. However, you don't get data below the virtual disk. For example, if the VM has snapshots, the data does not know about it. Also, a VM typically has multiple virtual disks (OS drive, swap drive, and data drive), so you need to add them manually if you use vCenter. In vRealize Operations, you use the "aggregate of all instances".

- If you look at the datastore counters, you can see VMFS and NFS, but not RDM. Because snapshots happen at the datastore level, the counter will include it. Datastore figures will be higher if your VM has a snapshot. You don't have to add the data from each virtual disk together as the data presented is already at the VM level. It also has the **Highest Latency** counter, which is useful for tracking peak latency.

- If you look at the disk counters, you can see VMFS and RDM, but not NFS. The data at this level should be the same as at the datastore level because your blocks should be aligned; you should have a 1:1 mapping between datastore and LUN, without extents. It also has the **Highest Latency** counter, which is useful for tracking peak latency.

vCenter 6.0 provides 17 counters for storage at the VM virtual disk level; 7 are new counters compared to vCenter 5.0. The new additions are number of seeks (small, medium, and large), latency in microseconds, and size of requests (read and write).

The next three screenshots show the counters available at the virtual disk group, datastore group, and disk group, respectively. For a typical VM, these counters will be the same as all the VMDK files are on the same datastore, which in turn is mapped 1:1 with the underlying disk.

Description	Rollup	Units	Internal Name	Collection Level
☐ Number of large seeks	Latest	Number	largeSeeks	4
☐ Number of medium seeks	Latest	Number	mediumSeeks	4
☐ Number of small seeks	Latest	Number	smallSeeks	4
☐ Write Latency (us)	Latest	Microsecond	writeLatencyUS	4
☐ Read Latency (us)	Latest	Microsecond	readLatencyUS	4
☐ Read workload metric	Latest	Number	readLoadMetric	2
☐ Average number of outstanding read requests	Latest	Number	readOIO	2
☑ Write latency	Average	Millisecond	totalWriteLatency	1
☐ Average write requests per second	Average	Number	numberWriteAvera...	1
☐ Write request size	Latest	Number	writeIOSize	4
☐ Read request size	Latest	Number	readIOSize	4
☐ Write workload metric	Latest	Number	writeLoadMetric	2
☐ Average number of outstanding write requests	Latest	Number	writeOIO	2
☑ Read latency	Average	Millisecond	totalReadLatency	1
☐ Read rate	Average	KBps	read	2
☐ Write rate	Average	KBps	write	2
☐ Average read requests per second	Average	Number	numberReadAvera...	1

VM virtual disk counters

The datastore metric group shows the metrics for this VM only and not for every VM in that datastore. To see the data at the datastore level, look at the datastore object:

Description	Rollup	Units	Internal Name	Collection Level
☐ Read rate	Average	KBps	read	2
☐ Highest latency	Latest	Millisecond	maxTotalLatency	3
☐ Average write requests per ...	Average	Number	numberWriteAvera...	1
☐ Write rate	Average	KBps	write	2
☐ Average read requests per ...	Average	Number	numberReadAvera...	1
☑ Read latency	Average	Millisecond	totalReadLatency	1
☑ Write latency	Average	Millisecond	totalWriteLatency	1

VM datastore counters

The disk is the physical LUN backing up the datastore. If the datastore does not span multiple LUNs, then disk counters will be very similar to datastore counters.

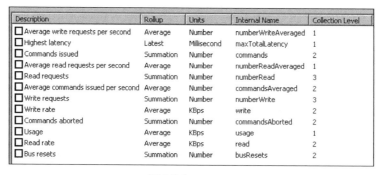

Description	Rollup	Units	Internal Name	Collection Level
☐ Average write requests per second	Average	Number	numberWriteAveraged	1
☐ Highest latency	Latest	Millisecond	maxTotalLatency	1
☐ Commands issued	Summation	Number	commands	2
☐ Average read requests per second	Average	Number	numberReadAveraged	1
☐ Read requests	Summation	Number	numberRead	3
☐ Average commands issued per second	Average	Number	commandsAveraged	2
☐ Write requests	Summation	Number	numberWrite	3
☐ Write rate	Average	KBps	write	2
☐ Commands aborted	Summation	Number	commandsAborted	2
☐ Usage	Average	KBps	usage	1
☐ Read rate	Average	KBps	read	2
☐ Bus resets	Summation	Number	busResets	2

VM disk counters

For latency, vCenter provides the **Write Latency** and **Read Latency** counters. There is no counter for total average latency, but there is a counter called **Highest Latency**.

If you have an RDM, use the counter at the **Disk** metric group. If you have NFS, use the counter at the Datastore metric group. If you have vmdk, you can use either.

vCenter provides the data in both milliseconds and microseconds. As you can see in the next chart, data in microseconds just provides a more granular view than milliseconds, which can be useful in latency-sensitive applications:

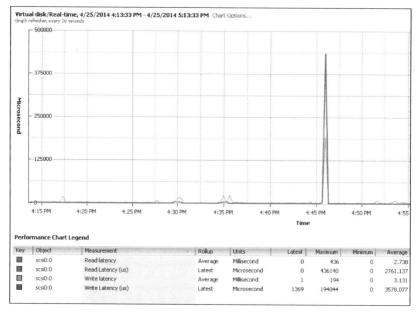

VM disk counters

At the datastore and disk levels, vCenter also provides the **Highest Latency** counter. This tracks the highest latency among all datastores and disks. It is based on the latest data. That means it is neither the average nor the peak of the sample period. You can see in vCenter that the rollup technique used is **Latest**. This is why it can be lower than the individual Disk or Datastore metric.

This metric is useful when the VM has multiple datastores or disks. It is also useful even if the VM resides on a single datastore or disk. Note that this is not total latency. **Highest Latency** is the peak of either **Write** or **Read**, not the aggregate of both. This can be used to track the peak as vRealize Operations takes an average of 5 minutes, which may hide any spike within the 5-minute period.

For utilization, vRealize Operations provides the **Workload (%)** counter. Because it is in percentage, it makes it easier to understand and manage. We will cover this counter in the *Storage counters at the datastore level* section.

Putting it all together

Let's now take an example to see how these three metric groups (Virtual disk, Datastore, and Disk) work together. We will use a vCenter 5.5 appliance in this example. The event causing the spike shown in the following screenshot was the vCenter web client server restarting. The administrator would have seen the message when attempting to log in to vCenter that the web client server was restarting.

At the virtual disk level, the total IOPS went up to beyond the 3000 mark of the VM level. The VM has two virtual disks, **scsi0:0** and **scsi0:1**.

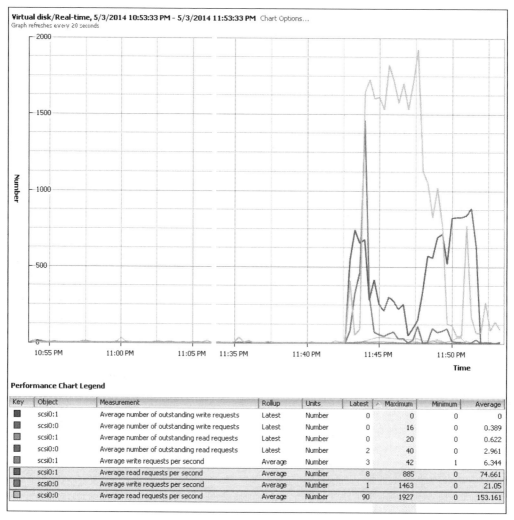

Virtual disk/Real-time, 5/3/2014 10:53:33 PM - 5/3/2014 11:53:33 PM Chart Options…
Graph refreshes every 20 seconds

Performance Chart Legend

Key	Object	Measurement	Rollup	Units	Latest	Maximum	Minimum	Average
■	scsi0:1	Average number of outstanding write requests	Latest	Number	0	0	0	0
■	scsi0:0	Average number of outstanding write requests	Latest	Number	0	16	0	0.389
■	scsi0:1	Average number of outstanding read requests	Latest	Number	0	20	0	0.622
■	scsi0:0	Average number of outstanding read requests	Latest	Number	2	40	0	2.961
■	scsi0:1	Average write requests per second	Average	Number	3	42	1	6.344
■	scsi0:1	Average read requests per second	Average	Number	8	885	0	74.661
■	scsi0:0	Average write requests per second	Average	Number	1	1463	0	21.05
☐	scsi0:0	Average read requests per second	Average	Number	90	1927	0	153.161

Metric values at the virtual disk level

At the datastore level, the pattern is consistent. While there are other VMs in the datastore, the counters are only showing the IOPS from this VM. Notice that we lose detail; there is no data at the virtual disk level. On the other hand, if we have snapshots, the result will be visible at this level.

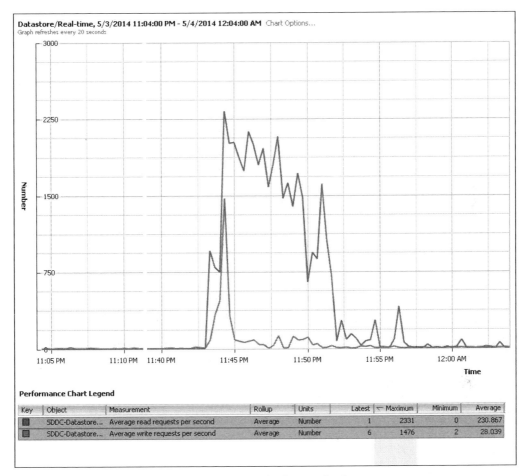

Metric values at the datastore level

The pattern is again consistent at the **Disk** level. The next screenshot shows the total I/O issued. If you divide the number by 20 (as the timeline is 20 seconds), you get a similar result with the IOPS you see at the datastore level.

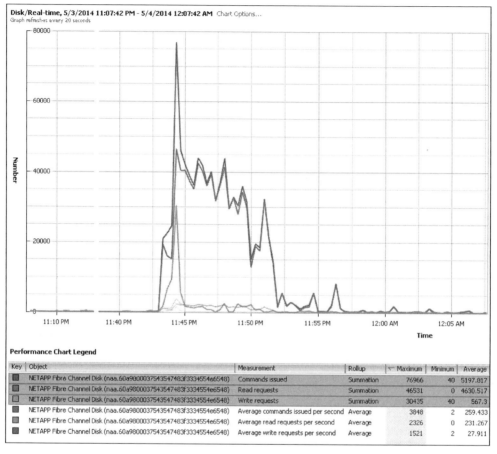

Metric values at the disk (LUN) level

All the previously shown charts are for IOPS. Let's now check the throughput.

In the following screenshot, the workload is small as the total value is less than 400 megabits per second, which is much lower than the physical limit. To get the total value, carry out the following steps:

1. Add the **Read** rate and **Write** rate to get the total throughput

2. Multiply the total throughput by 8 to convert from bytes to bits

3. Divide by 1000 to convert from kilo to mega

Please note that this is an average over 20 seconds. It is possible that there is a spike within the 20 seconds.

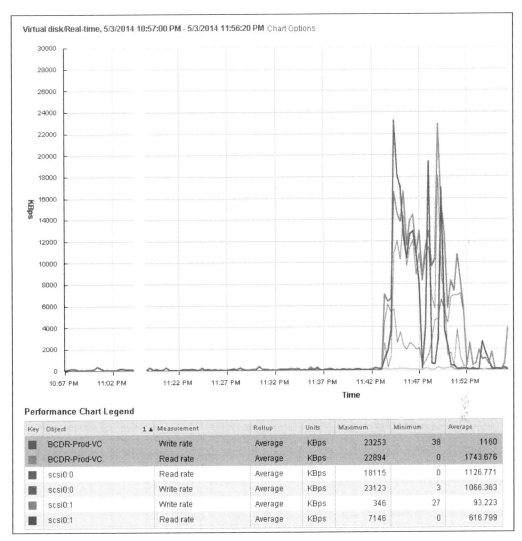

IOPS values at the virtual disk level

Even though the throughput is low, it does not mean latency is low. In our example, the latency went up to 25 milliseconds at the datastore level.

Note that the **Highest** latency counter can be a little lower than the **Write** latency or **Read** latency. Can you figure out why?

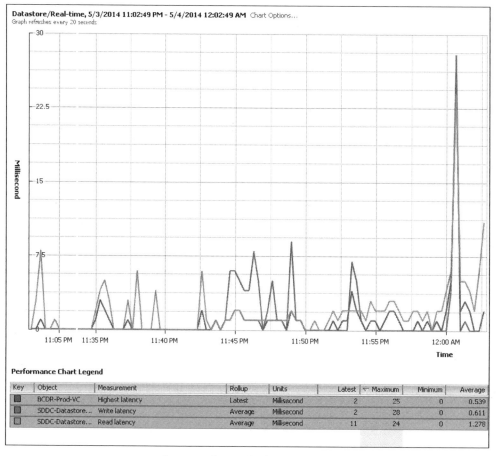

Latency values at the datastore level

It's because of the difference in the rollup technique. The **Highest** latency takes the last data in that 20-second sampling interval, not the average of the entire 20 seconds.

Shown in the next chart, the latency also went up to 25 milliseconds at the disk level. This is expected as we have a 1:1 mapping.

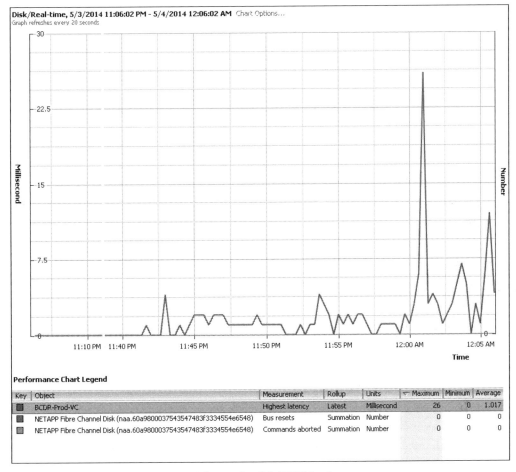

Values at the disk (LUN) level

VM storage counters – summary

We have talked about **Contention** and **Utilization** being the main areas you should check. The following table summarizes what you should monitor at the virtual disk level or VM level (which will be an average of all its virtual disks).

VM storage—virtual disk counters:

Purpose	vCenter	vRealize Operations
Contention	Read Latency Write Latency	Total Latency
Utilization	Average read requests per second Average write requests per second	Commands per second
Utilization	Write rate (KBPS) Read rate (KBPS)	Usage

For virtual disks, vCenter does not provide a total, which means you need to add them together manually (read and write). vRealize Operations provides both the summary and breakdown (read and write).

VM storage—VM counters:

Purpose	vCenter	vRealize Operations
Contention	Highest Latency (milliseconds)	Disk command latency (milliseconds)
Utilization	Commands Issued (number)	Commands per second
Utilization	Usage (KBPS)	Usage Average (KBPS)
Utilization		Workload (%)

vCenter also does not provide utilization in percentage. It only provides the raw data. I've left the table cell blank for ease of comparison.

Storage counters at the ESXi level

The storage counters at the ESXi level are similar to those at the VM level. They provide the same set of information (latency, throughput, and IOPS).

Naturally, each of the metric groups gives insight from the vantage point of the object. For example, the ESXi adapter metric group provides the data from each adapter (vmhba).

The following two screenshots show the sets of counters available for each ESXi adapter and their associated storage paths:

Description	Rollup	Units	Internal Name	Collection Level
☐ Read latency	Average	Millisecond	totalReadLatency	2
☐ Average write requests per second	Average	Number	numberWriteAveraged	2
☐ Average commands issued per second	Average	Number	commandsAveraged	2
☐ Highest latency	Latest	Millisecond	maxTotalLatency	3
☐ Read rate	Average	KBps	read	2
☐ Average read requests per second	Average	Number	numberReadAveraged	2
☐ Write rate	Average	KBps	write	2
☐ Write latency	Average	Millisecond	totalWriteLatency	2

ESXi Adapter counters

Notice in the screenshot that there is no total throughput counter, so you need to add write and read manually. vRealize Operations provides the total throughput counter via the **Total Usage** counter.

Description	Rollup	Units	Internal Name	Collection Level
☐ Read rate	Average	KBps	read	3
☐ Read latency	Average	Millisecond	totalReadLatency	3
☐ Write latency	Average	Millisecond	totalWriteLatency	3
☐ Write rate	Average	KBps	write	3
☐ Average read requests per second	Average	Number	numberReadAveraged	3
☐ Average write requests per second	Average	Number	numberWriteAveraged	3
☐ Average commands issued per second	Average	Number	commandsAveraged	3
☐ Highest latency	Latest	Millisecond	maxTotalLatency	3

ESXi Storage path counters

As shared earlier, you normally set four paths between an ESXi host and its target LUN. You set two HBAs (in case either one of them fails) and each HBA sees a port on each SP on the array (in case any SP fails).

This means that in the preceding Storage path counters, you will have four sets of values. You can use vRealize Operations to get their total, average, or peak.

At the datastore level, ESXi provides visibility into the operation of Storage DRS and Storage I/O Control. The Highest Latency counter is useful as, most of the time, an ESXi host will have multiple datastores. This tracks the highest among all the datastores.

Description	Rollup	Units	Internal Name	Collection Level
Storage I/O Control normalized latency	Average	Microsecond	sizeNormalizedDatastoreLatency	1
Storage DRS datastore outstanding write requests	Latest	Number	datastoreWriteOIO	1
Storage DRS datastore normalized read latency	Latest	Number	datastoreNormalReadLatency	2
Storage I/O Control datastore maximum queue depth	Latest	Number	datastoreMaxQueueDepth	1
Write rate	Average	KBps	write	2
Datastore latency observed by VMs	Latest	Number	datastoreVMObservedLatency	1
Storage DRS datastore read I/O rate	Latest	Number	datastoreReadIops	1
Average write requests per second	Average	Number	numberWriteAveraged	1
Write latency	Average	Millisecond	totalWriteLatency	1
Storage DRS datastore bytes read	Latest	Number	datastoreReadBytes	2
Storage DRS datastore read workload metric	Latest	Number	datastoreReadLoadMetric	4
Storage DRS datastore write workload metric	Latest	Number	datastoreWriteLoadMetric	4
Storage I/O Control aggregated IOPS	Average	Number	datastoreIops	1
Read latency	Average	Millisecond	totalReadLatency	1
Storage DRS datastore bytes written	Latest	Number	datastoreWriteBytes	2
Storage DRS datastore write I/O rate	Latest	Number	datastoreWriteIops	1
Read rate	Average	KBps	read	2
Storage DRS datastore outstanding read requests	Latest	Number	datastoreReadOIO	1
Storage DRS datastore normalized write latency	Latest	Number	datastoreNormalWriteLatency	2
Average read requests per second	Average	Number	numberReadAveraged	1
Storage I/O Control active time percentage	Average	Percent	siocActiveTimePercentage	1
Highest latency	Latest	Millisecond	maxTotalLatency	3

ESXi datastore counters

You can tell how much action has been taken by **Storage I/O Control (SIOC)** by following the **Storage I/O Control active time percentage** counter.

The next screenshot shows a datastore cluster with two members. The first chart shows SIOC was quite active because the datastore latency exceeded 30 milliseconds several times. The second chart shows the aggregate latency. The third and fourth charts show the latency of individual datastores, which are members of the group.

As you can see, the aggregate is the average of both. Note that the aggregate is the average per I/O; it is not just a simple averaging of the values on the different datastores, because the datastores had different amounts of I/O.

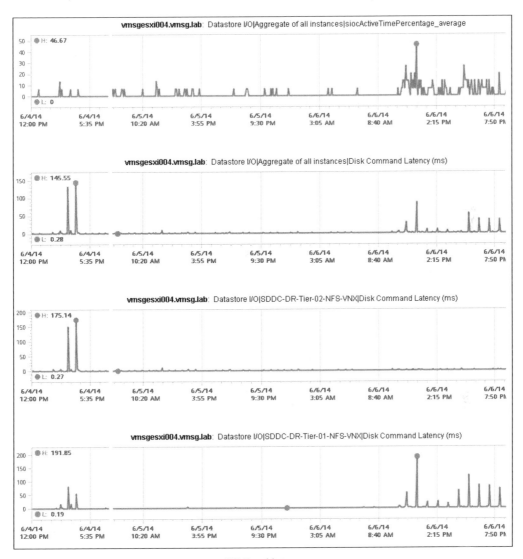

SIOC and latency

The ESXi Disk metric group, shown in the next screenshot, provides visibility into the vmkernel storage stack. For example, there are counters that track the amount of time a command is sitting in the kernel queue. As shared earlier, the vmkernel latency should be less than 1 millisecond most of the time, as the main bottleneck should be at the physical device layer. You can create a super metric that tracks the maximum of **Queue command latency** and **Kernel command latency** for all ESXi hosts in your data centers. You should expect a value of **0-1** for the super metric, indicating a healthy situation:

Description	Rollup	Units	Internal Name	Collection Level
☐ Queue command latency	Average	Millisecond	queueLatency	2
☑ Write rate	Average	KBps	write	2
☐ Bus resets	Summation	Number	busResets	2
☐ Write latency	Average	Millisecond	totalWriteLatency	2
☐ Average commands issued per second	Average	Number	commandsAveraged	2
☐ Kernel read latency	Average	Millisecond	kernelReadLatency	2
☐ Queue write latency	Average	Millisecond	queueWriteLatency	2
☐ Read requests	Summation	Number	numberRead	3
☐ Average write requests per second	Average	Number	numberWriteAveraged	1
☐ Physical device command latency	Average	Millisecond	deviceLatency	1
☐ Write requests	Summation	Number	numberWrite	3
☐ Maximum queue depth	Average	Number	maxQueueDepth	1
☐ Commands aborted	Summation	Number	commandsAborted	2
☐ Kernel command latency	Average	Millisecond	kernelLatency	2
☑ Read rate	Average	KBps	read	2
☐ Physical device write latency	Average	Millisecond	deviceWriteLatency	2
☐ Read latency	Average	Millisecond	totalReadLatency	2
☐ Average read requests per second	Average	Number	numberReadAveraged	1
☑ Highest latency	Latest	Millisecond	maxTotalLatency	1
☐ Commands issued	Summation	Number	commands	2
☐ Physical device read latency	Average	Millisecond	deviceReadLatency	2
☐ Queue read latency	Average	Millisecond	queueReadLatency	2
☐ Kernel write latency	Average	Millisecond	kernelWriteLatency	2
☐ Command latency	Average	Millisecond	totalLatency	3
☑ Usage	Average	KBps	usage	1

ESXi Disk metrics

The storage array provides access to many datastores, which are mounted by multiple ESXi hosts, sometimes in multiple clusters. Seeing the datastore counters at the ESXi or cluster level means that we do not get the full picture. To see the full picture, we need to look at the datastore or array level. Keep in mind that most ESXi hosts have a local datastore that gets included in the ESXi-level storage information. You need to manually exclude the local datastore information if you only need the data for a shared datastore.

Because of these reasons, we normally do not track storage performance at the ESXi or cluster level. The exception here is, naturally, distributed storage, as each ESXi also doubles up as a storage node.

Storage counters at the cluster level

vCenter does not provide information for storage at the cluster level but vRealize Operations does, including counters such as IOPS, Throughput, and Latency. The main reason why you should not look at storage at the cluster level when working with classic arrays is that the cluster is a compute cluster; it is not a storage cluster, so the boundary a cluster provides for compute may not apply to storage.

Can you think of another reason?

The data at this level, like for the ESXi host level, includes all the local datastores. This can impact the overall result, especially those that give an average of all the datastores. If you have a cluster with 10 nodes that share five datastores, you will have 15 datastores in the clusters. The 10 local datastores will skew the total result, masking important data such as average latency.

For a view beyond disk and datastore, the datastore cluster is what you should look into.

Storage counters at the datastore level

vCenter only provides the following screen for datastores. It is a fixed set of charts, with fixed configuration.

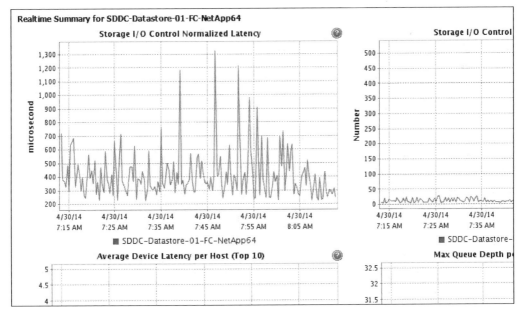

Datastore counters provided by vCenter

The complete list of charts available in vCenter is listed as follows:

- Storage I/O Control Normalized Latency
- Storage I/O Control Normalized Aggregate IOPS
- Average Device Latency per host (Top 10)
- Maximum Queue Depth per host (Top 10)
- Read IOPS per host (Top 10)
- Write IOPS per host (Top 10)
- Average Read Latency per VM vDisk (Top 10)
- Average Write Latency per VM vDisk (Top 10)
- Read IOPS per VM vDisk (Top 10)
- Write IOPS per VM vDisk (Top 10)

As you can see, the list is rather limited. For example, there are no counters for throughput, be it read, write, or total. Most charts only show the top 10 data points.

vRealize Operations provides a richer set of data for storage at the datastore level, including IOPS, throughput, latency, and outstanding I/O. For most of them, you get the data for read, write, and total.

In addition to these basic counters, vRealize Operations provides a **Workload (%)** counter, which provides good comparable information on the storage utilization. In reality, different datastores will experience different IOPS and throughput. Even in the same datastore, different VMs will have different demands. For example, when someone says, "the datastore has high storage workload", what does the person normally mean? Usually, they mean high IOPS, high throughput, or high outstanding requests. All these factors are considered by the **Workload (%)** counter, as you can see in the next chart.

Can you guess the counter that is not considered in Workload?

It does not consider the latency, as high latency does not necessarily mean the VMs in the datastore are generating a lot of workload.

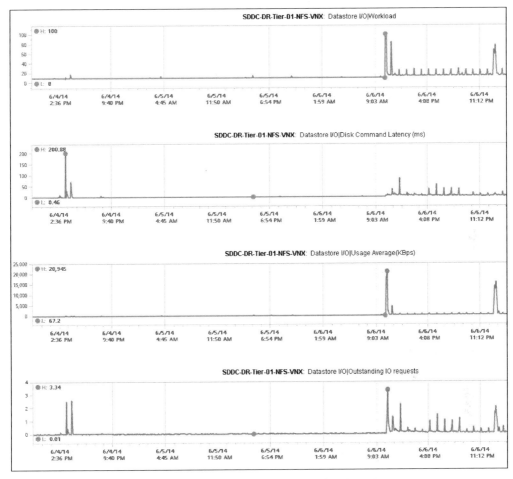

Some datastore counters provided by vRealize Operations

The **Workload** counter is useful to compare across datastores. Unfortunately, there is no **Workload** counter at the datastore cluster level. This means you need to compare it at the datastore level or create a super metric. The following are the counters you should check at the datastore level:

Purpose	vCenter	vRealize Operations
Contention	Not available at the datastore level	Disk command latency (ms)
Utilization	Not available at the datastore level	Commands per second
Utilization	Not available at the datastore level	Usage Average (KBPS)
Utilization	Not available at the datastore level	Workload (%)

Storage counters at the datastore cluster level

vCenter only provides the following screen for **Storage** at the datastore cluster level. Like for datastores, it is a fixed set of charts, the details of which cannot be modified.

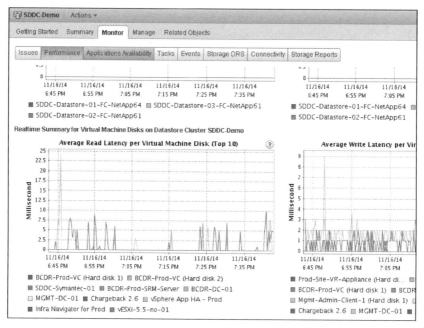

Datastore Cluster counters provided by vCenter

The complete list of charts provided by vCenter is as follows:

- Normalized Latency per datastore (Top 10)
- Aggregate IOPS per datastore (Top 10)
- SIOC Activity report per datastore (Top 10)
- Storage I/O Control Normalized Latency
- Storage I/O Control Normalized Aggregate IOPS
- Average Device Latency per host (Top 10)
- Maximum Queue Depth per host (Top 10)
- Read IOPS per host (Top 10)
- Write IOPS per host (Top 10)
- Average Read Latency per VM vDisk (Top 10)
- Average Write Latency per VM vDisk (Top 10)
- Read IOPS per VM vDisk (Top 10)
- Write IOPS per VM vDisk (Top 10)

As you can see from this list, it is rather limited. Just like with datastores, there are no counters for throughput, and most charts only show the top 10 data points.

vRealize Operations provides a richer set of data. You get the IOPS, throughput, latency, and outstanding I/O. For most of them, you get the data for read, write, and total.

Storage counters at higher levels

As you might expect by now, vCenter does not provide information for storage at this level, but vRealize Operations does. The following table lists the key counters. Except for the **World** object, the rest of the objects provide all the counters. Notice that their values include local datastores. If you want to exclude the local datastores, create a group.

The **Workload (%)** counter is easier for the operations team, as it uses percentage rather than raw data. For example, if you have 20 vCenter Servers and they show different KBPS numbers, it is difficult to understand at a glance the significance of that value—is it higher, lower or the same as last time? If you use the 0-100 range as a percentage, you can color code the range to help the operations team.

Object	Purpose	Counters	Roll up
Datacenter	Contention	Disk Command Latency (ms)	Average
Datacenter	Utilization	Usage Rate (KBPS)	Average
Datacenter	Utilization	Commands per seconds (number)	Average
Datacenter	Utilization	Workload (%)	Average
vCenter	Contention	Disk Command Latency (ms)	Average
vCenter	Utilization	Usage Rate (KBPS)	Average
vCenter	Utilization	Commands per seconds (number)	Average
vCenter	Utilization	Workload (%)	Average
World	Contention		
World	Utilization	Usage Rate (KBPS)	Average
World	Utilization	Commands per seconds (number)	Average
World	Utilization	Workload (%)	Average

Capacity monitoring

As we do capacity monitoring at the datastore cluster level, it becomes important that we know how the numbers are derived. Let's use an example as a way to test our understanding.

The following example uses a datastore cluster that has three datastores. Each has 1 TB, mapped to a 1 TB LUN. Let's verify what contributes to the **Free** column.

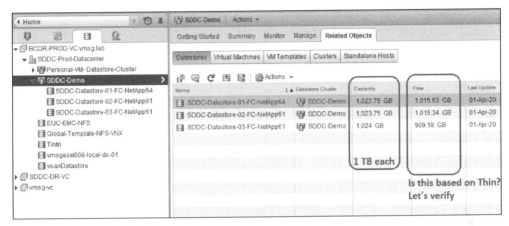

Datastore information in vCenter

To verify whether it is based on Thin, I added all the VMs in the datastore cluster, shown in the next diagram:

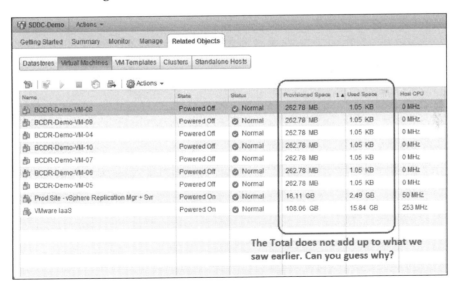

VM storage information in vCenter

Notice that they did not add up to what we saw at the datastore level. At the datastore level, it shows that the usage is more than 130 GB. At the VM level, the total used space is less than 20 GB. Something does not tally. Can you guess four reasons that can contribute to this discrepancy?

Let's browse the datastore. We find the first reason: we have non-VM objects. In this case, we have ISO files.

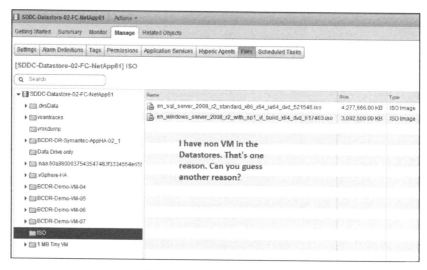

Datastore – the file-browser UI

The following diagram explains the next two reasons:

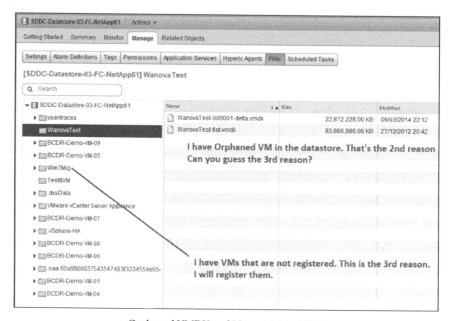

Orphaned VMDK and Non-registered VM

The following diagram shows the fourth reason. This particular VM has its CD-ROM coming from another datastore. Once we address the reasons, the total (**Used Space**) column makes more sense.

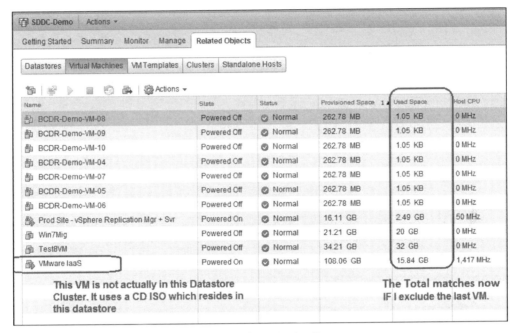

VM storage information in vCenter

Let's now see what the **Free** column at the datastore level shows. It is much closer to the 20 GB we saw at the VM level.

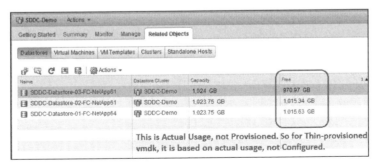

Datastore information in vCenter

This simple test confirms what we thought, which is that the **Free** column is based on the actual usage, not the provisioned number. Since we are using thin provisioning, the free space number is higher.

Now that we know how it is calculated, we can go to vRealize Operations and pick the right metric. I have plotted a few counters to show you which counters you should take:

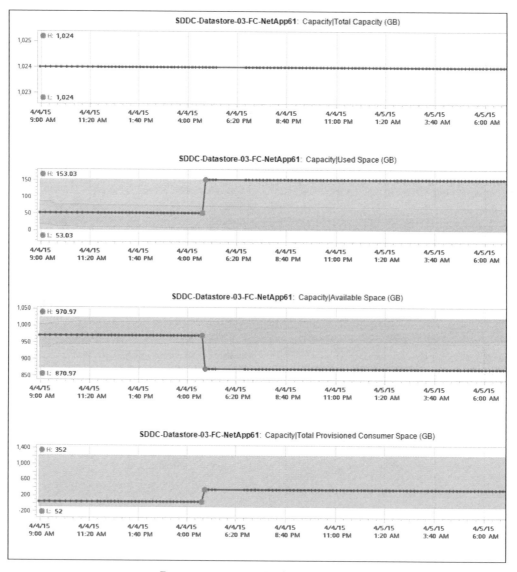

Datastore counters in vRealize Operations

I added a 200-GB thin-provisioned VMDK and 100-GB thick-provisioned VMDK to see how they impact the counters. So, the total is 300 GB.

Notice how different counters react differently:

- **Total Capacity** does not move. This is obvious, as it is the total capacity of the datastore, not the used or free capacity.

- The **Used Space (GB)** metric goes up by 100 GB, proving that it is based on actual usage. The 200 GB we added is not reflected as it is thin provisioned. It does not consume any space yet. As it is based on actual usage, it includes all files in the datastore, such as ISOs and VMs that are not registered to vCenter.

- **Available Space** goes down by 100 GB. This means it is also based on actual usage.

- **Total Provisioned Consumed Space (GB)** goes up by 300 GB. This makes sense, as it is based on provisioned space. This counter is useful is you are doing capacity planning based on provisioned space. Note that this number does not include non-VM (for example, ISO) files and VMs that are not registered to vCenter. The following screenshot proves that it does screenshot does not immediately follow.

I added a 20-GB file to the datastore. Notice that the **Used Space** counter went up by 20 GB. The **Provisioned** counter did not reflect that:

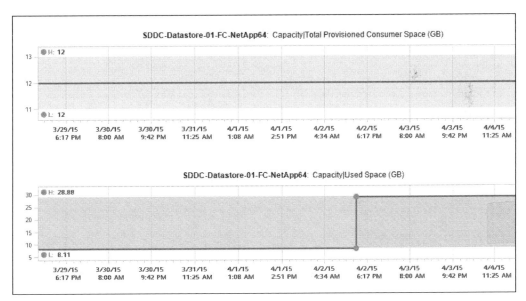

Datastore counters in vRealize Operations

Just in case you are wondering whether there is any change in vRealize Operations 6.2 since the preceding set of screenshots was taken in 6.0, here is what it looks like in 6.2. Other than a shortening of the counter name, the counter works in the same way. In the following example, I removed around 2 GB of ISO files from the datastore:

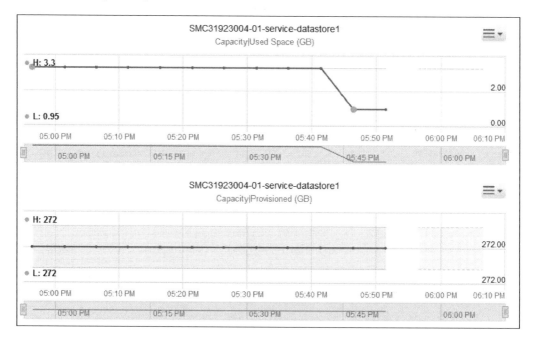

Datastore counters in vRealize Operations

At a glance

Thin provisioning allows you to provision more than what you actually have. As a result, you can run out of storage if you are not careful. You have two choices in capacity planning as a result:

- Plan based on utilized space. This results in aggressive sizing.
- Plan based on provisioned space. This results in conservative sizing, as your VMs do not fully use the provisioned capacity.

The correct method is to use both plans together. We covered a sample solution in *Chapter 7, Capacity-Monitoring Dashboards*.

Let's recap the counters you should use:

The information you need	Counter to use
The total capacity of a datastore	Capacity | Total Capacity (GB)
The actual space consumed in a datastore	Capacity | Used Space (GB)
The consumption number in %	Capacity | Used Space (%)
The actual free space in your datastore	Capacity | Available Space (GB)
The total provisioned space	Capacity | Provisioned (GB)

This works well for a datastore. What about at the datastore cluster level, since this is where you should be doing your capacity management?

There are fewer metrics at the datastore cluster level. If you do not see them, they are not enabled. Go to **Policy** and enable them. The following diagram shows you how to enable multiple metrics at the same time:

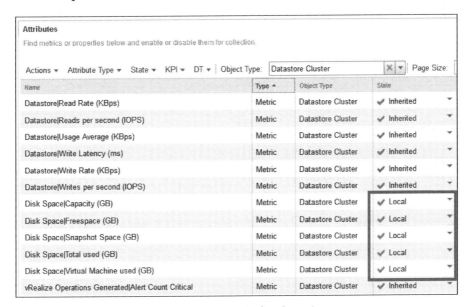

Enabling metrics in vRealize Operations

There are fewer counters, so we need to use super metrics in these cases:

- To see the total capacity in your datastore cluster, create a super metric as **Sum (Datastore: Capacity | Total Capacity (GB)) Disk Space | Capacity**

- To see the space consumed based on **Thin Provision**, use **Disk Space | Total Used (GB)**

- To see the free space based on Thin Provision, create a super metric as **Sum (Datastore: | Capacity | Available Space (GB)) Disk Space | Free Space**

- To see the total space consumed based on Thick Provision, create a super metric as **Sum (Datastore: Capacity | Provisioned (GB))**

- To see the free space based on Thick Provision, create a super metric as **Sum (Datastore: Capacity | Total Capacity (GB)) – Sum (Datastore: Capacity | Provisioned (GB))**

VMware VSAN

The preceding discussion applies to a classic physical array. Let's take a look at distributed storage. By distributed storage, we mean a storage architecture that uses local disks from servers to form virtual shared storage. There is no physical storage anymore. There are multiple ways to achieve this, and there are enough differences among the distributed storage products.

The differences result in different approaches for performance and capacity management. In this book, we will cover **VMware Virtual SAN (VSAN)**. You should not assume that you can apply the solution here to monitor other distributed storage products. Even within VSAN, there are differences in monitoring a hybrid VSAN and all-flash VSAN.

 Read *Chapter 16, VMware Virtual SAN Diagnostics and Troubleshooting Reference Manual* by Cormac Hogan (http://www.vmware.com/files/pdf/products/vsan/VSAN-Troubleshooting-Reference-Manual.pdf).

Let's see how monitoring VSAN differs from monitoring classic storage. As usual, we begin with the customer of our IaaS platform, which is a VM.

Remember all the VM storage counters we covered earlier? Do you expect all of them to be available? We are at the VM layer after all, above the storage layer.

A VM does not know whether it sits on top of a VSAN or classic array. Right?

Most of the counters are in fact no longer available. You might be wondering what I mean by that. Here is what the VM Datastore metric provides you if your VM is on VSAN:

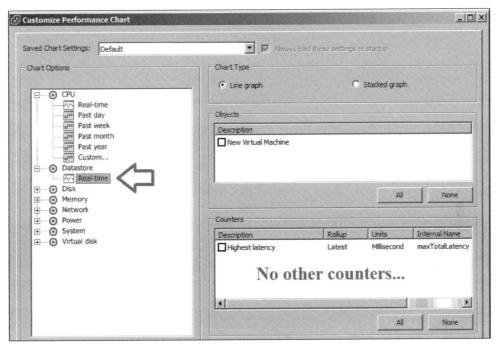

VM Datastore metrics on VSAN

You'll notice right away that all the counters at the VM datastore level are no longer available. The only counter left is Highest Latency. In addition, the VM Datastore counters are only available in real time. You do not have them after 1 hour.

The same situation applies to the VM Disk counter. The only counter available in VSAN is Highest Latency.

The reason they are not available is they are no longer relevant. In VSAN, VM storage sits directly on the local disk. Technically, there is neither datastore nor LUN. vRealize Operations shows this direct relationship.

In the following screenshot, the VM has its storage located on five physical disks. By physical, I mean the actual disk, not a volume or RAID group.

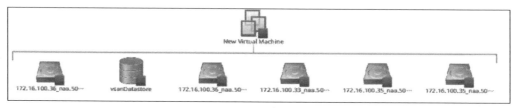

Where VM disks reside on VSAN

In VSAN, the ESXi host running the VM may not even host the VM storage. A VM now has a compute host and storage host. The VM in the screenshot has:

- Host **172.16.100.33** supporting it with one drive
- Host **172.16.100.35** stores in two drives
- Host **172.16.100.36** stores in two drives

In the view in the preceding screenshot, the device name is not shown in full. It is also not showing the ESXi where the VM is running. This is where the navigation panel comes in handy.

The following screenshot shows another VM. The VM is powered off and was running at ESXi **172.16.100.32**. Its storage, however, is stored on three different disks on three ESXi hosts.

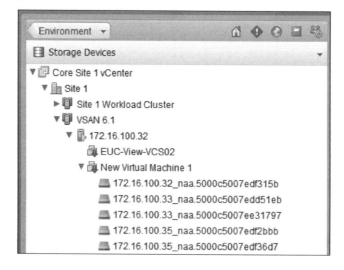

You can see the physical drive by clicking on the icon. This is another difference compared to classic arrays, where it is not easy to find out which actual physical drive has your VM data.

Monitoring VSAN

Now that we have seen how VSAN differs fundamentally from classic arrays from a performance-monitoring point of view, let's take a step back to see where we need to monitor. Once we know which objects or components to monitor, we can figure out what metrics to monitor.

Let's start with a single ESXi host so that we can highlight the differences. The following diagram shows the key components for performance monitoring. We have a single VM in this example. The VSAN kernel module in the hypervisor provides the storage function. It writes the VM data into the **Cache** layer. For a hybrid VSAN, it reads the VM data from the **Cache** layer. If it has a cache miss, it will go into the **Capacity** layer. This is obviously slower. For an all-flash VSAN, it reads the VM data from the **Capacity** layer directly.

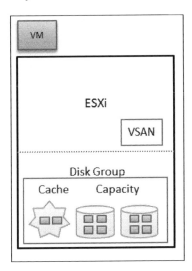

Both the **Cache** and **Capacity** layers form a disk group. While VSAN is capable of supporting multiple disk groups in a host, using just one disk group and defining your storage at the software level is a common configuration.

From this, we can see there are points where performance can be affected, as follows:

- The VSAN kernel module does not get enough CPU or RAM. If the ESXi host is busy, it can impact the VSAN kernel module. This in turn impacts its ability to serve the VM storage request.
- The **Cache** is not large enough and we have a cache miss.
- The **Cache** is not fast enough. It is unable to cope with the demand. Demand here can mean either a VM workload or VSAN internal operation. VSAN internal operations can be the destaging of data to the **Capacity** layer or synchronization among hosts.
- The **Capacity** layer is not fast enough. It is unable to cope with the demand. Again, the demand here can come either from VM or VSAN internal operations.

Since VSAN needs at least two hosts (four is the minimum recommended best practice), let's now extend our diagram to include multiple ESXi hosts.

Again, I have simplified the diagram. Only two hosts are drawn and I have simplified the disk group to keep the diagram tidy.

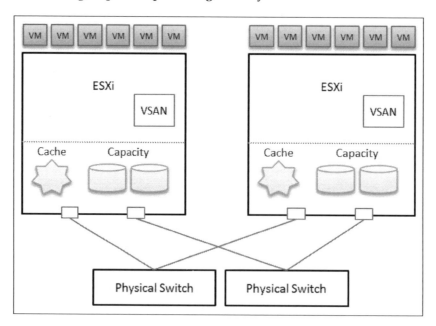

We now have the network component to monitor, too. Generally, you will have a pair of 10 GE for each ESXi. The same physical network cable carries traffic for VSAN and non-VSAN. That means we need to ensure that VSAN traffic is not affected and the overall network is able to cope with demand. For VSAN traffic, we can monitor at the distributed port group level. For overall traffic, we can monitor at the vmnic level.

You also need to monitor the physical switch. See the next chapter, where we discuss how you can extend vRealize Operations into physical networks.

Now that we know what objects to monitor, let's proceed with the first one.

Disk

A key component in VSAN performance is the cache, where an SSD is used. One VSAN disk group is supported by one and only one physical SSD. vRealize understands this and shows the relationship, as shown in the following screenshot:

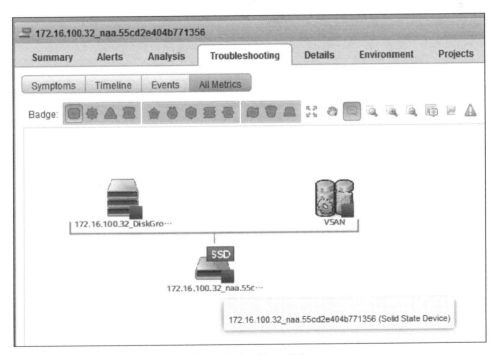

VSAN SSD relationship to disk group

You can click on the SSD icon to drill down and see its metrics. In addition to the performance and capacity metrics, you also get the **SMART (Self-Monitoring, Analysis and Reporting Technology)** statistics. SMART provides a set of counters that serve as a good indicator of drive (HDD or SSD) reliability. Refer to `https://en.wikipedia.org/wiki/S.M.A.R.T.` if you need more details. Here are the SSD metrics:

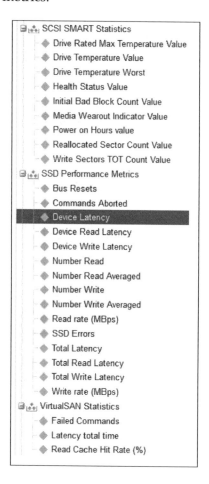

Among all these counters, a key one for VSAN performance is **SSD Cache Hit Rate**. VSAN uses the SSD as a read cache. In a **hybrid VSAN**, you want to see a high hit rate, ideally above 95 percent. We cover this in *Chapter 8, Specific-Purpose Dashboards,* where we create a super metric to track the hit rate across many SSDs on a single dashboard.

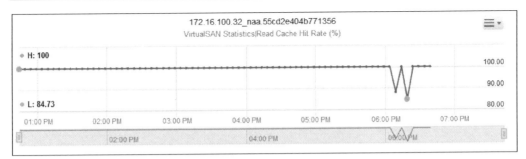

The VM SSD Read Cache Hit Rate metric

The data will eventually hit the magnetic disk. This can be due to write destaging from SSD or simply a read cache miss. vRealize provides a good set of metrics for the magnetic disks, as shown in the following screenshot. You can track performance, capacity, and availability.

Looking at all the spindles one by one is certainly time consuming. This is where you can be creative and create a super metric. A super metric differs from a regular one as it allows you to maintain details while viewing data across many objects.

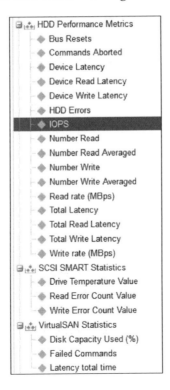

Disk groups

Both the SSD and HDD work together to form a **disk group**. A disk group forms the smallest logical building block. It does not span across ESXi hosts. A disk group is accessed via a **VMHBA** object and the following screenshot shows that vmhba2 is used by the **172.16.100.32** ESXi to access this particular disk group:

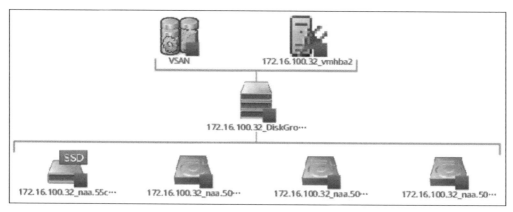

VSAN disk group relationships in vRealize Operations

The following screenshot shows the counters that you can monitor at the disk group level. You get both the performance and capacity metrics.

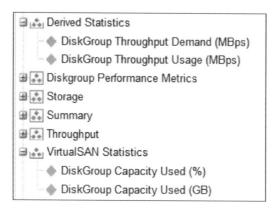

VSAN hosts

Moving up to a higher level, multiple disk groups belong to a host. If you have multiple disk groups per host, you can track at the host level to see information across all the disk groups in the host.

Now, there is a minor complication. There are two host objects; one has the VSAN counters and the other has the vSphere counters. Just make sure you select the correct one, as shown in the following diagram:

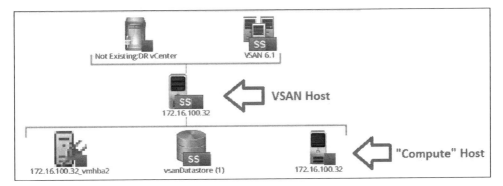

VSAN Host and Compute Host

VSAN datastore

Finally, at the highest level, the VSAN hosts form the VSAN datastore level. There is only one VSAN datastore per cluster, making operations easier. You can get the data at the host level, as each host is listed. The following screenshot shows that there are four hosts forming the VSAN cluster. You can also get the performance at the overall VSAN datastore level.

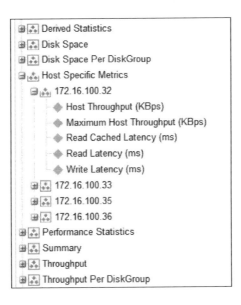

Summary

In this chapter, we covered storage counters. We cover both centralized storage and distributed storage. In 2016, the adoption of distributed storage will continue its rapid rise. I hope you can see that it requires a different approach with respect to monitoring and change your practice accordingly.

In the next chapter, we will cover the last of the infrastructure elements by diving into network counters.

15
Network Counters

We will complete our exploration of counters by covering network counters in this chapter. We will take the same approach we did with CPU, RAM, and storage. The layout of the chapter is as follows:

- Windows network counters
- VM network counters
- ESXi network counters
- Cluster network counters
- Distributed Virtual Switch network counters
- Network counters at higher levels
- NSX counters
- Physical switch counters

Network counters at the Guest OS level

Understanding network counters at the Guest OS level is important for an SDDC architect. The data inside the Guest provides better visibility.

The following screenshot shows Windows 7 **Resource Monitor**. You will quickly notice that a lot of this information is not available at the vSphere layer:

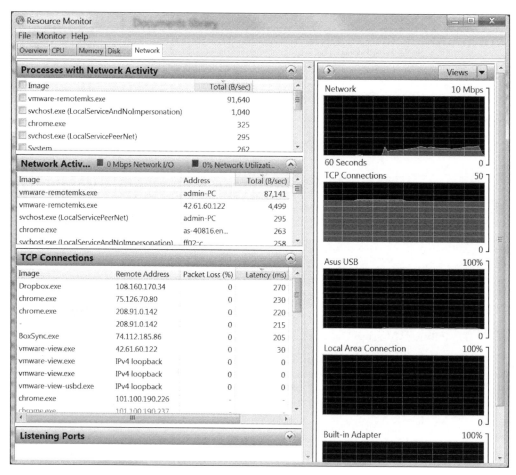

Windows 7 Resource Monitor

At the hypervisor layer, we can only see packet loss. Can you notice a counter that will tell you whether there is a network issue even if there is no packet loss?

Yes: latency.

It is in fact available at the process level. This is important as different processes can be talking to different destinations. It is in fact normal for a web browser to hit multiple sites. As you can see here, a single browser (Google Chrome) is talking to different websites.

In the preceding screenshot, the Windows 7 PC was playing an HD video over **VMware Horizon View**. Latency was good at below 50 milliseconds, and **View PCoIP** was using less than 100 KBPS of bandwidth. You can see from the green line chart that PCoIP was using around 1 Mbps.

Let's play a 4K video from YouTube and see what the counter looks like. The Windows 7 PC is connected via wireless to a home network:

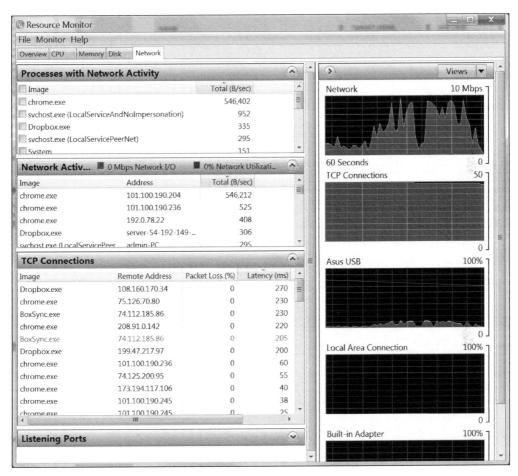

Windows 7 Resource Monitor

We can see that the bandwidth utilization rises to 546,212 bps. As you can see from the green line chart, it is in fact hitting my limit of 10 Mbps.

The **TCP Connection** widget contains more information. We can show additional columns, such as **PID** (or **Process ID**) and **Remote Port** (or simply port number):

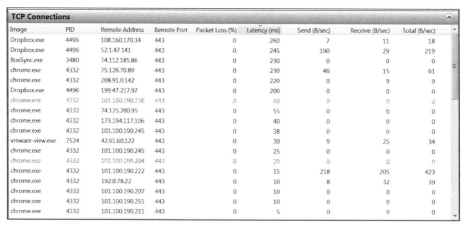

Image	PID	Remote Address	Remote Port	Packet Loss (%)	Latency (ms)	Send (B/sec)	Receive (B/sec)	Total (B/sec)
Dropbox.exe	4496	108.160.170.34	443	0	260	7	11	18
Dropbox.exe	4496	52.1.47.141	443	0	245	190	29	219
BoxSync.exe	3480	74.112.185.86	443	0	230	0	0	0
chrome.exe	4332	75.126.70.80	443	0	230	46	15	61
chrome.exe	4332	208.91.0.142	443	0	220	0	9	9
Dropbox.exe	4496	199.47.217.97	443	0	200	0	0	0
chrome.exe	4332	101.100.190.236	443	0	80	0	0	0
chrome.exe	4332	74.125.200.95	443	0	55	0	0	0
chrome.exe	4332	173.194.117.106	443	0	40	0	0	0
chrome.exe	4332	101.100.190.245	443	0	38	0	0	0
vmware-view.exe	7524	42.61.60.122	443	0	30	9	25	34
chrome.exe	4332	101.100.190.245	443	0	25	0	0	0
chrome.exe	4332	101.100.190.204	443	0	20	0	0	0
chrome.exe	4332	101.100.190.222	443	0	15	218	205	423
chrome.exe	4332	192.0.78.22	443	0	10	8	32	39
chrome.exe	4332	101.100.190.207	443	0	10	0	0	0
chrome.exe	4332	101.100.190.251	443	0	10	0	0	0
chrome.exe	4332	101.100.190.211	443	0	5	0	0	0

Windows 7 Resource Monitor – the TCP Connections screen

Besides **Resource Monitor**, Windows provides **Performance Monitor**. This tool is more useful for overall monitoring, as you can collect the information more easily. Unfortunately, the same level of detail is not available with this tool. For example, the latency counter is not available:

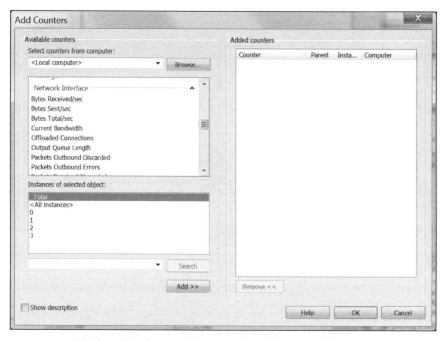

Windows 7 Performance Monitor – the Add Counters dialog box

Even when we check at the process level, the latency counter is not available:

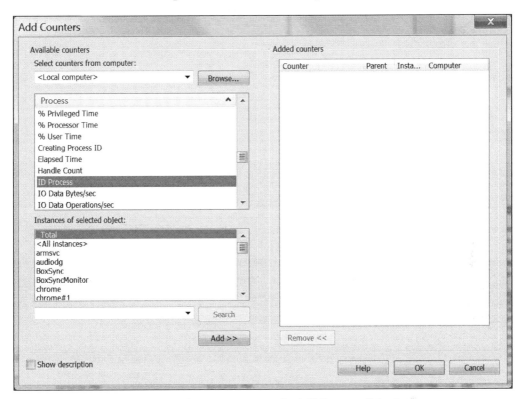

Windows 7 Performance Monitor – the Add Counters dialog box

Network counters at the VM level

The following screenshot shows the counters vCenter provides for network at the VM layer. The counters are available at each individual vNIC level and at the VM level. Most VMs will only have one vNIC, so the data at the VM and vNIC levels will be identical. The vNICs are named using the 400x convention.

This means that the first vNIC is 4000, the second vNIC is 4001, and so on:

Description	Rollup	Units	Internal Name	Collection Level
☐ Data receive rate	Average	KBps	bytesRx	2
☐ Broadcast receives	Summation	Number	broadcastRx	2
☐ Data transmit rate	Average	KBps	transmitted	2
☐ Multicast transmits	Summation	Number	multicastTx	2
☐ Packets transmitted	Summation	Number	packetsTx	2
☐ Data receive rate	Average	KBps	received	2
☐ Transmit packets dropped	Summation	Number	droppedTx	2
☐ Data transmit rate	Average	KBps	bytesTx	2
☐ Packets received	Summation	Number	packetsRx	2
☐ Multicast receives	Summation	Number	multicastRx	2
☐ Usage	Average	KBps	usage	1
☐ Broadcast transmits	Summation	Number	broadcastTx	2
☐ Receive packets dropped	Summation	Number	droppedRx	2

VM network counters

As usual, let's approach the counters, starting with *contention*. There is no latency counter, so you cannot track how long it takes for a packet to reach its destination. There are, however, counters that track dropped packets. Dropped packets need to be retransmitted and therefore increase network latency from the application point of view. vCenter does not provide a counter to track packet retransmits.

vRealize Operations provides a latency counter, which uses packet drops as an indicator. Using a percentage is certainly easier than dealing with the raw counters in vCenter. The packet drop percent age is based on the packets transmitted and received in that collection period. These two counters are not collected by default.

You certainly want to avoid having packet drops in your network. To monitor whether any VM is experiencing packet drop, you can build a super metric and develop a dashboard with a line chart and **Top-N** widgets. The super metric tracks the maximum packet drop of all VMs. You apply it at the appropriate level (for example, cluster, datacenter, vCenter) and plot a line chart. You should expect a flat line at **0** when the network is performing well.

The line chart, however, does not tell you which VM experiences packet drop if you have any. This is where the **Top-N** chart comes in. You can set it, say, to top-25 VM and make the time range long (for example, 1 month). This is available in an existing dashboard.

For **Utilization**, vCenter provides the data both in terms of the number of TCP/IP packets and network throughput. There is also a **Usage** counter, which is the sum of the Data **Transmit Rate** (**TX**) and Data **Receive Rate** (**RX**). The **Usage** counter cannot exceed the physical wire speed, even with full duplex. So, if the VM is sending 800 Mbps to another VM in another ESXi host, it can only receive 224 Mbps since the total (**TX** + **RX**) cannot exceed 1000 Mbps.

The limit can certainly be exceeded if the communication is between two VMs in the ESXi hosts, as the packets move at memory speed.

The following chart shows that **Usage** counter is the sum of RX and TX. In vRealize Operations, use the **Usage Rate** counter. The counter **4000 | Usage Rate** will only give the data for the first vNIC; hence, it will be incomplete if you have a VM with two vNICs (for example, those with LAN-based backup or having access to multiple networks):

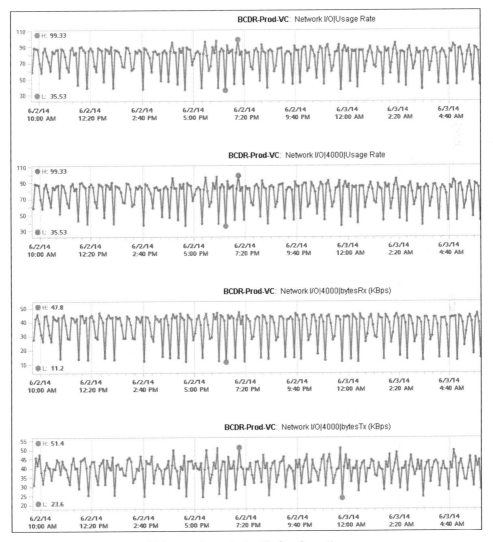

VM network metrics in vRealize Operations

You will notice that the numbers provided by vCenter and vRealize Operations are given in KBPS, while your vmnic is in Gbps. 1 Gbps equals 131,072 KBPS, so this is the theoretical maximum for a 1 GE physical card. Because vCenter takes a 20-second average, you will not see this number most of the time as it means that the throughput is sustained for the full 20 seconds. vRealize Operations will provide an even lower figure as the number is averaged over 5 minutes. You can reduce this to 1 minute if you have allowed for increased resource utilization (vRealize Operations VM and network infrastructure).

There are duplicate counters, as shown in the next screenshot. There are two data transmit rates and two data receive rates. The following data is from a vCenter 5.5 Update 1 appliance. As you can tell, there is a regular spike every few minutes or so. The load is primarily due to two vRealize Operations instances (5.8.1 and 6.0) accessing vCenter:

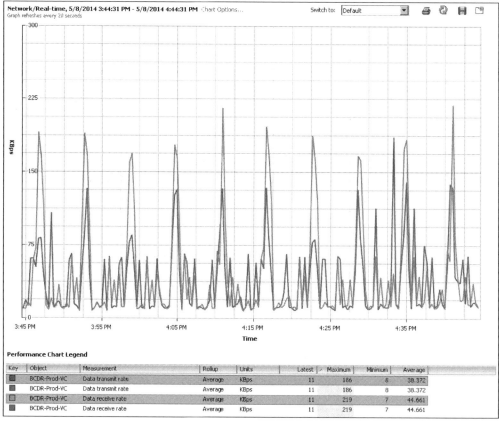

VM network metrics in vCenter

You may want to know whether any given VM hits the network limit. Assuming you are on a 1 GE network, you can do this by creating a super metric that tracks the maximum Usage (KBPS) of all VMs, multiplying that value by 8, and then dividing it by 1000 * 1000 to convert to Gbps. If you see a number nearing 1, it means you have a VM hitting 1 GE (which is the limit that the VM sees. The actual limit is likely to be lower since many VMs will be sharing the 1 GE vmnic).

Besides unicast traffic, which should form the bulk of your network, vSphere also provides information about broadcast and multicast traffic. If you are not expecting any of this traffic from certain VMs (or clusters) and want to be alerted if it does occur, you can create a group for the objects and then apply a super metric. The super metric would add the four counters that capture broadcast and multicast. You should expect a flat line as the total should be near 0.

We have talked about Contention and Utilization being the main areas you should check. The following table summarizes what you should monitor for the network. Notice that vCenter does not provide the total packet drops. Also, the unit is in the number of packet drops, not in percent. For utilization, vCenter does not have the equivalent of Workload. I've kept the table cell blank for ease of comparison:

Purpose	vCenter	vRealize Operations
Contention	Transmit packets dropped (number)	Packet Dropped (%)
	Received packets dropped (number)	
Utilization	Usage (KBPS)	Usage Rate (KBPS)
Utilization		Workload (%)

Network counters at the ESXi level

vCenter provides three additional counters at the host level. It can track packet receive errors, packet transmit errors, and unknown protocol frames. The counters are provided at either the host or vmnic level. They are not provided at the switch or port group levels.

This means you cannot gauge the performance at the port group or switch levels easily using vCenter:

Description	Rollup	Units	Internal Name	Collection Level
☐ Multicast receives	Summation	Number	multicastRx	2
☐ Usage	Average	KBps	usage	1
☐ Data receive rate	Average	KBps	bytesRx	2
☐ Multicast transmits	Summation	Number	multicastTx	2
☐ Unknown protocol frames	Summation	Number	unknownProtos	2
☐ Data transmit rate	Average	KBps	transmitted	2
☐ Packet receive errors	Summation	Number	errorsRx	2
☐ Packet transmit errors	Summation	Number	errorsTx	2
☐ Packets transmitted	Summation	Number	packetsTx	2
☐ Data receive rate	Average	KBps	received	2
☐ Transmit packets dropped	Summation	Number	droppedTx	2
☐ Receive packets dropped	Summation	Number	droppedRx	2
☐ Packets received	Summation	Number	packetsRx	2
☐ Broadcast receives	Summation	Number	broadcastRx	2
☐ Data transmit rate	Average	KBps	bytesTx	2
☐ Broadcast transmits	Summation	Number	broadcastTx	2

ESXi network counters

Just like vCenter, vRealize Operations also does not provide counters at the standard switch or port group level. This means you cannot aggregate or analyze the data from these network objects' points of view. This is one reason why you should use **Distributed Switch**. It simply has a much richer monitoring capability.

Usage, **Data Received Rate**, and **Data Transmit Rate** are all available at the host level and at the individual NIC level. For readability, only vmnic3 and the host are shown in this screenshot:

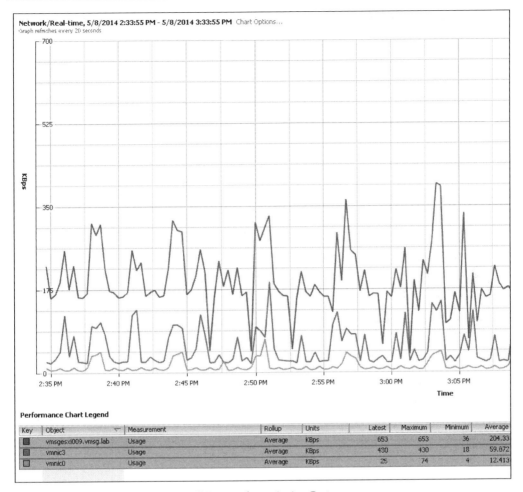

ESXi network metrics in vCenter

You should expect the values for packets dropped and unknown packet frames to be **0**. A packet is considered unknown if ESXi is unable to decode it and hence does not know what type of packet it is. Discuss with your network admin if you are seeing either a dropped packet or an unknown packet.

The packets dropped and unknown packet frames counters are available at the host level and individual NIC level. For readability, only vmnic1 and the host are shown in this screenshot:

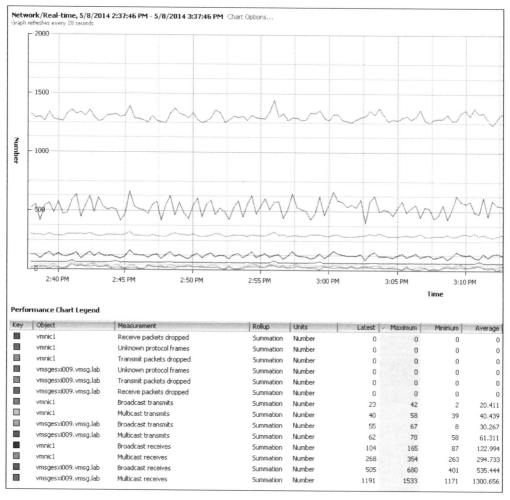

ESXi network metrics in vCenter

The key counters to track for ESXi are consistent with the key counters for a VM. Again, vCenter does not provide the total packets dropped and the equivalent of the Workload counter. I've kept the table cell blank for ease of comparison. Here's the table:

Purpose	vCenter	vRealize Operations
Contention	Transmit Packets dropped (number)	Packet Dropped (%)
	Received Packets dropped (number)	
Utilization	Usage (KBPS)	Usage Rate (KBPS)
Utilization		Workload (%)

Network counters at the cluster level

vRealize Operations provides a set of counters at the cluster level. Refer to *Chapter 4, Performance Monitoring*, as the approach is similar for network. Ensure that you create the super metrics so that you complement the average with peak. The following table lists the key counters:

Purpose	Counters	Roll up
Contention	Packet Dropped (%)	Average
Utilization	Usage Rate (KBPS)	Summation
Utilization	Workload (%)	Average

Network counters at the Distributed Switch level

As covered earlier in the book, vCenter does not provide information at the Distributed Switch level. This makes monitoring difficult, as you cannot slice the data from the switch point of view. vRealize Operations addresses this by providing the necessary counters at the Distributed Switch level and its port groups.

The next screenshot shows that vRealize Operations has network as a first-class citizen. The structure shows a Distributed Switch called **Site 1 Distributed Switch**. vRealize Operations shows the objects associated with it, such as these:

- Distributed port group
- Distributed port group (NSX)
- Uplinks
- ESXi host

This screenshot shows the metrics for a **Distributed Switch** object:

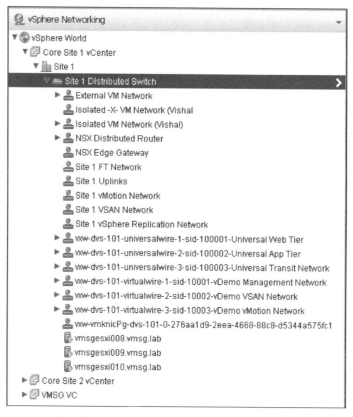

A vSphere Distributed Switch in vRealize Operations

As you can see, it has the usual network metrics you would expect. From the metric, you can also create a super metric. For example, you can create a super metric that tracks the maximum of **MTU Mismatch**, **Unsupported MTU**, **Teaming Mismatch**, and so on. You should expect a flat line with **0** as the value. You can then create an alert if the value goes beyond it:

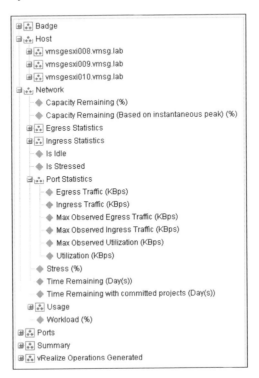

For Contention, vRealize Operations provides the **Packet Dropped (%)** metric. You will not find the **Contention (%)** metric.

For **Utilization**, you use both the **Usage Rate (KBPS)** and **Workload (%)** metrics. You need to use both due to the dynamic nature of the upper limit. The following screenshot shows an example of visibility at the Distributed Switch level:

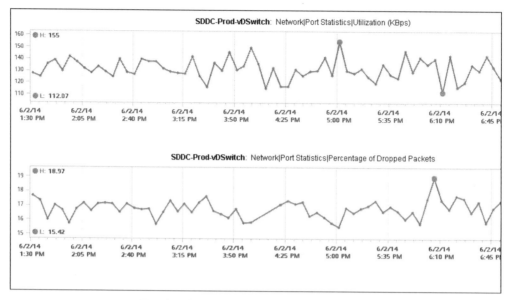

Distributed Switch metrics in vRealize Operations

Network counters at the distributed port group level

If you expand a distributed port group object, it will show all the VMs connected to it.

Metric-wise, you can expect the same set of metrics at the Distributed Switch level. After all, a port group is just a collection of ports with the same properties:

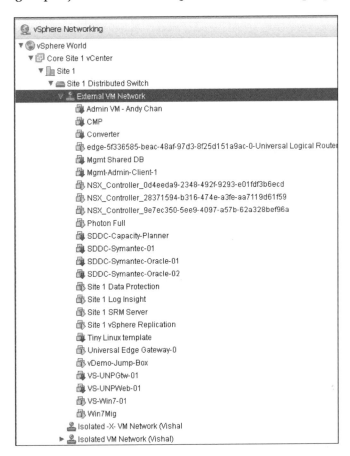

Network counters at higher levels

As covered earlier in the book, vCenter does not provide information for the network at higher levels (Datacenter, vCenter, World). vRealize Operations provides a set of counters for the network at these levels, which are useful for overall visibility.

This table lists the key counters. The only exception is that the packet dropped information is not available at the World level. I've kept the table cell blank for ease of comparison:

Object	Purpose	Counters	Roll up
Datacenter	Contention	Packet Dropped (%)	Average
Datacenter	Utilization	Usage Rate (KBPS)	Summation
Datacenter	Utilization	Workload (%)	Average
vCenter	Contention	Packet Dropped (%)	Average
vCenter	Utilization	Usage Rate (KBPS)	Summation
vCenter	Utilization	Workload (%)	Average
World	Contention		
World	Utilization	Usage Rate (KBPS)	Summation
World	Utilization	Workload (%)	Average

Network counters in NSX

If you are using VMware NSX, you need the vRealize Operations management pack for NSX to get visibility into the virtual network. As you can see from the following set of screenshots, NSX is a whole world in itself.

NSX for network is the equivalent of vSphere for compute:

NSX objects in vRealize Operations

Network monitoring tools need to support NSX monitoring from the ground up. It is not a simple extension that can be developed easily. It is much more than monitoring the VXLAN tunnel or **Transport Zone**. The preceding screenshots show many components that behave differently in a physical network. Take, for example, NSX Distributed Firewall. It does not exist in non-NSX networks.

Besides knowing the NSX objects, vRealize Operations also knows the relationships among the objects. The following screenshot shows an **Edge** named **Universal Edge Gateway** that belongs to an **NSX Manager** named **Production Site NSX**. The Edge VM has an uplink called **External Network**, which is mapped to a distributed port group called **External VM Network**:

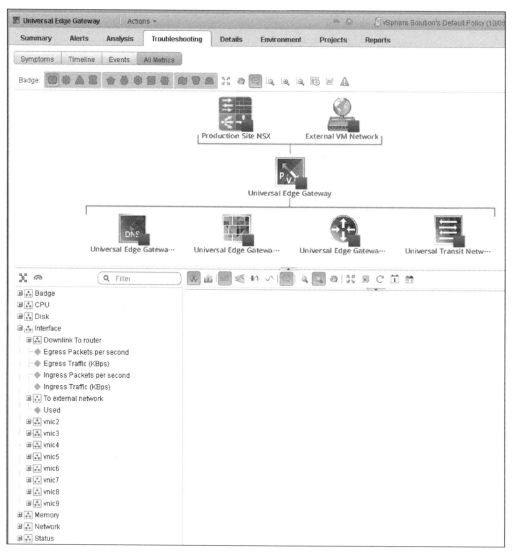

NSX object relationships in vRealize Operations

In the **Interface** metric group, you can see the 10 virtual interfaces that this Edge VM can have. There are two interfaces configured. They are labeled **Downlink To Router** and **To external network**.

Each of the NSX components has its own metrics in vRealize Operations. Most of them are just standard CPU, RAM, network, and storage metrics. The real value is in understanding the relationships among the objects.

Network counters for physical switches

A majority of VMware administrators do not monitor the physical network. The main reason is that their job scope and responsibility do not cover the physical network. This creates difficulty in network troubleshooting. At the minimum, you need to have visibility into the devices that are directly connected to the ESXi hosts.

Starting from December 2015, vRealize Operations provides this visibility. The metrics and configuration are collected by SNMP polling. Network devices themselves and topology are discovered with LLDP or CDP—protocols that need to be enabled on network devices. The following screenshot shows that it has discovered three switches using the SNMP V3 protocol:

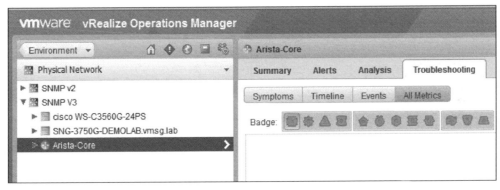

Visibility into physical switches

If we expand the switch labeled **Arista-Core**, we will see its relationship with other switches. We can see that it is connecting to two other switches. We can expand the hierarchy further and see the relationship with the ESXi host. This gives us visibility into which switch has which ESXi host.

If we expand a host, we will see the VM on that host:

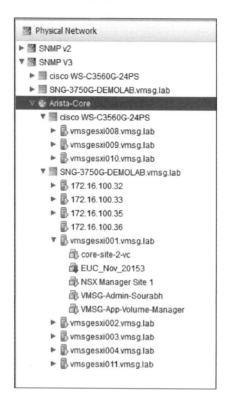

The counters that it collects are the standard counters you normally expect from a typical network monitoring tool, as shown in the following set of screenshots:

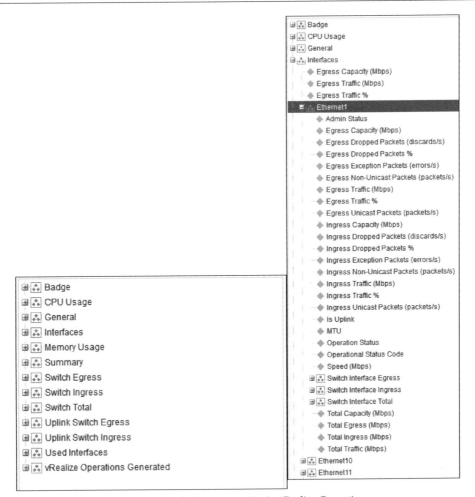

Physical network device – metrics in vRealize Operations

For each switch, you can drill down and see the statistics at the individual port level.

Summary

I hope you have found the content informative and realized that network monitoring cannot be done at the vSphere layer alone.

This chapter concludes *Part 3*, where we spent over 100 pages touring the counters in vCenter and vRealize Operations.

It also takes us to the end of the book. It has been a great pleasure sharing this knowledge, and I hope you enjoyed it as much as I did. Thank you for reading this all the way through. It is a heavy topic, so you should congratulate yourself on completing the review.

One thing I particularly liked about writing this book is that it's basically about documenting the collective experience I gained from dealing with customers. As someone working on the vendor side, I only know the theory. It is the customers who live with the implementation once the consultants leave, facing the production environment and end users directly.

Let's recap the key messages that you read. I hope they resonate and you see the practicalities in your environment.

The first part of the book set out to explain why virtualization is a much larger change in the evolution of IT. It highlighted the common misconceptions about virtualization, with the goal of setting a strong foundation for the rest of the book. Its chapters provided an extensive comparison between the physical server and the virtual machine and between the physical data center and the virtual data center. Collectively, *Part 1* explained how best practices in physical data centers became dated practices, and a set of new practices emerged.

Part 2, the book showed a practical solution for realizing the new practice. It provided real-life examples of the dashboards. I hope it gave you a good idea about what's possible with vRealize Operations.

Part 3 of the book was a reference section. The five chapters of this part went deep into the world of counters. It covered the four main elements of infrastructure: CPU, RAM, disk, and network. It also covered them from every vSphere object's point of view, so we can see the relationships among counters as they are rolled up to high-level objects. It is clear that vCenter does not provide you with the visibility you need when you look at your environment from high-level objects. This is where vRealize Operations and Log Insight complement it very well.

We covered a lot of ground, and yet, there is so much more to cover. We covered the areas that have been excluded in the Preface. These are just some of the areas we can cover as we embark on this once-in-a-lifetime journey into the weird and wonderful world of cloud computing.

In the meantime, let's continue learning from one another. You can reach me at LinkedIn and I will continue updating my blog.

There are many places online to network and socialize with your peers in the industry. A virtual place that I check in to regularly is a Facebook group that I set up more than six years ago. It started as a Singapore-based group, but then expanded to Asia Pacific with more users joining in. By now, it has become one of the largest VMware groups globally on Facebook. Join us at `https://www.facebook.com/groups/vmware.users` and network with your peers.

Index

H

hardware-defined data center (HDDC)
  about 19
  operations 45
hardware partitioning
  about 7
  versus virtualization 7, 8
heatmaps 264
Horizon View Agent 337
hybrid VSAN 478
Hyper-Converged Infrastructure (HCI) 19
Hyper-Threading (HT) 338

I

IaaS performance
  about 64, 105-107
  alerts 122-126
  dashboard, creating 111-114
  dashboard, for list of affected VMs 127-130
  dashboards, adapting to different
        environments 130
  performance SLA line 114
  super metrics, applying 110
  super metrics, creating 107-110
IBM DB2
  about 273-275
  DB2 on VM dashboard 273
  DB2 Top-N Queries dashboard 275
IBM Tivoli
  about 269, 270
  Environment Overview dashboard 272
  Linux OS dashboard 271
IBM Tivoli Monitoring (ITM) 272
Independent Software Vendors (ISVs) 42
Information Technology Infrastructure
        Library (ITIL) 47
Infrastructure as a Service (IaaS)
        operation 44
Infrastructure layer 63
infrastructure monitoring
  Blue Medora used 233
Input/Output Operations
        Per Second (IOPS) 15
Iometer
  URL 444

K

Key Performance Indicators (KPIs) 256
Knowledge Base (KB) 343

L

Latency 338
Lenovo compute
  about 246, 247
  Overview dashboard 246, 247
Logical Domain (LDOM) 7
Logical Partition (LPAR) 7
Logical Unit Number (LUN) 7, 10, 21
Low free threshold (KB) counter 420

M

Machine Demand (KB) 423
Managed VMware (dedicated) 22
Managed VMware (shared) 22
management changes, SDDC
  about 46
  asset management 48
  availability management 47
  capacity management 47
  compliance management 47
  configuration management 47
  financial management 48
  performance management 46
  security management 47
maximum CPU performance
  options 340
Max Limited counter 359
memory 385-388
memory counters
  at cluster level 433-438
  at Guest OS level 388-397
  at higher levels 438
memory counters, at ESXi level
  about 417-419
  Consumed, versus Active 424-432
  contention counters 419-422
  ESXi memory key counters 433
  utilization counters 422-424
memory counters, at VM level
  about 398-400
  contention counters 401-404

performance monitoring 53, 61

performance SLA
  about 67-70
  CPU SLA 71
  memory SLA 71
  network SLA 71, 72
  storage SLA 72

performance SLA line
  about 114
  group, creating 116, 117
  policies, creating 118, 119
  resultant dashboard 122
  SLA, adding to each line chart 120
  super metric, creating 115, 116
  super metrics, mapping to policy 119, 120

performance troubleshooting 53

physical server
  versus Virtual Machine 13-16

Physical-to-Virtual (P2V) process 9

power management
  URL 343

primary counters
  for monitoring 55

provider layer
  properties 50, 51

Provisioned Memory (KB) 424

pure cloud 22

Q

Quality of Service (QoS) 12

R

Raw Capacity 78
Raw Device Mapping (RDM) 15
Readiness 338
Ready 338
Recovery Point Objective (RPO) 79
Redundant Array of Inexpensive Disks
    (RAID) 15
Reserved Capacity (MB) 424
Reserved overhead counter 399, 409

restaurant analogy
  about 48, 49
  consumer layer 50
  provider layer 50, 51

S

SAP HANA
  about 275, 276
  configuration 278
  SAP HANA Environment Overview
      dashboard 277

SDDC capacity planning
  about 78-80
  at compute level 81
  at network layer 86
  at storage layer 81-85

SDDC key counters
  compute 283-287

SDDC management
  about 43
  architecturally 45
  changes, identifying 43, 44
  operationally 45

SDDC, versus HDDC
  about 35
  application 41, 42
  compute element 36-38
  data center 36
  networks 39, 40
  storage 38, 39

Service Level Agreement (SLA) 49

single-socket multi-core
  used, for VM configurations 337

Site Recovery Manager 8

SMART (Self-Monitoring, Analysis and
    Reporting Technology)
  reference 478

software-defined data center (SDDC)
  about 19-26
  compute function 27, 28
  management changes 46
  network function 28-30
  operations 45
  relationship, between key objects 33-35
  storage function 31, 32

specific-purpose dashboards
  about 179
  big-screen dashboards 179
  dashboards, for network team 216, 217
  dashboards, for storage team 200
  dashboards, for VDI team 226

Made in the USA
San Bernardino, CA
14 December 2016